Turkmenistan

The World Bank
Washington, D.C.

World Bank Country Studies are among the many reports originally prepared for internal use as part of the continuing analysis by the Bank of the economic and related conditions of its developing member countries and of its dialogues with the governments. Some of the reports are published in this series with the least possible delay for the use of governments and the academic, business and financial, and development communities. The typescript of this paper therefore has not been prepared in accordance with the procedures appropriate to formal printed texts, and the World Bank accepts no responsibility for errors. Some sources cited in this paper may be informal documents that are not readily available.

The World Bank does not guarantee the accuracy of the data included in this publication and accepts no responsibility whatsoever for any consequence of their use. The boundaries, colors, denominations, and other information shown on any map in this volume do not imply on the part of the World Bank Group any judgment on the legal status of any territory or the endorsement or acceptance of such boundaries.

The material in this publication is copyrighted. Requests for permission to reproduce portions of it should be sent to the Office of the Publisher at the address shown in the copyright notice above. The World Bank encourages dissemination of its work and will normally give permission promptly and, when the reproduction is for noncommercial purposes, without asking a fee. Permission to copy portions for classroom use is granted through the Copyright Clearance Center, Inc., Suite 910, 222 Rosewood Drive, Danvers, Massachusetts 01923, U.S.A.

The complete backlist of publications from the World Bank is shown in the annual *Index of Publications,* which contains an alphabetical title list (with full ordering information) and indexes of subjects, authors, and countries and regions. The latest edition is available free of charge from the Distribution Unit, Office of the Publisher, The World Bank, 1818 H Street, N.W., Washington, D.C. 20433, U.S.A., or from Publications, The World Bank, 66, avenue d'Iéna, 75116 Paris, France.

ISSN: 0253-2123

Library of Congress Cataloging-in-Publication Data

Turkmenistan / [Helga Müller ... et al.].
        p.   cm. — (A World Bank country study)
    ISBN (invalid) 0-8213-2832-8
    1. Turkmenistan—Economic conditions.   2. Turkmenistan—Economic
policy.   I. Müller, Helga W., 1960–   .   II. Series.
    HC 421.5 T88   1994
    330.958′086—dc20
                                                      94-10572
                                                      CIP

CONTENTS

Text Figures

Text Tables

PREFACE

Turkmenistan became a member of the World Bank on September 22, 1992. This report is based on the findings of a mission to Turkmenistan in September 1992 led by Enrique Lerdau. The report was discussed with the authorities in October and November 1993. The World Bank wishes to thank the Turkmen authorities for their support and cooperation in providing information and data on the Turkmen economy.

The report was prepared by Helga Müller (the main author), Ali Alikhani (industry), Stan Bereza (financial sector), Toby Burton (privatization/private sector development), Yusupha Crookes (energy), Arye Hillman (trade), Markuu Kaariainen (telecommunications), David Kunkel (agriculture), Muhammad Mustafa (telecommunications), Barbara Ossowicka (statistics) and Wayne Vromen (social safety net/labor market). Other staff contributing to the report included Isabel Guerrero, Katarina Mathernova, Costas Michalopoulos, Klaus Lorch, and Michael Mills. The study was carried out under the general supervision of Kadir Tanju Yurukoglu, Division Chief and Russell J. Cheetham, Director. The report was processed by Miranda Cookson and Robert Elings.

Since the mission was undertaken, several reform measures, addressing key reform areas discussed in this report, have been implemented by the government. The report has been updated according to these developments.

CURRENCY EQUIVALENTS

Currency Unit = manat (as of Nov. 1, 1993)
US$1 = 2 manats

WEIGHTS AND MEASURES

Metric System

GOVERNMENT FISCAL YEAR

January 1 - December 31

ABBREVIATIONS

CBR	Central Bank of Russia
CBT	Central Bank of Turkmenistan, Gosbank
CIS	Commonwealth of Independent States
CIT	Corporate Income Tax
CMEA	Council for Mutual Economic Assistance
EAMU	External Assistance Management Unit
EBRD	European Bank for Reconstruction and Development
EC	European Cmmunity
FDI	Foreign Direct Investment
FSU	Former Soviet Union
G-7	Group of 7 Industrial Nations
GDP	Gross Domestic Product
GNP	Gross National Product
Goskomstat	State Committee on Statistics
Gosplan	State Planning Committee
IBRD	International Bank for Reconstruction and Development
IFC	International Finance Corporation
IMF	International Monetary Fund
MNOU	Memorandum of Understanding
MOA	Ministry of Agriculture
MOEF	Ministry of Economics and Finances
MOI	Ministry of Irrigation
NMP	Net Material Product
OECD	Organization for EConomic Cooperation and Development
SOE	State Owned Enterprises
TCA	Turkmen Cooperative Alliance
UNICEF	United Nations Children's Fund
VAT	Value Added Tax
VEB	Vnesheconombank

EXECUTIVE SUMMARY

1.　　　　Turkmenistan became a member of the World Bank on September 22, 1992, having gained its independence on October 27, 1991. With 500,000 square kilometers, it is the fourth largest republic of the former Soviet Union (FSU). But with the Kara Kum desert covering 90 percent of the area, Turkmenistan's population is only 3.8 million, the fourth smallest of the FSU. Landlocked, Turkmenistan depends on its neighbors for access to international markets.

2.　　　　Although Turkmenistan has good potential for diversification into mineral resource-based industries, the economy is still predominantly agricultural. While agriculture represented nearly half of total production, industry was only a fifth of net material product in 1991. Agricultural yields are low by international standards because of years of inefficient water use, salinization, irrigation of inappropriate land, and overdevelopment of cotton cultivation. Furthermore, the high specialization in energy and cotton -- the two biggest sources of export revenues -- has made the economy heavily dependent on food imports.

3.　　　　Turkmenistan is well endowed with energy resources, primarily natural gas and oil. It is the second largest natural gas producer in the FSU after the Russian Federation and the fourth largest in the world. It is also the fourth largest oil producer in the region. Despite this natural wealth, Turkmenistan is one of the least developed republics, with the highest infant mortality and the lowest life expectancy. Per capita incomes were significantly below the union average in the 1980s.

Recent Economic Developments

4.　　　　Turkmenistan has been relatively less affected by the breakdown of the Soviet Union than other republics. However, production of gas fell by 30 percent in 1992 because of the inability of Turkmenistan's FSU trading partners to pay for imports from Turkmenistan. The decline in Gross Domestic Product is estimated at about 5 percent in 1992. The relatively lower drop in productivity than in other FSU countries was partly due to significant construction activity undertaken through new government investment. Agricultural output declined in 1992 by about 4 percent mainly due to bad weather. Industrial production declined significantly (about 20 percent) due to the disruptions in interrepublican trade, shortage of spare parts and inputs, and the inability of most public enterprise managers to adapt to changing circumstances.

5.　　　　*Trade*. Turkmenistan's hard-currency and interrepublican trade accounts were in surplus in 1992 and are expected to be in surplus in 1993. Exports were largely dominated by gas, oil and cotton. Turkmenistan's energy exports are hampered by two problems. Its interrepublican gas exports received an average free on board price of US$10 equivalent (=2000 rubles) per 1000 cm compared to the world market price of US$72/1000 cm in 1992. Turkmenistan increased this price substantially from R13,700 in January to R38,400 per 1000 cubic meters in June 1993 with the result that arrears with other FSU countries intensified over the year. Furthermore, Turkmenistan is dependent on the Russian gas pipeline for hard-currency sales to Europe. Russia pools its own gas with that of Turkmenistan and then uses it either domestically or for hard-currency exports to Europe.

6.　　　　*Monetary Policy*. Turkmenistan's participation in the ruble zone effectively removed from national control actions on the exchange rate and money supply in 1992 and 1993. With growing inflation in the ruble area the Government realized that national independence had to be complemented by monetary independence. The Government, therefore, decided to introduce its own currency. In preparation for the introduction of the currency the Government accumulated a hard currency reserve to support the national currency and the Central Bank took various administrative measures to stem the flow of ruble notes into Turkmenistan. The Government introduced its own currency -- the manat -- on November 1, 1993. Between November 1 and November 5 the official exchange rate was set at US$1 = manat 2. The Government has indicated its intention to introduce a managed floating exchange rate regime.

7.   *Prices*. Turkmenistan started to liberalize prices in early 1992 but several of the price liberalization measures were soon reversed. Developments of prices in 1992 and 1993 were basically influenced by the imported inflation from the ruble zone and the persistence of price controls for about forty consumer goods and services. With the introduction of the new currency in November 1993, the Government liberalized several prices. Eleven commodities are still subject to control at subsidized prices. Another 26 commodities are subject to a review by an antimonopoly commission which will negotiate with enterprises the maximum level of price adjustment. The Government has indicated that the ultimate goal is full price liberalization but the timetable is not clear.

8.   The minimum wage was increased several times in 1992 and 1993, at a rate much higher than most of the other FSU countries. On November 1, 1993, the Government established a new wage scale and an estimated average wage of manat 400. Given the limited scope of the price reform, with a conversion rate of R500 to the manat, these figures imply a sharp rise in real wages in November, 1993.

9.   *Fiscal Accounts*. With the breakup of the Union, Turkmenistan's budget has experienced both negative and positive shocks. The country had been one of the main beneficiaries of Union transfers, with direct transfers of up to 20 percent of total revenues. The Government's revenues dropped from 40 percent of GDP to 20 percent of GDP. At the same time, however, there was a positive shock when exports earnings became directly available to the country, rather than to the Union. Moreover, export prices increased as Turkmenistan started to gradually approach international market prices in its sales to the FSU and the country has large terms-of-trade gains.

10.   Although technically the 1992 budget was in deficit, there was a budgetary surplus of 14 percent of GDP after taking into account hard currency revenues which were channeled through an extra-budgetary fund. The situation began to deteriorate in 1993, as a result of accumulating arrears of some FSU countries on Turkmenistan's exports and the appreciation of the real exchange rate. This will deteriorate the budgetary surplus, since arrears have a substantially negative effect on revenues and 70 percent of total government revenues consist of hard currency receipts from the gas cooperation.

Medium-Term Prospects

11.   Despite its high proportion of desert land, Turkmenistan has strong economic potential. Energy resources are plentiful, and there is considerable scope for raising the productivity of irrigated land. Large gains in terms of trade as energy prices approach international levels should lead to increasing export revenues that could finance a substantial expansion of imports of both capital and consumer goods. Current account surpluses are expected throughout the nineties provided there is substantial investment to sustain current gas export levels and to develop basic transport infrastructure.

12.   The efficient re-investment of financial resources obtained from the energy sector is central to Turkmenistan's future development prospects. Other developing countries with large energy resources have confronted the same task. The experience shows that it is easier to obtain the financial resources from extracting the natural wealth than it is to reinvest them in a way that will generate long-term growth and a higher standard of living.

13.   To develop Turkmenistan's potential and maximize the rate of return on investments, careful economic management and comprehensive reforms are essential. Progress on structural and systematic reforms would provide enterprises and individuals with the right institutional and market incentive structures and strengthen substantially the sustainability of the supply response in the economy. Turkmenistan could indeed achieve some growth with little reforms by financing it from gas export revenues, all of which go to the government. It is expected to have smaller declines in GDP than other FSU countries. However, such slow economic growth would be insufficient to generate the increasingly larger employment opportunities that Turkmenistan would need in the longer term, given its rapid population growth. A slow path of reforms would imply continued reliance on public investment and continued low productivity, thereby increasing budgetary expenditures. The poor baseline situation on social indicators coupled with rapid population growth will also exert increasing pressure on budgetary expenditures over the medium term.

14.   Growth without significant reforms would also tend to be expensive because of the substantial waste and inefficiency which would continue under the existing system. As prices would not be allowed to fully play their role in allocating scarce resources because of the existing price controls and subsidies, efficiency gains from increased competition would be delayed. With limited reforms, increasingly larger investments would be required to generate the same output growth. In an environment in which most investment decisions are not based on adequate cost-benefit analysis within an overall investment strategy, a lot of investment could be unprofitable, inefficient or against the long-term interest of Turkmenistan.

15.   A decisive implementation of a comprehensive reform program could improve the pace of recovery and reduce the vulnerability to potential external risks. Through a more productive use of resources, growth rates with the same amount of investment could reach 4 to 5 percent by the late nineties, compared to much less with no reform. Progress on systematic reforms would provide enterprises and individuals with the right institutional and market incentive structures to grow and invest. It would, thereby, strengthen the sustainability of the supply response throughout the economy.

16.   *External Risks*. Turkmenistan's exports are concentrated on energy and cotton, whose prices are subject to movements in international markets. A decline in the price of energy can lead, even in resource-rich countries such as Turkmenistan, to serious long-term problems such as soaring budget and balance-of-payments deficits and declining growth. A $1/1000 cubic meters drop in oil prices would decrease Turkmenistan's exports by $50 million. Furthermore, the same effects would be caused by an increase in transport charges, since Turkmenistan has little leverage over the determination of regional gas transmission tariffs. A $30 decline in the export price of 1000 cubic meters of gas -- caused by a decline in the international price and/or an increase in transport charges -- would turn the trade balance into a deficit by mid-1990. Without the diversification which would come about from reforms, the country's future would be vulnerable to external developments beyond the control of policymakers. Some of these problems could result from the classic 'Dutch Disease' since strong growth in export receipts from one sector of the economy can significantly reduce the competitiveness of other sectors in the economy through currency appreciation. Experience in other oil exporting countries suggests that

macroeconomic crises have been a direct consequence of an inefficient economy overly dependent on a single commodity to export.

17.   Furthermore, Turkmenistan is tied by innumerable links to the FSU, and there is great uncertainty surrounding the evolution of interrepublican trade and the ability of other FSU countries to pay for their imports from Turkmenistan. Hard currency revenues will continue to be uncertain as long as the country is dependent on Russia for transport and access to hard currency markets. Demand for natural gas in Russia should decline as domestic prices increase and the industry is restructured. Then a considerable volume of gas supplies would be available for exports, potentially reducing the demand for Turkmenistan's gas.

18.   The risks of course will be magnified if there is no reform or there is poor implementation of reforms. As the range of decisions broadens and the complexity of issues increases, decentralization of authority will be necessary as well as substantial strengthening and adjustments of institutional capacities. Technical assistance will need to be mobilized to strengthen the Government's capacity in the critical areas of stabilization and reform.

19.   Other risks include the possibility of severe supply dislocations in the FSU, especially in Russia. Given Turkmenistan's remoteness, shortfalls cannot be easily made up by recourse to other sources. There could be considerable supply bottlenecks provoked by a shortage of raw materials, intermediate goods, spare parts and replacements for capital goods.

Policy Priorities during the Transition

Stabilization Program

20.   *Monetary Policy*. The success of a stabilization program depends on the monetary and exchange rate arrangements to be adopted by the Government of Turkmenistan. The Government introduced its own currency on November 1, 1993. However, maintaining a strong national currency will not only require strong export performance, but also macroeconomic stability. With a separate currency, the focus of monetary policy should be to reduce inflation. Interest rate policy would need to be consistent with exchange rate policy: if the return on domestic currency deposits is unattractive there will be capital flight.

21.   The availability of substantial hard currency reserves provides the country with some protection against external shocks. Turkmenistan intends to adopt a managed floating exchange rate system to maintain this reserve position and the Government has centralized its foreign exchange holdings at the Central Bank. It is very important, in light of the expected continued surplus of hard-currency reserves, that the Central Bank be allowed to manage reserves. This is not only necessary for maintaining a strong external reserve position, but also to manage the inflow of the surplus into the economy.

22.   *Fiscal Policy*. Macroeconomic stabilization will depend also on sound fiscal management. Deficit financing from the monetary system would be limited by the objectives of controlling inflation. The Government will have to undertake measures to increase revenues and cut expenditures since the budget surplus in the consolidated accounts is not likely to last for long. It is already declining due to lower than expected revenues from the energy sector and increasing expenditures for social services and

subsidies. Without reforms there is a strong likelihood that budget deficits will grow significantly and bring about balance of payments and macroeconomic instability.

23.   If the Government is to support a reasonable level of public investments and keep the deficit under control, overall accounts will have to be restructured. The taxation system should be strengthened and the tax base widened as much as possible. The exemptions from the VAT should be reconsidered. The tax system should be strengthened through such measures as reinstating the gasoline tax (abolished in August 1992), substantially reducing the exemptions from income and profits taxes, discontinuing the tax-free status of the cotton company, increasing user charges for many public services, and adjusting housing rents at least to cover operating costs. Subjecting all imports to the VAT would increase revenues and remove the distortions against domestic producers. Barter transactions need to be subject to an invoice verification by customs and to taxes. Since a high proportion of revenue comes from energy, the Government should review the sector's taxation and pricing system.

24.   For the Ministry of Economics and Finance to exercise full control over public finances, budgetary institutions and procedures will have to be reexamined at all levels of Government. Furthermore, all extrabudgetary funds, with the possible exception of the pension fund, should be included in the budget. Otherwise budgetary management becomes impossible.

25.   *Resource Management*. The critical task at hand is to manage the surplus generated from exports carefully and to maximize its rate of return. Whether the surplus flows back to the Government's budget, the banks, or public enterprises, the crucial issue will be the ability of these agencies to make effective use of these resources from the point of view of the country as a whole. To the extent that the surpluses flow back through the banks, commercial banks will need to have the capacity to make sound lending decisions. To the extent that resources flow back to the Government's budget, the Government will need to build up the management capacity in order to evaluate the costs and benefits of projects and to prioritize them. The Government should base its investment decisions on both an overall strategy and the profitability of individual projects. The Government is currently planning several projects with foreign promoters that involve hard-currency expenditures. Many of these projects have had no cost-benefit analysis. This lack of analysis is dangerous: the country could be investing in unprofitable industries that could quickly deplete hard-currency resources. Such losses would become a major burden on the budget.

26.   A public investment and financing plan should include economically and financially sound investment projects selected on the basis of a careful cost-benefit analysis. The plan's sectoral composition should follow a national development strategy elaborated by the Government. Projected annual expenditures -- built up from the forecasts for each project -- should match the financial resources available. And the foreign exchange impact should be consistent with developments in the balance of payments.

27.   If public enterprises outside the budget are allowed to use the surplus, it will need to be done in a context where these resources are used in a way that maximizes the welfare of the country as a whole. Finally, there is the option of leaving resources offshore until the Government decides which is the best way to re-invest, or, until these investment management capacities are built up.

28.   *Subsidies*. Subsidies and price controls distort the structure of relative prices and make meaningful cost-benefit analysis impossible. The current pricing policy greatly reduces incentives to cut production costs and resource allocation. With price controls in place, investments are delayed or of the

wrong kind. Without a clear signal on prices, investors and producers cannot determine the potential value of privatized assets. Most investment would be of a speculative nature or with strictly short run objectives. The rationale for price liberalization lies in eliminating the increasing inefficiencies caused by a highly distorted price structure and in countering high costs. Barter trade has appeared in part as a result of attempts to avoid price controls.

29.   Subsidies also influence the Government's financial requirements. Their elimination -- or reduction to a few items -- is desirable for efficiency and budgetary reasons. A medium term program to phase them out is needed which is compatible with the social objectives of the Government. Such a program should give priority to sectors where the supply response to higher producer prices is expected to be quickest.

Structural Reform Program

30.   *Domestic and Foreign Trade Policy*. Both imports and exports need to be liberalized to ensure a dynamic economy. The freedom to import will foster competition by providing alternative sources of commodities for state monopolies -- and for consumers. The freedom to export will help develop the domestic private marketing system -- and attract private firms to the development of markets abroad. Because of its immediate impact on supply, the reform should start with the removal of all domestic restrictions on trade and allowing free entry into the import-export business. So far, designated ministries follow bureaucratic, not market incentives. An international commodity exchange, covering a broad range of commodities, might also be set up in cooperation with other Central Asian countries.

31.   *Legal Framework*. In order to strengthen private sector development, there is a need to address significant gaps in property, contract, and bankruptcy laws, to harmonize existing legislation affecting foreign and domestic investors, and to strengthen the capacity to enforce the legal regime. If the privatization of land and state enterprises is to yield benefits, decisionmakers need to be assured of the right to retain the returns from their investments. Those returns must not be directed to the production of unprofitable commodities. If individuals and firms have the means to enforce legitimate contracts and are allowed to enter into business freely, they will foster competition and innovation.

32.   *Privatization*. Privatization has been negligible in Turkmenistan. If the Government wants to pursue it further the main priorities should be the enactment of a more liberal legislation for all aspects of privatization, the development of an overall strategy for privatization and a rapid expansion of the small-scale privatization program (covering most of the retail and service sector). Shops and service establishments should be auctioned. The Ministry of Agriculture should introduce flexible lease arrangements for state farms and cooperatives -- and consider introducing outright land sales as well.

33.   *Enterprise Reform*. The elaboration of a comprehensive and successful strategy for privatization needs to be accompanied by measures to strengthen the governance of enterprises that will not be privatized. The Government should transform SOEs into corporate entities managed according to commercial law; create an independent body in charge of SOEs, and abstain from new projects that can be taken on by the private sector. Furthermore, credit to enterprises should only be to finance their losses and should be conditional on restructuring or liquidation plans for clearly nonviable enterprises.

34.   *Private Sector Development*. The regulatory, legislative, and economic environment for private investment is rudimentary, with inadequate safeguards. Different incentives are applied to private

and public enterprises. State enterprises should not benefit from preferential credit extended by the banking system -- or from direct state subsidies in manufacturing and agriculture. Nor should they be given preferential access to both local and imported inputs.

35.   *Institutional Framework*. Turkmenistan needs to change the institutional framework for economic policymaking. In the past, policy decisions and the processing of information originated in Moscow, and the republican administration was only in charge of implementation. Therefore, there was little capacity to analyze economic developments. Turkmenistan should now start developing the institutional framework to formulate and implement reforms. Training to improve such capacity would be high priority.

36.   *Financial Sector Reform*. International experience shows that the financial system has been one of the most serious obstacles in the transition to a market economy. The intermingling of subsidy programs with credit programs makes the application of sound banking criteria -- or the performance of the banks' intermediation function -- virtually impossible. Reforms are necessary to liberalize and commercialize the financial system, to improve the payments system, and to strengthen the Central Bank, and legal, accounting, and prudential framework. Thereafter, financial sector reforms that will support economic growth include developing a merchant banking system, restructuring the State Savings Bank and other banks, and improving the flow of savings. Interest rates should increasingly play a greater role in mobilizing savings and in allocating credit. Their complete liberalization will be warranted once stabilization has been completed and once lending patterns are driven primarily by commercial rather than ownership criteria and confidence in the ability to withdraw deposits from the banking system has been restored.

37.   *Social Sector Reform*. Since Turkmenistan's social indicators are worse than elsewhere in the FSU, targeted and cost-effective measures are needed to address this problem. The current social safety net system is not capable of dealing with the social effects of an emerging market economy. If the government does implement major market oriented reforms it will need to restructure the social protection system in order to assist those negatively affected. Furthermore, the profile of those in need might change. For example, income differentials are increasing due to the trade disruptions and the break-up of the Soviet Union. Future developments will undoubtedly introduce other fundamental changes in the pattern of the poor and vulnerable. For the system to be affordable, social benefits should be focused on the poor, while remaining conducive to effective administration.

38.   Enterprises have not shed labor, despite the contraction of output. There is a tradeoff between improving the financial situation of enterprises and protecting employment. The implementation of a reform program would make it necessary to reduce legal restrictions and encourage labor mobility. Unemployment insurance could be financed by a payroll tax.

Sectoral Reforms

39.   *Energy*. Turkmenistan's energy sector offers good prospects for generating significant foreign exchange earnings and provides a basis for improved creditworthiness. But the prospects for the natural gas sector are clouded by low remaining proven reserves in developed fields, the limited capacity of the domestic industry to identify and develop new reserves, and the uncertainties surrounding export markets in the medium term.

40.   These challenges can be met if the Government attracts foreign expertise and capital to regenerate the sector's production potential and help diversify the export markets. The domestic industry lacks the capacity to undertake the scale of development required to sustain production at recent levels, and to reverse the trend toward premature liquidation. Moreover, the costs of such an undertaking are beyond the country's financing capacity. Inevitably, Turkmenistan needs foreign investors to realize its large resource potential.

41.   At present, the critical issues in the energy sector involve: (i) the arrangements for pricing and marketing of gas; (ii) the terms of access by third parties to the transmission network now owned and operated by Turkmengas; and, (iii) the taxation of foreign operators. Without a clear policy on the commercial aspects of gas production, promotional initiatives in gas-prone territories are unlikely to succeed. The Government needs to address these issues directly, within the framework of petroleum legislation.

42.   The country's capacity to market natural gas should be strengthened. While increasing gas exports to existing markets should be a short term priority, investments in new pipelines may be appropriate. This would allow Turkmenistan to diversify transport options and enter new export markets. The economic and financial viability of a large investment program under consideration has not been assessed. It would seem wise for the Government to postpone a decision until such analysis is available.

43.   *Energy Prices*. Turkmenistan has maintained a system of highly centralized control of all domestic energy prices. One feature of the present pricing framework is that it provides little incentive for the efficient management of enterprises and the efficient use of energy by consumers. Price controls, based on average enterprise operating costs, encourage the cross subsidization and continuation of non-viable activities, particularly in the absence of competition or regulatory monitoring of efficiency.

44.   The Government should ensure that energy prices fully reflect the cost of supply or, when traded in world markets, the export value. In applying this general principle, a distinction should be drawn between energy resources that can be supplied only with dedicated infrastructure that would be economically inefficient to duplicate. In the case of Turkmenistan, the latter situation would cover the network industries -- electricity and natural gas supply -- which require extensive transmission and distribution systems and enjoy inherently large economies of scale. For these natural monopolies, prices for specific consumers should cover operating cost plus an allowance to finance the cost of investments in order to maintain an acceptable service. Some regulation of these prices and the provision of effective service needs to be maintained.

45.   The Government's recently implemented directive that the main natural monopolies in the sector -- the power and gas distribution industries -- supply electricity and gas on a more or less free-of-charge basis has important policy implications. Currently, the estimated implicit subsidy of the supply of gas to residential and commercial consumers of gas is $40/per 1,000 cubic meters and $4/1000 cubic meters to industrial customers. The level of the implicit subsidy will be about $200 million with the full implementation of the distribution system currently under way, assuming that the present policy of free gas to residential consumers is maintained. This system is not only unsustainable, but also does not provide incentives for the efficient use of energy. The objective should be the progressive adjustment of prices. The Government may wish to have services to some customers below cost for a defined period of time. However, in order to avoid increasing the cost of services to other customers or reducing the efficiency and cost effectiveness with which these resources are used, this subsidy should be provided directly by the Government to the consumer.

46.   *Agriculture*. The priority in agriculture is to liberalize prices and establish a proper system of ownership. State production orders need to be eliminated to allow the market to work. Input subsidies should be phased out, and food prices adjusted to competitive levels. Price liberalization should be accompanied by the liberalization of distribution and trade, as well as by allowing imports and exports to provide alternative sources of commodities to state monopolies and help develop the domestic private marketing system. A hard budget constraint should be imposed on all state and collective farms, accompanied by lifting all geographical restrictions on buying inputs and selling outputs.

47.   Once the institutional and legal framework is put in place, privatization of small-scale agro-processing enterprises, input dealerships, and retail food outlets can begin. Furthermore, sectoral policies should be implemented including the withdrawal of the state from the direct distribution of agricultural inputs, the privatization of most processing, wholesale and retail trade, the development of small-scale transport operations, and the reform of agricultural credit, research, information, and marketing services.

48.   *Transport/Telecommunications*. Turkmenistan's geographic remoteness from hard-currency markets makes adequate transport and international telecommunications particularly important. The availability of transportation is critical for the competitiveness of agriculture and the industrial sector. Transport costs are highly subsidized, and thus these costs are given little consideration in production decisions. In reforming this system, the elimination of these subsidies and privatization is a key requirement. Thus a program should be developed as rapidly as possible that legalizes and regulates individual ownership of transportation services, privatizes small and medium-sized trucking enterprises, auctions off excess inventories of trucks and spare parts (with preference given to currently employed drivers), and auctions off surplus military trucks. Encouragement should be given to the breakup of huge trucking enterprises and the spinning off of the transportation units of various ministries. Agroprom, economic enterprises, municipalities and state and collective farms should to be changed into independent companies. Even with these steps, large investments will be needed in road improvements, all sizes and types of trucks, service facilities, logistics management, long-haul tractor-trailers, refrigerated trucks and transfer nodes between different types of transportation facilities.

49.   A restructuring program for the telecommunications sector should be defined including sectoral policy, regulation, legislation, and operating arrangements, before a long-term investment program can be developed. In the short-term the highest priority areas include the continuing maintenance and operation of the existing network and the expansion of revenue generating services.

50.   *Environment*. A major reform of environmental policies and institutions is required along with economic reforms. The appropriate pricing of resources -- such as water and energy -- will induce greater efficiency in resource use. The key reforms for environmental protection are price reform, privatization, and the establishment of a competitive industrial structure. But it will also be important to establish mechanisms for the development and implementation of environmental policy measures -- including an adequate monitoring system and effective procedures for standards setting and enforcement. Pollution fees and fines will help finance administrative costs, and user charges can help fund future environmental investments.

External Financing and Donor Participation

51.   Turkmenistan could have current account surpluses throughout the nineties provided there is substantial investment to sustain current gas export levels and develop basic transport and

telecommunications infrastructure. While Turkmenistan would be able to obtain some financial assistance from multilateral agencies, most capital requirements will need to be sourced from foreign direct investment (FDI) and loans from international commercial banks. Equity could be a natural financing source, specially for investments in natural resource development, provided the conditions to attract FDI are in place. The Government would also need to borrow since it is important to strike the appropriate balance between equity and borrowing. In addition to an adequate framework for FDI, the immediate external financing task faced by the Government is, therefore, to build up access to international capital markets.

52.   The Government of Turkmenistan needs to develop a foreign borrowing strategy. Among other principles, debt should only be incurred if it is going to generate higher rates of return or export growth than the interest rates incurred. Higher returns than the international cost of capital will require to have an adequate policy framework in place, including an environment conducive to exports and good investment projects. Moreover, a necessary condition in gaining access to capital markets is to ensure the continuation of a strong debt servicing capacity position, since it provides banks with the security that Turkmenistan will be able to service debt on commercial terms.

53.   Once a foreign borrowing strategy is in place, foreign borrowing should be monitored and governed by clear policies and ceilings. Linking loans to a sound investment program provides an insurance against returns that are lower than the cost of capital. Containing future external debt requires monitoring and regulating the activities of public entities entering into individual foreign loan agreements. It also requires extremely careful use of government guarantees for private projects.

54.   External financing, either for investment or for larger-than-anticipated external shocks, will be easier to obtain if Turkmenistan implements a strong reform program. To design and implement such a program, the Government will require substantial assistance in developing the institutional capability to manage the transition. The international donor community could provide technical assistance to develop this capability. It would not only support the design and implementation of economic reforms but also the preparation of investment and project proposals to be presented to the international community.

55.   The risk factors which could affect Turkmenistan's financing requirements are mostly exogenous developments. However, their impact could be minimized by appropriate Government policy. Adverse changes in terms of trade, further deterioration in interrepublican trade, and a slower than anticipated move to world prices for gas exports constitute the most important sources of risk. Long-term economic growth will depend on the country's policy environment which will be one factor determining the quality of investment decisions. Multilateral agencies could be of assistance to Turkmenistan in establishing the economic policies necessary to achieve its goal of long-term economic growth. Although lending would be small relative to the country's needs, the Government could use agencies like the World Bank to mobilize and to attempt to maximize the benefits from different external financing sources.

Part I

The Macroeconomic Framework

Part I of the report analyzes recent economic developments and the political and macroeconomic conditions (Chapter 1). Furthermore it discusses the policy priorities during the transition, assesses the medium-term outlook (Chapter 2), and provides an analysis of external financing issues (Chapter 3).

Despite its high proportion of desert land, Turkmenistan has strong development potential. Its energy resources are plentiful, and there is considerable scope for raising the productivity of irrigated land. Despite its mineral wealth, natural factors are a major constraint to Turkmenistan's development. Water is scarce, and the country is remote from markets. Furthermore, prosperity may be vulnerable, however, since there is great uncertainty surrounding the evolution of interrepublican trade and the pricing of gas exports. Turkmenistan's potential could be developed through appropriate economic management and a comprehensive program of structural reforms. The country could achieve some growth with little or no economic reforms, by financing it from the high export earnings expected for the medium term. However, with slow reforms growth would be limited below Turkmenistan's potential. The substantial waste through efficiency losses would limit the supply response of the productive sectors to new investment. Furthermore, without reforms, the lack of export diversification would leave the economy tied to the fate of energy-related earnings. A comprehensive reform program could bring about a strong recovery and reduce the impact of potential external risks.

It is expected that the country will have a substantial surplus in interrepublican and hard-currency trade over the medium-term. However, the trade surplus is underpinned by gas exports. The strength and speed of the recovery will depend critically on Turkmenistan's ability to sell its gas for hard currency and the ability of the country to expand its export base. Furthermore, the efficient re-investment of financial resources from the energy sector is central to Turkmenistan's future development prospects. The critical task at hand is to manage the surplus generated from exports carefully and to maximize its rate of return.

Even if there is no need for balance-of-payments support, investment needs in basic infrastructure and public services are high. The existing network is in poor condition and oriented to almost exclusive trade with the FSU. Furthermore, technical assistance is needed in a wide area of activities to assist Turkmenistan implement a reform program. While Turkmenistan would be able to obtain some financial assistance from multilateral agencies most capital requirements will need to be sourced from foreign direct investment and loans from international commercial banks.

CHAPTER 1

RECENT ECONOMIC DEVELOPMENTS

Turkmenistan in Perspective

1.1   Turkmenistan formally declared its independence from the USSR on 27 October 1991. On 21 December 1991 it joined other republics in the Commonwealth of Independent States (CIS). President Niyazov, elected uncontested on 27 October 1990 was previously chairman of Turkmenistan's Supreme Soviet and first secretary of the Central Committee of the republic's Communist Party. Enjoying strong executive powers he is assisted by an appointed Presidential Council. After independence, the Communist Party was formally disbanded, and many of its former members joined the Democratic faction in the Supreme Soviet. A new constitution was adopted by referendum on May 8, 1992, followed by presidential elections in which President Niyazov was reelected.

Geography and Demography

1.2   The Republic of Turkmenistan lies in the southernmost part of the former USSR bordering Uzbekistan in the north and the east, Kazakhstan in the north, the Caspian Sea in the west, and Iran and Afghanistan in the south. Covering 488,100 square kilometers, it is the fourth largest republic of the former Soviet Union. With the uninhabitable Kara Kum desert taking 90 percent of the total area Turkmenistan had only 3.5 million people in 1989, making it the fourth smallest republic in population (see Table 1.1). The native Turkmen population makes up 72 percent of the total (see Table 1.2). Other ethnic groups include Russians (9.5 percent), Uzbeks (8 percent), Kazakhs, Tatars, Ukrainians, Armenians and Azeris.

Table 1.1
Selected Demographic Data
for The Central Asian Republics

	Land Area (sq. km.)	Population 1989 (mln.)	Average Growth Rate 1979-89	Population Density (persons/ sq. km.)
Kazakhstan	2,717,300	16.464	1.2	6.0
Uzbekistan	447,400	19.906	2.6	44.0
Kyrgyz Republic	198,500	4.291	2.0	22.0
Tajikistan	143,100	5.112	3.0	36.0
Turkmenistan	488,100	3.534	2.5	7.0
Total	3,994,400	49.307	2.3	12.3
Russia	17,075,400	147.386	0.7	9.0
Turkey	779,000	55.000	2.4	71.0
Pakistan	796,000	109.900	3.2	138.0
United States	9,166,600	246.079	0.4	27.0
France	550,100	55.863	1.0	102.0

Source: *l'URSS en Chiffres 1989, USSR Facts and Figures Annual 1991, FAO Yearbook 1988, Gosplan World Development 1991,* IMF, IBRD, OECD and EBRD, *A Study of the Soviet Economy 1991,* vol. I, Table 32, p. 230.

Table 1.2
Percent Nationality Composition By Republic, 1989

	Russ.	Ukrai.	Balt.	Kaz.	Turk.	Uzbek	Taj.	Kyrg.
Kazakhstan	37.8	5.4	1.3	39.7	--	2.0	0.2	0.1
Uzbekistan	8.3	0.8	0.1	4.1	0.6	71.4	4.7	0.9
Kyrgyz Republic	21.5	2.5	0.2	0.9	--	12.9	0.8	52.4
Tajikistan	7.6	0.8	0.1	0.2	0.4	23.5	62.3	1.3
Turkmenistan	9.5	1.0	0.4	2.5	72.0	9.0	0.1	--

Source: *A Study of the Soviet Economy 1991*, vol. I, Table 4, p.207

Economic Structure

1.3   Turkmenistan's economy is highly dependent on the production and processing of energy resources and cotton. Rich in mineral resources, the republic has an estimated total of about 4.0 trillion cubic meters (tcm) of non-associated gas which has been identified and 1.1 billion tons of oil reserves. Total remaining identified reserves of natural gas amount to 2.7 tcm. Its proven gas reserves per capita are as high as those in Saudi Arabia (See Table 1.3) and it has large reserves of iodine bromine, sodium sulphate and various salts. There are also indications of gold and platinum. Turkmenistan extracts about 60 billion to 80 billion cubic meters of natural gas a year. Most of it is exported because there are no domestic facilities for chemical processing of natural gas. The main domestic use of gas is as fuel for thermal power-generating plants; two thirds of the production from these plants is also exported. The production of chemicals from other mineral resources is highly developed and includes the production of mineral fertilizers, sulfuric acid, ammonia, sulphur, synthetic detergent, sulphate and chloride salts, iodine and bromide iron. Oil is refined at the Krasnovodsk refinery, which has a capacity of 5 million tons per year.

1.4   Despite its mineral wealth, natural factors are a major constraint to Turkmenistan's development. Water is scarce, and the country is remote from markets. The industrial structure, is a result not only of this resource base, but also of the former Soviet Gosplan, with its heavy emphasis on large plants designed to service the whole former Soviet Union market. In 1991, about a third of Turkmenistan's industrial production came from 61 textile enterprises, another third from 38 large state enterprises in   chemical, gas, oil-processing and electricity-generation.

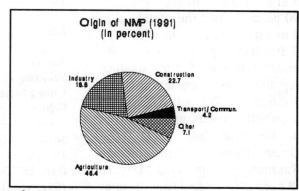

Figure 1.1

1.5   Industrial production contributed about a fifth of net material product (NMP) in 1991, and construction about a fourth. But there is a large volume of unfinished construction, and transport and telecommunications links with the rest of the world remain weak.

1.6   Even though Turkmenistan has considerable potential for diversification into mineral resource-based industries, the economy remains predominantly agricultural. In addition to cotton, other major crops include grains, vegetables and fruits. Livestock products accounted for nearly one fourth of total gross agricultural production in 1991. In the past three years, agriculture accounted on average for 46 percent of net material product (see Figure 1.1) and for 42 percent of employment. Agricultural production relies heavily on irrigation with about half of all arable land irrigated. Agricultural yields remain low by international standards, however, because of years of inefficient water use, salination, irrigation of inappropriate land and overdevelopment of cotton cultivation.

1.7   Exports are dominated by gas, oil products and light industrial goods, mainly cotton fiber. Of the 74.5 billion cubic meters of gas and 380,000 tons of cotton fiber exported in 1991, 84 percent was exported to other republics. The main imports from other republics in 1991 were machinery and metalwork (a third of the total), light manufactured goods (19 percent) and processed food (15 percent); the major imports from the rest of the world in 1991 were light industry products (37 percent) and food products (27 percent).

Table 1.3
Gas and Oil Reserves in Selected Countries

	GNP per capita (US$, 1990)	Population (mln)	Crude oil Reserves (bln bbls)	Proven Gas Reserves (tcm)	Crude Oil Reserves per Capita	Gas Reserves per Capita
Turkmenistan	1,357	3.7	2.5	1.3	0.68	351
Kazakhstan	2,159	16.7	12.00	1.6	0.72	96
Saudi Arabia	7,060	14.9	255.00	5.2	17.11	349
Venezuela	2,580	19.0	58.5	3.0	3.08	158
Algeria	2,060	25.00	9.2	3.2	0.37	128
Nigeria	290	114.00	16.00	2.8	0.14	25
Canada	20,370	26.5	-	2.7	-	102
Indonesia	510	178	8.2	2.6	0.05	15
Norway	22,830	4.2	na	2.3	na	548

Sources: J. Homer, *Natural Gas in Developing Countries,* World Bank Discussion Papers, Washington D.C., 1993; World Bank staff estimates.

1.8   Turkmenistan's growth rate in the 1980s was high compared with that of other republics of the former Soviet Union. Although income per capita was significantly below that of Russia and the Soviet Union averages (about 0.7 compared with the union average of 1.0 in the 1980s), it was supposedly higher than corresponding incomes for citizens of the other Central Asian countries, excluding Kazakhstan. Nevertheless, Turkmenistan's social indicators have been very low by Western standards and in comparison with other Central Asian countries (see Table 1.4). The country had the highest infant mortality in the former Soviet Union and the lowest life expectancy (65.2 years). The average family size is 5.6, compared with 3.5 in the former Soviet Union; and the annual population growth rate is high (2.5 percent from 1985 to 1990, and projected at 2.1 percent for 1990 to 1995). The average growth in the working-age population was 2.7 percent from 1979 to 1989 and is increasing (compared with 0.4 percent in the former Soviet Union and 0.1 percent in Russia). More than 40 percent of the population is less than 14 years old compared with 25 percent in the former Soviet Union overall (see Table 1.4). That will create pressure on the labor market in the future.

Table 1.4
Social Indicators

	Turkmenistan	Russia	Former Soviet Union	Lower middle-income countries	Upper middle-income countries
Infant mortality (per 1,000), 1989	54.7	17.8	22.7	51.0	50.0
Life expectancy at birth (years), 1989	65.2	69.6	69.5	65.0	67.0
Average family size, 1989	5.6	3.2	3.5	na	na
Doctors (per 10,000), 1989	35.5	47.3	44.4	na	na
Hospital beds (per 10,000), 1989	111.0	139.0	133.0	na	na
Birth rate (per 1,000)	35.0	14.6	17.6	30.0	27.0
Fertility	4.5	1.7	2.4	3.6	2.7
Income distribution, 1989 (percentage of total population)					
- Less than R 75	35.0	5.0	11.1	na	na
- R 75-100	22.6	11.0	13.7	na	na
- R 100-150	26.2	31.1	na	na	na
- R 150-200	10.1	25.1	22.1	na	na
- Greater than R 200	6.1	27.8	21.8	na	na
Age of population, 1990 (in percentage of total)					
- 0-14	41.3	23.6	25.7	37.6	33.8
- 15-65	54.7	65.1	65.1	57.8	60.9

Source: IMF, World Bank, OECD and EBRD, *A Study of the Soviet Economy,* February 1991, World Bank, World Development Report 1991 and 1992.

Economic Performance before 1992

Aggregate Demand and Output

1.9   Turkmenistan's economy, like that of the other former Soviet Union republics, was hurt by instability in the USSR at the end of the 1980s. In 1990, however, NMP increased, despite a 22 percent drop in industrial production mainly because of growth in the agricultural and transport sectors (see Figures 1.2, 1.3 and 1.4).   In 1991, Turkmenistan's economy was less severely affected by disruptions in trade and the breakup of the Soviet Union than were many of the other republics. NMP declined less than 1 percent in real terms (compared with 11 percent in Russia). Sustained growth in oil and cotton processing, the rise in the production of consumer goods and the construction activities

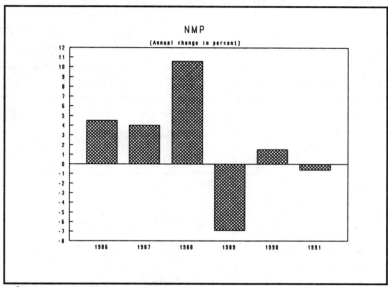

Figure 1.2

associated with the Chardzhou plant nearly offset the decline in agricultural production that resulted from bad weather and a sharp contraction in trade and the transport sector. Total investment levels were sustained by a high level of inventory investment (see Figures 1.4 and 1.6). However, personal consumption declined both in 1990 and 1991 (see Figure 1.5).

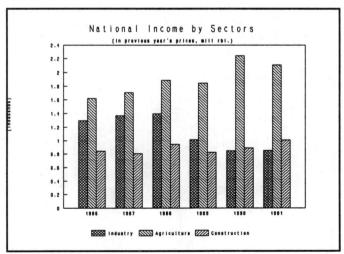

Figure 1.3

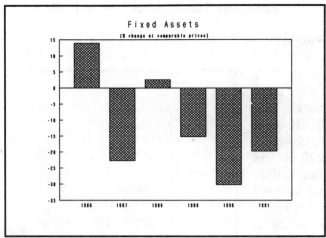

Figure 1.4

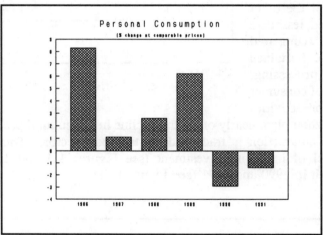

Figure 1.5

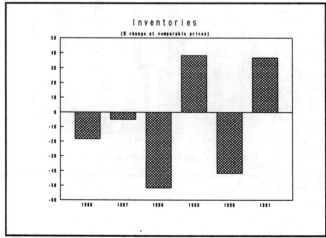

Figure 1.6

External Trade

1.10   Trade, measured as an average of exports and imports, was some 35 percent of GNP prior to independence, 92.5 percent of which was interrepublican. This proportion is the highest of all the former republics. But this dependency is based on exports that are relatively homogeneous and have world markets. Some of these exports could be diverted outside the FSU if certain conditions are met. The consolidated balance of payments in domestic prices is estimated to have been in surplus in 1991 of about 17 percent of GNP. The trade account with foreign countries ran a persistent deficit before 1991, but these numbers did not include any shipments of natural gas, Turkmenistan's principal hard-currency earner. Before independence, the gas was valued at a domestic USSR price that was a small fraction of the world price, and it was pooled with Russian gas for distribution within Russia and for sale to the economies of Eastern Europe that were members of the Council for Mutual Economic Association (CMEA). With the end of the CMEA on 1 January 1991, trade with the USSR was initiated at world prices with payment in hard-currency. For 1991, Turkmenistan gas exports made up 11 percent of the total USSR gas exports, with exports assigned to Hungary, Poland, Czechoslovakia, Yugoslavia and Romania. However, this quota was only part of Turkmenistan's gas sales to Russia, which is the only market connected to Turkmenistan by pipeline. Turkmenistan's trade balance with foreign countries improved substantially in 1991, after 12 billion cubic meters of natural gas were reassigned from interrepublican to foreign exports. Since in 1991 these exports were not undertaken in hard-currency but in rubles at an artificially low exchange rate, it seems more consistent to include them in the interrepublican trade figures. If the gas exports are excluded, hard-currency exports declined. Prior to 1991, Turkmenistan's interrepublican trade account also operated in persistent deficit. But in 1991 the trade balance shifted into a surplus of about 23 percent of gross national product -- a result of a sharp increase in the value of exports.

Price Performance

1.11   Under central planning and the central allocation of real resources, prices were generally an accounting tool with little effect on consumption, investment or production decisions. Prices remained fixed for long periods at levels unrelated to the pattern of scarcities. The official price index, did not reflect the "hidden" inflation associated with the introduction of supposedly new products and the costs to consumers and society as a whole of goods rationed by store-by-store searches and long queues, favoritism and corruption.

1.12   In 1991, retail prices increased by 173 percent, and wholesale prices by 296 percent, following the January-April 1991 price reforms in Russia and the accommodative monetary policy in the former Soviet Union as a whole. The increasing differential between wholesale and retail inflation was partially associated with increasing subsidization of consumer goods.

Fiscal Policy before Independence

1.13   Turkmenistan's fiscal accounts for the second half of the 1980s show a small surplus. However, the budgets of the republic's governments were ultimately always in balance, because the union automatically financed any revenue shortfall or expenditure overrun by allowing higher revenue retention or by direct budgetary transfers. Before 1990, fiscal policy in the USSR was strictly centralized to ensure conformity with plan objectives and in contrast with a genuine federal fiscal system, in which revenue-sharing arrangements between central and local governments are relatively stable and unified, in the former USSR they were changed annually and on an ad hoc basis. Revenue-sharing arrangements served only as an administrative device to simplify a system of centrally controlled resource allocations by republics. Most major taxes were to be shared on the basis of negotiated arrangements between the union Ministry of Finance, and the ministries of finance of the 15 republics. Expenditures were mainly guided by spending directives issued by Gosplan.

Table 1.5
USSR: Breakdown of Planned State Budget Revenues of Union Republics,
By Republic, 1990

Union Republic	Total Revenue (bln rbl)	Personal Turnover Tax (allocation and share of revenue)		Income Tax (allocation and share of revenue)		Enterprise Taxes (allocation and share of revenue)		Union Grants (as a share of revenue)	Other Sources (as a share of revenue)
All Republics	248.7	82	37.5	57	8.2	14	6.6	3.5	44.2
RSFSR	137.5	84	37.7	50	9.2	12	7.6	--	45.5
Turkmenistan	2.3	100	34.8	100	5.2	20	2.2	30.9	26.9

Note: Consolidated budget of union republics and local soviets of people's deputies. Data refer to budget plan for 1990, unless otherwise noted. Allocation refers to the proportion of revenue to be retained by union republic from revenue collected within the republic in a given revenue category. Revenue from profits of union-subordinated state enterprises from allocation of profit tax, as shown; 100 percent allocation of tax on labor resources; and 100 percent of water charges.

Sources: IMF, World Bank, OECD and EBRD, *A Study of the Soviet Economy,* February 1991

1.14   Turkmenistan was one of the main beneficiaries of the transfers from the union budget. Direct transfers from the union budget accounted for up to 20 percent of total revenues (see Table 1.6) or 10 percent of GDP. Furthermore, the retention rate of its main revenue sources, the turnover tax and the personal income tax was 100 percent in the late 1980s (see Table 1.5), that is, all of the revenues from these taxes collected on the territory in Turkmenistan were retained in Turkmenistan's budget. Therefore, Turkmenistan's financing share on expenditure items which were financed solely by the union budget (including defense, justice, internal security, subsidies to the external sector, most budgetary investment in the economy, and enterprises of the so-called "group A", for example, transport and heavy industry) was close to zero. This constituted an additional net indirect net transfer from the union to Turkmenistan's budget[1]. Capital expenditures were also fully centralized and all capital investments were financed and implemented by the Ministry of Economics in Moscow, with the exception of those directly funded by public enterprises. Unused investment funds had to be returned to the central government in Moscow.

---

1.   The following example illustrates the magnitude of these indirect budget transfers. In 1990, direct transfers from the union budget accounted for about 10 percent of GDP. In addition Turkmenistan received 20 percent of the profit tax of union-subordinated state-enterprises. Capital expenditure and defense related expenditure accounted each for about 14 percent of total expenditure in the Union budget. If these expenditure shares are applied to Turkmenistan's budget the direct transfers and the indirect transfers--the distribution of the profit tax of union-subordinated enterprises and capital and defense-related expenditure undertaken by the Union-- amounted to 25 percent of Turkmenistan's GNP in 1990.

Table 1.6
Consolidated Government Budget, 1985 - 91
(in millions of current rubles)

	1990	1991	1991 %
Total Revenue	3,236.4	6,486.6	100.0
Tax Revenue	1,037.8	1,971.4	30.4
- Turnover Tax	779.8	668.8	10.0
- Company Profits Tax[a]	..	517.5	8.0
- Sales Tax[a]	..	314.1	4.8
- Income Tax from Coops.[b]	92.0	121.7	1.9
- Personal Income Tax	166.0	349.3	5.4
Non-tax revenue	1,470.5	3,106.2	47.9
- Foreign Economic Activity[c]	..	10.8	0.2
- State Duties	15.4	33.8	1.1
- State Lottery	3.2	2.6	0.1
- Funds from Social Security	187.2	..	..
- Profits Transfers[d]	312.2	..	..
- State Bonds[e]	35.6	5.5	0.1
- Fixed Payments	..	1,551.0	23.0
- Other Revenue	916.9	1,503.0	23.2
Union Transfers	728.1	1,409.0	21.7
Total Expenditure	3,114.0	5,895.6	100.0
National Economy[f]	1,848.2	2,302.3	32.5
- Social & Cultural	1,162.1	3,354.7	56.9
of which:			
- Education & Science	655.2	1,158.8	19.7
- Health, Physical Education	282.9	555.7	9.4
- Social Security	206.8	1,571.7	26.7
Internal Security & Admin [g]	48.8	161.0	2.2
Other Expenses	54.9	77.6	1.3
Surplus/Deficit (Percent of GDP)	122.4	591.0	
Revenues	42.7	44.2	
Expenditures	41.1	40.2	
Union Transfers	9.6	9.6	

Note: Includes all levels of government, but excludes the hard-currency fund
a/ Introduced in 1991
b/ Same as company income tax
c/ Income arising from the sale of goods imported with hard-currency
d/ Transfers from state-owned enterprises (formerly of the Soviet Union)
e/ Not a financing item: state bonds were issued by the former Soviet Union government and sold in Turkmenistan. The receipts were divided evenly between the union and Turkmenistan. However, these bonds were the liability of the union making Turkmenistan's share a transfer from the union
f/ Including development (capital) expenditure, and subsidies on account of price differentials
g/ Includes police and administration

Source: Ministry of Economics and Finance

1.15   As in many other republics, the management of public finances was particularly difficult in 1991, as efforts for full independence intensified. First, the tax laws of the union were superseded by regional regulations. Second, while the April 1990 law gave the republics primacy in determining expenditure policies in several areas, Turkmenistan also started to pursue its own independent investment, subsidy and social support policies without consultation with the union government. The government of Turkmenistan imposed an additional profit transfer from the state-owned Cotton Cooperation and a one-time export duty on raw materials.

1.16   Expenditures for the "national economy", - mainly of subsidies to account for price differentials and development capital expenditures - amounted to about 12.4 percent of GDP in 1991. These large subsidies reflected mainly the compensation paid to agencies and enterprises required to sell food and medicine at controlled wholesale prices. Expenditures for education, culture and arts, health and social security accounted for over 18 percent of GDP in 1991. Many social security funds were administered through extra budgetary accounts such as the pension fund or the Social Insurance Fund. Transfers from the union were 22 percent of total revenue, and the budget for 1991 closed with a surplus of R591 million (see Table 1.6).

Money and Credit

1.17   Under central planning the Soviet Gosbank did not formulate and implement monetary policies in the sense generally understood in market economies. Credit and cash plans were constructed as the financial counterparts of the planning of the real flows of goods and services in the economy. Therefore, monetary policy in Turkmenistan was highly accommodative. For 1991, domestic credit extended to the non-government sector and the broad monetary aggregate M2 increased threefold. Currency in circulation increased by 145 percent, compared with a 14 percent in 1990. The main source of monetary expansion was the rapid rise in credit to the non-government sector, which rose by 195 percent. This outweighed the contractionary impact of government operations on domestic liquidity and contributed to a threefold increase in the net domestic assets of the banking system. Overall, the ratio of broad money (M2) to GDP increased to 98 percent by the end of 1991.

1.18   The level of nominal interest rates increased markedly during 1990, with some consumer loan rates increasing by as much as 17 percentage points (from a prevailing maximum of 8 to 25 percent). During 1991, on instructions from the USSR Gosbank, refinance rates were increased from 3 to 5 percent to 6 to 12 percent. Other interest rates remained broadly unchanged and all interest rates remained highly negative in real terms despite the increases. The bulk of credit given by banks was short term (repayable within a year) with long term credit accounting for only 6 percent of the total at the end of 1991. Industry was the major recipient, (absorbing about 46 percent of bank credit outstanding at the end of 1991), followed by the trade sector.

Table 1.7
Preliminary Summary Monetary Accounts
End of Period Stocks (in billion rubles)

	Dec 1991	Dec 1992	Aug 1993
Central Bank (SCBT)			
Assets	4.0	26	189
Net Foreign Assets (NFA)	-6.0	-125	316
NFA in hard currency	--	-1	699
NFA in rubles a/	-6.0	-124	-383
o/w: with Russia	-6.0	-125	-325
Net Domestic Assets	9.0	150	-127
Credit to Government (net)	--	199	-541
Credit to banks	2.0	48	549
Credit to the economy	--	--	165
Other items net b/	8.0	-96	-300
- Correspondent Accounts	-3.0	-99	-187
Liabilities	4.0	26	189
Currency outside SCBT c/	3.0	19	108
Reserves	1.0	7	78
Other Deposits	--	1	2
Banking System			
Assets	12.0	106	800
Net Foreign Assets	-4.0	50	456
NFA in hard currency	--	173	704
NFA in rubles a/	-6.0	-124	-251
LT Claim on Sberbank USSR	2.0	2	3
Net Domestic assets	16.0	56	344
Credit to Government (net)	-1.0	21	-720
Credit to the economy	10.0	86	1,272
Other items net b/	7.0	-52	-208
Liabilities	12.0	106	800
Currency outside banks c/	3.0	13	75
Deposits	10.0	93	725

a/ Excludes ruble shipments from Central Bank of Russia (CBR).
b/ Consists of interbank loans, correspondent and settlement, and unclassified accounts.
c/ For SCBT: currency received from CBR less vault holdings;
      for the banking system: currency emitted by SCBT less commercial banks' vault holdings.

Source: IMF

Developments in 1992 and 1993

1.19   Although there are strong indications that Turkmenistan was less affected by the breakdown of the Soviet Union than the other former republics, preliminary Goskomstat data are inconsistent and many of the indicators are of doubtful reliability. Especially the national income estimates are contradictory. Therefore, staff estimates of basic economic indicators are likely to be revised when more reliable data is available. Furthermore, comparisons of economic indicators between 1991 and 1992 have to be undertaken very carefully as far as the governments budget is concerned since the 1992 budget was the first one implemented by the Turkmen government and it includes significant changes in the revenue structure and expenditure responsibilities.

Aggregate Demand and Output in 1992

1.20   There are indications that output dropped much less than in other countries of the former Soviet Union in 1992, in part because of significant construction activity. With a surplus in the consolidated budget, the government was able to engage in several investment projects like the construction of the new airport in Ashkabad. Agricultural output declined by about 4 percent because of bad weather and large increases in input costs, while industrial production fell by about 17 percent because of disruptions in interrepublican trade, shortage of spare parts and inputs traditionally supplied by other FSU countries and the inability of most enterprise managers to adapt to changing circumstances. Estimates set the decline in real NMP at 5 percent for 1992, assuming declines in all sectors except construction. The decline in total consumption was about 7 percent. Imports from the former Soviet Union countries declined less than in other countries of the former Soviet Union.

Table 1.8
Main Economic Indicators

NMP Growth Rate	-5
- Agriculture	-4
- Industry	-17
- Construction	23
- Other	-10
Investment (% of NMP)	25
Trade Surplus (% of NMP)	17
Government Revenues (% of NMP)	
- excluding hard-currency fund	25
- including hard-currency fund	66
Government Expenditure (% of NMP)	38
Price Changes (Dec. 1991=100)	
- Wholesale Prices (Dec. 1992)	1615
- Retail Prices (Dec. 1992)	964

Source: Goskomstat

1.21   For 1993, Goskomstat data show an NMP increase of 8 percent for the first 8 months. This is mainly due to an increase in gas output after the decline of about 30 percent in 1992. Furthermore, agricultural output is increasing after the low yields in 1992. However, industrial output has declined by about 10 percent in the first 8 months.

Price Liberalization

1.22   On January 4, 1992, a presidential decree stipulated that prices of most consumer, industrial, and agricultural goods in Turkmenistan would be determined according to the market principles of supply and demand beginning January 10, 1992. Gosplan was given the responsibility of regulating, monitoring, and modifying the processes of market price determination and of revaluing the existing stock of goods. The decree also defined a number of "socially important" goods whose prices would remain controlled.   The prices of most of those goods, however, were increased significantly on January 10, 1992. The decree also specified a number of measures intended to guard against abuses of the new price regime.

Reversals in the Liberalization of Prices

1.23   On January 17, 1992 the authorities reversed some of the above price liberalization measures. The reversals included lengthening the list of products whose pricing is subject to state control to include grains, fish, children's products, and natural gas sold by intermediaries to households and providers of community services. The decree also reduced the controlled increase in the prices of some meats, liquified gas, electricity, and heating.

Price Increases

1.24   Price indicators have to be interpreted with caution. Since the indices for commodity groups are unweighted averages, increases in prices of a few goods lead to a large increase in the overall index, irrespective of the weight of these goods. Inflation rates will be overestimated if indicators are used that are derived from monthly data (see Table 1.9).

Table 1.9
Price Changes in 1991/1992

	1991[a]	1992[b]	Average Change 1991	Average Change 1992	Dec 1992[c]
Retail	273	744	113	371	964
Wholesale	396	8,899	152	2,735	1,615

Source: Goskomsat
a/ 1990 = 100; based on monthly price changes
b/ 1991 = 100; based on monthly price changes
c/ December 1991 = 100

1.25   Overall, wholesale prices increased 16 fold from December 1991 to December 1992, and average prices for consumer goods rose more than nine fold. The wholesale price increases were especially high on oil, chemical, machinery, and food products. Consumer price inflation declined sharply during the year before registering about 15 percent in December (see Figure 1.7). Consumer price inflation is lower in Turkmenistan than in other countries of the former Soviet Union but wholesale price inflation has been quite dramatic (see figures 1.8 and 1.9). Consumer prices rose by 364 percent in January-May 1993, reflecting 200-300 percent increases in many controlled prices in February 1993. The difference between producer and consumer price inflation again reflects extensive budget subsidies for consumer goods. While inflation has been high in Turkmenistan, it has been less than in the Russian Federation for both consumer and wholesale prices. This can be explained, by price liberalization being less complete in Turkmenistan than in Russia -- most of the prices of basic food and consumer goods are still administered -- and price differentials can be expected to persist, given transport costs and remaining trade barriers.

1.26   With the introduction of the new currency in November 1993, the Government liberalized several prices. Eleven commodities are still subject to control at subsidized prices. Another 26 commodities are subject to a review by an antimonopoly commission, which will negotiate with enterprises the maximum level of price adjustment. The Government has indicated that the ultimate goal is full price liberalization, but the timetable is not clear.

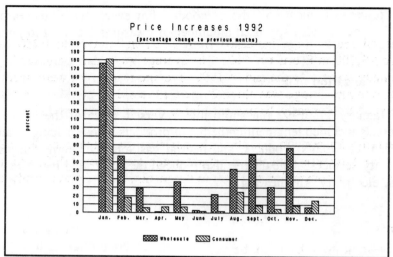

Figure 1.7

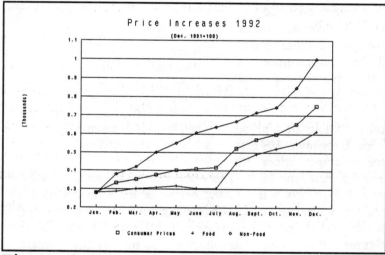

Figure 1.8

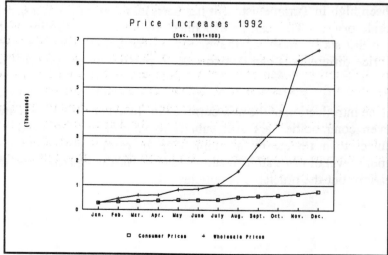

Figure 1.9

Wages

1.27   The minimum wage increased from R350 in January to R750 in July to R1,600 in October 1992 and to R3,200 in February 1993. The average wage also increased in 1992, but somewhat faster than the minimum wage. At the end of 1992, average real wages were unchanged from the 1990 level, while the real minimum wage was about 20 percent less than in 1990. In May 1993, the average real wage was estimated to be nearly 20 percent higher than at the end of 1990.

1.28   After the introduction of the new currency on November 1, 1993, the Government established a new wage structure with the minimum wage set at manat 150, and an estimated average wage of manat 400. With a conversion of R500 to the manat, these figures imply a sharp one-time rise in the real wage.

Fiscal Developments

1.29   The breakdown of the old union revenue and expenditure sharing system made major changes in Turkmenistan's fiscal system necessary. The 1992 budget was the first implemented by the Turkmen Government after the breakdown of the Soviet union and it included significant changes in the revenue and expenditure structure.

Public Finances in 1992

1.30   After the Soviet Union dissolved in 1991, the old revenue-sharing system became inadequate and new tax laws had to be introduced. The budget for 1992 included significant changes in the structure of taxation and new expenditure categories. On the revenue side, the turnover tax and the sales tax were replaced by a value-added-tax (VAT) and a number of excise taxes levied on a small number of goods. But the excise tax on vodka and gasoline were eliminated on August 1, 1992. The VAT was levied at a rate of 28 percent. Imports from outside the FSU are not subject to the VAT, and the tax paid on capital goods purchases is not deductible. A tax on enterprise profits (CIT) at a flat rate of 35 percent, was adopted in 1991. The personal income tax has now a schedular structure with progressive marginal rates which leaves a large part of nonwage income free of personal income tax.

1.31   The major tax sources in 1992 were the VAT (about 26 percent of total revenues) and the enterprise profit tax (20 percent). Another major source of revenue in the 1992 budget was fixed payments to the budget by the state-owned gas and cotton companies; these payments account for 29 percent of total revenues. These are profit transfers payable to the government over and above company income tax and VAT payments. Furthermore, export companies had to surrender a proportion of their foreign exchange earnings, typically about 70 to 75 percent. In return they received in rubles -- except for the gas corporation which received no payment -- the domestic price equivalent for the goods exported. As domestic prices are well below international prices, the system constituted a substantial implicit tax on exporters. Furthermore, the ruble amounts spent to purchase the hard-currency earned by enterprises are budgetary expenditures while the hard-currency retained was kept in an extrabudgetary account and was used to accumulate reserves. It is estimated that the net inflows to the extrabudgetary foreign exchange fund were about 400 million dollars (R80 billion at an average exchange rate of 200 rubles to the dollar) in 1992.

Table 1.10
Consolidated Budget, 1992-1993
(in millions of rubles)

	1992 Budget Est.	1992 Actual	1992 % of Total	1993 Jan-June Actual
REVENUE	47,963	64,009	100.0	256,157
Tax	22,351	34,447	53.8	214,268
Value-added Tax	14,058	17,400	27.2	87,836
Gas Corp.	7,856	6,563	10.3	..
Cotton Assoc.[a]	2,465	0	0.0	..
Other	3,737	10,837	16.9	..
Company Profits Tax	5,771	12,875	20.1	69,963
Gas Corp.	3,409	3,754	5.9	..
Cotton Assoc.[a]	2,285	0	0.0	..
Oil Corps	0	1,823	2.9	..
Other Coops/				
Public Companies	77	7,298	11.4	..
Excises	1,502	1,187	1.9	..
Personal Income Tax	1,020	2,985	4.7	7,012
Tax on Raw Materials[b]	..	..	..	49,457
Nontax	25,612	29,562	46.2	41,889
Fixed Payments[c]	17,354	18,253	28.5	..
Gas Corp.	13,830	10,183	15.9	..
Cotton Assoc.	3,524	7,500	11.7	..
Electricity Corp.	0	570	0.9	..
Sale of Imported Food	7,100	56	0.1	14,418
Other Revenue	1,158	11,253	17.6	27,471
EXPENDITURE	52,150	92,665	100.0	211,898
National Economy	25,952	58,059	62.7	132,380
Price Subsidies	15,203	28,558	30.8	..
Capital Expenditure	7,340	17,670	19.1	..
Other	3,409	11,831	12.8	..
Social and Cultural	15,477	26,396	28.5	58,155
Education and Science	6,820	13,423	14.5	..
Health Care	3,375	6,202	6.7	..
Social Security	4,101	5,256	5.7	..
Defense	38	493	0.1	1,762
Other	10,683	7,717	8.3	19,601
SURPLUS (+)/DEFICIT(-)	-4,187	-28,656		44,259

Note:
[a] Raw cotton is exempted from all taxes.
[b] Tax on Raw Materials was introduced in 1993.
[c] Fixed payment was abolished in 1993.

Source: Ministry of Economics and Finance, Ashkabad 1993 and IMF

1.32   Initially, the government projected a budget deficit for 1992 at R4.2 billion assuming that the price for expenditures and revenues would increase five fold (see Table 1.10). The budget was prepared by the Ministry of Economics and Finance, and the expenditure estimates were primarily based on budget norms and the previous year's expenditures, with limited attempts to adjust for new policy measures and price changes. The actual budget outcome differed, therefore, significantly from the planned figures. The budget for 1992 showed a deficit of R32 billion (12.4 percent of GDP). However, it is very important to point out that when the hard-currency revenues are taken into account (valued at the average exchange rate for 1992), the budget was in a substantial surplus of R70 billion.

1.33   One major factor in the budget outcome was the greater-than-expected increase in prices. The actual realized increase in prices exceeded the budget estimates, and there was a shortfall in real terms in all major tax revenues. The introduction of new taxes like the VAT in place of the turnover tax resulted in a significant shortfall of tax revenues in the first months of 1992, that is, VAT collections in January amounted to only R6.6 billion; in February they went up to R732 billion With the lack of experience among tax collectors and taxpayers, a certain decree of noncompliance should have been anticipated. Furthermore, although the planned budget included R7 billion from foreign economic activity, actual revenues from this source were close to zero. Besides, real budgetary revenues were overestimated. Inflation eroded a substantial proportion of revenues which were fixed on a nominal basis. The payments of the gas company were even lower than in the budget plan for 1992 because the dispute with the Ukraine over gas prices led to a reduction in the fixed payment of the gas company. The VAT revenues were also affected by problems with gas exports, because the gas company pays a large share (30 to 40 percent) of all VAT revenues. On the expenditure side, the price increases led to a substantial increase in nominal expenditures, whereas real expenditures -- especially on education and health care -- declined by about 30 percent. As a result, price subsidies accounted for about one third of total expenditure.

Budget for 1993

1.34   The planned budget for 1993 was balanced. However, since the plan was drawn up under unrealistic assumptions regarding inflation and sales and prices of energy exports, substantial revisions were done already in February. The 1993 budget includes significant changes in the overall revenue structure. Raw cotton is exempted from all taxes in 1993 in order to support investments in cotton processing. The VAT rate was reduced to 20 percent with several exemptions and the CIT rate to 25 percent. Instead of a fixed payment a "tax on raw materials" is now levied on sales of raw materials. The rate for oil and mineral fertilizer is 10 percent of sales, on chemicals 5 percent and on gas 22 percent. Essentially, 95 percent of the revenues from this tax will be paid by the gas company. The tax is not levied on hard-currency exports.

1.35   The budgetary situation in 1993 is severely affected by the increase in arrears of some FSU countries on Turkmenistan's exports and lower ruble gas receipts. Furthermore, the appreciation of the real exchange rate of the ruble causes a lower share of hard-currency receipts, because the nominal ruble/dollar exchange rate depreciated less than the rate of increase in the GDP deflator. The overall fiscal position in 1993 is projected to show a deficit of about 5 to 7 percent of GDP, financed mainly through the banking system.

Monetary Policy

1.36   The mechanism for issuing and distributing money in 1992 was essentially unchanged from that under Soviet central planning. Turkmenistan has very limited control over monetary policy and inflation outcomes as long as the country remains in the ruble zone because inflation will be imported through the price-exchange rate mechanism. The rate of currency issue by the Central Bank of Turkmenistan in 1992 is the result of an interaction between the requests for currency from the Central Bank of Turkmenistan to the Central Bank of Russia and the volume of new currency received from the Central Bank of Russia.

1.37   The Central Bank of Turkmenistan obtained its rubles through the debiting of Turkmenistan's settlement account with the Russian Central Bank. Cash was then passed on to commercial banks for distribution to enterprises to meet wage bills in particular after debiting these banks' correspondent accounts with the Turkmenistan Central Bank. As price liberalization has proceeded and inflation has increased in the countries of the former Soviet Union, much more frequent adjustments were needed in the amount of cash required to meet wage payments. The adjustments and requests for currency to the Russian Central Bank were made on a 10-day basis in late 1992.

1.38   In the early part of 1992, currency issue lagged behind the rise in prices that began in January. Due to the problems with the availability of currency in late 1991 and early 1992, a Presidential decree was signed on January 4, 1992 requiring that: (i) the authorities should not service or redeem union bonds for 1992; (ii) financial instruments issued by other republic's governments not be cashed in Turkmenistan; (iii) checks issued outside the country not be honored by the financial institutions; (iv) banks not transfer their surplus ruble resources to the other republics; and, (v) deposits made through non-cash means of payment could not be withdrawn in the form of cash for six months. Currency issue was much larger in the second quarter of 1992. However, the currency question was complicated by the open borders between countries in the ruble zone. Currency can be carried into and out of Turkmenistan without restraint, and the comparatively low subsidized prices in Turkmenistan might have attracted large amounts of currency into the country for the purchase of goods. The amount of currency inflow was unknown, however, and more broadly the stock of currency actually circulating in Turkmenistan was unknown.[2]

1.39   There are indications that total credit to state enterprises rose by 630 percent in 1992, with a large share being allocated by the Credit Committee of the Cabinet of Ministers. Once a decision for credit allocation had been reached, commercial banks were authorized to borrow from the Central Bank at a refinance rate of 2 percent and on-lend to the appropriate enterprise at 3 percent. Banks may also borrow at 15 percent from the Central Bank and on-lend at 18 percent to enterprises or the private sector that have not been included in the "directed credit" plan. Credit policy was extremely accommodating in early 1993 and access to credit by the Central Bank at highly negative real interest rates by state enterprises and agricultural cooperations increased dramatically.

1.40   The increase in currency in circulation and the associated increase in enterprise borrowing from banks to finance their wage payments, has had a severe impact on the structure of the commercial banks balance sheets. At the level of individual banking institutions, the inflation has resulted in a deterioration in their standing as the Government has persisted in its policy of providing credit at highly

---

2.   Gosbank Russia has estimated a net migration of cash at 60 percent of emission.

subsidized rates to industrial and agricultural enterprises. As a result, the capitalization of the banking system has declined dramatically in relative terms with the capital to assets ratio falling.

Developments in 1993

1.41   Monetary developments until November 1993 were still dominated by the ruble allocation to Turkmenistan and the size of the reserve position at the Central Bank of Russia. These resources formed the base for domestic credit expansion, since hard currency reserves were sterilized. The Central Bank of Russia eased its monetary policy in the second half of 1992, which led to increased currency shipments to Turkmenistan and credit policy continued to be expansionary in the first eight months of 1993. A large volume of directed credit was authorized in mid-1993. Much of the directed credit was intended for enterprise imports from the FSU. Since Turkmenistan had exceeded its technical credit lines with the Central Bank of Russia, however, payment requests to the suppliers in Russia were denied. The funds were credited to the bank's correspondent accounts for return to the enterprises that originated the payment requests.

Introduction of the Manat

1.42   Turkmenistan introduced its own currency, the manat, on November 1, 1993. The initial exchange rate was 2 manat per U.S. dollar during the conversion period. Following the adoption of a new foreign exchange law in October 1993, there are currently no restrictions on current account transactions. In preparation for the introduction of the currency, the Central Bank took various administrative measures to stop the flow of rubles into Turkmenistan. The Government withdrew from circulation 5,000 and 10,000 ruble notes, limited conversion only to deposits at the Savings Bank as of September 1, 1993 plus the accumulation of wage payments subsequently made into these accounts, required that purchases of commodities costing more that R25,000 be made by check, and limited the amount of cash subject to conversion into the manat to R30,000 per adult.

External Trade

1.43   Turkmenistan's interrepublican and hard-currency trade accounts were both in surplus in 1992 (see Table 1.11). The increase in ruble exports is mainly due to the increase in the ruble price of natural gas from R34 per 1,000 cubic meters which was the USSR price, to R167 in late 1991, to R870 at the beginning of 1992, to R3,500 on July 1, 1992, which was about 10-15 percent of the international price. Planned sales to the ruble zone for 1992 were 60 billion cubic meters, which included 28 billion cubic meters to Ukraine. In January and February 1992 Ukraine took 5 billion cubic meters at R260 (the internal Russian price) before shipments to Ukraine ceased when Ukraine refused to pay the higher price Turkmenistan requested.

1.44   Under an agreement with Russia, Turkmenistan supplies Russian regions with gas and receives in return a quota for Russian gas, which is exported on Turkmenistan's behalf for hard-currency to European markets. The total gas export quota for 1992 for Russia was 103.5 billion cubic meters. Of this, Turkmenistan has been assigned 11.28 billion cubic meters for hard-currency export. Some 1.6 billion cubic meters of it was sold through dollar clearing with the former CMEA countries of Central and Eastern Europe, and 1.08 billion cubic meters was bartered for transmission and other expenses to the Russians. Net hard-currency sales were 8.6 billion cubic meters, which was exported via Russia and for which Turkmenistan received approximately $75 per 1,000 cubic meters, which is close to the international price. Thus, 87 percent of these proceeds were in hard-currency, 13 percent exchanged through dollar clearing. Hard-currency proceeds for 1992 were about $700 million. Eighty percent of the hard-currency proceeds were transferred to the government's special hard-currency fund with no ruble compensation. In the first six months of 1993, hard currency exports to Eastern Europe were 5.9 billion cubic meters at a price of $75 per 1000 cubic meters

Table 1.11
External Trade, 1988-92

	1988	1989	1990	1991	1992 (est.)
Hard-Currency Trade Account (mln. US$)					
Foreign balance	-101	-234	-397	-472	206
Merchandise exports	179	197	195	146	1,324
Oil and gas exports	0	5	30	na	881
Merchandise imports	280	431	592	618	949
Services	na	na	na	na	-169
Interrepublican Trade Account (mln. rbl.)					
Interrepublican balance[a]	-97	-328	-458	1,095	98,700
Interrepublican exports	2389	2,418	2,469	6,731	193,500
Oil and gas exports	801	745	705	na	78,800
Interrepublican imports	2486	2,746	2,927	5,636	-89,800
Services	na	na	na	na	-5,100

a/ There is a great uncertainty about the trade data reliability and the valuation of trade flows in the former Soviet Union. Especially for 1992, the reported imports seem to underestimate total imports significantly.

Source: Statistical Office Ashkabad 1992, Trade Division.

1.45   The second major source of hard-currency earnings is cotton. Before independence, cotton was shipped from Turkmenistan by the all-union cotton organization. Turkmenistan received the Soviet Union domestic price for cotton. After independence, cotton was shipped via Agroindustry Processing, with domestic delivery arrangements initially maintained basically on the lines of the previous planned system and with interrepublican agreements to supply cotton. There has been a substantial increase in hard-currency exports since independence. Total exports to the ruble and non-ruble zones in 1992 were between 250,000 to 300,000 tons, from a total output of 450,000 tons. The ruble zone took 100,000-150,000 tons, with some 100,000 tons being exported for hard-currency. Half of the non-ruble zone exports of cotton are bartered (in 1992, mostly with Italy). Prices are determined with reference to the Liverpool exchange, with a discount because of quality problems with Turkmen cotton. The Liverpool price is currently around $1,145 per ton for 33 to 34 millimeter length. The Cabinet of Ministers allocates cotton also for barter to permit essential imports that are lacking or are not being supplied via the Interrepublican Trade Agreements. Cotton earnings are around $150 million per year. In 1993, Turkmenistan expects to export about 250, 000 tons of cotton for hard-currency at a price which is close to the world market price ($1.100 per ton).

1.46   The consolidated current account is expected to be in surplus in 1993 in spite of continued inability of some FSU countries to pay for their gas imports from Turkmenistan and increasing arrears. In hard-currency trade, Turkmenistan reported a surplus of about $280 million until June 1993.

CHAPTER 2

THE REFORM PROGRAM AND THE MEDIUM-TERM OUTLOOK

2.1   Despite its high proportion of desert land, Turkmenistan has strong economic potential. Energy resources are plentiful, and there is considerable scope for raising the productivity of irrigated land. Large gains in terms of trade as energy prices approach international levels, should lead to increasing export revenues that could finance a substantial expansion of imports of both capital and consumer goods. Current account surpluses are expected throughout the nineties provided there is substantial investment to sustain current gas export levels and to develop basic transport and telecommunications infrastructure. External investment, however, will be easier to obtain if Turkmenistan implements a strong reform program.

2.2   Prosperity in the medium term may be vulnerable. Turkmenistan's exports are concentrated on energy and cotton, whose earnings are subject to movements in international prices which are beyond the control of policymakers. Simulations of the impact of a permanent $1 decline in the export price of 1000 cubic meters of gas would imply a $50 million decline in export receipts per year. Furthermore, the same effects would be caused by an increase in transport charges, since Turkmenistan has little leverage over the determination of regional gas transmission tariffs. A $30 decline in the export price of 1000 cubic meters of gas -- caused by a decline in the international price and/or an increase in transport charges -- would turn the trade balance into deficit by mid-1990. Three country-specific factors also cause concern: the poor social indicators coupled with rapid population growth; remoteness from foreign markets; and the inefficiency of the economic apparatus inherited from the Soviet system. Furthermore, there is great uncertainty surrounding the evolution of interrepublican trade and payments, the trade regime, and the pricing of gas exports in the FSU.

2.3   The efficient re-investment of financial resources obtained from the energy sector is central to Turkmenistan's future development prospects. Other developing countries with large energy resources have confronted the same task. While many have failed, a few countries have managed to transform these resources into productive assets. The experience shows that it is easier to obtain the financial resources from extracting the natural wealth than it is to reinvest them in a way that will generate long-term growth and a higher standard of living.

2.4   The critical tasks at hand is to manage the surplus generated from exports carefully and to maximize its rate of return. Whether the surplus flows back to the Government's budget, the banks, or public enterprises the crucial issue will be the ability of these agencies to make effective use of these resources from the point of view of the country as a whole. To the extent that the surpluses flow back through the banks, commercial banks will need to have the capacity to make sound lending decisions. To the extent that resources flow back to the Government's budget, the Government will need to build up the management capacity in order to evaluate the costs and benefits of projects and to prioritize them. If public enterprises outside the budget are allowed to use the surplus, it will need to be done in a context where these resources are used in a way that maximizes the welfare of the country as a whole. Finally, there is the option of leaving resources offshore until the Government decides which is the best way to re-invest, or, while these investment management capacities are built up. Furthermore, if payment arrears of other FSU countries increase, Turkmenistan might also want to consider leaving gas and oil in the ground as a physical asset and reserve.

2.5   To develop Turkmenistan's potential and maximize the rate of return of investments, careful economic management and comprehensive reforms are essential. Progress on structural and systematic reforms would provide enterprises and individuals with the right institutional and market incentive structures and strengthen substantially the sustainability of the supply response in the economy. The country could achieve some growth with little or no economic reforms, by financing it from the high export earnings expected for the medium term. With slow reforms however, growth would be limited much below Turkmenistan's potential. The substantial waste which would come about under the existing system, would limit the output generated from new investment. As the price system would not play its role of allocating scarce resources, switching into areas of comparative advantage would be constrained, and efficiency gains from increased domestic competition would be delayed. With slow reforms, increasingly larger investment expenditures would be required to generate the same output growth.

2.6   Without significant reforms, the lack of export diversification would leave the economy tied to the fate of energy-related earnings. The unfortunate consequences of such a situation in the experience of some energy-exporting countries are described in Box 2.3. The experience shows that a decline in the price of energy can lead, even in resource-rich countries such as Turkmenistan, to serious long-term problems such as soaring budget and balance-of-payments deficits and declining growth. While some of these problems would be in part a result of the classic "Dutch Disease," (see Box 2.1), they usually are a direct consequence of an overly vulnerable, undiversified economy.

Economic Prospects

2.7   Turkmenistan's reform program was set out in a document adopted in January 1991. The document included a list of legislative, fiscal and monetary measures, the principles for price formation, privatization, the development of industrial infrastructure, and agricultural reform. The Government has so far:

- Drafted a five-year investment plan.

- Removed price controls on several goods, and increased subsidies on others (see Chapter 1).

- Restructured the fiscal system through the introduction of the VAT, excise taxes and changes in the taxation of energy and exports.

- Transferred the hard currency fund to the Central Bank. The Government plans to incorporate it in a single budget in 1994.

- Drafted new laws in some areas, particularly foreign direct investment and privatization.

- Started pilot privatization programs in agriculture.

- Introduced its own currency, the manat, on November 1, 1993.

- Made substantial progress on monetary reform. The Government's intention is to follow strict fiscal and monetary policies to support the new currency.

- Undertaken a number of steps to liberalize the trade regime.

2.8   Overall reforms have so far lagged behind other countries of the former Soviet Union. The Government has a five-year plan that includes large investments in infrastructure and energy to be financed by both foreign direct investment and the budget.   One of the main goals of the plan is to achieve food self-sufficiency by 1995.   Another is to increase cotton processing.   The 1993 budget included specific programs to promote grain production and cotton processing.

2.9   There have been important reversals in the initial union-led price liberalization of January 1992.   In early 1993, a presidential decree stipulated the free provision of water, electricity and gas to the population.   Elements of price liberalization were introduced on October 1, 1993, but were suspended on October 5, 1993.   With the introduction of the new currency in November 1993, the Government liberalized several prices.   Eleven commodities are still subject to control at subsidized prices.   Another 26 commodities are subject to review by an antimonopoly commission which will negotiate with enterprises the maximum level of price adjustment.   The Government has indicated that the ultimate goal is full price liberalization, but the timetable is not clear.

2.10   The previous industrial structure is still intact, and there has been very little privatization; the private sector has hardly developed.   The Government plans to undertake privatization in several stages until 1997, with small-scale privatization starting in 1994 and medium-scale privatization in fiscal year 1995/96.   The privatization program has still not been approved however.   And, the pilot privatization housing program was suspended in early 1993.

The Key Elements of A Successful Reform Program

Stabilization

Monetary Policy

2.11   The stabilization program depends crucially on the monetary and exchange-rate arrangements adopted by the Government.   As long as Turkmenistan remained in the ruble zone, it had limited control over monetary policy.   The Government introduced its own currency on November 1, 1993 since monetary instability in the ruble zone had serious negative effects on stability. Maintaining a strong national currency will not only require strong export performance but also macroeconomic stability.   In view of the uncertainty surrounding the new currency and the trade relationships with other FSU countries, tight monetary policy has to be advanced to control inflation.

2.12   The availability of substantial hard currency reserves provides the country with some protection against external shocks.   Turkmenistan intends to adopt a managed floating exchange rate system to maintain this reserve position and the Government has centralized its foreign exchange holdings at the Central Bank.   It is very important, in light of the expected continued surplus in hard-currency reserves, that the Central Bank be allowed to manage reserves.   This is not only necessary for maintaining a strong external reserve position, but also to manage the inflow of the surplus into the economy.   The inflow of the surplus into the economy could also be managed by keeping the resources abroad to sterilize them.   This gives the country a higher rate of return on its hard currency earnings than accumulating an unreasonably high hard currency reserve.

Fiscal Policy

2.13   Macroeconomic stabilization will also depend on sound fiscal management. Budgetary deficit financing from the monetary system has to be consistent with the objective of controlling inflation. Budget deficits can either be financed by savings (foreign or domestic) or from the monetary system. Turkmenistan's current savings could finance large investments and budget deficits for some time.

2.14   Expenditures will have to be restructured substantially if the Government wants to support a reasonable level of public investments and keep the deficit under control. This would imply a cut in subsidies and transfers to enterprises. It would not be wise, however, to cut expenditures on an ad hoc basis or proportional across the board: they should reflect priorities both within and across sectors. Better targeting of social expenditures and greater efficiency in investment spending should be the main objective.

2.15   The budgetary revenues will continue to be extremely sensitive to the ability of other FSU countries to pay for Turkmen gas exports. To make the budget less dependent on revenues from taxes on gas exports, the tax system should be strengthened, and the tax base should be broadened. Exemptions from the VAT have grown, with adverse effects on revenues (fruits, vegetables, canned goods, cotton fiber, among others are exempted). Exemptions create distortions in the economy and lead to a loss of revenues. Measures to strengthen the tax system should also include the reinstatement of the gasoline tax (abolished in August 1992), a substantial reduction in the exemptions from income and profits taxes, the discontinuation of the tax-free status of the cotton company, increases in user charges for many public services (for example, transport, telecommunications, electricity and irrigation) to cover, eventually, the costs of providing these services and adjusting housing rents to cover at least operating costs. Subjecting all imports to the VAT would increase revenues and remove distortions against domestic producers. Barter transactions need to be subject to an invoice verification by customs. They should also be subject to import and export taxes and duties, as well as to the company profit tax. Since such a high proportion of total revenues are from energy sector, the Government should review very carefully taxation of the energy sector. An important move towards a more rational tax system and a more efficient taxation of energy resources in the 1993 budget is the elimination of the fixed payments because these payments were not related to actual profits.

2.16   The Government should also review the system of tax exemptions for foreign direct investment. Tax exemptions, special tax deductions and tax holidays have the same effects as direct subsidies. They lead to a misallocation of resources and increase the financing requirement of the Government. Furthermore, they may not be effective in attracting foreign investment since the home country often repatriates profits which results in a transfer from Turkmenistan's treasury to the home country's treasury.

2.17   For the Ministry of Economics and Finance to exercise full control over public finances, budgetary institutions and procedures will have to be reexamined at all levels of government. Technical assistance from the International Monetary Fund has already been received for strengthening fiscal institutinos and enhancing the effectiveness of fiscal management. However, current and capital expenditures have not been reexamined yet. Furthermore, the operation of extrabudgetary funds makes transparent budgetary management impossible. The channeling of foreign exchange transactions through an off-budget fund creates great difficulties with the overall assessment of the budgetary situation. These difficulties would be eliminated if all extrabudgetary funds, with the possible exception of the pension fund, were to be included in the budget. The Hard Currency Fund has already been transferred to the

Central Bank and hard currency transactions will be incorporated on a single budget beginning in fiscal year 1994, which is a positive step toward more fiscal transparency.

Subsidies and Price Liberalization

2.18   Subsidies distort relative prices and resource allocation and are a major burden on the Government's overall financial requirements. While their elimination-or reduction to a few carefully targeted items-is desirable on both micro (efficiency) and macro (financial) grounds, it is understood that an immediate complete removal might provoke unacceptable social and economic dislocations. A medium-term program to reach the desired goal may therefore be preferable. Meanwhile, fiscal measures to finance the remaining subsidies will have to be taken or continued. The medium-term program of eliminating price controls and subsidies should be structured so as to give priority to those sectors in which the supply response to higher producer price is expected to be quickest; this will minimize the burden that price increases will place on consumers. The selection of specific items and sectors for immediate decontrol should depend not only on the physical conditions of production, but also on the degree of efficiency and the level of privatization of the sector. The Government plans to extend all interest subsidies, transfers, and some lending and grants to enterprises through the budget beginning with fiscal year 1994, which will make the magnitude of the subsidies and transfers more apparent.

Structural and Sectoral Reform Program

2.19   Macroeconomic stability alone will not ensure sustainable growth or generate employment. The success of the transition to a market economy will also depend on the Government's willingness and ability to implement a comprehensive program of structural and sectoral reforms. The pace can be gradual but the reform program has to be comprehensive. The major elements of this reform program are discussed in part II and part III, and they include:

- Establishment of an appropriate legal and institutional framework compatible with a market economy.

- Liberalization of domestic and foreign trade.

- Enterprise restructuring and privatization.

- Financial sector reform.

- Establishment of an appropriate social safety net that includes unemployment insurance.

- Development of the sectors with the greatest supply response, that is, the energy, industrial and agricultural sectors of the economy.

Institutional Reform

2.20   Turkmenistan faces a need for substantial change in the institutional framework for economic policymaking. In the past, policy decisions and the collection and processing of information originated mostly in Moscow. Since the function of republican administration was to implement economic policy decisions made at the union level, there was little capacity to analyze macroeconomic developments. Policymaking personnel were scarce in virtually every branch of Government. Turkmenistan is now developing the institutional framework necessary to formulate and implement the economic policies needed to advance the transition toward a market economy. Training to improve the capacity to implement economic policy should therefore be of high priority.

Domestic and Foreign Trade Policy

2.21   Since early 1993 the Government has taken some steps toward liberalizing the trade regime. However, interstate trade agreements remain in place and the licensing and quota arrangements for some products continue to apply. Quantitative and price restrictions are also still imposed on exports of cotton and other raw materials to protect domestic supplies. Furthermore, all exports to non-FSU countries require a special license. Substantial measures are required in the area of trade policy, given the major role of exports earnings in ensuring a successful transition. Both imports and exports will need to be liberalized to ensure a dynamic economy. The freedom to import will foster competition by providing alternative sources of commodities to state monopolies. The freedom to export will help develop the domestic private marketing system. As a starting point, the government should consider removing all domestic trade restrictions on farms and other economic enterprises. This might be followed by allowing free entry of individuals into the import-export business. So far, the prerogative of designated ministries to trade results in international economic transactions following bureaucratic rather than market incentives. The freedom to export will attract private firms to undertake development of markets abroad. There are likewise gains from permitting competition in the supply of imports to domestic consumers. At present, imports are only allowed via the Ministry of Trade and other authorized importers. Finally, an international commodity exchange covering a broad range of commodities might be advantageous to set up in cooperation with other Central Asian countries.

2.22   A strong supply response could come from the energy sector. The large revenues that are expected to continue flowing from the gas sector provide Turkmenistan with the opportunity to accelerate adjustments in the non-gas sectors. The resource has to be managed properly however, or large energy exports may constrain the development of other sectors (see Box 2.1). Given international fluctuations in energy prices, the economy needs a broad expansion of its export base. On the other hand, diversification should not be viewed as an end in itself. Emphasis should be placed on eliminating most of the market distortions which would lead to a national allocation of resources among sectors in the longer term. This can be achieved in part through the implementation of an open trade regime since it would increase competition in the non-energy sector of the economy. This might be achieved by opening up the economy to increased foreign competition.

Enterprise Reform

2.23   Privatization is at the core of the transformation to a market economy. While it is important to start privatizing state-owned enterprises (SOEs) as soon as possible, improving management of those enterprises that will not be privatized is also needed. The Government should start by elaborating on a comprehensive strategy for privatization. It should also transform SOEs into companies managed according to commercial law; create an independent body in charge of the SOE; and, for the most part, abstain from involvement in any new industrial project wholly or partly owned by public sector entities. A mass incorporation decree could force a clarification of ownership and will sort out the relationship between enterprises, the branch ministries and concerns. The Government should not get involved into any activities that can be undertaken by the private sector. Furthermore, enterprises should only be granted credit to finance their losses conditional on restructuring plans for sectors with excess capacity or liquidation plans for clearly non viable enterprises.

Box 2.1
Dutch Disease

The term "Dutch Disease" was coined to describe the reaction that an economy may have to the emergence of a new major export industry or, alternatively, to a significant rise in the international price of one or more existing exports. Strong growth in export receipts from one sector of the economy can significantly reduce the competitiveness of other sectors in the economy through currency appreciation. Such appreciation, which results from high export earnings of one commodity, leads to stagnation and decline of other manufactured exports. This problem takes its name from the experience in the Netherlands following the development of new natural gas fields under the North Sea. Similar problems have affected to various degrees Algeria, Australia, Mexico, Nigeria, Norway, Venezuela and the United Kingdom. Dutch Disease is a threat to full employment.

It is this phenomenon that has driven many developing countries that export mineral resources to intervene. This has been done by establishing multiple exchange rates or by protecting domestic agriculture and industry through tariffs, quantitative restrictions, etc. Mostly these measures have been found to stunt efficiency and progress in the protected sectors. The least harmful intervention has been found to be to let the exchange rate be determined by the cost/price levels of the non-mineral export sectors and to levy special taxes on the resulting windfall profits of the mineral sector. This requires purposeful management of the exchange rate by the central bank. It permits keeping the tax burden on the non-mineral export sectors relatively low.

Privatization

2.24   Privatization has been so far negligible in Turkmenistan. To strengthen the basis for and launch the privatization process, the main priorities should be:

- Define and implement a comprehensive privatization program.

- Clear definition of a lead agency for each type of privatization; the development of the work program of the agency which implement the privatization program, including training, and development of a database of enterprises both to monitor progress and to provide information for investors.

- Promulgation of adequate legislation for retail, housing, agricultural and industrial privatization. The Ministry of Agriculture should introduce flexible lease arrangements for state farms and cooperatives and consider introducing outright land sales as well.

- A rapid expansion of the small-scale privatization program, with calendar of targets (covering most of the retail and service sector).

2.25   A rapid expansion of the small-scale privatization program, with definition of targets covering most of the retail and service sector is critical. Small-scale privatization can be key signal for transformation. Not only can the privatization of smaller enterprises be accomplished relatively quickly, but the failure to embark upon small-scale privatization before other stages of reform, can have a negative impact on the overall success of the reform program.

Private Sector Development

2.26   The development of a legal framework consistent with a market-oriented economy is necessary especially to strengthen private sector development. In particular, there is a need to address significant gaps in the areas of property rights, contract and bankruptcy laws; harmonize existing legislation affecting foreign and domestic investors; and strengthen the capacity to enforce the legal regime. The current regulatory and legislative environment for new private sector investment is rudimentary and lacks many safeguards. If privatization of both land and state enterprises is to yield benefits, decision makers need to be assured of the right to retain the returns from their investments. They must not be directed to produce unprofitable commodities. Individuals and firms must have the means to enforce legitimate contracts and be allowed to enter into business freely. This will in turn foster competition and innovation.

2.27   Furthermore, the same competitive environment should apply equally to private and public enterprises. This is currently not the case. State enterprises should not benefit from preferential credit extended by the banking system or from direct state subsidies in manufacturing and agriculture. Neither should they be given preferential access to both local and imported inputs. Given Turkmenistan's small economy, new ventures will almost inevitably compete with domestic monopolies. But if import restrictions are removed, concerns about monopolies in Turkmen markets may largely disappear.

Financial Sector Reform

2.28   In a market-based economy the financial system helps channel savings toward their most productive use. It also provides the payments systems necessary for carrying out transactions. International experience shows that the financial system is proving to be one of the most serious obstacles both to sound short-term macroeconomic management and to the long-term development of a market economy. In part, it is the result of ascribing fiscal as well as banking functions to the state banks. The intermingling of subsidy programs, maintained for social reasons, with credit programs makes the application of sound banking criteria -- or the performance of the banks intermediation function -- virtually impossible. These are two separate objectives and one instrument. Overall, reforms must aim to liberalize and commercialize the financial system. This includes a rapid improvement in the effectiveness of the payments system, restructuring of the main commercial banks, development of a merchant banking system, restructuring of the State Savings Bank, improving the flow of savings, reform of the legal, accounting and prudential framework, reform and strengthening of the central bank and human resource development.

2.29   Interest rates should play a greater role in mobilizing savings and in allocating credit. Complete liberalization of interest rates would be warranted once lending patterns are driven primarily by commercial rather than ownership criteria, and when confidence in the ability to withdraw deposits from the banking system has been restored.

Social Safety Net

2.30   A social safety net for the poorest and most vulnerable groups will be required in the context of a reform program. Apart from the objectives of efficiency and affordability, the benefit system as a whole should prevent individuals and families from falling into extreme poverty. Furthermore, it should be affordable and conducive to effective administration. At the same time reform in this area should aim to reduce disincentives to work and the tendency to overly rely on the State.

2.31   Although unemployment is not yet a serious problem in Turkmenistan, if reforms are undertaken it is important to initiate steps leading to appropriate social security arrangements. The Government's expectations of the maintenance of unemployment at modest levels during the near future seem to be based on the extremely low level of current unemployment and the fact that the share of industrial employment is comparably low. Enterprises are not shedding labor yet, despite the contraction of output. A trade-off between improving the financial situation of the enterprises and protecting the level of employment seems inevitable, however.

2.32   The implementation of a reform program, therefore, will make it necessary to implement an active labor market policy. A first step would be to encourage labor mobility and to reduce legal restrictions on the geographic location of work. To accomplish this, considerations should be given to modify the propiska requirement and to launch housing privatization. Furthermore, local labor offices should post job vacancies for all areas in Turkmenistan. Workers would then know where the jobs are. To put this suggestion into operation, however, a computerized system is needed to make job availability known outside of local labor markets. There is also a strong case for action to prevent long- term unemployment through appropriate use of adult retraining programs. It is most cost effective to apply these remedies before the onset of long-term unemployment. Otherwise the social costs of making the person employable are much greater.

2.33   Unemployment insurance could be financed by either a payroll tax or general revenues. At present, the Government anticipates levying a new 2 percent payroll tax on enterprises to finance both unemployment insurance and the new training initiative. Employees could pay part of this however, since they would be the beneficiaries of these new programs. It would be desirable to evaluate such a system promptly, since it will require years before sufficient funds are accumulated to make it effective.

Energy

2.34   Central to future development prospects is the efficient exploitation of Turkmenistan's energy sector, which offers good prospects for generating external creditworthiness and financial surpluses needed to reform the economy and ease the hardships of the adjustment. Prospects for the natural gas sector to be the motor of economic growth are clouded, however, by the relatively low remaining proven reserves in developed fields, the limited capacity of the domestic industry to identify and develop new reserves, and the uncertainties surrounding export markets in the medium-term.

2.35   Most of these challenges can, however, be met if the Government can create a favorable environment that will attract both foreign expertise and capital to regenerate the gas sector's production potential and help to diversify the export markets. The domestic industry does not have the capacity to undertake the scale of development required to sustain production at recent levels and to reverse the trend toward the premature liquidation of the industry. Moreover, the cost of such an undertaking (US$3 billion to US$4 billion) is beyond the country's financing capacity. Inevitably, Turkmenistan will have to attract foreign investors to realize the large gas resource potential of the country. This will only materialize if the institutional framework for large-scale private sector involvement is in place.

2.36   At present, the critical issues in the energy sector involve: (i) the arrangements for pricing and marketing of gas; (ii) the terms of access by third parties to the transmission network, which is currently owned and operated by Turkmengas; and, (iii) the taxation of the foreign operators. Furthermore, experience shows, that in the absence of a clear policy on the commercial aspects of gas production, promotional initiatives in gas-prone territories are unlikely to succeed. The Government needs to address these issues directly, preferably as integral elements of a petroleum law. Increasing the volume of exports to Europe will depend on the willingness of the Russian Gasprom, which controls the pipeline access to European markets, to transfer market shares. An important first step to get access to this market would be the strengthening of the country's capacity to market natural gas independently.

2.37   While increasing the value of gas exports to existing markets should be the sector's main priority in the short term, in the longer term, investments in new pipelines to diversify transport options and enter new export markets for natural gas may be an appropriate objective. The economic viability of such investments needs to be first established. The sector has a large investment program under consideration at present. Final decisions on these plans should be deferred until their economic and commercial viability has been determined. Moreover, it would seem wise for the Government to minimize the exposure of the public sector to the capital risk entailed in most of the proposals likely to be implemented, particularly where they are export oriented. By and large, it is reasonable to expect that for financially viable export projects, foreign venture capital can be found on acceptable terms.

2.38   In general, the Government's objective should be to ensure that energy prices fully reflect their cost of supply or, where the resource is easily traded in world or regional markets, their export value. For natural monopolies, prices for supplies to specific classes of consumers should cover the operating cost of such provision plus an appropriate allowance to finance the cost of investments to maintain an acceptable quality and level of service. While some form of regulation of prices and efficiency of service provision would need to be maintained, this should seek to carefully balance the need to protect consumers with the need to ensure that entities remain commercially viable and can take the actions necessary to promote this.

Agriculture

2.39   The priority in agriculture is to establish a proper system of incentives for production and processing. This has two facets: ownership and prices. Regarding ownership, either privately owned plots or long-term, secured leases may be more effective in generating appropriate responses to price signals than the present state and collective farms. State production orders need to be phased out to let the market work; input subsidies need to be eliminated, and prices of food commodities adjusted to competitive levels. Price adjustments should be accompanied by the liberalization of imports and exports to provide alternative sources of commodities to state monopolies and help develop the domestic private marketing system. A hard budget constraint should be imposed on all state and collective farms and should be accompanied by lifting all restrictions on where farms and enterprises may purchase inputs and sell outputs.

2.40   Once the institutional and legal framework is developed and put in place, rapid privatization of small-scale agro-processing enterprises, input distribution and retail food outlets can begin. Furthermore, a sectoral policy should be implemented that provides market signals. This policy should include the withdrawal of the state from the direct distribution of agricultural inputs; privatization of most processing, wholesale and retail trade; small-scale transport operations; and reform of agricultural credit, research, information and marketing services.

Reform Scenario

2.41   A scenario for Turkmenistan's future development is based on the assumption that the Government will reform comprehensively between 1994 and 2000 (Table 2.1) and will be able to attract the large foreign investment needed to sustain energy production at current levels. The privatization plan, as currently envisaged, would start with small-scale privatization by fiscal year 1994. Since the balance of payments situation and economic developments are highly uncertain for 1994 and beyond, the figures in the medium-term scenario should be viewed as simulations of possible outcomes rather than projections. They will have to be revised as trends in trade become clearer.

2.42   A fast, comprehensive implementation of a reform program -- such as the one described above -- could have significant effects on the pace of the recovery and reduce the impact of external risks. The country is vulnerable to movements of a few international prices by its concentrated export base, a high population growth rate, its remoteness from foreign markets, and the inefficiency of many of its inherited economic institutions. These vulnerabilities could be reduced in a more diversified economy. In a reform scenario, underpinned by higher productivity, access to international commercial financing and private investment, output growth may be significantly faster than in the slow reform case. Higher growth would generate more new employment opportunities. It would also bring about higher income per capita and welfare levels for the growing population.

Resource Management

2.43   One of the most critical tasks for Turkmenistan will be to manage the surpluses generated from exports carefully and in a way that will maximize their productivity. Central to future development prospects is the efficient exploitation of Turkmenistan's energy sector and the efficient use of the resources obtained. As a depletable resource, the extraction of gas and oil constitutes a consumption of a depletable wealth asset rather than a current output attributable to factors of production. The quantity of the resource which is being extracted and used exhausts itself and eliminates its availability for future use. Two important questions arise with regard to gas and oil production, price policies required to maximize producers' profitability and the use of the surpluses obtained through energy exports. The first relates to the rate of production and price of the resource which maximizes its rate of return. The second relates to the rate of savings and investment which would be needed to replace asset consumption and create an alternative source of income substituting for the progressive exhaustion of the depletable asset.

2.44   The first policy decision is therefore to determine the minimum level of gas production that would be needed to satisfy consumption and investment requirements. The level and composition of government expenditures have important consequences in a market economy in terms of overall macroeconomic effects, as well as more microeconomic implications for industries and consumers. Experience shows that following favorable shifts in their terms of trade, many countries pursued unsustainable expenditure policies, financing them with the windfall gains of positive shocks or external borrowing. The medium-term effect depended significantly on whether the additional spending was directed to consumption or investment.

2.45   The second step is to decide on three alternative investment options:

- to use the gas revenues not consumed or invested domestically for investments in foreign assets with a positive future return;

- to extract the gas and use its proceeds in domestic capital formatting, creating alternative productive physical assets which would contribute to the future flow of goods and services;

- to leave gas and oil in the ground as a physical asset and reserve with potential earnings in the form of price rises or to prevent the further build-up of payment arrears.

2.46   The key policy issue will be the productivity of the investments undertaken. To the extent that the surpluses flow back through the Central Bank, the Government would have to determine what share of those resources to distribute to the commercial banks. In this case it would be important that the commercial banks have the capacity to make sound lending decisions. To the extent that resources flow back to the Government budget, decisions would have to be made regarding where they should be reinvested. The issue then is the capacity within the Government to evaluate the costs and benefits of projects and to prioritize them at the Government level. A public investment review process would need to be put in place to ensure that the most viable projects are selected for inclusion in the public investment program (see Box 2.2). Another avenue for resource management is to allow public enterprises to use, outside the budget, the resources that flow back to the economy. The issue in this case is the ability of these enterprises to make effective use of the resources from the point of view of the country as a whole. Finally, there is the option of leaving resources offshore until the Government decides which is the best way to invest the resources.

Box 2.2
Improving Public Expenditure Management

Effective public expenditure management makes heavy demands on government institutions. Each of its sub-activities -- the formulation of the macroeconomic framework, project preparation and investment programming, the link between planning and budgeting, the coverage, preparation and classification of the budget, and budget implementation and expenditure control -- has an institutional and political, as well as a technical or economic dimension. A review of the experience of many countries trying to address these issues reveals an awesome array of problems which are at least as likely to have institutional roots as technical ones. Economic analysis and forecasting, even in the relatively short term, is often so deficient that it leaves the authorities unprepared for major deviations from the program necessitated, for example, by a substantial external shock. Unable to cope with the uncertainties inherent in the planning and budgetary processes, governments are forced to react with damaging, ill-thought-out, across the board cuts. Frequently, it will be found that the linkages between the macroeconomic framework and the investment program, and between both and the budget process, are fragile or non-existent. Many governments encounter considerable difficulty in formulating an investment program that is more than an aggregation of wish-lists drawn up by the different spending agencies. Control over the external borrowing of government agencies is frequently less than desirable. Phasing of capital spending is often inadequate or non-existent, while the recurrent cost implications of public investment are rarely taken into account. Classification of budgetary items may not facilitate a policy or objectives oriented approach to public expenditure planning. Budgetary coverage, both in terms of institutions and major categories of expenditure, may be partial, impeding the ability of the core ministries to exercise effective control. On the other hand, the organization of the spending agencies, their technical capabilities for financial and economic analysis, and their linkages with core ministries may be such that an integrated and coordinated approach to revenues and expenditures is, at best, severely impeded.

<u>Investment Programming and Project Preparation</u>. The institutional arrangements which exist for the preparation of medium-term plans and investment programs vary enormously from country to country, but in only rare cases could the be described as acceptably satisfactory. Nevertheless, among the difficulties are:

●   Considerable and deliberate overprogramming, reflecting an unwillingness or inability to make hard decisions as to priorities. This leads not only to the formulation of programs way out of line with domestic or foreign resource availability, but also to too many projects being started at the same time, excessive dispersion of available skills, slowdowns in project implementation and lower returns from investment.

●   The lack of criteria for choosing which projects should or should not be included in the program. Relatively few countries have systematically established procedures or institutional capacity for economic project appraisal at either sectoral or core ministry level. <u>Cost-benefit analysis</u> can lead to a vast improvement in public-investment programming since the projects with the highest rate of return are selcted.

●   The lack of priorities and ranking of projects. Government has tried to address this through the formulation of <u>"core" investment programs.</u> An agreement is reached that the government abandon a policy of partially funding all or most projects, and distinguishes between "core" projects which should receive funds under all circumstances

Box 2.2 (cont.)

and standby projects which are funded only when additional resources are available. It is important to emphasize here that "funding" includes not merely capital, but all current resources required to complete and operate a priority project. "Core" programs should also be concentrated on strategic projects and should exclude white elephants even where funding is assured.

- Poor coordination between macro-analysis and expenditure planning can also lead to a lack of appreciation of the impact of the general policy framework on the success of a public investment program. Chief among inappropriate policies are: (i) pricing policies leading to large subsidies which are not only a direct strain on the budget but may also discourage production and hence reduce resources; (ii) substantial and unproductive overemployment in the public service; (iii) inadequate control over the expenditures of local authorities and autonomous agencies; (iv) public ownership of inefficient and loss-making enterprises, established with the intention of remedying market failures or achieving social objectives, but in practice doing neither; and, (v) the general incentive and policy framework. If there is, in broad terms, a failure to encourage efficiency through economic incentives, then this will, of course, affect the quality of both public and private investment. Poor private investment decisions can in turn feed back on the public sector through not only fewer resources but also a sense that the public sector "must do everything."

Source: World Bank Discussion Paper; Managing Public Expenditure, World Bank 1989.

Supply Response

2.47   In the reform scenario it is assumed that Turkmenistan will be able to mobilize sufficient capital to finance the required investments to keep up energy production at current levels, and reforms in domestic energy pricing are undertaken. In this case energy exports to the FSU could be sustained at higher levels than in the slow reform scenario (see Table 2.5). In contrast to allowing the progressive depletion of existing developed fields, currently proven and probable reserves in undeveloped fields could be brought into production to offset the declining output from existing producing fields. Production could be further augmented by bringing identified possible reserves and newly discovered reserves into production through intensified exploration efforts. A strong trade performance could support increased domestic absorption, allowing a higher level of consumption and critical imports of capital goods. Increased capital goods imports, in particular, could speed the recovery of the economy.

2.48   Since new investments would be directed to its most efficient use in a reform scenario, rather than to capture economic rents, the supply response would be higher than without reforms. With a growing private sector and increasing foreign direct investment, the Government could withdraw fairly quickly from those investment activities which are best undertaken by private enterprises. This would lead to a significant increase in productivity and output. Investment flows associated with foreign direct investment in the energy sector are expected to prevent a sharper contraction in aggregate investment starting in 1994. Investment could increase from 10 percent in 1994 to as high as 13 percent per year in 1996, if the Government is able to attract substantial foreign investment. The Government wants to increase investments by about 20 percent per year, in part based on very high estimates of foreign direct investment flows.

2.49   Reforms that give the enterprises and consumers the right incentives are the best way to generate supply response. Early support to private sector development and enterprise restructuring should result in an early growth in the private sector, which would, to some extent, compensate for the decline in the state enterprise sector. Industrial output could increase significantly by 1996 and 1997. Small-scale privatization in trade and services could lead to increases in the service sector of up to 5 percent by 1995.

Table 2.1
Economic Scenario with Reform
(constant 1992 prices)

	Projections			
	1994	1995	1996	1997-2000 (avg.)
	(percent change)			
Growth Real GDP	2.0	2.0	3.5	3.5
- Agriculture	0.0	1.0	2.0	4.0
- Industry	-2.0	1.0	2.0	4.0
- Energy	0.0	0.0	0.0	0.0
- Construction	7.0	7.0	10.0	6.0
- Services	2.0	4.0	5.0	6.0
Consumption	2.5	0.0	0.5	2.5
Consumption/Capita	-0.5	-3.0	-2.0	0.5
Investment	10.0	10.0	13.0	10.0
Resource Balance				
- Exports	0.5	1.0	1.5	2.5
- Imports	5.0	4.5	4.5	3.5

Source: World Bank Staff estimates.

2.50   If the Government decides to proceed fast with reforms in the agricultural sector, this might also have a positive effect on agricultural output. Higher economic returns to farmers will increase agricultural productivity. The increased private control could be expected to have a positive production response by 1995.

2.51   Consumption might take about one year to adjust if the Government starts to implement comprehensive reforms in 1994, and can be expected to be stagnant in 1995. Due to the high population growth rate, however, consumption per capita will decline during the adjustment period. After about 2-3 years, consumption will start to grow even to a level where consumption per capita increases.

External Trade Prospects

2.52   The trade surplus will need to be underpinned by gas exports. But, the uncertainty about the agreements with Russia on the quota for hard-currency gas exports, the use of barter trade, the uncertainties in interrepublican trade and the instability in the ruble zone make trade prospects very difficult to forecast. The strength and speed of the recovery will depend critically on Turkmenistan's ability to sell its gas for hard currency and to approach international prices for its exports to the former Soviet Union market and on the ability of other FSU countries to pay for its gas imports. However, the exportable gas surplus would decline dramatically if Turkmenistan were not able to attract investments to develop additional reserves and if there were large energy consumption increases due to the provision of free gas to the population.

Exports

2.53   FSU Exports. In January 1993, the export pricing basis was revised. Toward the end of 1992, Turkmenistan linked its pricing strategy explicitly with that adopted by Gasprom of Russia. Export prices to the former Soviet Union republics were set on a uniform basis (at the Turkmenistan border) at 60 percent of the price of exports to areas outside of the former Soviet Union, based on a exchange rate of R400 per dollar, revised quarterly. Turkmenistan encountered significant problems in implementing its pricing strategy, however, and accounts receivable on exports have grown dramatically since the new pricing policy has been implemented. As a result, trading has been switched largely to a barter basis.   Since most of the FSU trade is now through barter transactions, valuation of exports and imports under these arrangements is arbitrary. The estimates for trade with these countries would have to change if Turkmenistan is unable to obtain the world market price for the FSU exports.

Table 2.2
Turkmenistan - Trade Simulations
(millions of US dollars)

| | Projections | | | |
	1994	1995	1996	1997-2000 (avg.)
FSU Trade				
Exports[a]	2,100	2,200	2,200	2,300
- Gas	1,700	1,700	1,700	1,700
Imports	1,300	1,400	1,500	1,700
Trade Balance	700	800	700	600
Foreign-Currency Trade				
Exports	1,100	1,150	1,200	1,400
- Gas	705	705	705	705
Imports	850	1,000	1,100	1,500
Trade Balance	250	150	100	-100
Trade Balance Total	950	950	800	500

[a] Transport charges for exports to the former Soviet Union and the hard currency are set at R400 per mcm per 100 kilometers with an underlying initial exchange rate of R400 per US dollar.

Source: World Bank staff estimates.

2.54   However, the macroeconomic framework presented in Table 2.1 assumes that average export prices to the former Soviet Union will increase to an average of net export revenues for non-former Soviet Union exports by 1995. These price increases imply substantial terms-of trade gains in Turkmenistan's trade with states of the former Soviet Union.

2.55   While countries of the former Soviet Union are expected to increase gas production, Turkmenistan should remain competitive, given its strong comparative advantage. In 1992, Turkmenistan supplied around 80 percent of gas consumption of the republics in Central Asia and the Caucasus, excluding Uzbekistan. In addition, it supplied around 25 percent of Ukraine's consumption. Even in the medium-term these supplies will be difficult to replace. Without them, Gasprom will find it difficult to ensure supply to European hard-currency markets via Ukraine.

2.56   However, already in 1993, arrears of other FSU countries to Turkmenistan increased rapidly as the price of gas exports to FSU countries was raised. The Government so far has been reluctant to cut off the supply of gas to countries in arrears and prefers to seek a negotiated solution to this problem. If this problem cannot be resolved, it would imply that a large proportion of the trade surplus with the FSU cannot be used for imports. Subsequently, this would lead to lower than projected increases in output and consumption.

2.57   Hard-Currency Exports. With the rest of the world, export allocations in hard currency through the Russian pipeline system could face a potential bottleneck. This possibility is not taken into account in the projected scenario. We assume that Turkmenistan will be able to keep the current quota and that tariffs for gas transport to the former Soviet Union and Central Europe would continue to be paid in rubles. Under these assumptions, hard-currency receipts from oil and gas are estimated at $700 million in 1993 (see table 2.2)..

Imports

2.58   Turkmenistan's export growth potential is needed to support continued growth in real import demand. New investments will make it necessary to increase imports from the hard-currency countries significantly. Capital goods imports will be essential if the economy is to implement investments. Also, non-CIS imports are expected to increase as consumers substitute higher quality foreign imports for competing domestic and other CIS imported products.

2.59   Provided exports are growing, hard-currency imports are likely to grow significantly in the medium-term. Imports from non-CIS markets were $500 million in 1991 and grew to $545 million in 1992. Since much of this import demand, especially for capital goods, cannot be fulfilled by interrepublican trade hard-currency imports are projected at a range of $850 million in 1993 to $1.5 billion in 1996 (see Table 2.2). Also, a normalization of trading conditions within the former Soviet Union will take some time. Imports from the former Soviet Union can be expected to increase at a slower rate than hard-currency imports. Some increase in former Soviet Union imports is expected as a counterpart of the substantial gas exports, which are being undertaken on a clearing basis.

2.60   Reforms in the enterprise and agricultural sector should also have a positive effect on the trade balance, through higher light industry and agricultural exports to the FSU. This would enable the country to increase its former Soviet Union-imports to even higher levels and, combined with the positive income effect, this would prevent the declines in per capita consumption, likely in the slow-reform scenario.

2.61   The implementation of more substantial reforms would also improve the fiscal accounts. Tax revenues from the private sector would increase. Budgetary outlays for price subsidies, loss-making enterprises and investment would decline. It could then lead to a substantial reduction of the budget deficit. This would give the Government the possibility to maintain a certain level of well-targeted social expenditures without the danger of macroeconomic instability.

Slow Reform Scenario

2.62   Experience in other countries shows that failure to reform can lead to serious problems in the medium to long term even in resource-rich countries like Turkmenistan (Box 2.3). Some oil-rich countries -- such as Nigeria or Algeria -- seeing the apparent abundance of foreign exchange after the oil price increases in the 1970s believed they could afford to implement reforms very slowly or not at all. Indeed, favorable shifts in the terms of trade fueled domestic booms in several countries. However, very large unprofitable and inefficient investments -- poorly designed and implemented -- were undertaken by the Government and government spending ᵥ especially for social expenditures -- increased more than revenues. Furthermore, high population growth rates increasingly posed severe social pressure. In countries like Turkmenistan, the need for new job opportunities and higher income, imposes a very high minimum rate of necessary economic growth.

Box 2.3
Country Experience

Nigeria: Nigeria's response to the oil windfall after the first increases in oil prices in 1974 was to increase Government spending by more than the rise in revenues, financed with external borrowing from the monetary system. The response to the second oil price boom in 1979 was similar (large budget deficits and a continuing overvaluation of the currency), except that the mix of public spending shifted further toward consumption. Nigeria failed to offset the appreciation of the currency between 1974 and 1984 caused by the large export revenues from oil; large premiums were charged in the parallel currency market, and foreign exchange was rationed. The oil price boom, together with poor marketing and pricing policies, disrupted the farm sector, causing a steep decline in the production of traditional cash crops and heavy migration to the cities.

A telling statistic about this oil exporter is that its per capita growth rate, which averaged 1.1 percent a year in the period 1960-73 declined 2.8 percent a year after the oil price increase of the early seventies. Public spending was largely responsible for the decline. Between 1973 and 1981, public employment tripled from 0.5 to 1.5 million. Government expenditure rose fivefold between 1972 and 1974 and accounted for almost 80 percent of total oil revenue. Public investment increased from 5 percent of GDP in 1974 to 17 percent in 1977 and accounted for more than half of total investment that year. The budget turned from surplus to a deficit averaging 24 percent of retained revenue from 1975 through 1978.

From a broader perspective, the origins of Nigeria's problems lay in structural trends and policies pursued since the early 1970s. The sharp increases in oil prices in 1973/74 -- and again in 1979/80 -- dramatically altered Nigeria's resource position. Gross real national income increased by 80 percent in real terms between 1972 and 1977, and then by another 17 percent in 1978-80. This was used as a fast expansion of public spending. Substantial investments were made in physical infrastructure, and there was also major growth in expenditures in the health, education and social sectors throughout the economy. There was much waste, with many projects being poorly designed and implemented. The increasing oil revenues created expectations about still higher -- and permanent -- revenues. This generated, in particular from the mid-1970s onwards, very optimistic development programs. The development plan assumed an increase in Government capital spending of about 100 percent in 1979. In order to finance large-scale infrastructural projects, the Government resorted in the early 1980s to substantial international borrowing.

Algeria: Although the first Five Year Plan (1980-84) aimed at ambitious objectives; growth of GDP at 7.1 percent per year, an investment rate of 48.6 percent of GDP. GDP grew only by 4.3 percent per annum in real terms and the investment rate settled at 38 percent. Most of these shortfalls in performance were the result of two series of factors: (1) a downturn in the hydrocarbon market trend that made it necessary, once the danger of a perilous slippage in foreign indebtedness was noted, to constrain imports that were essential for maintaining a high growth rate for the industrial sector; and (2) poor productivity in the production apparatus.

With the plummeting of hydrocarbon prices during the 1985-89 period, the projections had to be drastically modified: unit prices dropped by at least 40 percent on international markets and triggered chain reactions. These affected the overall macroeconomic equilibrium in Algeria, resulting in a drastic compression of imports, a downward revision of investment opportunities and a substantial weakening of economic growth. The growth of GDP practically came to a standstill in 1986 while investments were reduced by 25 percent and imports by 27.6 percent.

Source: Country Economic Memorandum, Nigeria, World Bank 1985; Algeria, The 1985-1989 Development Plan and the Medium-and Long Term-Prospects, World Bank, 1987.

2.63   The experience in these countries showed that structural weaknesses and downward trends could be hidden by the financial facilities allowed by energy profits, but not forever. However, in the early 1980s, growth and investments declined. Budget deficits soared, and the substantial investment cutbacks resulted in a large number of unfinished, highly capital-intensive projects. Declining export revenues and increased import demand resulted in a severe foreign-exchange shortage and a sharp deterioration of the countries' credibility on international capital markets.

2.64   While some of these problems were in part the result of the classic "Dutch Disease," they were mostly a direct consequence of government action or lack of action. Underlying these trends were structural problems caused by a combination of factors: excessive government spending, inadequate incentives to increase efficiency and production, and a price system that did not play its role of allocating scarce resources. The overreliance on public sector investment and production rather than on private investment and production as the main engine of growth was another common factor behind these experiences. Furthermore, the lack of export diversification made these economies vulnerable to risks. It also resulted in policies that were overly focused on maximization of mineral earnings.

2.65   If reforms are not implemented and existing enterprise structures are perpetuated, the reallocation of resources to new operations will not take place. Lower domestic production results in higher import needs to satisfy consumption. A lowering in the trade surplus would reduce Turkmenistan's ability to import capital goods, thus delaying access to new technology and increased production efficiencies. Without privatization, private sector response would be limited. Efficiency gains derived from increased domestic competition would be delayed. Overall, the very slow implementation of reforms can lead to severe macroeconomic problems such as high budget and balance-of-payments deficits and rising inflation.

Supply Response

2.66   Under a slow reform scenario, the prospects for substantial growth would be severely limited: output is projected to be stagnant in real terms until 1996 (see Table 2.3). In the initial years, continued supply disruptions and contracting consumer demand in the former Soviet Union will hurt production. Industrial output is expected to decline by at least 5 percent in 1994, specially since stocks are already very high. The impact of industrial contraction on aggregate GNP, however, will be limited as the sector is very small. In the medium-term, the Government is assumed to continue to subsidize loss-making enterprises. This should lead to smaller declines in production than those in other economies in transition. But without major reforms,

Table 2.3
Economic Scenario with Slow Reforms
(percentage change at constant 1991 prices)

	1994	1995	1996	1997-2000 (avg.)
Growth real GDP	-4.0	-2.0	0.0	1.5
Agriculture	-2.0	0.0	0.5	2.0
Industry	-5.0	-3.0	-1.5	1.5
Construction	5.0	5.0	7.0	7.0
Energy	-10.0	-7.0	-5.0	-4.0
Services	-2.5	-1.0	0.0	1.5
Consumption	-0.5	0.0	1.5	2.0
Consumption per capita	-3.0	-2.0	-1.0	-0..5
Investment	5.0	5.0	6.0	7.0
Resource balance				
Exports	-2.5	-1.5	-1.5	-1.0
Imports	2.0	2.0	2.5	2.5

Source: World Bank Staff Estimates

productivity is expected to continue to fall. Large investments will be required to avoid contractions in industrial output.

2.67   The public investment projects currently planned for infrastructure and the energy sector may bring about an increase in construction activity of about 5 to 7 percent a year. Furthermore, private investors seeking to use natural resources or cheap energy could keep industrial output from collapsing in the short run. Agricultural output is expected to stagnate during the 1993 to 1996 period, since there will be no improvements in the incentives to increase production and yields. Services should at best grow in parallel to GDP, given the lack of private sector development.

2.68   By 1996, part of the service sector and part of the small-scale industrial sector is expected to be privatized. As a consequence, a small increase in growth is expected in the late nineties. Investments in the resource-based sectors of the economy should also continue to stimulate growth. The development of the gas sector, however, will be particularly capital intensive, with only a small spillover effect on the rest of the economy in the short term.

2.69   In the slow reform scenario Turkmenistan will not be able to attract the very large foreign investment flows needed to develop the gas reserves and the productivity of the investments undertaken is much smaller than in the reform case due to the inefficient use of resources. The lack of a price liberalization program implies also an unstable relative price structure in the short term that is also likely to act as a disincentive to investment. In addition, as long as the relative price structure is distorted through extensive subsidies and price controls investment resources will most likely not be directed to their most efficient use. Furthermore, the Government's intention to keep social expenditures at the current levels will either lead to substantial deficits in the budget or will restrict the funds available for direct investments by the Government.

Trade

2.70   The provision of free gas on the domestic market sets the wrong incentives for investors in energy-intensive industries. It will also lead to an increase in domestic demand for gas that will affect the tradable surplus. Despite its low level of industrialization and the lack of heavy industry, Turkmenistan's per capita energy consumption is very high. In spite of declining GDP, which would usually bring about a drop in domestic demand for energy, overall energy demand in Turkmenistan has continued to grow since 1990. With free domestic gas coupled with the increase in population and the creation of new energy-intensive industries, domestic energy demand will grow significantly. Such growth in demand can only be satisfied by reductions in exports (see table 2.4).

2.71   Furthermore, given current conditions, the prospects for sustained future gas production at recent levels are poor. While the total remaining identified reserves (2.4 trillion cubic meters) can sustain production at recent levels until the mid-2010s, the ability of the domestic industry to develop the remaining undeveloped and identified reserves is limited (see Chapter 9). Under this scenario, it is assumed that future production is confined to exploitation of total reserves in the already developed fields plus continued production of associated gas at current levels. This scenario assumes a limited field development program consistent with the current drilling capacity of the industry. In these circumstances, the exportable gas surplus is likely to drop substantially. This will lead to a substantial decline in the trade balance with the FSU. Furthermore, the increase of gas prices for FSU gas exports might imply a significant reduction in the quantity of gas exports, as few FSU countries are able to afford these increases. Already many FSU countries face major difficulties in paying for their imports.

2.72   Agricultural exports may start to increase after 1994, especially exports of cotton. Improvements in the quality of cotton could help reduce the discount from the world price that Turkmenistan is currently obliged to accept for its cotton exports. The receipts from agricultural exports may vary, however, depending on the magnitude of barter trade and developments in the other FSU-countries.

Implications of Energy Price Changes

2.73   The previous section concluded that Turkmenistan's export revenues are vulnerable to changes in international energy prices or in the export arrangement with the Russian Gasprom. Simulations of the impact of a permanent 1$/1000 cubic meters decline below the price levels assumed in the slow-reform scenario suggests that on average over the period 1994-2000, Turkmenistan would likely register a 2.1 percent decline in export receipts from gas exports, amounting to about $50 million per year. Therefore, under the slow reforming scenario, the projected trade surplus in the medium term could disappear if energy prices decline. Furthermore, the same effects would be caused by an increase in transport charges since Turkmenistan has little leverage over the determination of regional gas transmission tariffs.

Table 2.4
Turkmenistan - Trade Simulations
Slow Reform Scenario
(millions of US$)

	1994	1995	1996	1997-2000 (avg.)
FSU Trade				
Exports[a]	2,100	2,000	1,950	1,800
- Gas	1,700	1,550	1,450	1,200
Imports	1,500	1,700	1,800	1,900
Trade Balance	600	300	150	-100
Foreign-Currency Trade				
Exports	1,100	1,150	1,200	1,300
- Gas	700	700	700	700
Imports	850	900	1,000	1,300
Trade Balance	250	250	100	0
Trade Balance Total	850	550	250	-100

[a] Transport charges for exports to the former Soviet Union and the hard-currency are set at R400 per mcm per 100 kilometers with an underlying initial exchange rate of R400 per US dollar.

Source: World Bank staff estimates.

Implications for the Fiscal Accounts

2.74   In 1992, Turkmenistan's overall government accounts were in surplus, taking into account the large revenues received from the foreign-exchange retention tax. But prospects for even the overall surplus are tenuous; the Government plans to undertake several investment projects that may easily lead to substantial fiscal deficits. Furthermore, the changes in the tax structure and the exemption of the cotton company from paying taxes makes the 1993 budget very dependent on revenues from the gas sector.[1]   Given the build up of payments arrears for gas exports, there is uncertainty if the Gas

---

1.   In 1992, about 45 percent of total revenues were received from the gas sector which included the VAT, the CIT and the fixed payment. In 1993, the gas sector is expected to pay 73 percent of total revenues whereas 39 percent are from the tax on raw materials.

Corporation will be able to collect the expected revenues. Substantial efforts will be required to maintain the Government's targets for hard-currency reserves as well as to maintain financial stability following the introduction of the new currency. Furthermore, the continuation of current policies, especially on subsidies, could have very negative implications for the fiscal accounts. Thus, the 1994-budget is projected to be in deficit of about 10 percent of GDP in 1994. This significant turnaround reflects both a decline in the share of revenues of GDP, mainly those from gas exports, and a considerable increase in expenditure under the present system of price subsidies. If price subsidies would be eliminated the expected deficit could be reduced by several percentage points.

2.75   In Turkmenistan's fiscal accounts, social expenditures are a major item. Since the population growth rate is very high, total social expenditures will have to be increased substantially in the next years if the Government wants to maintain the current level of social expenditures. If the Government wanted to improve the existing low welfare indicators the budgetary impact would be even higher. Table 2.4 shows for illustrative purposes how social expenditure will increase if they are maintained constant on the per capita level of 1992. Since GDP growth is likely to be slower than population growth, the share of social expenditures to GDP and total Government expenditures will increase over time. High population growth will also put substantial pressure on the labor market. It is expected that the work force will grow from 2 million in 1992 by 0.26 million until 1995 and 0.41 million until the year 2000. If no additional employment is created, unemployment payments will grow rapidly, and total social expenditures including unemployment benefits will increase from 11.6 percent of GDP in 1992 to about 17 percent in the year 2000.

Table 2.5:
Simulation of Social Expenditures

	1992	1995	2000
Social Expenditures[a]			
- % of GDP	11.0	11.4	12.3
- % of Total Government Expenditure[b]	27.7	29.8	32.5
Social Expenditure incl. Unemployment Benefits[c]			
- % of GDP	11.6	15.3	16.7
- % of Total Government Expenditure	27.7	38.5	55.6

a/ Social Expenditures are assumed to stay constant at a per capita basis at the 1992 level.
b/ Government expenditures are assumed to grow at the GDP growth rate.
c/ Unemployment benefits are assumed to be paid at the level of the minimum wage in 1992. Furthermore, it is expected in this scenario that no additional employment is created and the workforce will grow by 0.26 million until 1995 and 0.41 million until 2000.

CHAPTER 3

EXTERNAL FINANCING

3.1   Turkmenistan could have current account surpluses throughout the nineties provided there is substantial investment to sustain current gas export levels and develop basic transport and telecommunications infrastructure. The existing network is in poor condition and oriented to almost exclusive trade with the FSU. Inadequate basic infrastructure could represent a major constraint to foreign investment and private sector development.

3.2   While Turkmenistan would be able to obtain some financial assistance from multilateral agencies most capital requirements will need to be sourced from foreign direct investment (FDI) and loans from international commercial banks. Equity could be a natural financing source, specially for investments in natural resource development, provided the conditions to attract FDI are in place. The Government would also need to borrow since it is important to strike the appropriate balance between equity and borrowing. It would provide some flexibility and maybe even better terms for the countries' overall portfolio. Moreover, it might represent a competitive source of funds for non-energy investment requirements. In addition to an adequate framework for FDI, the immediate external financing task faced by the Government is, therefore, to build up access to international capital markets.

3.3   The Government of Turkmenistan needs to start by developing a foreign borrowing strategy. Among other principles, debt should only be incurred if it is going to generate higher rates of return or export growth than the interest rates incurred. Higher returns than the international cost of capital will require to have an adequate policy framework in place, including an environment conducive to exports and good investment projects. Moreover, a necessary condition to gain access to capital markets is to ensure the continuation of a strong debt servicing capacity position, since it provides banks with the security that Turkmenistan will be able to service debt on commercial terms.

3.4   Once a foreign borrowing strategy is in place foreign borrowing should be monitored and governed by clear policies and ceilings. Ideally most external financing should be mobilized on the basis of investment projects, with attractive rates of return. Linking loans to a sound investment program provides an insurance against returns that are lower than the cost of capital. It can prevent the type of crisis that some Latin American countries suffered in the eighties: they borrowed to finance consumption and, in doing so, faced major debt servicing problems. Containing future external debt requires monitoring and regulating the activities of public entities entering into individual foreign loan agreements. It also requires extremely careful use of government guarantees for private projects.

3.5   Managing external resources is more challenging in Turkmenistan, however. It goes beyond articulating a debt strategy. Liability management needs to be complemented by a strategy to manage the countries foreign assets. Given the existing situation, Turkmenistan is in the unusual situation of being a creditor in FSU trade. While this is likely to continue in the foreseeable future, as it stands it is clearly sub-optimal. Turkmenistan is not being paid by several important trading partners. This constitutes a potential resource drain which could quickly build up. Arrears are already so large that non-payment of principal obligations by Ukraine, for example, could wipe out the balance of payments surplus in one year. Turkmenistan could find itself in the situation of financing other countries' deficits through transferring capital which might never be repaid.

3.6   The risk factors which could affect Turkmenistan's financing requirements are mostly exogenous developments. However, their impact could be minimized by appropriate Government policy. Adverse changes in terms of trade, further deterioration in interrepublican trade, and a slower than anticipated move to world prices for gas exports constitute the most important sources of risk.

3.7   External financing, either for investment or for larger-than-anticipated external shocks, will be easier to obtain if Turkmenistan implements a strong reform program. To design and implement such a program the Government will require substantial assistance in developing the institutional capability to manage the transition. The international donor community could provide technical assistance to develop this capability. Assistance is needed not only to support the design and implementation of economic reforms but also to prepare investment and project proposals to be presented to the international community.

Debt

3.8   In November 1992, the Group of Seven (G-7) signed a communique with the original eight signatories of the Memorandum of Understanding on servicing the debt obligations of the FSU. Official creditors agreed to a partial deferral of amortization payments on medium and long-term debt due in 1992 (see box 3.1). Under an external debt agreement between eight of the countries of the former Soviet Union--in November 1991, Turkmenistan's share in total USSR external debt was set at 0.7 percent, or about US$420 million, excluding letters of credit. On this basis, scheduled debt service payments were estimated at US$95 million in 1992, of which US$41 million were interest payments. Turkmenistan would have been eligible for a deferral of US$50 million in principal payments in 1992 if arrears were reduced by about US$29 million.

3.9   Turkmenistan signed an agreement with Russia in July 1992 for the zero debt option: to transfer its share of the debt of the former Soviet Union and servicing obligations to Russia in exchange for relinquishing most claims on former Soviet Union assets. As a result of this agreement,

---

Box 3.1: Interrepublican Debt Agreement

Interrepublican Memorandum of Understanding, October 1991.   The Memorandum of Understanding committed the signatories to the following:

- To be jointly and severally liable for the external debt of the former Soviet Union. It is generally understood that this liability is to cover all debt obligations contracted by the Government of the USSR outstanding at the date of the Memorandum of Understanding.

- To designate the Vnesheconombank (VEB) or any successor to be determined as the Debt Manager with full authority to be sole interlocutor with creditors, negotiate and enter into commitments on their behalf, and service the debt as an agent on behalf of the republics.

- To conclude an agreement on the procedures and mechanism for debt service and another on the participation in the settlement of the debt of the three Baltic States.

Turkmenistan has practically no hard-currency debt. Ruble servicing obligations, although small, are not clear. They are not included in the following projections of financing needs.

External Financing

3.10   Although external financing estimates are preliminary and subject to uncertainty, the balance of payments is likely to be in surplus under both a slow and a fast reform scenario in the medium term (Table 3.1 and Table 3.2). The figures, however, should be viewed as simulations of possible outcomes rather than projections. They will be revised as trends in trade become clearer.

3.11   Although Turkmenistan is expected to have a substantial trade surplus in the near term, hard-currency revenues projections are conservative, given the uncertainty about Turkmenistan's ability to increase its earnings from gas exports. Those exports depend on an agreement with Russia on the quota to Western Europe, which the Government cannot directly influence in the short term.

3.12   Moreover, the current account surpluses throughout the nineties will require substantial investment to sustain current gas export levels and develop basic transport and telecommunications infrastructure. The existing network is in poor condition and oriented to almost exclusive trade with the FSU.

3.13   The simulations in Tables 3.1 and 3.2 assume that the surplus from hard currency exports to the rest of the world is used to build-up international reserves. The hard currency reserve is estimated at US$500 million in early 1993 (over two months of imports). The simulations in Table 3.1 assume reserves will increase to six months of imports by the year 2000. These simulations do not take into account the possibility to leave some of these earnings in interest-bearing accounts off-shore which would increase the surplus. However, it does represent a viable alternative for the Government while it builds up its capacity to manage the re-investment of energy related revenues.

3.14   Earnings from FSU trade are assumed to be non-convertible and are projected to be provided as export credits to FSU importers. The surplus with the FSU countries should be between US$600 and US$800 million in the medium term. However, if Turkmenistan continues to accumulate large non-interest bearing arrears like in 1993, which are not repaid and do not pay any interest, the financing requirements would increase by about US$ 100 million in 1995 and US$500 million by the year 2000.

3.15   Turkmenistan has no immediate need for official external capital. However, if FSU balances continue to be in arrears or unconvertible, or a large proportion of gas trade takes place on a barter basis, Turkmenistan will not be able to self-finance its pressing investment needs. The FSU trade surplus would, in that case, be of little use for Turkmenistan.

Table 3.1
Medium Term Simulations: External Financing: Reform Scenario[a]
(in million U.S. dollars)

| | 1994 - 1996 (Annual average) | | 1997 - 2000 (Annual average) | |
| | Lower | Upper | Lower | Upper |
	Bound		Bound	
Current Account (-deficit)	600	950	500	700
Change in Reserves[b] (-increase)	-400	-660	-470	-650
Capital Account (+net capital export, -net capital import)	200	290	30	50
Direct Foreign Investment	180	360	460	560
Net Credits: (+credit, -loans)	-380	-650	-430	-510
- Export Loans[c]	-440	-750	-480	-620
- Multilateral	40	60	30	70
- Bilateral	20	40	20	40

Table 3.2
Medium Term Simulations: External Financing: Slow-Reform Scenario[a]
(in million U.S. dollars)

| | 1994 - 1996 (Annual average) | | 1997 - 2000 (Annual average) | |
| | Lower | Upper | Lower | Upper |
	Bound		Bound	
Current Account (-deficit)	450	500	-200	-400
Change in Reserves[b] (-increase)	-320	-350	0	0
Capital Account (+net capital export, -net capital import)	130	150	-200	-400
Direct Foreign Investment	70	110	90	120
Net Credits (+ credit, -loans)	-200	-260	110	280
- Export Loans[c]	-225	-310	80	220
- Multilateral	15	30	20	40
- Bilateral	10	20	10	20

Source: Bank Staff Estimates

a/ The ranges indicated above reflect uncertainties around the midpoint of each of the components rather than alternative policy scenarios. Thus, neither the lower nor upper bounds can be added up to represent an independent balance of payments scenario.

b/ Surpluses in hard-currency are used to build up the hard-currency reserve.

c/ It is assumed that surpluses in FSU trade are used to provide export credits to other former Soviet Union countries (see paragraph 3.14).

3.16   <u>Investment Needs in the Energy Sector</u>. In the medium to long term, the realization of the potential for the sector to be the motor for the transformation of the economy will depend on substantial investments to regenerate its production potential and, possibly, to gain access to new markets. Given the claims of the Government on the sector's cash generation and the composition of such cash flow, the sector cannot finance such investments on its own. The effective management of the surpluses that are generated by the sector in the next few years would be crucial to managing any future decline in gas export revenues and to establishing a degree of creditworthiness that would be crucial to mobilizing the magnitude of external financing that would be required to implement these investments. In the slow reform case, Turkmenistan's current account is expected to be in deficit in the late nineties (see Table 3.2) since energy exports will decline substantially if the country is not able to attract enough foreign investment in the energy sector to sustain gas exports. To assure the future of the gas industry, the country may need to invest at least US$3 billion by the end of the decade. This can only be financed with significant external investment participation.

3.17   To maintain its medium-to long-term production capacity, the industry would need to invest around $3 billion in appraising and developing identified reserves in the next 5 to 10 years in addition to stepping up its exploration efforts. The timing of significant investments in alternative pipeline systems or major petrochemical diversification is uncertain. However, while the incentives for such investments may be strong toward the end of the period covered by this medium-term scenario, particularly if the projected significant increases in exportable regional gas surpluses materialize, these investments will be beyond the capacity of the country to finance. In addition, there is little prospect of any investor being willing to finance such investments unless the outlook for gas production improves. In summary, the country may need to invest a total of at least US$3 billion in gas fields development and US$5 billion in alternative export pipelines by the end of this decade to ensure the future of the gas industry.

3.18   <u>Government Investment Estimates</u>. The Government's projected investment requirements in the gas industry are substantially greater than the need identified above. The Government projects a financing requirement of (i) US$20 billion to find, appraise and develop gas (and associated oil) reserves; and (ii) US$1.5 billion for a pipeline to Iran and Turkey. Given the potential market constraints on gas exports, it does not appear prudent to devote the proposed large expenditures on exploration and development unless it is targeted at oil production, with most associated gas produced expected to be reinjected. Moreover, the proposed pipeline costs are very low by international norms while the pipeline capacity, at a maximum of 28 bcm, is not consistent with the projected exportable surplus to outside the former Soviet Union.

3.19   The current investment program of the Government both to develop wells and create the infrastructure necessary for expanded exports is extremely large. Such a program would cost at least US$20 billion spread over six to eight years. It may be too optimistic to expect the required magnitude of capital inflows over such a short period of time or the ability of the economy to develop the large absorptive capacity to make such an inflow effective. Nonetheless, given the country's favorable geology, it is clear that with a well-articulated strategy for addressing the technical, market and financial constraints on gas production capacity, gas production could be maintained at recent levels in the medium term and significantly expanded in the longer term if prospect market conditions permit.

Possible Financing Sources

3.20   Turkmenistan, unlike most other FSU countries, has a real chance of getting access to international capital markets once the country has established some track record with the international financial community. The appropriate mix of financing should be determined on the basis of relative costs and conditions. The returns from such financing, however, are also linked to the type of financing that will be chosen. Alternative financing venues include direct foreign investment, project related financing, suppliers or exports credits, and commercial bank lending.

Private Sources

Foreign Direct Investment

3.21   The Government wants foreign investors to play a crucial role in providing capital and introducing new technology. Foreign direct investment in convertible currency would most likely be in the energy sector. Although some foreign direct investment has already taken place it could be limited, however, by the lack of transparency in rules and regulations and the uncertainties about future political and economic developments. The key elements to create a stable investment climate would be:

- macroeconomic stability and a convertible currency;

- guarantees for the free movement of foreign capital, dividends and capital gains;

- simple and transparent procedures to grant necessary approvals and licenses in connection with business and investment activities; and,

- permission for foreigners to fully own local companies, with the exception of clearly defined areas in which the government wants to retain control.

- A satisfactory legal and fiscal framework for foreign investment in the energy sector and a classification and standardization of existing procedures for promoting the country's petroleum potential to foreign investors.

3.22   <u>Foreign Direct Investment in the Energy Sector</u>. Turkmenistan has considerable potential to expand oil and petroleum production and reduce its dependence on gas. The Government is engaged in formulating a revised long-term strategy for addressing the key problems facing the domestic industry. Central to the energy sector strategy is attracting foreign technology and capital to relieve the key potential constraints on gas production capacity.

3.23   The extensive experience of the World Bank in the development of natural gas resources suggests that, in the absence of a clear policy on the commercial aspects of gas production, promotional initiatives in gas-prone territories are unlikely to succeed. An energy sector strategy would need to:

- establish a clear and comprehensive legal, contractual and taxation framework to assure potential investors of a stable operating and commercial climate for their activities in the oil and gas sector;

- change the system of promotion of the country's petroleum resources from the current promoting foreign participation in small low-risk development and rehabilitation ventures in the oil sector to one more appropriate for high risk and large-scale exploration and development activities;

- establish pricing and marketing gas arrangements, as well as the terms of access by third parties to the existing gas transmission network within the country; and,

- articulate the Government's strategy to address the key export market risks in the short-term and for establishing alternative infrastructure access to export markets in the medium to long-term.

3.24   Foreign Investment in the Oil Sector. In the short run, the Government needs to address the industry's underlying lack of financial resources for essential maintenance activities. Both remedial operations and maintenance may require significant upgrades of technology and techniques. Reversing the declining oil production will require considerable foreign capital and technology. So far, institutional structures and the legal and financial framework to attract foreign capital are effectively absent. The Government would need external advisory assistance and training of its staff to manage such an activity effectively. A petroleum law to clarify the respective role and obligations of the Government, its operating agencies in the sector and potential external investors has yet to be drafted. A global natural resources law was recently enacted by the Government. This law is not appropriate, however, to the needs of the oil industry, and petroleum should ideally be removed from its ambit or, at the least, the areas of conflict between this law and provisions more appropriately tailored to the oil industry resolved explicitly. Finally, the potential tax and financial arrangements governing the industry are unclear and would require some form of codification.

Export and Supplier Credits

3.25   Export and supplier credits are expected to become a significant source of financing over the medium term. In the current distorted and uncertain environment, export credit agencies will need to pay attention to the financial and economic viability of projects proposed for financing under export credits. Furthermore, the Government will need an overall investment program because the interest of each individual ministry or sector might not always coincide with what is best for the country. This is even more urgent because export-import banks will need guarantees and have lending limits by country. Since the government will have to ration and guarantee credits, a prioritization of projects is a sine qua non.

Role of Multilateral Institutions

3.26   Long-term economic growth will depend on the country's policy environment which will be one factor determining the quality of investment decisions. Multilateral agencies could be of assistance to Turkmenistan in establishing the economic policies necessary to achieve its goal of long-term economic growth. Although lending would be relative small relative to the country's needs, the Government could use agencies like the World Bank to mobilize and to attempt to maximize the benefits from different external financing sources.

3.27   Since the country has no need for balance-of-payments support, Turkmenistan could seek from multilateral institutions non-project related technical assistance and support to design and implement general economic reforms[1].   There is an immediate need for technical assistance in many areas. Assistance is required for the Central Bank, monetary policy, banking supervision, banking education, profitability assessment, portfolio reviews and diagnostic audits of the major financial institutions.   In agriculture it is needed for improving water management and preparing a national water strategy, improving the drainage system, promoting a policy environment conducive to agricultural output growth. If the Government wants to keep social spending under control, an immediate review of the current benefit programs is needed to target social expenditures to the most vulnerable.   Other areas that need immediate attention are training in general economic management and assistance in drafting a comprehensive public investment strategy (see below).

Public Investment Program

3.28   The Government is currently considering several projects. These investment proposals involve the use of public funds, by requiring equity contributions on infrastructure investments, either through tax abatements or exemptions.   Since many of these projects lack adequate economic and financial cost-benefit analysis, the country could end up investing in unprofitable industries that will deplete its hard-currency resources. Learning from international experience the Government should base its investment decisions on careful calculations of the profitability of its projects and on an overall public investment strategy.   Private owners calculate the profitability of new investments carefully.   Since in Turkmenistan investment decisions are made almost wholly in the public sector, it is particularly important that similar assessments be made for the projects being considered. Linking loans to a sound investment program could help prevent the debt crisis that many countries suffered in the eighties.

3.29   A public investment program should have the following characteristics:

- A list of the investment projects that are economically and financially sound, ranked on the basis of cost benefit analysis. However, since a meaningful cost benefit analysis can only be undertaken if the relative price structure is right. Domestic distortions caused by price controls and the extensive subsidies have to be minimized.

- A sectoral composition that follows the national development strategy, approved by the Government.

- Projected annual expenditures that match the available financial resources (budgetary savings and external loans).

- An aggregation of the total foreign exchange impact of these projects to ensure consistency with balance-of-payments projections.

3.30   A central unit should set spending guidelines--such as minimum rates of return on projects and maximum foreign borrowing in order to avoid ad hoc criteria and to simplify the management of the investment program.   Such a unit would add sectoral spending plans, match them with resource

---

1.   Specific proposals on Turkmenistan's technical assistance needs in the structural and sectoral reform areas are described in part II and III of this report.

availabilities, make program adjustments to the spending agencies when imbalances appear, and elevate irreconcilable differences to the competent authority.

Creditworthiness

3.31   Turkmenistan should be able to service future debts on commercial terms. However, the country's sustained creditworthiness over the long run will depend on Government policies. The country is vulnerable to external shocks, especially in the energy sector. To reduce these risks, the Government needs to implement a comprehensive reform program and has to undertake careful economic management.

3.32   The country has large investment needs which can in part be met by domestic savings but will also require substantial foreign investment and assistance. The possibility of fruitful interaction with multilaterals exists but will only materialize if the legitimacy of a dialogue with such lenders about the reform and general economic management is recognized. Some external assistance and investments make sense only in the face of particular reforms. In any event, lenders, whether public or private, have a legitimate interest in the future ability of borrowers to service their debt. In the case of sovereign risk, such ability is largely a function of macroeconomic management, structural reform and the external environment.

Major Risks and Uncertainties

3.33   One of the key uncertainties around Turkmenistan's gas exports are the developments in the Russian domestic gas market and their impact on regional gas supplies. Domestic demand for natural gas in Russia is expected to decline by 1996, as prices of gas increase and the industry is restructured. If the expected restructuring of the Russian market occurs, a considerable volume of Russian gas will be released for export to the region and abroad. This could reduce demand for Turkmenistan's gas. But increasing cooperation in pricing between Turkmenistan and Gasprom of Russia may reduce competition and raise prices.

External Environment

3.34   Turkmenistan gas export receipts depend heavily on the prices agreed with Russian and other FSU buyers. They also depend on Turkmenistan's agreed share in the Western European market, on the pipeline charge, and on movement of Russian internal prices toward international prices.

3.35   Another risk is the possibility of severe supply dislocations in the FSU, especially in Russia. There could be considerable supply bottlenecks in raw materials, intermediate goods, and spares and replacements for capital goods. Turkmenistan's remoteness from other sources might make import substitution from other countries difficult. Its inexperience with direct procurement in market economies is another factor which might play against the alleviation of these import shortages in the short term.

3.36   In addition, financial and macroeconomic developments in Russia will have repercussions on the Turkmen economy. Even with its own currency, it will not be able to completely insulate itself from macroeconomic events in the FSU, given the large proportion of its trade with these countries. In this connection, the most important external risk may be that the countries of the FSU continue to trade in nonconvertible currency and are not able to pay for its imports. It might then be of little use for

Turkmenistan to accumulate large arrears of other FSU countries, while rapidly having shrinking surpluses with the rest of the world.

3.37   Lower revenues from gas will result in slower growth and a substantially lower trade surplus. If gas export prices to the FSU do not increase at the pace assumed above, if most of the gas exports are on a barter basis for a long period, or if the increase in gas prices leads to a higher-than-expected decline in demand, this will greatly reduce the surplus with countries of the FSU. There also are substantial risks with hard-currency gas exports. Future hard-currency revenues will continue to be uncertain as long as Turkmenistan depends on Russia for both transport and marketing to hard-currency markets. Finally, a decline in the world market gas price would also affect the trade balance and the budget.

Implementation Capacity

3.38   Even if the external environment is good and the political will for reform exists, there is a risk that the implementation of reforms will be poor. As the range of decisions broadens and the complexity of issues increases, decentralization of authority will be necessary. Timely and effective implementation of the structural and sectoral reform program will require a substantial strengthening of institutional capacities. Because the pace of reforms may be constrained by the inability of the administration to implement policy measures, training to improve the capacity to implement economic policy is therefore a high priority. The lack of experience and skills of managers and workers in banks and enterprises, so far shielded from responsibility and accountability, is another possible constraint.

Part II

Structural Reforms

No significant changes have yet taken place in the state-owned enterprise sector. Not only is the previous industrial structure still intact but enterprises also have failed to adjust. It will be very important to promote faster adjustment, especially through privatization and private sector development to foster a faster supply response. Furthermore, Turkmenistan's state enterprises require radical restructuring. Restructuring will include reforms in the ownership and legal structure, financing, staffing, and technical assets. Some restructuring measures will represent institutional changes. Others will concern the treatment of existing assets such as the financial debts, environmental problems and the cost of laying off staff. Finally, some physical restructuring might be needed to address the operational problems. These include the need to upgrade products to international standards and the acquisition of new equipment, technology and skills. A description of the current status and proposed reforms for privatization, private sector development and the governance of state enterprises is provided in Chapter 4.

The financial system is proving to be one of the most serious obstacles in the FSU, both to sound short-term macroeconomic management and to the long term development of a market economy. Reforms must aim to liberalize and commercialize the financial system through a rapid improvement of the payments system, restructuring of the main commercial banks, and reform of the legal, accounting and prudential framework. Chapter 5 describes the current status of the financial sector and proposes reforms.

The success of the transition to a market economy will depend on the Government's willingness and ability to implement a comprehensive program of structural reforms. Substantial measures are required in the area of trade policy, given the major role of export earnings in ensuring a successful transition. Chapter 6 describes the current trade system and the changes required to help to begin to reap some of the considerable gains of foreign trade.

A necessary element in the agenda for structural reforms is the provision of an adequate social safety net to protect the poor and those who are adversely affected by the reforms. Chapter 7 contains a description of the existing system of social protection, the labor market and the system of education and training, and assesses the adjustments that will be required.

CHAPTER 4

PRIVATE SECTOR DEVELOPMENT
AND GOVERNANCE OF STATE ENTERPRISES

4.1   Privatization and private sector development are occurring slowly at the margins of the economy, while state involvement is expanding in some sectors. Most private activity is in the service, agricultural and trading sectors and is not, with the exception of a few joint ventures, directly productive. The regulatory, legislative, and economic environment for private sector investment is not comprehensive, and Government plans to reduce entry barriers are limited. Few foreign or domestic investors are considering significant equity investments, and most major projects will be Government controlled for several years. No substantive transfer of ownership of agricultural, industrial, or other assets has occurred. The Government's program is to proceed step by step, commencing with small service units, followed by leases for retail premises and some agricultural land. The Government gives concerns over equity, social hardship, and control priority over increasing the economic efficiency of the state sector, through privatization or other means.

4.2   Performance of state owned enterprises will remain poor as long as ambiguity in the ownership and inadequate control over SOEs continues. Inaction is likely to result in increased stripping of assets and declining output. Without structural changes in the sector, enterprises continue to hold the Government accountable for output declines and accumulation of inventories, while the possibility of a financial crisis mounts. Thus, the fate of a stabilization program and reforms in general depend to a large extent on transforming SOEs into economic entities that respond to market signals.

Structure of the Industrial Sector

4.3   In 1991, Turkmenistan's industry's share of net material product amounted to 19.6 versus 46.4 percent for agriculture. Production of gas and generation of electricity are the most important activities within the industrial sector. Some minerals, particularly sulfur, magnesium, iodine, bromide and salt, are also extracted. Though Turkmenistan is a large cotton producer, the textile industry has not been adequately developed. Other industrial activities consist mainly of producing building materials, fertilizer and chemicals, some electrical equipment and consumer goods. In 1991, 10.6 percent of the work force was employed in the industrial sector. Employment increased from 1980 to 1990 on average by 1.5 percent a year.

4.4   From 1987-1991 industrial production increased by over 3 percent in real terms. However, in 1992 production dropped by about 17 percent. This situation was due to the disruption of the Former Soviet Union's market. Not only were exports and imports disrupted, but SOE managers all over the FSU had to face changing conditions.

4.5   The average size of SOEs is slightly more than 100 employees. This is lower than in other republics of the FSU (e.g. more than 800 in Lithuania). Although some industries are highly concentrated, many are of medium scale (see Table 4.2).

4.6   Most industrial policy is formulated by the Office of the Council of Ministers and the Ministry of Economics and Finance. The supervision of most industrial and commercial enterprises is the responsibility of various Ministries. Power generation and gas industries are under the supervision of independent concerns (holdings).

Table 4.1:
Turkmenistan: Output of Selected Industries

	1990	1991	Growth Rate 1990/1991	1992 (Jan-Aug)
Turkmen Minerals (1000 tons):				
Sulfur	477.9	343.1	-28.0	162.4
Sodium sulfate	241.4	259.4	7.4	163.2
Sulfuric acid	842.6	788.1	6.3	254.6
Magnesium sulfate	40.1	22.5	44.9	26.0
Oil Refining (1000 tons)	5,464.2	7,132.2	30.5	4,082.4
Heavy Duty Pumps (unit)	1,064.0	1,068.0	0.3	744.0
Cement (1000 tons)	1,084.6	903.5	-16.7	707.4
Bricks (million units)	718.3	624.6	-13.1	188.7
Flat Sheet Glass (1000, square meters)	5,085.0	6,098.0	19.9	3,928.0
Knitwear (million pieces)	11.6	10.5	-9.5	3.9
Hosiery (million pairs)	18.5	12.7	-31.4	6.5
Ashkabad Footwear Corp. (1,000 pairs)	5,142.0	4,246.0	-17.5	2,341.0
Vegetable Oil (1,000 tons)	108.2	106.0	-1.9	61.0

Source: Goskomstat, 1992.

4.7   The Office of the Council of Ministers has a special department dealing with industry. It is in charge of coordination and control of industrial activity. In practice this department has replaced the former Gosplan and has the final say on any new industrial project to be financed by the Government. It also monitors, and to some extent supervises, through its specialized divisions, the activity of independent enterprises. The Ministry of Economics and Finance has specialized divisions in charge of heavy industry (energy, chemicals and mechanical); consumer goods and services; agro-industrial complexes; transport and communications; social and economic development and investment policy and coordination.

4.8   The relationship between the supervisory ministries and SOEs is not uniform; it varies according to the type of activities of the latter and the function of the former. Some enterprises enjoy a great degree of independence, while others are treated as an administrative extension of the relevant Ministry. In some cases, SOEs under the supervision of the same Ministry are treated differently. The budget of the supervisory Ministry is normally financed by their respective SOEs. Government officials argue that this practice is justified because it constitutes a legitimate tax on SOEs. But such a system is against the basic rules of fiscal management in the public sector. Moreover, it may result in the supervisory Ministry becoming dependent of SOE's, which it is supposed to control, thus leading to a situation where the supervisory Ministry and the SOEs collude against the best interest of the state.

Table 4.2:
Number of Workers

	Enterprise	Number of Workers	Share of Total (%)	Average Number of Workers per Enterprise
Total Industry	1,381	139,934		101
Electricity	23	6,958	4.9	303
Fuel	6	9,177	6.6	1,530
Chemicals and Petroleum Products	9	8,915	6.4	991
Machines and Metallurgy	434	226,07	16.2	52
Wood and Paper Products Duty Pumps (unit)	119	4,750	3.4	40
Construction Materials	287	195,19	13.9	68
Glass	1	968	0.7	968
Light Industry	197	450,54	32.2	229
Textiles	(61)	(239,23)	(17.1)	(392)
Food Processing	255	175,30	12.5	69
Medicines	1	301	0.2	301
Printing	10	1,495	1.1	150
Other	39	2,660	1.9	68

Source: IMF Pre-Membership Economic Review

Procurement and Distribution

4.9   Few enterprises are free to determine their production level. Most of them receive a production quota from the Ministry of Economics and Finance, in cooperation with the supervisory ministries. This practice was carried out under the centralized command economy of the overall Soviet system. However, they are no longer adequate to address the new problems enterprises face: need for major maintenance work, unavailability of spare parts and so forth. Because they still had to meet the unchanged production targets, enterprises concentrated on quantity, leading to quality degradation.

4.10   The worsening quality of the enterprises' products is accentuated by the combination of two additional factors. First for practical reasons, no industrial standard is enforced: it may prevent the achievement of quantitative production targets. Second product marketing is usually performed by other organizations. This keeps the enterprises from being concerned with the ultimate quality of their output, which might not meet the need or the expectation of the consumers. As a result, various SOEs, particularly under the Ministry of Consumer Products, are faced with large unsold or unsalable inventories.

4.11   The disruption of the previous marketing setup and interrelationship between enterprises in the former Soviet Union has exacerbated the predicament of the SOEs. Until 1989 all input requirements of various industries were specified and handled by ministries or special organizations based mainly in Moscow. The production of some enterprises was also distributed by central state organizations throughout the former Soviet Union. Currently the enterprises themselves or their supervisory ministries have to deal with procurement and marketing, a task for which they have not been prepared. They have to identify--sometimes with much difficulty--their old suppliers or customers. The former often claim to have been paid in hard currency or paid prices much higher than the enterprises' expectations. Previous customers are generally no longer under any obligation to purchase from them. Moreover, the quality of inputs or outputs is often below the market requirement.

Prices

4.12   Prices of the great majority of consumer products are set by the Ministry of Economics and Finance. This is usually done without regard to the real cost of production. No consistent rule is followed for determining prices. The same products can have different prices according to the enterprise or the market. For items considered basic necessities a two-tier price system has been established (see Table 4.3). For each item, a quota is allocated to individual consumers (lower price) or to enterprises (higher price). The lower prices are systematically below the official cost of production. This price policy has already resulted in the emergence of a black market for some items. Such price differentiation is applied at enterprise levels as well.

Budget and Auditing

4.13   Except for enterprises under the supervision of the Ministry of Bread Products and, in some cases, the Ministry of Construction Materials, the budget of each SOE is prepared by its accounting department and approved only by the managing director. Contrary to the past, there is no authority in charge of auditing the enterprises. Although it is hoped that many enterprises will be privatized eventually, in the meantime there is a need for effective review of the way they are managed. The Government does not yet seem to perceive the urgency of supervising the enterprises while preserving their autonomy. Even the controllers assigned by the supervisory ministries to examine the accounts of the SOEs are not given access to the information they need. For some enterprises, there is a tacit agreement that the controllers will not ask for documents considered by the management to be business secrets.

Table 4.3
Turkmenistan: Two-Tier Price System
of Selected Items
(rubles)

Item	Enterprises	Individuals
Bricks (1,000 units)	2,500	924-955
Corrugated asbestos sheet	89	46
Cement (ton)	766	578
Glass (m²)	47	18
Construction stone (m³)	320	162
Gas (m³)	185-200	105

Source: Ministries of Construction Materials and Consumer Goods, September 1992.

4.14   Many SOEs employ far more people than are needed. For instance, the two local refineries with a combined annual production of 6 million to 7 million tons have a work force of about 3,770. The international norm for the number of employees at a refinery of 10-million-ton capacity is less than 600. Absenteeism is also noticeable in some cases. Another problem is the high rate of emigration for non-Turkmen technical staff. This trend, if continued, may seriously harm the whole industrial sector because the local know-how is insufficient to sustain the enterprises.

Profits and Financial Position

4.15   If international norms of cost accounting were applied, probably most -- or perhaps all -- SOEs would be unprofitable. The majority of SOEs lack adequate amortization provisions and any possibility of renovation of machines and equipment depends on soft credits from the banking system. Various administrative and price interventions result in enterprises marketing their output below its real cost of production. Nonetheless, most enterprises claim to make profit and are expected to do so. In calculating the profit, firms:

- Take the difference between the cost of production and the total amount of total amount of output, whether sold or kept as inventory.

- Underestimate or totally disregard inflation.

- Underestimate amortization provisions.

Managers are interested in showing profit in order to receive bonuses and keep their position. Furthermore, part of the profit is distributed as social benefits among enterprise employees. Thus, maintenance is deferred and fictitious profits are shown, leading to decapitalization of the enterprise. Financial data for the sector need to be treated with caution, both because of these accounting practices and because of the distorted input and output price structure. However, in principle, the viability of an enterprise could be assessed on the basis of this type of activity, dimension, technology and location. This, nonetheless, needs further study.

Accounting

4.16   Beginning in January 1993, enterprises and organizations (besides banks and budget-supported institutions), including enterprises with foreign investment, began to use the Plan of Accounts of Financial and Business Activity of Enterprises and the Instruction for its Application approved by a decree of the former Ministry of Finance of the USSR, dated November 1, 1991. These documents were developed with the United Nations Center on Transnational Corporations. A number of new accounts are stipulated; they are intended for generalization of information of individual types of property, obligations, and business transactions. New forms of annual accounting reports and instructions for their compilation are being developed. Annual accounting reports are mandatory for enterprises and organizations regardless of the forms of ownership, including enterprises with foreign investment. The balance sheet of the enterprise is compiled using a net balance sheet. Restructuring of assets has been done on the basis of the degree o liquidity of the types of enterprise property. A Statute of Accounting and Reporting has also been elaborated which calls for publication of financial reports which include an estimate of assets and liabilities which should be periodically checked by internal and external audits. At present structural internal and external audit subdivisions have been set up in the Ministry of Economics and Finance. An Audit Activity Statute is being prepared.

Investment

4.17   Enterprises can invest their net profits freely without prior approval of any supervisory body. Some of the "rich" corporations -- gas, power generation, cotton processing -- have invested their funds in activities selected by the managing director, without regard to their main line of activity. For example, the power-generation company is engaged in food processing--wine, milk and dry fruit -- and also in leather and carpet thread production. New projects for production of cheese, sugar and textile are under study. SOEs with available financial resources of their own are free to invest as they choose, but are expected to inform the Ministry of Economics and Finance. As for the SOEs in need of investment financing, their projects are prepared in cooperation with the Ministry of Economics and Finance before being submitted to the Office of the Council of Ministers.

Future Viability

4.18   Many SOEs could become economically and financially viable in an open market economy if the major problems mentioned above were addressed. Core factors of competitiveness are location, scale, integration, linkages and technology. Some units badly located, or with products destined mainly for markets of the Former Soviet Union may be forced to shut down or to restructure. Some industries have no comparative advantage; for example, the production of aluminum sulfate was destined for water purification all over the Former Soviet Union. The sulfur that goes into the aluminum sulfate is brought from a remote southern part of the country and aluminum oxide from as far away as St. Petersburg. Such a relatively low-price commodity has to be produced close to the market because high transportation costs make it uncompetitive. On the other hand, although Turkmenistan has an important gas industry, no extraction or processing equipment is manufactured in the country. Even though some could be produced efficiently using existing local know-how. The country annually produces 650,000 tons of salt, four fifths of which is exported. But ground table salt is not produced locally and has to be imported from Armenia.

Private Sector Development

Current Role of the Private Sector

4.19   Little of Turkmenistan's economy is in private hands, although there is significant marginal activity in the agricultural and trading sectors. The Tax Inspectorate's register for July 1992 shows 8,940 taxable enterprises (including agricultural entities), of which only 2,600 small-scale enterprises are fully private (mostly trading or distribution outlets, home-worker operations, small brick factories, and the like). There are 14 foreign enterprises (mostly shops) and 10 joint ventures (mostly trading operations, with a few production ventures and 1 gas exploration agreement).[1] Another 300 shops and small-scale production facilities belong to the semi-state Turkmenistan State Cooperative Alliance, which operates a countrywide barter system in rural areas, that trades surplus rural produce for foreign consumer goods. In the first six months of 1993, the number of small-scale private increased to 3000.

4.20   These figures somewhat understate the volume of economic activity not directly planned or monitored by the state. Around 23 industrial enterprises have farms, and many agricultural cooperatives have, for example, small brickyards, which produce tradable goods for their own consumption. In estimating the size of other unofficial and semi-private activity, some evidence suggests widespread rigging of enterprise production figures and accounts. It does not appear, however, that most enterprises systematically engage in unofficial sale or barter either with each other or with entities outside Turkmenistan.

---

1.   Ministry of Economics and Finance figures are higher, showing 38 joint ventures registered by July 1992, and 52 by September 1992.

The Regulatory and Legislative Environment

4.21   Despite the legislative changes in late 1993, the regulatory and legislative environment for new private sector investment still needs improvement. While the court system has undergone significant reform, a lot needs to be done for it to be independent of the executive branch of Government. Historically, Turkmenistan used two court systems: one organized by the Ministry of Justice (the "Government system") and one operated by line ministries, with courts specializing in particular sectors. Under the Soviet system, economic disputes among SOEs were adjudicated by the state "arbitration" courts, which followed a separate procedure from the regular civil courts. In 1992, the "arbitration" courts were abolished and, in their place, new economic courts were created. As a result, there are three levels of regular courts which adjudicate civil and criminal matters, and, in parallel, three levels of economic courts. The Government is currently considering merging these 2 court systems, and creating only separate economic panels in the regular courts. Not unlike the experience in other countries of the FSU, neither the civil nor the economic courts have sufficient personnel or skill to handle complex commercial disputes.

4.22   Registration of new companies is relatively straightforward, with detailed registration first required at the oblast level. For registration involving foreign investment, one needs to seek Government approval. Registration problems appear to be mainly practical. First, because there are no local consulting or other firms to help prepare the initial documentation, previous examples are copied, leading to errors. Second, municipal workers are poorly qualified and lack legal training, which can make their demands unrealistic. It normally takes around one month to register, with a payment of R2,000 for a local firm and (by administrative practice rather than law) $500 for a foreign firm. A bank account cannot be opened without registration at the oblast level. The legal framework to protect businesses is still evolving, and important technical issues are still being worked out. Although a law on small businesses is extant, the new bankruptcy law has not yet been tested in practice.

4.23   Legislation on foreign trade and investment in Turkmenistan is also undergoing significant changes. Among the basic laws are laws on Foreign Investment, Secessions, Free Trade Zones, and Foreign Economic Activity. There is no bankruptcy law. Incentives for foreign investors appear generous. However, in certain cases they also lead to tax losses and unequal competition with local firms. Where investors contribute 30 percent or more of the capital, 100 percent of earnings are tax free until the original investment is recovered. However, critical provisions are not tightly drafted and could be subject to abuse. For example, the definition of investment is very broad, including paid services and trade-marks, as well as, apparently, additional paid-in capital subscribed later. All of these can be netted off against tax obligations, allowing companies to avoid taxes for many years. Procedures for remittance of profits are also unclear, as it appears that hard currency income from sales abroad can be held in foreign branches, rather than consolidated with company financial statements prepared in Turkmenistan. Import of any production-related item is supposedly permitted without a license (but does not automatically entitle the importer to foreign exchange). As a final example, the rate at which foreign currency investments, or ruble dividends, are exchanged is specified as the Bank of Turkmenistan exchange rate, but it is not clear if investors can benefit from different ruble rates offered, for example, in Moscow by physically transferring rubles. Many such detailed issues are yet to be raised by the small number of foreign companies currently active. Such companies generally prefer to sign "special" joint-venture agreements that can give them even greater advantages. Foreign investors are allowed to take part in the privatization process (including retail and land privatization), but in the event of similar bids, that from a domestic buyer will be preferred.

Taxation

4.24   Tax matters are handled by the Tax Inspectorate, formed by special decree on 6 January 1992 as an independent body reporting directly to the President. Taxation had previously been a function of the Ministry of Economics and Finance. The new body has a central establishment of 112 professional staff (40 currently at post), with 1,250 staff at oblast and district levels. The head of the Inspectorate was appointed on 5 August 1992, and staff followed (mainly from the Ministry of Economics and Finance) in mid-September.

4.25   The oblast authorities notify the Tax Inspectorate when a new enterprise is registered. Submissions have to be made every three months to the Tax Inspectorate. Failure to pay taxes due can result in punitive taxation of the company or, in certain cases, in taxes being levied personally against the manager. In the period January-July 1992, 1,860 enterprises (21 percent of the total) and 1,200 managers (13 percent) were fined this way. Inspectorate officials are very concerned over this level of non-compliance and may take more vigorous action to prevent it. The new structure does, however, incorporate a new Department of Appeals and Legal Issues.

4.26   The enterprise profit tax applies to the profits of all enterprises after distribution of dividends and was applied at a rate of 35 percent with a number of exemptions and deductions. This rate was reduced to 25 percent in 1993. Collective and state farms, and a list of enterprises with specific activities, are exempt from the tax but should be subject to the tax. Newly created enterprises in particular sectors are exempt or partly exempt during their first two years. In addition to the profit tax, enterprises pay 37 percent of the wage bill to the pension fund.

The Competitive Environment

4.27   State enterprises benefit from cheap credit extended by the banking system and from direct state subsidies in manufacturing and agriculture. They are given preferential access to both local and inputs imported by the Government, and their parent Ministries exercise considerable control over transport and distribution arrangements. There is no effective utilization of the bankruptcy law to ensure that inefficient state producers exit. Private enterprises, nevertheless, have some benefits where they are not required to fund substantial social expenditures, including upkeep of schools, health facilities and the like, borne by existing large state enterprises, but can instead pay higher salaries.

4.28   Given Turkmenistan's small economy, larger new ventures will almost inevitably either comprise or compete with domestic monopolies, but neither antimonopoly legislation, nor any institution exists to adjudicate on related issues. The problem of monopoly power is referred to in the Privatization Law (Article 5.3), but there are no current plans to establish any antimonopoly institutions. The Ministry of Economics and Finance is instead expected to deal with specific monopoly issues as they arise during the privatization process.

4.29   In the case of monopolies, demonopolization should precede or accompany incorporation. Production in some industries is highly concentrated. Some industries appear significantly oversized, and the demand for their output at appropriate prices is likely to be far below present capacities. Plans have to be formulated for the overall restructuring and modernization of the industry including the elimination of excess capacity, import liberalization and retraining of workers before these assets undergo commercialization and privatization. Most industrial restructuring and demonopolization could occur as an outcome of the market process itself, rather than as an administered prerequisite to the introduction of market forces or the reform of ownership. Enterprise owners disciplined by market forces are generally in the best position to determine which lines of activity to shed and which to expand. It is also very important to liberalize and demonopolize trade and transport for a sound industry sector.

Small-Enterprise Development

4.30   The Government is currently working on a plan to create a fund to provide capital for small entrepreneurs, possibly involving the Chamber of Commerce, and a state commercial bank.

Investment Promotion

4.31   Investment promotion is currently handled, *de facto*, by the Chamber of Commerce, a non-governmental "public" organization containing both private business persons and state enterprise managers. Its Chairman characterizes its current mission as "protecting private enterprise against the state." It will also lobby to secure public investment (for example, state contributions to small milk-processing facilities started by co-operatives). The Chamber will derive most of its revenues from organizing trade fairs, the first of which was arranged in conjunction with a Turkish firm. The Chamber also performs miscellaneous services including inspection of imports to avoid disputes over whether items were supplied.

4.32   The Chamber may in the longer term have difficulty in combining its function as a center for private sector activity and promotion of investment. The latter ideally requires a "one-stop shop" where investors can receive official guidance on registration procedures; about taxation, law and government policy; on professional services, and on potential investments.

4.33   The President has announced a new body, the Innovation Fund of Turkmenistan, to act as an investment promotion entity. Its responsibilities will include investor search; provision of legal and financial services, and, apparently, registration of companies and conclusion of agreements. It may also have a role in promoting small businesses. Some funding may come from the proceeds of privatization sales. Details of this fund are not yet available.

Response of Existing Entrepreneurs

4.34   There is limited evidence of rapid growth of some domestic private sector activity. Most of the small enterprises need new equipment and training; are short of capital, and can only make limited use of the banking system. They are often critically short of inputs, which may previously have been provided by the state sector. Without new methods of financing, and an ability to source raw materials outside the state system, such small firms cannot grow rapidly.

Foreign Economic Activity

4.35   The list of joint ventures registered with the Ministry of Economics and Finance shows that foreign economic activity is increasing slowly, but with a wide range of nationalities represented. Interviews with foreign business persons suggest they generally try to negotiate special joint-venture contracts and rely on personal contacts rather than working inside a properly developed and transparent legal and fiscal framework. The risks involved and lack of competition tend to encourage over-pricing, which has in other countries led to scandals and a poor public perception of foreign and domestic private business persons. Although a small number of joint-venture partners claim to be equity investors, this should be treated with some caution. Equity is frequently injected in the form of plant and services that, in an environment where Government does not seek competing bids, can be difficult to evaluate quantitatively. Particular concerns raised by foreign business persons were the poor transport and communications infrastructure and difficulties with the banking system, which cannot support trade finance effectively.

Government Program on Privatization

4.36   Little privatization has occurred to date. The Government is still working on a privatization program to be implemented.. To implement the privatization program, a subdivision was created within the Ministry of Economics and Finance. This division is very small and 5 of the 10 positions have been filled yet.

The Legal Framework

4.37   The law on privatization passed in early 1992 is largely based on Russian legislation, with minor amendments generally favoring more rather than less state control. The details permitting actual transactions are issued by the President. A set of more detailed laws on agriculture, retail sales, housing and industrial privatization is currently under preparation.

Institutional Arrangements

4.38   Institutional arrangements to administer the program were completed in July 1992, with creation of a Ministry for Economics and Finance (MOEF). In addition to the MOEF, the municipal authorities and the Ministry of Agriculture are expected to take leading roles by executing privatization. No conflict of authority is evident between these different bodies, partly because so little has been sold. The MOEF will resist involvement of line ministries, which have obvious vested interests and derive part of their administrative budgets from enterprises. In some republics, municipal authorities have prevented asset sales because they would be forced to assume social and other obligations currently met by state enterprises. This problem may arise in Turkmenistan for the agricultural sector. Because privatization, in other than the small scale services sector, has yet to commence, detailed questions over ownership have not yet arisen. Box 4.1 contains a brief summary of the Government plans for each asset described below.

The Program for Privatization

4.39   The Ministry of Economics and Finance is working with the Economic Research Institute and key Ministries to draw up a comprehensive Privatization Program for consideration by the Cabinet of Ministers. Drafts propose a phased program, starting with small-scale privatization (trading and services such as shops, canteens, cafes and hairdressers and small industrial enterprises). This will be followed by a larger number of retail sales, and then by medium and finally by large-scale enterprises. Social facilities such as cinemas will be left till even later, to "preserve the social fabric." The law on privatization specifically excludes certain state assets (related to defense, state security and protection of the environment). Sale mechanisms are likely to include auctions, distribution of non-voting stock to workers and sale of stock to the general public.

Box 4.1
Turkmenistan: Draft Privatization Program
Summary of Ownership Arrangements for State Assets (September 1992)
and [MOEF Draft Privatization Approach for Each]

Housing	Municipal authorities (oblasts and districts) [Give away or sell with 10-year resale restriction]
Shops and Services	Municipal authorities where shops are part of housing blocks Ministry of Economics and Finance, municipal authorities in cases where they are separate
Industrial Enterprises	Ministry of Economics and Finance [Minority holding given/sold to workers:
State Farms/Cooperatives	Municipal authorities: cooperatives own equipment and buildings [Encourage 10-year or longer leases: move to "service company + farmers" structure]
Land	Municipal authorities (oblasts and districts) [Land transfer in longer term. Long leases for industrial sites and agricultural production]
Natural Resources Sector	Ministry of Economics and Finance [No privatization at present: some joint ventures]
Infrastructure	Ministry of Economics and Finance [No privatization at present: some joint ventures]

4.40   Privatization schemes using vouchers are not a Government priority. Although such schemes are difficult to design and administratively complex, they hold the promise of rapid change in ownership, even where assets are not very valuable. They also have the potential of improving the equity and transparency of asset disposals; increasing the pressure for asset auctions and stimulating the creation of intermediate management companies. The Ministry of Economics and Finance should keep the progress of such schemes, particularly in neighboring republics, under review to see if part or all of successful modes can be transplanted.

Housing Sales

4.41   Residential property and land sales will be handled by the six oblasts that own the properties, with the Cabinet of Ministers setting overall policy. Each oblast will delegate administration to the relevant district authority, each of which has established special committees to deal with this. Housing sales throughout Turkmenistan began in 1988 under a special law that permitted sales only to war veterans, with the price determined by committees that visited the premises. This process was administered through "self-financed" offices in each of Ashkabad's three districts, which charged a fee for each sale. The price paid was R3,000 - 10,000, the stock being mainly old single-story buildings, built in the 1950's. Around 3,000 apartments were sold in Ashkabad, from a total stock of around 125,000.

4.42   A new law for Ashkabad passed on 1 January, 1992 permitted residents living or working in the city for more than 15 years to obtain ownership free. Those with less than 5 years' residence were not eligible. For apartments between 5 and 15 years, a special commission visits and values the premises. All those with physical disabilities or war veterans were entitled to apartments free. Variants of this scheme were also launched in Turkmenistan's other five oblasts. This program was considerably slowed by a presidential decree of 12 March 1992 that forbade new owners to sell housing for 10 years after purchase. This decree was applied retroactively to those who had purchased since January. A special committee will buy back homes from those who want to dispose of them, selling 70 percent to state enterprises and giving 30 percent free to those on housing waiting lists. This decree was apparently directed against those who wished to sell their apartments and leave the country. The biggest exodus of this type has been to Russia. Market forces would allow new owners to dispose of apartments to foreign business persons for large sums. This was considered intolerable while long housing waiting lists persist. New owners can rent however, as long as tenants have the correct passport stamp and income is registered with the tax authorities.

4.43   Officials do not expect many applications for privatizing apartments. Current occupiers will not be ejected if they do not apply to buy their apartment, and they can pass property on to their children whether it is private or public. Many prospective purchasers are concerned over potential high maintenance charges, although when apartments forming part of a state block have been sold, the state appears to continue to supply overall maintenance and services at no additional charge to the new owners. This provision will need to be examined in the future as the number of private apartments increases. There are currently no plans to privatize public utilities.

Retail Privatization

4.44   There are 5,477 registered shops in Turkmenistan: 2,172 state-owned and 3,305 owned by co-operatives and a few joint-ventures. State shops are controlled by trade distribution organizations which report both to the Ministry of Trade and to various sector Ministries (e.g., the Ministry of Bread Products). Where shops are part of a housing complex, they are owned by the relevant municipal authority. Ownership of co-operative shops is also apparently with the municipal authorities.

4.45   The state distribution system operates from 9 very large warehouses in Ashkabad, through a system of regional and municipal warehouses. Two warehouses deal with food (one has a 30,000 - ton capacity for refrigerated goods; the other is for dry goods). Most of the food products are subsidized and often bought at high cost, for example, from the Ukraine. More than 7,000 people are involved in the distribution system countrywide, with 2,500 people in the food sector alone in Ashkabad. Seventy staff in the Ministry of Trade "monitor" these organizations.

Privatization Prospects

4.46   The privatization process will be managed by Privatization Committees composed mainly of representatives from the municipal and regional authorities, the Ministry of Economics and Finance, banks and enterprises. Shops will be divided by each committee into three categories:

●   Fewer than five staff, where they are given free to employees.

- Small shops, (5-100 staff) sold at auctions by the Ministry of Economics and Finance.

- Larger shops, where 25 percent of residual value will be given to employees as non-voting shares; 5 percent to management and 10 percent to suppliers or other enterprises with a close working relationship. The remaining 60 percent will be auctioned to suppliers or other enterprise with close business ties to the enterprise, with employees able to purchase at a discount (probably 30 percent).

Shops will be required to keep the same product line during normal opening hours for 1 to 2 years.

Medium- and Large-Scale Enterprise Privatization

4.47   The model for most enterprises will allow 25 percent of the "value" to be given to employees as non-voting shares; 5 percent to management; 10 percent are sold to workers and 60 percent retained by the Ministry of Economics and Finance for eventual sale when a buyer can be found. A version of the Russian asset valuation method (using historical accumulated depreciated cost) seems likely to apply to the final sale.

Enterprise Managers' Response to Privatization

4.48   Visits to industrial and agricultural enterprises demonstrated differing levels of understanding and enthusiasm for the privatization process. Managers already exporting to the CIS or elsewhere generally appeared less concerned over Ministry support and were more aggressive in their plans. Others, dependent on state-supported prices and inputs negotiated by Ministries from the CIS, were more nervous. It appears that relatively few of the enterprises visited would constitute profitable private sector entities without significant reinvestment and work force re-organization at both white- and blue-collar levels. It was also evident that the skills and capital to achieve this are in very short supply in Turkmenistan.

Support Services for Privatization

4.49   Privatization requires an active professional services sector to provide accounting, legal and consulting support. There are very few firms that exist in these areas in Ashkabad. Although some Turkmens have expressed an interest in setting them up, growth will be slow and will lag behind demand. Furthermore, substantial training will be required to develop adequate services in these areas. Since similar problems exist in neighboring republics, while cross-border service firms could in time give some support, they are currently severely under-resourced even for their own domestic markets. Much of the required expertise can also be provided through technical assistance.

Financing Private Sector Development and Privatization

4.50   Capital to finance both private sector development and privatization is in very short supply. Inflation has eroded the value of domestic savings, even if these could be accessed through the unreformed banking system. The latter is not currently organized to provide debt finance on a commercial basis. Some wealthy domestic individuals are likely to provide equity capital for a few particularly attractive enterprises, but this source is quite limited. Foreign investment, particularly from Turkey and Italy, may fund a small number of medium - and large - scale projects in the agricultural and energy sectors, but smaller ventures in other sectors may not justify appraisal costs by foreign investors. Turkmenistan's economy is not thought to be large enough to support a full stock exchange, although regional possibilities may exist in the long term.

The Social Impact of Privatization

4.51   Turkmenistan is fortunate in having only a small heavy industrial sector, which will relatively limit the social impact of closures. Only 56 plants employ more than 500 people, almost all in the textiles sector. Some down-sizing here will nevertheless be required to achieve international competitiveness. More casualties are likely in the 50 to 500 - employee range.

4.52   Current Government thinking is firmly set against any enterprise closures or down-sizing, even where the latter might save a facility in the longer term. Visits suggest this attitude is shared by managers - only one claimed to be consciously reducing his labor inputs. Agricultural privatization may have limited labor retrenchment consequences, as productivity gains are possible on most farms through encouraging farmers to diversify. New, more labor-intensive technologies may also be introduced.

Enterprises and Public Expenditure

4.53   Enterprises in many formerly socialist economies, provide a number of services for their employees and their families which are typically thought of as falling into the government's jurisdiction. Some construct and support hospitals, undertake the construction and maintenance of housing, build and run kindergartens and preschools, make voluntary donations towards the financing of public transport systems and local governments extrabudgetary funds. In the case of some larger enterprises, capital expenditures by public enterprises have been extended to other areas such as roads and water lines. However, structural change and the privatization process will require that enterprises disencumber themselves of these non-production related responsibilities, and make it necessary for the public sector to take over some of these services provided by enterprises in the past. Provision will have to be made for the financing of these new public expenditure.

Transparency of the Privatization Process

4.54   It is too early to assess this, as neither the institutions nor the legislation is sufficiently developed, and very few transactions have occurred. First transactions are often given special privileges to ensure that they will work, which can later backfire. This route appears to have been followed when dealing with some of the first foreign investors. Intensive exposure to case studies from other republics, combined with a good choice of pilot transactions, should reduce the risks.

Development of the Privatization Program

4.55   To develop a privatization program and launch the privatization process the main priorities are:

- A review of the Government's current privatization program with a view towards strengthening and accelerating it.

- An intensive study of foreign legislation to ensure that recent lessons and changes are fully incorporated, and the accounting and other implications understood.

Existing legislation has to be redefined, and amendments and implementing legislation adopted.

- Institutional planning to ensure that the Ministry of Economics and Finance devolves functions and authority where appropriate, along with clear definition of a lead agency for each type of privatization, development of its own work and resourcing program, including training, and development of a database of enterprises both to monitor progress and to provide information for investors.

- Research of fiscal incentives for investments offered elsewhere, including the level and structure of tax relief offered and special arrangements for natural resources.

- Establishment of a small business agency with one or two regional offices and development of a pilot project approach.

- Examination of current investment promotion arrangements and the set up of a "one-stop" agency.

- Rapid promulgation of improved and more liberal legislation for retail, housing, agricultural and industrial sales.

- Requirement for all enterprises to become defined corporate entities.

- Distribution to enterprises of a circular describing how to prepare transformation and privatization documents for the Ministry of Economics and Finance.

- Selection of two medium-sized industrial and agricultural enterprises (probably farms) to act as pilot privatization candidates, under close supervision from the Ministry of Economics and Finance.

4.56   A rapid expansion of the small-scale privatization program, with definition of targets covering most of the retail and service sector is critical. A strategy for each state asset is described in Box 4.2. Small-scale privatization can be key signal for transformation. Not only can the privatization of smaller enterprises be accomplished relatively quickly, but the failure to embark upon small-scale privatization before other stages of reform, can have a negative impact on the overall success of the reform program.

Box 4.2
Suggested Strategy For Each State Asset

Housing
- Devolve to municipal authorities, with monitoring role. Seek relaxation in 10-year resale and renting/subletting rules

Shops and Services
- Devolve to municipal authorities for auction where possible
- Restructuring/privatization of trucking/wholesale

Industrial Enterprises
- Introduce corporatization program by set date
- Commence pilot privatization program (4 enterprises)
- Encourage "bottom-up" privatization of viable enterprises
- Propose "financial monitoring" relationship for non-viable enterprises
- Study possibility of vouchers

State Farms/
Cooperatives
- Assist Ministry of Agriculture to introduce flexible lease arrangements
- Devise method of separating municipal functions, service company and independent farmers
- Introduce competition into supply of inputs and marketing of outputs

Land
- Need for transparent program
- Move to irrigated land sales following progress on steps above
- Recommend outright sale or long leases from municipal authorities for industrial developments

Natural Resource
- Bring some assets into joint ventures

Infrastructure
- Encourage telephone/ railway/ utilities to sell off non-core assets
- Encourage management contracts

4.57   The principal privatization approach to emerge so far in most of the FSU countries relies on a balanced use of "top down" and "bottom up" approaches (see Box 4.3). In general most republics have adopted a "top down" approach to setting rules and establishing an approval process, while adopting a "bottom up" approach that allows the enterprises themselves to put together their privatization plans and to implement the transactions. With regard to medium and large scale enterprises, Russia has opted for the "bottom up" approach for enterprise proposals while setting the rules of the game at the central authority, or from the top down. In small scale privatization, both rules and program initiatives have largely been delegated to local authorities, leaving the enterprises and central authorities with a notable passive role. As for larger enterprises, the "top down" approach has been, so far, limited to a few transactions where either hard currency earnings or demonstration effects have been sought. In light of the relatively slow progress achieved in large privatizations relying on initiatives from outside buyers -- or, more typically, enterprise employees -- some FSU countries, such as Kazakhstan and Kyrgyz Republic, are considering more centralized state initiatives in the future. It is clear that regardless of the approach, there is a need for transparent rules and regulations governing the process.

Box 4.3
Privatization Experience

Small-scale Privatization: The most common method for privatizing small SOEs is through sale at auctions. Kazakhstan, Kyrgyz Republic, Latvia, Lithuania, Estonia, Georgia and Russia have chosen some type of organized bidding process as the primary method of divesting the small enterprise sector. The majority have opted for cash auctions, but some allow the use of other instruments as well. This decentralized method is highly efficient and provides capital for the local selling governmental agency. Some other widely-used methods for privatizing small enterprises among the FSU republics include divestment by competitive bidding, tender offers, or leasing.

Although most of the FSU republics have leased a portion of state property to the private sector -- some with option to buy -- the use of leases predominates in the republics with the more conservative privatization programs. Nearly all of the leases have been made to employees and labor collectives. The process of tender offers or competitive bidding is more cumbersome and time consuming than other methods, particularly when based on the most attractive social and economic offer, as well as on price. In addition, potential investors may become discouraged when the restrictions imposed are not compatible with profit maximization. For example, new owners may be required to continue existing operations for a number of years as opposed to immediately converting to a more profitable business. In Kyrgyz Republic, for example, the evaluation of tender offers that are based on restrictive social and economic plans has slowed the pace of privatization.

Large-scale Privatization: The privatization of medium and large SOEs has presented a greater challenge to the FSU republics. The common approach has been to corporatize the large enterprises into joint stock companies. Thereafter, the decision remains as to whether to dispose of these enterprises case-by-case (commercial privatization) or en masse (voucher privatization) to the general public. The commercial privatization approach can consist of competitive sales of shares, either by auction or by tender, to strategic investors or employee-management buy-outs. The traditional advantage of commercial privatization is that it provides better corporate governance through ownership concentration and that it raises capital for the government. Its drawbacks are that: (i) it can be a slow process, since firms are sold on a case-by-case basis; and, (ii) it targets a limited number of investors and excludes the general population. Russia has adopted an innovative blend of mass privatization with case-by-case auctions that are organized rapidly with minimal enterprise preparation. In most republics, larger SOEs are generally privatized case-by-case due to the extensive pre-sale preparation that they require.

Mass Privatization: Mass privatization schemes are also being widely adopted in order to speed up the process of divestment and to promote wide-spread participation through distribution of vouchers to the population. Russia, Ukraine, Latvia, Lithuania and Georgia have all devised some form of voucher scheme in their mass privatization programs. To date, Russia and Lithuania are the only republics to have made real advances in implementing their voucher programs. There are certain important distinctions between the two strategies, however. First, the Russian vouchers all have identical face values of 10,000 rubles, while Lithuanian vouchers have face values based on citizens' age brackets. Secondly, Russian vouchers are fully tradable for cash or other assets, while Lithuanian vouchers are not. Finally, Russia has gone through the lengthy and expensive process of printing and distributing its vouchers in a physical format, while Lithuania simply credits the individual's savings account with the value of the voucher.

Box 4.3   (cont.)

In addition, Russia and Lithuania have different auction mechanisms for acquiring shares in large SOEs. In Russia, all bids are made through the use of vouchers, while in Lithuania auctions, bidders must use a combination of vouchers and a cash quota to bid for shares. Kazakhstan is opting for a slightly different method of mass privatization: shares of medium and large SOEs will be given to investment funds and the public will be given certain Privatization Investment Coupons to invest in them.

In designing a method to incorporate vouchers in a mass privatization scheme, a number of factors were considered, including: the number of SOEs to be privatized using vouchers; the percentage of total shares to be offered through vouchers; the strength of the banking system; the rate of inflation; and especially the level of public support. These and other factors were used to determine: (i) whether to have vouchers with or without face value; (ii) whether or not to make vouchers tradable, and, (iii) how to distribute the vouchers, whether in a physical form or through savings accounts. The designers were also concerned that vouchers would be part of a broader program of creating effective and equitable ownership, and therefore gave priority to the following criteria:

- Administrative simplicity,
- Speed and security of distribution,
- Making shares of enterprises available for bidding as soon as distribution of vouchers is complete.
- Widespread public acceptance.

Russia has also emphasized the use of investment funds to act as financial intermediaries, but has chosen a laissez-faire approach to their development. By March 1993, 300 funds have emerged and registered with the state. Investment funds can be an effective way to concentrate ownership and provide effective governance of enterprises. These funds also reduce the risk exposure of individual investors through diversification.

Source: Soo. J. Im, Robert Jalali, and Jamal Saghir, <u>Privatization in the Republics of the Former Soviet Union: Framework and Initial Results</u>, World Bank, Washington, D.C., June 1993.

Governance of State Enterprises

4.58   Privatization has proven to be a complex and time-consuming process. And given the large number of SOEs, no matter how successful the process of privatization is, it is likely that many SOEs will remain in state hands at least temporarily. Thus, improving the performance of the remaining SOEs both during the transitional period and in the long run is vital. While the Government should privatize the SOE sector as soon as possible, it should also strengthen the governance for those enterprises that cannot be privatized immediately.

4.59   SOEs lack any coherent set of rules defining their status and regulating their operation. The enterprises have no board where the supervisory ministry, as shareholder, could be represented. The extent of authority and the level of responsibility of the management varies widely from one enterprise to another. Paradoxically the Government, on the one hand, interferes in what should normally be within the competence of the management (price and volume of production) and, on the other hand, neglects its duties as shareholder and manifests total disinterest in the way the SOEs are managed.

4.60   It is crucial that management structures be installed that closely approximate private sector norms. An efficient ownership and governance structure for enterprises would provide:

- A clearly defined ownership.

- An enterprise supervisory body responsible for the longer term strategic issues and oversight of management performance.

- Substantial operational autonomy and incentives for enterprise management.

- A hard budget constraint.

Ownership Reform in the Transition

4.61   At present, the Government is the principal -- or the only -- shareholder in the enterprises but does not exercise shareholder functions. Therefore, it is most important that the Government starts to exercise its ownership rights over the SOEs through a mass incorporation decree. The decree will force a clarification of ownership and will sort out the relationship between enterprises, the branch ministries and concerns. The shares of SOEs that will not be immediately privatized should be held by a Government agency representing the owner. A broad incorporation program, that is, the conversion of state enterprises into legal corporations with properly defined capital, charter, legal identity and board of directors, should make easier both the privatization of firms and the supervision of firms that remain state owned.

The Hard Budget Constraint

4.62   Enterprises, whatever their ownership, respond only to market signals and to the pressure of competition if the owners hold managers truly responsible for the financial results of their decisions. Market discipline is undercut when there is a soft budget constraint, that is, when losses are covered by transfers from other enterprises, the state budget or automatic credits from the financial system. The imposition of a hard budget constraint makes enterprises financially independent.

4.63   However, financial autonomy has to be accompanied by managerial autonomy that permits enterprises to adjust to changing constraints and opportunities that is to adjust prices, outputs, employment and other inputs in response to the signals given by the market. The importance of a hard budget constraint, in turn, highlights the urgency of rapidly eliminating current price distortions. If price distortions remain, relatively efficient enterprises could become financially inviable, while other enterprises that are made profitable only by virtue of the distorted price could be encouraged to expand -- an undesirable outcome. The imposition of a hard budget restraint needs also to be accompanied by elimination of existing differentials in the tax treatment enterprises receive accordance to their size, branch, mode of organization or other factors.

Ministries

4.64   Implicit in the reorganization of enterprise ownership, control and management is a dramatic change in the roles and responsibilities of the existing branch ministries. Several Government agencies currently deal with this issue without being effective or coherent. Objectives could be better achieved if all industrial problems were handled by a single Ministry of Industry, whose functions would include the formulation and monitoring of the Government's overall industrial policies and study of sectoral policy issues. It would not become involved, however, in control or management of enterprises. Several ministries, such as the Ministries of Consumer Goods, Construction Materials, and Bread Products -- the remnants of the old centrally planned system -- should be abolished.

Management

4.65   A central factor in the poor performance of SOEs has been the absence on the part of those making the fundamental decisions regarding the enterprises' activities and policies, of any stake in the efficient use and future value of their capital assets. Management of commercially oriented SOEs should be accountable for their performance. Moreover, the top management of the SOEs should clearly realize what their future function would be and what is expected from them in an increasingly competitive environment. All this probably requires a well-designed, consistent training program at top and middle management levels because the shortage of trained and experienced managers is likely to be one of the most serious bottlenecks to rapid improvement in enterprise performance.

Accounting

4.66   The existing system of enterprise accounting needs to be revised to meet the requirements of a market economy. The publication of financial accounts, incorporating a proper valuation of assets and liabilities, would begin early in the transition. Accounts should be audited (externally and internally) and should aim to represent a full and fair view of the financial position of an enterprise for the information of shareholders, creditors and those entrusted with supervisory authority. Such accounts would also allow managers to evaluate performance and take key decisions, for instance, on investment.

Investments

4.67   Investment decisions have to based on a careful assessment of the profitability of new investments no matter whether they are made in the public or private sector. At present, this is not the case, and the ministries need training and assistance in understanding how to undertake these decisions. Currently, there seems to be a lack of capability as well as demand for the economic and financial evaluation of projects according to modern, market-based criteria.

Liquidation and Bankruptcy

4.68   Without the threat of liquidation and bankruptcy, even the best-designed management system may fail to harden the budget constraint. In a market economy insolvent or illiquid enterprises would be restructured or liquidated by their owners or their creditors unless they are considered economically viable. It is therefore important that the Government implement the new Bankruptcy law, including the development of efficient and adequate procedures, institutions, and enforcement mechanisms.

4.69   An important issue is how to deal with loss-making enterprises. Many of them might become viable after restructuring. Those considered not to have any chance of survival in a competitive environment should be gradually phased out. The sudden liquidation of some insolvent enterprises, particularly if they are labor intensive, might be socially and politically difficult. In such cases, losses should be financed in a transparent manner by the budget and not, as is currently done, through allocation of soft credits by the banking system. The rate of subsidies to concerned enterprises should decline with time and be accompanied by a phased program of lay-offs of their employees and sale of their assets.

Box 4.4
Technical Assistance Recommendations

Private-Sector Development

Assistance may be required in the following areas:

- **Legislative Area.** This would principally involve review of existing legislation, proposals for amendments, and assistance in the development of implementation and enforcement mechanisms.

- **Tax Treatment of Foreign and Domestic Investors.** This would require an expert view on what tax advantages will benefit Turkmenistan, compete with other centers and prove relatively simple to administer.

- **Competition Policy.** Expert advice will have to concentrate on the preparation of the legislative and regulatory basis in the antimonopoly area, including the creation of appropriate institutions that will carry out these policies.

- **Small-Business Promotion.** This area requires significant support to help bring credit and training to Turkmenistan's new businesses, through either the existing banking system or new institutions.

- **Investment Promotion.** The Government's approach to new investors needs to be carefully coordinated, and advice sought on the kind of incentives that might be offered.

Privatization

- **Institutional Support for the Ministry of Economics and Finance.** Assistance in overall program planning; establishment of an enterprise database; preparation of materials to distribute to enterprises; technical advice on valuation methods; managing transactions; and developing a public relations strategy would all be invaluable assuming that privatization acquires more momentum. In addition, regular updates on "best practice" from other parts of the CIS would be very useful.

- **Program Development.** Immediate priorities would be assistance with speeding up the retail and services program; putting forward more inventive options on housing sales, and developing a properly sequenced agricultural program.

- **Support for Specific Transactions.** If the pilot approach recommended for larger sales is adopted, expertise in consulting and business planning; valuation; law, and negotiation will be essential to ensure the pilots are successful and provide suitable models.

CHAPTER 5

FINANCIAL SECTOR REFORM

5.1   The challenge for Turkmenistan, like for other post-socialist economies, will be how to undertake the complex task of liberalizing and commercializing the financial system while achieving and maintaining financial stability. A common practice is that financial institutions cave in to pressure from state enterprises for increased lending and thus undermine monetary policy. Such practices, which would institutionalize hyperinflation, threaten long-term growth. With this in mind, proposals in this chapter take the view that stabilization must have priority. It is important that the institutional reforms introduced, help Turkmenistan authorities exercise monetary restraint while developing an efficient structure of financial intermediaries as quickly as possible.

Turkmenistan Financial System under Central Planning and the 1988 Reforms

5.2   Until independence the Turkmenistan financial system was a regional component of the Soviet financial system, which contained regional divisions of the main Soviet Union-wide banks. Under the central planning system the financial system did not play an independent role in the allocation of resources to their highest value use but allocated funds in accordance with the decisions of the central planning bodies in Moscow. The regional branch of Gosbank in Turkmenistan was the main channel of resource allocation through the financial system. Soviet policies appear to have resulted in positive fiscal flows into Turkmenistan and other Central Asian republics, although the mix of financial and fiscal flows makes it difficult to assess the magnitude of the net transfer.

5.3   Within the central planning system the banking system was an integral component in the three stage process of mobilization and allocation of resources:

- The collection of tax revenues and financial resources from individuals, enterprises and organizations in the various republics.

- The aggregation of these resources at the federal level.

- The allocation of the total volume of resources through both financial and fiscal channels according to central plan directives.

5.4   Until 1988 most enterprise credits were provided by the regional branch of the Gosbank in Turkmenistan and funded by resources transferred from Gosbank Moscow. Some investments were financed by long-term lending extended by the construction bank. The Turkmenistan branch of the Foreign Trade Bank extended some credit to enterprises engaged in foreign trade and conducted all foreign exchange operations.

5.5   In early 1988 the Soviet authorities established a two-tier banking system. The central feature of the reforms was the separation of the commercial banking operations from the Gosbank, establishment of 3 new commercial banks from a segmentation of the commercial portfolio (the Agriculture, the Industry and Construction Bank and the Social Bank) and allowing for the establishment of new commercial banks. The Savings Bank and the Foreign Trade Bank continued in a broadly unchanged role. The current structure of the Turkmenistan banking system is little changed from the structure established at the time of the 1988 reforms, with the three main state commercial banks being the regional successors of the three Soviet-wide organizations. They were converted into joint stock banks whose shareholders were specific Government Ministries and large enterprises in 1990.

The Current Structure of Financial Institutions in Turkmenistan

5.6   The financial system in Turkmenistan consists of a central bank, two specialized state banks and seventeen commercial banks. Apart from the three state commercial banks only the Senegatbank is of any significance. There is also a state insurance company (Gosstrakh).

The Bank of Turkmenistan (Gosbank)

5.7   Under the newly established banking laws issued in June 1992 Gosbank was established as an independent central bank responsible for the conduct of monetary policy, management of the payments systems and the supervision and regulation of the banking system. In addition, the bank is charged with setting preferential rates and administering subsidies to the priority sectors of the economy (see also Box 5.1). It is clear that much development work needs to be done in adjusting the bank's role from that of a regional branch of Gosbank to that of a national central bank since most of the particular functions were carried out by Moscow or, alternatively, did not exist under central planning.

The Savings Bank (Sberbank)

5.8   The Savings Bank collects the bulk of household ruble deposits through its more than 500 branches. It also acts as the payments agent of the Government with respect to households. The bank has only since 1988 begun to develop a limited personal lending portfolio but remains a net provider of funds to the banking system. Prior to independence the surplus savings of Sberbank were transferred from, Moscow to Gosbank and then channeled back according to central plan directives. As a result, by the beginning of 1992 Sberbank held claims on Moscow of nearly R1.7 billion. These claims, together with interest owed, amounted to a current debt of nearly R2.5 billion in September 1992, which has not been settled by Moscow but replaced by an equivalent Turkmen Government bond issue held as an asset on the Sberbank balance sheet. The Government bond is not currently yielding any interest.

5.9   The presence of a large proportion of non performing assets (2.5 billion compared with 4.7 billion rubles of customer deposits) has clearly created financial difficulties for a bank that has virtually no capital base. At the beginning of August 1992 Sberbank's deposit rates rose to 20 percent, and the bank was given the right for the first time to on-sell 50 percent of its surplus deposits directly to commercial banks rather than at a low rate to the Gosbank. It is nevertheless unlikely that this is sufficient to stabilize the parlous situation of this institution, which appears to be technically insolvent. (To safeguard the position of this bank, the Government has also guaranteed its deposits and has promised to provide the bank with R2.5 billion.)

Box 5.1
Central Bank: Current Status

The central bank (Gosbank) is charged with supervisory responsibilities over the banking system but has no appropriate legal or accounting framework in which to function. Of great importance is lack of supervisory experience, and lack of human resources. The supervisory role is also undermined by clear directives transmitted to the central bank to assist in the extension of credit to priority sectors that break the Gosbank's own prudential norms. Currently the Gosbank conforms to the five prudential rules issued for the entire Soviet banking system in 1990 that require banks, for example, to maintain a capital-to-deposits ratio of 5 percent. These regulations are far too lax for application to banking conditions during transition.

The central bank also has a key role in developing the payments system. Delays in payments have, according to the accounts of all the commercial bankers interviewed, increased dramatically since the break-up of the Soviet Union, despite the introduction of local regional settlement centers whose role was to assist in check clearing. The central bank has a clear role in coordinating activity in this area, but it appears that many banks are now going their own way in the areas of payments and automation; this might lead to considerable problems of coherence.

The State Banking Law places on the bank the responsibility of ensuring that an annual credit plan is presented to the President of Turkmenistan for approval. However, in actual practice, because of the high level of inflation, the central bank's active management of policy appears to have been limited to the distribution of cash to enterprises according to their needs after adjustments have been made for inflation. It thus appears at this stage that no detailed credit plan is in place, although there is evidence of directives saying that support for priority sectors is to be maintained at the expense of others, particularly the private sector. As a consequence the staff within the central bank are under the conflicting pressures of understanding the need for exercising monetary restraint and responding to the demand for distress borrowing by enterprises.

The new state banking law has not established a clear separation between the new functions of the central bank and its role as a quasi-fiscal agent of the government. An example of the continuing role as practiced under central planning is the request that the bank create capital funds to finance certain commercial and quasi-governmental activities. This mixing of roles makes the emergence of a central bank which can work with the necessary degree of autonomy difficult.

Agroprombank

5.10   Agroprombank, by virtue of the size of its balance sheet, is the largest bank in Turkmenistan (loans represent 70 percent of the total loans granted by banks). The bank has 53 branches, and its shareholders include the Ministry of Agriculture as well as state agricultural processing enterprises and cooperatives. Its main liabilities include deposits of agricultural enterprises and Government deposits, but mainly loans from other banks and predominantly from the Gosbank. The lending of this institution is directed to collective farms, the agricultural processing industry and the irrigation industry.

5.11   It appears that in view of the policy of subsidizing agriculture, the rates charged by this bank are in many cases lower than those charged to other enterprises, particularly by the commercial banks. In august 1992 a special credit line was introduced by presidential decree that supports lending to collectives at a rate of 2.2 percent. Agricultural enterprises obtain only 0.5 percent for the deposits

Table 5.1: Turkmenistan Banking System (Selected Balance Sheet Items)
(millions of rubles)

	Deposits (enterprises, organizations, individuals)		Lending (enterprises, organizations, individuals)		Capital		Capital Ratio[a] (%)	
	Dec 91	Jun 92	Dec 91	Jun 92	Dec 91	Jun 92	Dec 91	Jun 92
Investbank	734	3,524	1,316	12,298	81	296	6.2%	2.4%
Agronpronbank	3,361	2,884	6,228	33,851	175	207	2.8%	0.6%
Turkmenbank	509	2,362	1,023	9,284	42	129	4.1%	· 1.4%
Vnesheconombank	723	242	574	1,244	1	19	0.2%	1.5%
Gosbank	26	319	11	44	5	43	45.5%	97.7%
Senegatbank	229	476	386	1,190	45	42	11.7%	3.5%
Gasbank	9	240	10	296	5	9	50.0%	3.0%
Sberbank	3,618	4,767	-	-30	24			
TOTAL	9,209	1,4814	9,548	58,207	384	769		

a/ Capital/Lending
Sources: Central Bank, Ashkabad 1992

they are compelled to make at the bank. The lending of this institution has increased dramatically in the first half of the year by R27.5 billion to R33.8 billion at a time when the capital base of the bank has only marginally increased to R207 million over the same period (see Table 5.1).

The Industry Bank (Investbank)

5.12   The Industry Bank serves the industrial and construction sector. Its main shareholders are drawn from the Government and the state enterprise sector. The largest single shareholder is Gasprom. The bank sees its main function as supplying credit to all the industrial sectors of the economy. A high proportion of this bank's liabilities are represented by enterprise deposits, and this bank is clearly less dependent than the Agroponbank on support from Gosbank. Nevertheless, over the first half of 1992 the lending of this bank has increased ten-fold to R12.3 billion (see Table 5.1). The vast majority of this lending was short term with a three-month maturity profile; it was essentially being done to meet enterprises' working capital needs particularly wage payments. Over the same period the bank also managed to increase its capital from R81 million to R296 million, which was still not sufficient to prevent a significant fall in the bank's capital ratio.

5.13   A "hard budget constraint" is not being applied as far as large state enterprises are concerned. According to bank sources, their priority is to help "productive" manufacturing industry rather than less socially beneficial trade-related enterprises. The bank receives funds from Gosbank currently at 15 percent and, like other banks, is obliged to on-lend these to state enterprises at no more than 18 percent (a maximum 3 percent margin). The bank receives a limited amount of other funds from its own clients, for which it pays rates of more than 20 percent, and is able to on-lend these at higher rates (25 percent). Virtually all of the credit supplied is short term, but the bank is putting forward a proposal to set up an investment fund to develop industry by providing money for periods longer than five years. The management of the bank is acutely aware that it would require significant additional capital if it were to play an active role in this area.

Social Bank (Turkmenbank)

5.14   The Turkmenbank had originally been formed at the time of the Soviet reforms of 1988 to serve municipalities, schools, hospitals and universities. The Government was also an important customer. It is clear that this bank acts more as a fiscal agent than as a bank. Nevertheless, like the two other state commercial banks, it has been transformed into a joint stock company with 41 branches as of December 1993. It is now a significant lender, and this trend was apparent over six months to the end of June 1992, when its lending had increased nine-fold to R9.2 billion. This increase had clearly been accomplished only through considerable increases in funds received from the Gosbank. Again, capital resources standing at R129.2 million in July 1992 were inadequate.

5.15   The Turkmenbank is placing a great deal of emphasis on the development of its foreign exchange services. It holds the foreign currency accounts of some major enterprises. Having a foreign exchange license allows it to conduct foreign trade activities through correspondent banks on behalf of its clients. It is also placing considerable emphasis on the development of automation with some success already having been achieved through a network of microprocessors linking the branches of the bank by telephone lines, allowing more efficient balance sheet and payments management.

The State Foreign Trade Bank (Vnesheconombank)

5.16   The Vnesheconombank was developed from the Turkmenistan branch of the Soviet parent trade bank. Its functions are:

- To play a role in the management of the foreign exchange reserves. This includes the development of schemes for managing foreign exchange funds. However, certain functions may be taken over by the State Central Bank of Turkmenistan.

- To be a fiscal agent for the Government, capturing the hard currency foreign exchange earnings of exporters such as Gasprom at source.

- To disburse intergovernmental hard currency loans or grants such as those already arranged from Turkey (technical) and the EEC (food aid).

- To provide foreign exchange services for all the major enterprises such as Gasprom.

- To be an export development bank.

5.17   The Government of Turkmenistan clearly has considerable aspirations for this institution in spite of its current modest size of only 100 employees and a small capital base. There are also plans to capitalize this institution to a level of R500 million in 1993. However, there are clear difficulties this institution might face in attempting to combine commercial and central banking functions. There is also the question of division of powers with the central bank referred to above.

Box 5.2
Management of Banks

The Turkmenistan banking system continues to function as an integral component of the central planning mechanism rather than as an autonomous mechanism for financial intermediation. Indeed, in many ways even the structural reforms introduced in the Soviet Union in 1988 creating a two-tier banking system have had only a cosmetic impact on the methods of operation of both state and state-commercial banks. In particular the 3 main sectoral commercial banks -- Agroponbank (Agriculture), Investbank (Industry) and Turkmen bank (budgetary units) -- remain committed to the support of the enterprises within their sectors rather than to working in a profit-maximizing manner. The strong links between state enterprises, bank shareholders and management and the various sectoral ministries make it extremely difficult for the banks to resist requests for distress borrowing in the current difficult economic climate.

In all banking institutions management faces the fulfillment of two different and effectively incompatible tasks. The first task is to carry out a range of quasi-fiscal duties on behalf of the state, which includes the provision of highly subsidized funds to their clients, disbursements of funds (for instance, in the case of the Turkmen Bank to budgetary units), collection of tax revenues and the development of commercial banking activities. Management exercises limited control over the overall structure of their balance sheets and the levels of remuneration of the large subsidized element of their loan portfolios, where restrictions are placed on the margin the bank can earn. As a consequence, there has been a strong element of effective cross subsidization of priority sectors and indeed, particularly in the case of the State Savings Bank, of the budget by "commercial" customers through relatively lower deposit rates and higher lending rates. The element of cross subsidization increased as the Government has failed to adjust its subsidization guidelines in the face of increasing inflation.

The absence of a modern accounting system of loan classification systems and of formal procedures for assessing loan decision makes it extremely difficult to assess the magnitude of problem loans in the Turkmenistan banking system. Nevertheless, it can be suggested that an increasing number of enterprises are facing severe financial difficulties. For example, Investbank has suggested that 400 of its client enterprises are facing payments difficulties. There is also evidence of payments arrears developing between enterprises. In the latter case it is of course impossible to discern how much of this increase is part of a process of adjustment to normal commercial practices of extending trade credit, since trade credit was not allowed under the central planning system.

Virtually all the credit advanced to enterprises has been of a short term nature (average term of 3-months) and lending has been justified by the need to meet short term working capital requirements, particularly wages, rather than long term investment requirements. Even before the surge in lending at the end of 1991 only 6 percent of bank lending was longer term, with the bulk of investment resources provided directly by the government to enterprises. The skills of bank officials were thus very much focused on the administration of the so-called cash plans which essentially were geared to the working capital needs of enterprises. This background suggests that bank staff will have considerable difficult in adapting their skills to a situation whereby short term bank loans are rapidly transformed into "hard-core" borrowings as financial distress increases.

Other Commercial Banks

5.18   Of the other commercial banks, only the Senegatbank with 15 branches is of any significance. The shareholders of this bank are smaller enterprises, and it receives relatively modest support from Gosbank in terms of deposits. Its clients are drawn from state enterprises. It is clear that prudential norms are more strictly applied to the new commercial banks than to the state specialized and commercial banks. Nevertheless, these new banks have an important advantage over the state commercial banks in that they have more diversified lending portfolios and certainly in the case of Senegat and Gasbank, more diversified ownership structures.

Banking Sector Trends

5.19   The period of high inflation and the deliberate policy of subsidization followed by the Government has resulted in a real change in the relationship of the agricultural and industrial sectors to the banking system. These changes are reflected in the balance sheets of both the Investbank and the Agroponbank, which over the first half of 1992 became much more dependent on funds from the central bank to finance their lendings to their respective sectors. This trend is likely to have reflected both the difficulties of the sectors in responding to the partial price liberalization and the absence of direct sources of financial support from the government. Clearly this enhanced role of the banks as providers of finance to enterprises must be taken into account in the design of a financial restructuring program.

Financial Sector Reform

5.20   The key issues that reforms in the financial system must address are the following:

- A rapid improvement must be achieved in the effectiveness of the payments system, which currently is a major impediment to economic development.

- Urgent measures must be taken to augment the supply of individuals' savings significantly and to establish efficient channels of intermediation to direct them to high-value uses.

- A bank accounting system based on international standards should be introduced to provide transparency in the assessment of institutions for bank managers, Government policymakers and potential investors (see Box 5.4). This is particularly important to attract foreign capital and banks.

- A prudential framework should be developed that, while conforming to international standards in terms of scope and consistency with the new accounting system, should set prudential norms in a realistic manner to provide a safety set that will evolve with the necessary restructuring of the banking system.

- The banking system's staff must acquire the skills needed to assess the risk-reward trade-off between different proposals to ensure an appropriate flow of funds for both short-term working capital requirements of enterprises and long-term investment projects.

- A vigorous strategy must be pursued both inside the commercial and state banks and through the educational system to augment greatly the trained human resources available for developing the financial system.

- A legal framework must be put in place that, while providing an operating environment consistent with the development of profitable commercial banking activity, avoids an excessively wide banking mandate, given the narrowness of the skills base in Turkmenistan (see Box 5.4). In formulating the law, the option of licensing institutions to provide a narrow spectrum of services (e.g., payments services and commercial banking, investment banking), should be considered.

- A monetary control mechanism should be put into place that takes into account the limited credit-assessment skills and the priority of maintaining effective control.

- All subsidies should be recognized as such directly in the budget, and the ad hoc use of the banking system should be phased out to ensure that commercial assessment of lending projects becomes the predominant criterion for resource allocation.

Bank Lending

5.21   At the heart of the reform problem is the need to develop an institutional context whereby the lending skills of commercial bankers can be developed in a controlled manner so that their evolution does not undermine macroeconomic stability. Experience has shown in other post-socialist societies that semi-autonomous state commercial banks with no lending skills and the interconnection among banks, enterprises and government agencies as clients and shareholders represent a weak point, as far as the imposition of conditions of monetary restraint is concerned, as long as ownership relationships remain unchanged.

5.22   What is possible to achieve in Turkmenistan must conform to a financial sector reform program. In particular it is clear that in the absence of significant privatization of state enterprises, the three major banks -- Agroponbank, Investbank and Turkmenbank -- should be placed under especially firm control as far as their lending decisions are concerned. There are considerable dangers for macroeconomic stability if such banks were to be given unlimited discretion, considering the undeveloped lending skills in the banks. In the absence of ownership changes, these dangers multiply. Consequently it is essential to have a mechanism to impose on these banks uniform reserve requirements.

5.23   Although controls through capital ratios could be an important method of restricting the activity of banks, their effectiveness as real prudential controls would depend on the availability of a modern accounting system capable of assessing the quality of the bank's loan portfolio and experienced lending staff who can determine the required levels of provisioning. In these circumstances it is certain that an overhasty recapitalization of banks from the levels indicated above would pose significant "moral hazard" problems, since it may create an expectation of future bail-outs if necessary and inhibit responsible behavior by bank management.

5.24   In conclusion, therefore, it would be appropriate to retain a strong brake on the lending activities of these banks in the first phase through high levels of obligatory reserves. These should be remunerated but should exclude Government securities. As the banking, accounting and lending controls of the banks and property relationships are slowly transformed, prudential capital limits can become much more important as instruments of control.

Commercialization and Restructuring of the Main Commercial Banks

5.25   The need to reduce the reliance on credit from the central bank is fundamental to increasing the commercial orientation of Turkmenistan's banks. This dependency has increased dramatically in 1992 and undermines the development of risk-management skills, particularly given the weakness of their capital base. Since such credit is only available if directed to specific sectors at fixed and limited margins that do not reflect the full balance sheet costs, the distribution of such credits requires that they should be cross subsidized by commercial credits. It is thus essential that subsidies are adjusted as quickly as possible to reflect costs fully. As stabilization policies begin to take effect the banks must move toward providing the majority of their lending at real rates reflecting the risks and rewards of their projects. Nevertheless, over the short term and in the absence of transformation in the ownership structure of industry, the quality of the loan decisions is likely to be poor. Therefore, prudential requirements, particularly credit controls on banks should be very severe. This clearly has implications for the supply of credit to a nascent private sector that may have to depend on the development of smaller but well-supervised banks.

5.26   The transformation of Investbank, Agroponbank and Turkmenbank into private commercial banks is bound to be a long, drawn-out process that involves the development of new accounting and operating systems as well as the development of a wide range of technical skills. It is also likely that the first two institutions at least will have to be separated into multiple components because of their sectoral dominance. Fundamental restructuring of the main commercial banks does not at this stage appear to be feasible given the necessity of maintaining coherence in the banking system while essential technical improvements in the payments system are effected. At the same time, the likely slow pace of enterprise privatization would appear to a preclude changes in the ownership structure of banks. Nevertheless, some measures could be taken now with a view to easing the path of fundamental restructuring and ownership change in the future and providing a better basis for "commercializing" the relationships between bank management and clients. As has been suggested, the Government's policy of suppressing interest rates during the period of hyperinflation has effectively decapitalized the banks, and this process will continue until macroeconomic stabilization is achieved. If the banks are to play any autonomous role in credit decisions, then their capital resources must be significantly augmented. To achieve this, banks must be given flexibility to increase the spreads on lending; they must be compensated for the full cost of preferential lending, and their obligations to pay dividends to enterprise shareholders should be waived. These three actions should improve the banks' flow of retentions and thus their capital position, but they must clearly be supplemented by other recapitalization measures.

5.27   The current low level of capital of the banks has some advantages in that it may allow the government to buy out the enterprise shares (the dollar equivalent value of the capital of the banking system is only a few million). Direct ownership of the banks by the Ministry of Finance in the transition period may promote commercial relationships with clients and ensure compliance with prudential norms better than if clients are also majority shareholders. Direct ownership would also provide a better base for the fundamental restructuring and changes in ownership structure that will be required over the longer term.

Development of Merchant Banking Subsidiaries

5.28   A key problem is allocation of funds to effective long-term investment projects on the basis of market-based decision making. This skill must be developed in Turkmenistan. Our suggestion is that development finance departments should be set up in the Investbank, Turkmenbank, Agroponbank and Vnesheconombank with a focus on long-term investment activities. Even in the initial stage these development finance departments should be as autonomous as possible from the parent commercial bank, with a separate physical location and a separate management structure. They would nevertheless retain the basic client relationships and knowledge of the parent organizations; eventually they could develop a more diversified portfolio with the freedom to acquire an interest in both agricultural and industrial enterprises. Basic to the development of these long-term finance divisions would be the allocation of a fund (denominated in dollars), that would effectively mean the operations would be separately capitalized. These operations, which would look favorably upon projects that intended to develop exports, could provide the essential context for the development of banking skills.

5.29   The construction of the departments must be established from the outset as interim stages toward the development of fully capitalized merchant banking subsidiaries of each of the banks. While the precise range of services offered by these institutions requires much further discussion, they would certainly have the potential to undertake not only a venture capital role in the economy but also eventually a part in restructuring and privatizing state enterprises. Such subsidiaries would be subject to the highest standards of prudential supervision and may be particularly attractive as partners for foreign banks looking for joint venture possibilities in Turkmenistan and as conduits for business development finance attracted from abroad. The acid test of this proposal is, of course, the willingness of the authorities to dedicate capital, premises and people to the autonomous development finance departments. Clearly the legal and prudential framework under which such institutions should be established would have to be carefully considered.

Development of the Payments System

5.30   No element of the banking sector reforms has a higher priority than improving the payments system in Turkmenistan. An efficient payments system is necessary to enable all markets to function effectively and to connect Turkmenistan with the world economy. On a day-by-day basis, efficient payments enhance the enforceability of contracts in every market and are a prerequisite for the development of efficient capital and money markets. The current payments system described in Box 5.3, based on the central bank's settlement centers, is not operating properly. A priority for technical assistance now is to activate the network of computers in the centers that will enable same-day transfers between accounts. This system will not, however, lead to a consolidation of the correspondent account of each bank and therefore liquidity management will continue to be a problem for the banks. A measure should be introduced immediately to ensure that banks do not get free credit through the payments system; such free credit provides an incentive to delay settlement.

5.31   In the long term the banking system should move toward being responsible for its own document processing and clearing. This is not an abstract, theoretical concept; it reflects technical possibilities that exist. In particular the Turkmenbank links all its branches through a network of microprocessors using existing telecommunications channels and has the possibility of settling through a single settlement center in Ashkabad rather then through the regional network of centers. The bank's offer of providing a settlement service for other banks has been refused but nevertheless represents a very good example of how competitive forces could be usefully harnessed to assist developments in this key area. Indeed, the sale of efficient settlement services could provide income to banks during the transition period when their lending will need to be strictly controlled.

Box 5.3
The Payments System

The payments system in Turkmenistan is highly inefficient and a source of considerable difficulty for day-to day banking transactions by both enterprises and individuals. The central bank of Turkmenistan is responsible for the organization of the payments system and, as in all economies moving away from the centrally planned model, carries out all the back-office settlement tasks normally done by the banks themselves in a developed market economy. Bankers throughout Turkmenistan highlight difficulties in the payments system as one of the greatest obstacle in the development of the banking system and generally as an impediment to economic activity.

While the break up of the Soviet Union has clearly increased difficulties with interstate payments that have largely been conducted through the post, there has also been a dramatic increase in delays in domestic transfers. Thus, despite the relatively low volume of transactions, transfers between branches of different banks in Ashkabad can take more than three weeks to process, the delay often being attributed to the inefficient functioning of the central bank's settlement center. Settlement between banks in Turkmenistan is accomplished through the intermediation of the interbank settlement centers that are run by the central bank and that exchange the main settlement documents of the banks: the credit transfers, or AVISAS. Branches of the same bank in different regions of Turkmenistan will settle through the use of different settlement centers and different correspondent accounts rather than through a single, consolidated settlement center and correspondent account at the central bank. Since delays in computerization keep communication between settlement centers on a postal basis, the system exacerbates delays in payments and leads to a large, variable and growing payments float.

It is clear that at a time of high inflation there are strong incentives for customers and banks to delay payment, and since there is no payments system law that clearly identifies the risk taker and accountability, little discipline is currently being exercised. A recent innovation to the system has been the introduction of guaranteed checks. These checks may add significantly to the payment system risk in Turkmenistan (as has been the case in other economies in transition, such as in Poland) since there are no mechanisms for monitoring and control.

Restructuring the State Savings Bank and Improving the Flow of Savings

5.32   A particular area of concern has been the disastrous erosion of personal savings through high inflation. This erosion of personal wealth has shaken confidence in the banking system. This confidence must be rebuilt as a matter of urgency if Turkmenistan is to build a banking system capable of mobilizing significant resources for financial intermediation and investment. The importance is exacerbated by the absence of other financial intermediaries (the rapid emergence of a significant stock market is highly unlikely). Two immediate steps must be taken: restrictions must be removed on the interest rates paid to depositors, and the asset side of the Sberbank balance sheet must be restructured to remove the non performing component that has emerged as a consequence of the breakdown of the Soviet Union. Restructuring should now be much more feasible, given the erosion of the total value of deposits. The dollar equivalent value of all deposits is little more than $15 million.

5.33   Currently the position of Sberbank is unassailable with its 500 branches (five times more than the total of all the commercial banks), the state guarantee on deposits and the restriction that commercial banks cannot hold personal deposits greater than their capital. Apart from removing restrictions on rates paid, it should be possible to allow commercial banks to bid freely for personal deposits beyond the capital restriction. The Government guarantee to the Sberbank could be removed and possibly replaced later by deposit insurance on all small value irrespective of location. Clearly phasing out subsidized rates and replacing non performing assets will enhance Sberbank's ability to pay competitive rates.

5.34   If Sberbank is to function as an autonomous bank, it must be endowed with capital. However, other options exist over the longer term, particularly the possibility of distributing the branches of the Sberbank among the three main commercial banks. Doing so would provide these banks with the basis for developing a more diversified liability base. Alternatively, Sberbank could concentrate and develop expertise in the key area of home mortgage finance. The development of lending instruments whose rates were linked to inflation would enhance the bank's ability to pay attractive rates to depositors.

Reform of the Legal, Accounting and Prudential Framework

5.35   While the restructuring of domestic financial institutions will necessarily be a long process in Turkmenistan, the creation of an appropriate legal, accounting and prudential framework is an issue that must be addressed promptly (see Box 5.4). All three parts of the framework are vital ingredients of an operating environment in which domestic players can gain experience and potential overseas players are reassured that the rules of the game are clearly defined. The most cost-effective way of proceeding with this work is to ensure that republics such as Turkmenistan have full access to the development work being done on new systems of accounts in Russia. This work is particularly relevant because of the identical starting point and objectives. It is important in this area that both the International Monetary Fund and the World Bank assist the republics in obtaining access to this work.

5.36   The accounting framework is the issue that must be addressed with greatest urgency because of the necessary lead time before a new framework can be implemented. Bank managements need to begin to think systematically about their role in managing stand-alone financial enterprises. Adoption of a structure of accounts and balance sheets consistent with international practice is an essential step in this process. In addition, clearly defined rules for the proper accounting of interest earned but not paid and the creation of adequate provisions for potential loan losses (reinforced by prudential regulations -- see below) will provide the necessary focus on questions of risk related to clients. It is therefore recommended that a task force be set up as soon as possible within the central bank to work on this issue.

5.37   The new banking legislation is not fully compatible with a movement toward a market economy. In particular, the central banking law assigns functions to the central bank that are still closely related to a central planning mechanism. Amendments would, therefore, need to be made to ensure that subsidies to enterprises are clearly identified in the fiscal budget rather than achieved through ad hoc manipulation of the interest rate structure. Similarly, strict rules of independence for the central bank are necessary to cut the Gordion knot of state intervention. Of considerable concern also are the lax rules of licensing banks (the entry threshold is too low, and there is no "fit and proper" persons test). These condition need to be reassessed.

Box 5.4
The Legal, Accounting and Prudential Framework

The legal framework for the functioning of the Turkmenistan banking system is provided by the Law of Turkmenistan on the State (Central) Bank of Turkmenistan and the Law of Turkmenistan on Banks and Banking issued in May 1992 by the President of Turkmenistan. The former assigns an independent role to the central bank for maintaining the stability of the currency and for supervising the banking system. As suggested below, for a variety of reasons the central bank is currently unable to carry out either of these roles effectively. The central bank legislation may actually impede the development of most of these functions because, while it asserts the autonomy of the central bank, the law ascribes control and allocative functions to the bank that represent a continuation of the central planning system. In particular, the central bank is accountable for developing a credit plan for the banking system that involves direction of credit at appropriately low rates to priority sectors according to Government directives.

In addition, the intermediation role of the financial system is undermined by a clause giving the central bank a role in the disposition of surplus funds of both the state insurance agency (Gosstrakh) and the Savings Bank (Sberbank). The law also ascribes responsibilities for prudential supervision that, as noted, the central bank cannot fulfill because there is no framework of prudential rules, no modern accounting system, no legal remedies and limited human resources.

The Law of Turkmenistan on Banks and Banking establishes the conditions for operating commercial banks in Turkmenistan. The model of the commercial bank is that of a universal bank empowered to take equity positions as well as to undertake a wide range of retail and wholesale financial operations. While technical conditions will in any event militate against the introduction of a wide range of services in the short run, the large scope of the license may exacerbate supervisory problems in the medium term because of the absence of risk-management skills in Turkmenistan. The law also establishes the savings bank as a state bank whose deposits are guaranteed by the state. Finally, the law establishes conditions for the licensing of banks that do not represent an effective barrier to entry into the banking system. In particular the minimum capital level required of each bank is set far too low (including that set for foreign banks), while there is no "fit and proper persons" test that would formally require verification of ethical and professional credentials.

The new central banking law requires commercial banks to conform to a number of prudential rules that cover the main dimensions of risk: minimum amount of authorized capital, minimum capital ratio, liquidity, large exposures, foreign exchange interest rate and price risk and the establishment of loan loss reserves. These rules have not actually been translated into detailed instructions released to the banks, and indeed, the work on a modern bank accounting plan that would need to precede the introduction of the prudential framework has yet to begin in Turkmenistan. For the time being the prudential rules in force are those released for the Soviet Union as a whole, which have been in force since 1990. These regulations consist of five prudential rules: a minimum capital-to-deposits ratio of 5 percent; limitations on large exposures; a limitation on personal deposits to the amount of the capital base; limitations on short-term liquidity, and limitations on long-term liquidity. Although these rules appear incomplete and lax compared with norms established in developed market economies, all the banks in Turkmenistan are failing to achieve the required norms, particularly in the key areas of capital adequacy and large exposures. The prudential measures are calculated each month from the monthly balance sheets received by the central bank on the basis of the old Soviet plan of accounts.

Box 5.4 (cont.)

The accounting plan in use in Turkmenistan is the Soviet plan of accounts introduced in December 1989, with some minor changes. The prudential regulations in force in Turkmenistan are consistent with this plan of accounts. This accounting plan is geared to the role of banks under central planning and does not provide a transparent assessment of their standing as autonomous financial intermediaries. Neither does it form a basis for the collation of statistics essential to conducting monetary policy. In particular, the construction of the accounts does not provide a way for assets and liabilities to be clearly presented in a format necessary for the appraisal of banks. Nor does it provide a clear separation between transactions conducted between budgetary entities as distinct from non budgetary units. (It is thus difficult to define transactions with the non bank, non government sector necessary to compile monetary statistics.) Other problem areas include:

- In contrast with Western accounting practice, accounting profits are measured on a cash rather than on an accrual basis.

- There is no recognition of the need to provide systematically for potential loan losses and to suspend interest on loans to clients in difficulties.

- While not a feature of all developed accounting systems, it is essential in the evolving environment of the TSE that the quality of the assets be assessed as an integral part of the accounting system. This assessment is not part of the old Soviet plan of accounts.

- The accounting plan does not provide a basis for the accounting of off-balance sheet instruments (e.g. foreign exchange transactions) and Government securities.

- Finally the accounting system makes no allowance for inflation, which increased dramatically in the first half of 1992, increasingly distorting all financial information relating to banks.

The current bank accounting plan does not provide an information base for the prudential supervision envisaged in the new central banking law, but work on a new law has not yet commenced.

5.38   The banking law allows banks obtaining a banking license to be involved in a wide range of services far beyond basic commercial banking. But in the absence of the basic commercial banking skills, it is unwise to extend banks' operating agenda so far. A narrowing of the scope of the basic banking license will not only correctly focus bank management on the development of fundamental lending skills, but will also assist the bank supervisors. It is clear that, given the very close relationships between banks and customers, the provision of a capacity to take equity position is likely to undermine attempts to conduct relationships between banks and clients at an " arm's length". An alternative to the current formulation in the banking legislation may thus be to exclude investment banking activity from the basic banking charter and place such activity under separate regulatory control. The suggested development finance subsidiaries of the main commercial banks may be the correct vehicles to develop wider banking services and shareholding relationships under separate but strict regulatory control with limits on risk defined by evolving risk-management experience.

Reform and Strengthening of the Central Bank

5.39   The central bank has a particularly important role in the reform of the financial system since it must both improve and supervise established financial practice and more particularly, be an agent for change in a number of key areas, for example, banking supervision, the management of monetary policy and the development of the payments system.

5.40   As indicated above, there was no banking supervision department under central planning which checked compliance with legal regulations. As a result, the banking supervision function needs to be constructed from first principles:

- The banking supervision department must be endowed with sufficient authority to ensure compliance with the regulations, including an appropriately high entry threshold for new banks. It is also important that the law not give the supervisors an agenda of activities impossible to control.

- The new banking law requires the central bank to monitor the activities of banks in accordance with a set of prudential rules that seem broadly compatible with international practice. But the rules need to be transformed into detailed prudential notices and monitoring systems; for example, there is no basis for the monitoring of foreign exchange exposure. This change may require foreign assistance; it is also important to note that the rules themselves, such as in the area of capital adequacy, will give a realistic picture only when a new accounting plan is in place that realistically assesses the bank's position. The central bank must, as part of its prudential responsibility, be the agent and instigator for the introduction of a new accounting plan.

- It is important for banking supervisors to ensure that prudential norms be set realistically. In particular, rules limiting industry concentrations for the main state commercial banks can become more stringent (indeed current norms are broken by all banks) only if the fundamental restructuring and privatization of banks indicated above is accomplished and also some of the major industrial concentrations (such as Gasprom) are broken up. At the same time it will take time for the banking system itself to evolve financing mechanisms, such as loans syndications that will allow the dilution of concentrations. Thus, for now, banking supervision may only be able to limit further growth in concentrations. This is not to say of course that newly formed banks should not be subjected to strict prudential ratios (indeed, uncertainties and inexperience would imply prudential norms for, say, capital to be significantly higher than those defined for a first-class international bank). Indeed, strict prudential limits for those institutions unencumbered with the past are essential in transforming inexperienced bankers into good bankers and in making these banks attractive vehicles for foreign technical assistance and joint ventures.

- The development of a banking supervision capability will require accounting systems, a legal framework and prudential rules and information systems both in the central and commercial banks. Above all, it will require good people to supervise the systems. This will require an efficient recruitment and training program, which will in turn require foreign assistance. The new supervisors will have to be trained in the skills of both on-site and off-site supervision. The development of a capacity to conduct a thorough investigation of each institution in the field (on-site) is a priority.

5.41   Of particular importance for the evolution of the national central bank is the development of a capability to manage monetary policy. A clearer statistical framework within which to conduct monetary policy is a priority. The derivation of this framework will require a more comprehensive identification of the Government's fiscal activities, including direct and indirect subsidies as well as a better integration of the external sector into the monetary control aggregates. Attributing some of the central bank's external function to the state foreign trade bank does not promote coherence in this area. In the long term, the bank will want to develop a capability to manage monetary policy through indirect instruments, and the training of staff for this task should begin now.

5.42   The central bank also has a key role to play in the coordination of policy relating to the development of the payments system. The immediate task is to get the settlement centers to function properly, but the use of such centers may also be considered only an interim stage. The goal is to have the banks handle their own back-office processing of documents and (like the Turkmenbank today) conduct their affairs with the central bank through a single correspondent account and a single settlement center probably run by the banks themselves. The central bank will have to ensure that during the period of rapid change the technical parameters of the payments system are adequately defined to ensure compatibility between each bank's internal system, and make sure that control is exercised over payments system risk. Again, in this area, foreign assistance will be required, and staff will need to be prepared.

Human Resources Development

5.43   In the above section emphasis was placed on the training of staff. To put the problem into perspective, it is important to note that there are only approximately 5,000 staff employed within the Turkmenistan banking system, and this will need to be significantly augmented in both quantity and quality to allow the necessary growth in the banking system, particularly since many of the staff are currently doing low-level clerical work. Priority must therefore be given to setting up a local banker's association and an associated banking school (perhaps affiliated with, say, a Turkish institution) with the immediate task of developing core material in the local language for the training of bankers. A major contribution could be made to the development of the banking system if perhaps 20 "high fliers" could be now identified and sent for a year of intensive internships in banks abroad before returning to the major financial institutions.

Box 5.6
Technical Assistance Recommendations
Financial Sector

Central Bank

Every central banking function requires strengthening in Turkmenistan. The most appropriate vehicle for providing technical assistance may be the International Monetary Fund with responsibilities for different functions assigned to advisers from various central banks. The areas requiring attention (and an individual program and adviser) include:

- Monetary policy management and programming. Even before a program developing management of monetary aggregates can be considered, a statistical framework for management must be implemented and individuals trained in its use.

- The banking supervision function must be developed. This will involve the review and development of appropriate prudential rules for banks and the development of a system of on-site and off-site supervision of the banks.

- A new plan of account must developed for the banking system to allow the proper assessment of banks' profitability and in particular an assessment of the quality of the loan portfolios.

- Technical advice is essential for the central bank to play its vital role in coordinating the development of the payments system.

- The central bank requires advice in improving the legal framework for the operation of the banking system. (A number of areas of the current legislation require development and attention.)

Commercial Banks

As with the Central Bank every area of commercial banking activity will require improvement. Some areas of potential support which have been identified include :

- Portfolio reviews and diagnostic audits of the major financial institutions. This will be necessary not only prior to any major restructuring or ownership transformation but will also introduce Turkmen bankers to the question of loan appraisal and modern accounting methods. It will be essential for the central bank to have an involvement in such audits.

- It is vital to develop banking education for the system to allow the rapid acquisition of skills. This may be through programs directed at a local banker's association or alternatively through assistance in setting up a banking school. Alternatively more modest contributions could be made through for instance providing courses in such areas as foreign transaction procedures.

- It may be appropriate to place teams of advisers in certain identified institutions to develop them as centers of excellence for the banking system. One focal point may be the State Trade bank which is interested in developing an export development finance capability and has requested assistance. Alternatively one of the smaller commercial banks could be identified.

CHAPTER 6

FOREIGN TRADE

6.1   Although Turkmenistan's foreign trade potential is affected by serious external uncertainties, the articulation of a trade system will have an important influence in its success in the world economy. A liberal foreign trade regime could facilitate the transition to a market economy. Import competition would impose discipline on domestic markets that are in general less than competitive by virtue of the past concentration of production. Whether international trade plays this facilitating role depends to a large extent on the policies adopted toward the foreign transactions of domestic enterprises. The liberalization of foreign trade is part of a broader domestic transition to a decentralized market economy in which the behavior of enterprises, rather than Government decisions, determines the conditions under which enterprises buy and sell domestically and abroad.

Trade Policies

6.2   Before Turkmenistan's independence in October 1991, trade was conducted and organized as part of the overall economic plan specified by and directed from Moscow. Since independence. Trade has been decentralized, under the independent barter transactions of ministries and state enterprises and the discretionary spending of retained hard-currency earnings.[1] But the ministries and enterprises are subject to export quotas or licensing requirements from the Ministries of Finance and Economy.

6.3   Turkmenistan has kept the system of centralized state trading. In the beginning, the Turkmenistan Committee for Foreign Economic Connections negotiated trade agreements with governments of other republics and with enterprises in countries outside the ruble zone, principally via barter of cotton. The committee was disbanded in August 1992. Trade is now conducted by agencies closely tied to the Government, government ministries, and state-owned enterprises.

Policies Relating to the Ruble Zone

6.4   While independence provided the opportunity for a new beginning in the trade and payments regime, in many ways the institutional structure adopted reflects the old Soviet type trade regime. Turkmenistan remained a member of the ruble zone. Since full convertibility of the ruble to dollars was not in place, international trade has taken place in segmented markets on a hard-currency basis, and in rubles.

6.5   The Government's prominent role in ruble-zone trade preempted market forces. Trade occured through negotiated interrepublican agreements. Turkmenistan maintained a ruble account (the "correspondent account") in Moscow, for all trade with Russia. Since mid-1992 Russia had agreed to a provision of a credit ceiling in this account. Similar arrangements regulated ruble clearing between Turkmenistan and the other states of the ruble zone. This mechanism constituted ruble clearing, however, and did not permit multilateral clearing of payments imbalances.

---

1.   While there is no formal monitoring of enterprises' expenditures of hard currency holdings, reformed monitoring inhibits the use of the retained hard currency for consumption purposes.

Export Policies

6.6   The dichotomy between ruble-zone and hard-currency trade, with different prices applying to the same goods in the two regimes, led to inefficiencies in the allocation of exports. Turkmenistan's participation in the ruble zone was an inheritance of its previous integration into the Soviet system. Prior to independence trade (measured as the average of exports and imports) constituted some 35 percent of GDP of which 90 percent was interrepublican. While other republics also depended heavily on interrepublican trade (Estonia 91.6 percent, Armenia 90.1 percent, Uzbekistan 89.4 percent, Georgia 85.9 percent and Ukraine 82.1 percent), Turkmenistan's case was exceptional because interrepublican trade dependence was based on exports that are relatively homogeneous and are traded in world markets, making them readily divertible to markets outside the ruble zone. However, the prospects for diverting natural gas exports from ruble-zone trade to hard-currency trade remain hampered by transportation logistics that provide a strategic bargaining advantage to Russia in designating shares of Russian and Turkmen gas for hard-currency sale. Cotton, Turkmenistan's other important export, is not subject to the same transportation logistics and strategic considerations as natural gas.

6.7   Before 1993, exporting firms could keep between 20 and 50 percent of their hard-currency earnings. They had to surrender the remainder to the Government at artificially low exchange rates, based on domestic wholesale prices. The Gas Company had to surrender 80 percent of its hard-currency export revenues without any compensation which is an implicit 80 percent tax on exports. This implicit tax on foreign exchange earnings could be avoided through engaging in barter transactions at artificially low exchange rates based on domestic wholesale prices. On January 1993, Turkmenistan introduced an export tax at differentiated rates. The rate for exports of natural gas remained the same, there is a 30 percent tax for exports of gas condensate, 20 percent for petroleum products, 20 percent for cotton products, 15 percent for chemical products and 10 percent on all other goods. In addition, 10 percent of all the foreign exchange earnings have to be transferred to the 'Foreign Exchange Food Fund' of the Government.

6.8   There is substantial barter trade in Turkmenistan's dominant non-energy export commodity, cotton, by state enterprises and ministries. Cotton, in effect serves the role of foreign exchange reserve holdings, in that allocations of cotton for barter are routinely provided as a means of import financing. There are evident inefficiencies in seeking simultaneously to trade internationally in goods with the foreigner to whom cotton is sold. The higher transaction cost reduce the net price received for cotton exports.

Foreign Exchange and Import Policies

6.9   Both ruble and non-ruble trade has been subject to controls. This control is exercised through the allocation of both ruble balances and hard-currency balances. Not all hard-currency earnings had to be surrendered to the special government fund; some 20 to 50 percent of foreign exchange earnings were left to the discretionary use of the enterprises and ministries. In practice, there is a dual system of highly regulated and not regulated import transactions. Ruble-zone trade has been more regulated than hard-currency trade, since ministries and enterprises that have accumulated hard-currency via the retention scheme are not subject to foreign-exchange control on all of their own hard-currency earnings. Under the conditions of the ruble trade mechanism, agents were potentially regulated on all of their ruble-zone import transactions. Since most prices were still highly subsidized in Turkmenistan non-controlled ruble trade would have led to outflows of goods into other republics i.e. neighboring countries will be indirectly subsidized by Turkmenistan's budget. However after many of the prices will be liberalized, trade could be decontrolled.

6.10   The highest priority for imports is to ensure an adequate food supply. "Free imports," (not state orders) are conducted by the responsible ministries or enterprises using their own hard-currency earnings. At the same time, balanced bilateral trade agreements have been negotiated with governments of other republics. These agreements are very similar to those that used to determine CMEA trade, with an emphasis on the physical volume rather than the value of the goods exchanged. Centralized imports outside the agreements take place when shortages are perceived, with import financing at the discretion of the Cabinet of Ministers, which approves import requests and allocates hard-currency from the retention fund or cotton for barter. For consumer goods, the relevant ministry decides if there are shortages that necessitate imports and seeks hard-currency or cotton for barter from the Cabinet of Ministers. It also decides what to buy, and where to buy it.

6.11   With the dissolution of the CMEA trade and payments arrangements at the onset of 1991, the arbitrary prices of the CMEA system were exchanged for trade in hard-currency at world prices. For Turkmenistan, the new terms of trade imply a substantial gain, but the adjustment to world prices has been gradual among the states of the former Soviet Union. However, there are several changes Turkmenistan can make on its own, however, to help it begin to reap some of the considerable gains of foreign trade.

Recommendations

Movement to World Market Prices

6.12   A liberal trade regime transmits world relative prices to the domestic market, providing market indicators for domestic resource allocation and providing domestic producers with a means of judging comparative advantage in international markets. But as long as the exchange rate is highly undervalued the link to international prices is cushioned by the exchange rate. Policies are needed first to bring inflation under control and move the exchange rate closer to the purchasing power parity for tradable goods.

Multilateral Clearing

6.13   A system of multilateral clearing with short settlement periods should be introduced. A system of this kind will benefit both the countries that stay in the ruble zone and those that adopt a national currency. For countries that adopt a new currency, as Turkmenistan did on November 1, 1993, the multilateral clearing is a way of economizing on international reserves.

Enterprise Autonomy and International Trade

6.14   Under a planned socialist system, enterprises exercise little autonomy in the conduct of international trade. International trade, like economic activity in general, is planned and conducted by government agencies with a monopoly to trade in particular goods. Thus an important element in the transition to a market economy is the elimination of these trading monopolies and the introduction of a trading system that allows enterprises to make their own decisions about trade. This autonomy is particularly important for allowing an emerging private sector to directly participate in international trade, without the intermediation of government agencies.   The private sector has not yet emerged in Turkmenistan, however, because the transition from the old economic system has not proceeded far enough. Enterprises do have some autonomy in the conduct of trade as far as they can retain part of their hard-currency earnings.

CHAPTER 7

THE LABOR MARKET AND SOCIAL INFRASTRUCTURE

7.1   The legacy of the former Soviet Union in the newly independent countries is not only a particular political and economic structure but also a particular type of welfare state. In Turkmenistan this old system has not been replaced by a new system yet. If the Government embarks on a transition to a market economy, the welfare system will need to be changed substantially.[1]

7.2   Social indicators show Turkmenistan to be one of the least-developed countries in the Former Soviet Union. However, Turkmenistan has a low level of unemployment and an expensive system of social security provision. An extensive system of cash benefits makes payments to more than half the population. However, these social measures are not well targeted at those most in need, and eligibility requirements for benefits are low.

7.3   Since there is much more of an underlying poverty problem in Turkmenistan than elsewhere in the FSU, targeted and cost-effective measures are needed. The current social safety net system would not be appropriate to deal with the social effects of an emerging market economy if the government starts to reform the economy. A transition to a market economy, therefore, requires restructuring of the social protection system. Furthermore, the profile of those in need might change as income differentials are increasing.

7.4   In considering an appropriate strategy for the future, whether for the short term or for the long term, it is necessary to establish certain requirements that labor policies and social safety programs should fulfill. Apart from the objectives of efficiency and affordability, the benefit system as a whole should prevent individuals and families from falling into extreme poverty; it should not have undue disincentive effects, and it should be capable of low-cost and effective administration. In the early stages of transition the existing systems of income support, employment services and social services need to be adjusted to satisfy these principles. One of the most important priorities would be the development of an unemployment insurance system and active labor market policies.

7.5   These problems will be considered within the following framework:

- An analysis of the social safety net including the pension fund and the social insurance benefits.

- An examination of labor market issues and unemployment insurance.

- An analysis of the training and education system and its impact and linkages to labor market issues.

- A description of problems facing the health sector.

---

1.   The Government has announced plans to reform the social safety net system after the introduction of the new currency in November 1993. These plans include changing the structure of the pension fund, incorporating all cash benefits in the tax base, increasing salaries for teachers substantially, introducing a new law on the social insurance fund and adopting a new law on the minimum wage. Reforms implemented by November 1993 have been taken into account in this chapter. However, since most of the reform proposals were at an initial planning stage when the report was finalized, they have not been included.

The Social Safety Net

Pension Fund

7.6   The pension fund has two main areas of expenditures: retirement and disability payments and children's allowances, 85 percent are spent for pension payments. The pension fund is financed by an employee's payment of 1 percent of the wage, in addition to the employer's contribution equal to 80.5 percent of the total payroll contribution of 37 percent. The enterprise rate is 26 percent for state farms and cooperatives. However, because the pension fund's expenditures exceed its receipts, there is also a transfer from the budget that finances more than half of child allowance payments. The rationale for the division of payments for child allowances is that the pension fund is responsible for children up to age 6 while children aged 7 to 16 (up to 18 for non students) are the responsibility of the budget.

Pensions

7.7   As in the other former Soviet Union countries, the normal retirement age is 60 for men and 55 for women.   However, persons in "hazardous occupations" can retire five or ten years early. There is also a large number of survivor pensioners (about 80,000) who receive benefits on the basis of deceased spouses' earnings. In 1992, there were about 350,000 retirement and survivor beneficiaries. Life expectancy at retirement is 22 years for women (life expectancy is 77 years) and 15 years for men (life expectancy is 75 years). There is a net annual increase of 17,000 new pensioners each year. In early 1993, the number of pensioners was 404,000

7.8   Basic monthly benefits are 55 percent of average monthly earnings subject to a minimum and a maximum.   In September 1993 the minimum was R9,600 per month and the maximum was R50,400. Benefits are based on the average monthly earnings for the highest two consecutive years of the last 10 years before retirement or the highest five consecutive years overall. There are also significant longevity premiums and awards for meritorious services (see Box 7.1). To be eligible for benefits a man must have worked for at least 25 years and a woman for at least 20 years. Pensions can be received regardless of current earnings if there is an explicit agreement between the enterprise and the worker or if the worker is a member of a special group (for examples, war veterans, doctors and teachers in villages and rural areas). About 13 percent of old-age pensioners work.

7.9   Unlike in other republics, the pension system is indexed to the minimum wage, and both are periodically adjusted for inflation. When the minimum wage is revised, the minimum pension is adjusted by the same percentage. Adjustments occurred in March 1991 (from R70 to R135), January 1992 (to R350), July 1992 (to R750), October 1992 (to R1,600), February 1993 (to R3,200), and in May 1993 (R9,600). The adjustment is a discretionary decision of the President with the input of an advisory committee and heavily influenced by -- but not automatically equal to -- a calculation of changes in the cost of a market basket for households.

Disability Benefits

7.10   Permanent disability is determined by the findings of a medical-labor expert panel. There are three levels of disability. Category 1 is for persons with permanent total disabilities who were injured at work or who have contracted serious occupational diseases. Category 2 covers persons with serious conditions whose benefit costs are to be partially financed by the enterprise. In 1992 half of their payment is to be financed by the enterprise. This enterprise obligation is to rise by 10 percentage points annually and reach 100 percent in 1996. The distinctions between categories 1 and 2 are not important for cash benefit calculations since both are awarded benefits equal to 100 percent of average monthly earnings. Disability category 3 identifies persons who can still work and are expected to work albeit at jobs with reduced physical requirements. These persons receive monthly benefits equal to 30 percent of average monthly earnings. In January 1993 there were 53,638 disability pensioners: 3,275 in category 1; 22,528 in category 2; and 7,835 in category 3. Most persons in category 2 did not work and most in category 3 did work. Unlike old-age pensioners, disability pensioners can receive benefits without an upper limit, and there is no limitation on their earnings. On average monthly payments to disability pensioners average 85 to 90 percent of the old-age pensions. In 1992 disability was awarded to 4,490 people. For beneficiaries, continuing disability is reviewed periodically.

Box 7.1
The Pension Fund: Premiums

The actual monthly payment to a person from the pension fund can differ significantly from the amount suggested by the basic calculation formula. For persons with more years of service than the minimum number (25 for men and 20 for women), 1 percent is added for each year above the minimum to the basic replacement rate of 55 percent. As much as 20 percentage points can be added to the replacement rate under this provision (up to 75 percent). For men with 45 years of continuous service at retirement there is also a 10 percent addition to the monthly payment. Continuous service is defined as having no break in earnings of more than one month. Time spent in technical school training, university and military service is considered the same as employment for this calculation. For women the continuous service requirement is 40 years. The retirement payment can be increased in recognition of meritorious service to the Turkmen state. For retirees with dependents, an amount equal to half of the minimum pension is added (a single addition regardless of the number of dependents). All of these additional payments are multiplicative.

To illustrate the potential effect of this pyramiding, consider a male retiree whose high five-year earnings average is R2,000 per month. The 55 percent replacement rate would yield a monthly award of R1,100. However, with 45 years of continuous service the basic replacement rate would be 75 (not 55) percent, and 10 percent would be added for continuous service. Add to this a 20 percent bonus for service to the state and a dependent's benefit. Combining all of these factors, the R1,100 basic award would actually lead to a monthly payment of R2,355, an amount that exceeds the R2,000 per month pre retirement average.

Children's Allowances

7.11   There are 7 categories of child allowance beneficiaries for children up to age 16 and non students aged 17 and 18. Monthly payments depend on age and on the marital and employment situation of the family. In September 1993 the minimum child allowance was R110 per month and was paid to families where there was no pensioner. The maximum of R270 per month was paid to children under guardianship or trusteeship and to certain other children. Average monthly payments in September 1992 were R320 for children aged 1 to 6 and R214 for children aged 7 to 16. In September 1992 child allowances were paid to 682,000 children up to age 5; 896,500 children aged 6 to 16, and 153,000 children aged 17 and 18. These payments are financed partly by the general budget (for 6 to 18 year olds) and partly by the pension fund (for those younger than 6).

7.12   There are also maternal allowances for non working mothers. The monthly payment in September 1992 of R130 was received by 150,000 women. Additionally, special payments equal to half of the minimum wage are made to "mother heroes," roughly 25,000 women who have 10 or more children. These expenditures are on-budget items.

Box 7.2
Social Insurance Payments

Sick Leave. These payments are made according to a sliding scale that depends on years of work experience (from all jobs). Those with fewer than five year's experience receive 60 percent of their previous monthly earnings; those with five to eight years receive 80 percent, and those with more than eight years receive 100 percent. However, persons with three or more children receive 100 percent of earnings regardless of seniority. The first three days of annual sick leave are granted automatically, while longer leaves require that evidence of illness be supplied by a medical authority. A person may receive up to four months of sick leave in a year for a single sickness and five months for all illnesses. When an illness extends past four months the person is examined by a medical panel for an invalidity (permanent disability) determination. Average sick leave usage is about eight days per person per year.

Maternity Leave. This can be received for up to 140 days in uncomplicated births, for 154 days for multiple births and 160 days for complicated births. The woman receives full salary. Eligibility extends from 70 days before the birth to 70 (or more) days after the birth.   The current 140-day eligibility period is an increase from 100 days during the Soviet period. Ministry of Social Protection officials indicated the increase to 140 days was done partly to reduce infant mortality.

Birth Allowances. These are one-time payments to mothers, made at the time of the birth. As of September 1992 the allowance was R680 per child.

Burial Fee. This is a payment made to families after providing a receipt from the local Zachs (Vital Statistics) office that verifies the death.

Sanatorium and Rest Home Expenses. These services are available to employees and family members after a determination made by a medical expert panel. The trade unions administer six sanatoria and three rest homes. Payments are also made to individuals who enter enterprise-operated rest homes.

Pioneer Camps. These are summer camps for certain children.   Expenses for attendance are paid by the fund.

Work Injuries. Compensation for work injuries is paid as a wage continuation, that is the worker's actual wage at the time of the accident, regardless of worker seniority. After making the payment to the worker, the fund is reimbursed by the employer. Thus the fund administers payments, but the payments do not actually reduce the fund balance as do the other payments. Rather, they are directly financed by the wage fund at each enterprise.   Trade union representatives indicated the fund paid out R178 billion in 1991 (exclusive of payments on collective farms). Because the employer tax rate for collective farms is 26 percent, not 37 percent, they are subsidized both by this fund and by the pension fund. Trade union officials indicated the subsidy represented more than half of social insurance expenditures associated with state farms.

Social Insurance Fund

7.13   The Social Insurance Fund provides allowances and benefits and is administered by the trade unions. The Social Insurance Fund receives 19.5 percent of the employer payroll tax receipts. There are seven distinct types of payments (see Box 7.2), but sick leave and maternity leave account for 70 percent of expenditures from the Social Insurance Fund.

Payments to Students

7.14   Students in elementary and secondary school receive child monthly allowances appropriate to their age and to the marital and employment situation of their parent(s), ranging from R1,300 to R1,560 in September 1993. Additionally there are payments for school lunches. All student stipends are tied to the minimum wage.

Recommendations

Social Protection

7.15   Given the need to limit budgetary outlays for social expenditures and to protect the living standards of the poor at the same time, the main focus of reforms must be on efficiency in spending. It is expected that a market-oriented price system will lead to increases in the relative price of many wage goods, including most agricultural goods. There are a number of different methods of ensuring social protection in the transition period. However, to be able to target these payments to the groups most affected, it is important to assess the size and characteristics of the target population. It is necessary that data on the living standards based on the minimum consumption basket be processed and the income levels required to purchase this basket be derived. The minimum consumption basket should represent a basic benefit and should take the size of the family, family composition, location and so forth into consideration.

7.16   A number of different methods can ensure social protection in the transition period. However, attempts to compensate households fully for all adjustments in prices would exacerbate inflation. Options include:

- Undifferentiated benefits perhaps through a system of coupons, could serve to ensure the provision of a limited quantity of goods at predetermined prices or the cash equivalent.

- Food stamps, which could be either means tested or targeted by individual characteristics, such as age or disability.

- Means-tested cash compensation.

7.17   For the choice among these alternatives, one basic question is whether the benefits should be universal or restricted. If it were relatively easy to identify the poor and vulnerable, the preferred approach would be targeted transfers. One approach would be to issue food stamps to the needy on the basis of household characteristics, such as to the elderly, to families with a large number of children or to the disabled; this might be easier than the means test. However, there is a concentration of individuals at or just above the poverty line (see Box 7.3). Therefore, necessary adjustments of the poverty line in accordance with price increases would spread the net much wider and reduce the budgetary savings. Administrative costs and feasibility are also important. Where the majority of the population is at a relatively low income level, and is in danger of poverty after the price changes, universal provision may be the more cost-effective option. It could take place by continuing to provide certain quantities at subsidized prices. Market clearing prices would apply for producers and for quantities in excess of the ration. While cash transfers are recommended on grounds of simplicity, resalable in-kind benefits may have the advantage of shielding consumers from price increases.

· Box 7.3
Household Consumption Basket

For purposes of minimum wage-determination, there is a household market basket with expenditure weights taken from a periodic survey of household expenditures. The survey asks questions on 336 areas of expenditures. About 50 percent of the expenditure weights are associated with food expenditures, 30 percent with non food expenditures and 20 percent with services. Monthly price statistics are gathered for each detailed expenditure category and are calculated as weighted averages of state-controlled and market prices. These average prices are then applied to the expenditure weights to arrive at an average price (cost) of the market basket for a family. The food items in the basket have weights set by an assessment of the basic caloric intake needed for adequate nutrition.

7.18   A clear distinction should be made between social assistance and social insurance. The former should be transferred to the budget, while the latter should be covered through contributions.

7.19   **Pensions.** Candidates for selective cutting of expenditures that might have to be reduced for fiscal reasons are the following:

- Raise the normal age of retirement from the current age 60 for men and age 55 for women, and make it equal for both men and woman. This needs to be phased in over a lengthy period as it will raise labor supply in a period when there may be a substantial excess labor supply.

- If this should occur, oblige working pensioners to choose between wage and pension or reduce pension by a given amount for each additional ruble earned.

- Reduce longevity premiums in retirement benefits (these can raise the basic 55 percent wage replacement rate up to 75 percent) and other perks to the basic retirement benefit calculation, (e.g., awards for meritorious service to the state or payments to ""hero mothers").

- Treat pensions as a part of taxable income.

7.20   The administration and budget of pensions and allowances should be treated separately, because pensions relate to longer-term risks that should be treated on social insurance principles. Only the operations of the pension fund should take an extra budgetary form. Other benefits and contributions should be fully reflected in the budget.

7.21   The current system of cash benefits for retirement and child-maternity allowances is complex. The benefit determination for the individual applicant is obtained from a table of monthly benefits for child and maternity allowances, which has 20 separate entries with several distinct benefit amounts depending on the age of the child and the marital and employment status of the parent. This needs to be simplified, so it would be more transparent and easier to administer.

7.22   Child allowances along with all other cash benefits should be included in the tax base, since the number of children is already considered in the personal income tax. Furthermore, child allowances have to be restructured to ensure that they contribute as much as possible to poverty reduction. One option is to keep them as a universal benefit. Another option is to consolidate them and introduce means testing.

Social Insurance Fund

7.23   A number of the functions of this fund could be amalgamated with the provision of allowances, in particular the provision of the birth grant and work-injury allowances. Furthermore, some benefits could be reduced, like the length of maternity leave (paid at full salary) from 140 days to 100 days (its length prior to 1991). Employees could assume a greater responsibility, and user charges for some services like recreation facilities could be introduced. Some payments could be eliminated.

7.24   It is also important to implement measures to avoid abuses of the social security benefits like the sick pay system. Abuses of sick pay could be avoided by adopting a system in which workers pay the first day of sick leave themselves. Furthermore, firms could finance the first 3-4 weeks of sick leave. The Social Insurance Fund should pay only for long-term sick leave.

Cash Benefits

7.25   At present, cash benefits in Turkmenistan are quite generous, and for fiscal reasons they might have to be reduced. However, effecting reductions in social safety net expenditures in a society with a narrow income distribution presents a difficult challenge. In the short term, it might be difficult to improve targeting, the value of the benefits instead might have to be reduced in real terms by underindexation. When the minimum wage changes (as it appears it will on a quarterly basis for the near future) the percentage increase in cash benefits should not be allowed to follow in lock step with minimum wage changes. The example of the child-maternal allowances increases of mid-1992 (30 percent increases rather than the 114 percent increases of the minimum wage) could be applied to pension benefits as well. Selective benefit reductions and underindexation can both be applied to reduce real expenditures on cash benefits. Underindexation is simpler to administer, and it has the added advantage of allowing the spread between average wages (compensation for work) and average benefits to grow wider with the passage of time. This will increase the attractiveness of work relative to other uses of time.

7.26   All cash benefits represent a part of the taxable income and should therefore be taxed.[2] Exemptions for child allowances, severance pay and pensions should be withdrawn. Tax exemptions cause distortions and generate inefficiency in the allocation of the resources. Equity can be achieved without extensive tax preferences through expenditure policies and the basic income tax exemption limit.

The Labor Market

7.27   Although unemployment is not yet a serious problem in Turkmenistan, it is important to initiate steps leading to appropriate social security arrangements. If nothing is done now, the scope for long-term reforms becomes more limited. One example is the need to lift administrative restrictions on labor mobility that inhibit labor market adjustment and aggravate the mismatch of labor supply and demand. If reform is postponed, the system will become increasingly unmanageable. There is also a strong case for action to prevent long-term unemployment through appropriate use of adult training. It is most cost-effective to apply these remedies before the onset of long-term unemployment, since otherwise the social costs of making the person employable are much greater. More important, a contributing unemployment insurance system requires years of fund accumulation before it can cope with serious unemployment.

Structure

7.28   Turkmenistan's labor market shares several features with other CIS economies and also diverges from them in important ways because of its particular demographic and industrial economic base. The agricultural share of total employment is unusually high. In 1990, 37 percent of workers were employed in agriculture (state collective farms and cooperatives). Industrial employment accounted for only 15 percent of non agricultural employment and about one fourth of this was in agriculture-related industries. The employment structure did not change significantly in 1980s.

7.29   A significant background factor in Turkmenistan's employment situation is a slowdown in employment growth which has been present for more than a decade. Recent five-year employment growth rates in the nonagricultural state sector were as follows: 1970-75, 20 percent; 1975-80, 24 percent; 1980-85, 14 percent; and, 1985-90, 6 percent. The employment growth slowdown of the 1980s stands in contrast with population growth, which was essentially unchanged.   Although employment on state farms grew more rapidly than non agricultural employment during 1980-85 and 1985-90, it too has fallen short of growth in the working-age population. Turkmenistan is characterized by a high level of economically active population; the participation rate in the work force is more than 84 percent. Sixty -one percent of the work-force was employed in the state sector in 1990.

7.30   Data on employment by gender indicate that almost as many women work as men. Conditions of female employment are difficult to ascertain since many women work at or near the home as agricultural workers and as piece workers at such tasks as making carpets and sewing. Women also form the majority of the work force in service areas such as elementary, secondary and higher education and health protection. All of the latter occupations have below-average pay as indicated below.

---

2.   It is important in this respect that the minimum consumption level is exempted from the personal income tax.

7.31   Official unemployment in Turkmenistan has remained low, averaging 37,000 in 1991. During January - June 1993, 8,040 persons were registered as seeking jobs at local employment offices. At present, open unemployment is concentrated among highly skilled employees from ministries and scientific institutes where staffing is being reduced.

7.32   There were 8,606 vacancies on average during the first six months of 1993: 7,855 for workers and 751 for employees (or 9.7 percent white-collar listings). On average about half of registered job applicants found jobs during the first six months of 1993. The January-June national totals were 8,037 job applicants and 4,810 placements for a placement rate of 60 percent. The corresponding national totals for the first six months of 1992 were 13,499 job applications and 6,444 placements, for a placement rate of 48 percent.

Migration and Mobility

7.33   There appears to be some out-migration from Turkmenistan. Starting in 1990 measurable numbers of Russians and other non-Turkmen ethnic groups have emigrated.   The five principal destinations have been Russia, Ukraine, Kazakhstan, Azerbaijan and Armenia. Many of these people are urban residents with high educational qualifications who have traditionally held senior jobs in Turkmenistan. The out-migration suggests a strong need for training. The gross numbers involved in immigration and emigration between these five destinations combined and Turkmenistan were as follows: emigrants in 1990, 25,097; immigrants in 1990, 15,669; emigrants in 1991, 21,193; and, immigrants in 1991, 14,574. Thus, net emigration to these five republics amounted to 9,428 in 1990 and 6,619 in 1991, respectively 1.1 percent and 0.8 percent of non agricultural employment. In both years more than half of the net emigration involved working-age adults between the ages of 30 and retirement age (60 for men and 55 for women). Net immigration, in contrast, has largely involved Turkmen refugees from southern CIS republics. During the first eight months of 1992, 556 ethnic Turkmen families (2,300 people) immigrated to Turkmenistan.

Unemployment Compensation

7.34   Turkmenistan has a proposed unemployment insurance law that authorizes 50 percent wage replacement for up to six months. It is to apply to the non agricultural sector and to be financed by part of the proceeds of the proposed 2 percent payroll tax on employers. To date nothing has been done to implement this program. Questions associated with intake procedures, verification of previous earnings (the basis for cash benefits), work search requirements and so forth, have yet to be addressed.

7.35   Currently, the local labor offices administer the payment of severance pay when workers' jobs are terminated. Turkmen labor law requires employers to give two months' notice of an impending job termination. After the termination, the worker must register for employment to receive severance pay. The first two months of severance pay are received routinely with payments made by the employer. To receive a payment for a third month, however, the local employment office has to indicate that it cannot find a job for the person. Severance payments equal the person's monthly salary.

Wages

7.36   The average monthly wages of agricultural workers were similar to those of industrial workers until 1991 (see Table 7.1). At the end of 1990, for example, the economy wide average was R243.7 per month, whereas it was 245.8 for those on state collective farms and 288.7 for workers on cooperatives. Thus the average for agriculture (R275) actually exceeded the industrial average (R265). However, in 1992 wages in agriculture declined considerably compared with the average wage. Few industry averages are also considerably above average: railway transport, waterway transport, construction, science and technology, finance and state insurance and public administration including economic bodies and budget organizations (R306). This final group increased its average monthly salary from 11 percent below average in 1988 to 26 percent above average in 1990. On the low side of the 1990 sectoral wage distribution were monthly wages in health care, culture and fine arts.

Table 7.1: Relative Wage by Sector 1980-92

Sector	1980	1985	1988	1990	1991	1992
Industry	1.12	1.13	1.14	1.09	1.18	1.30
Agriculture	0.97	0.99	1.04	1.13	1.01	0.71
State Farms	0.99	1.00	1.07	1.19	na	na
Transportation	1.21	1.18	1.18	1.16	1.19	1.19
Communication	0.96	0.95	1.03	0.99	1.13	1.05
Construction	1.37	1.43	1.44	1.28	1.25	1.17
Trade, Catering	0.86	0.84	0.77	0.85	0.84	0.75
Information Services	0.74	0.74	0.80	0.86	0.89	0.70
Housing	0.80	0.83	0.85	0.81	0.79	0.76
Health	0.78	0.74	0.72	0.68	0.78	0.69
Education	0.90	0.94	0.93	0.78	0.71	0.99
Culture	0.72	0.72	0.60	0.63	0.67	0.75
The Arts	0.79	0.82	0.77	0.75	0.73	0.75
Science	1.17	1.21	1.33	1.31	0.95	1.20
Banking/Insurance	0.89	0.89	0.87	1.32	2.04	1.43
Public Admin.	0.95	0.91	0.92	1.26	1.11	1.17
Collective Farms	0.90	0.89	0.90	1.01	na	na

Source: National Economy Statistical Yearbook - 1990 for monthly wages in Rubles, 1991 and 1992 data. Statistical Office, Ashkabad 1993, staff estimates.

7.37   Establishing the level of the minimum wage and its periodic adjustment is central to the macro-level price-wage feedback link in the inflation process. Periodic presidential decrees on the minimum effectively determine how much of the recent price inflation feeds back into money wages and cash transfer payments. Money wage determination in Turkmenistan can be described as tripartite. Wages for individual workers are influenced by decisions made at three different levels: national, individual industrial sectors and individual enterprises. National-level wage determination focuses on the change in the minimum wage (R9,600 per month in September 1993). The minimum wage is set by presidential decree. The process of setting the minimum wage draws upon advice of a committee with representatives from several ministries. A key technical element in this determination is a calculation of the change in the cost of living as reflected in a minimum market basket of consumer expenditures.

7.38   The second level of wage determination involves bargaining between trade unions and enterprises at the industry level (there are about 25 sectors). For profitable sectors the agreed minimum wage may exceed the national minimum. "Profits" are defined to include some bonus wage payments and social benefits.

7.39   The third level is wage determination at individual enterprises. Again, there is the possibility that the enterprise minimum can exceed the sector minimum if the enterprise is profitable. All of these sub-national adjustments apply in an asymmetric manner, that is they can raise but cannot reduce the minimum wage. All changes are triggered by the change in a national minimum wage.

Box 7.4
The Educational System in Turkmenistan

In Turkmenistan's educational system each student attends primary and secondary school at least through the eighth grade. Significant percentages attend high schools (grades 9 and 10) while others participate in specialized training for job preparation. Technical training of workers and employees takes place in some 90 institutions that offer courses of differing lengths. Additionally there are nine sectoral technical and polytechnical institutions and the University of Ashkabad with four-year programs leading to bachelor's degrees and six-year master's degrees. Three main divisions of the educational system are: 1) pre schools and elementary and secondary schools, 2) specialized secondary schools and higher educational institutions and 3) institutions for specialized technical training of workers and employees.

Pre schools.   Children aged 1-3 attend creches, and those aged 3-7 attend kindergartens. Throughout Turkmenistan there are 1,600 pre schools with a total enrollment of about 220,000 in 1992. From population statistics it appears the pre school enrollment covers about one fourth of children aged 1-7. Between 1984 and 1991 the country experimented with a system whereby children aged 6 entered the first grade. This was discontinued in 1992 in favor of starting first grade at age 7 as had been the practice prior to 1984.

Elementary-Secondary.   Turkmenistan has 1,730 elementary and secondary schools with a total enrollment of 831,000 in 1991-92. In this ethnically diverse country, the schools differ in their primary language of instruction. Turkmen, taught in all schools, is the primary language in some 1,355 schools. Predominant languages in the other schools are as follows: mixed language (Turkmen and Russian) 123; Russian 107; Uzbek 88; and Kazakh 38. The majority of schools (77 percent) are in rural areas. Primary school is considered to extend from grade 1 to grade 3 while secondary school extends from grade 4 to grade 10.

Specialized Secondary Schools.   There are 36 secondary schools with specialized curricula emphasizing subjects such as math, chemistry and topics relevant to the Ministry with which they are associated. Graduates often attend institutions of higher education. Students usually enter these schools at the end of the eighth grade for a four-year course of study or after the tenth grade for a two-year curriculum. During the past school year about 40,000 attended schools for workers, and about 12,000 attended schools for junior engineers and other employee specializations. Secondary school extends through grade 8 for all students. About 90 percent leave the school system after grade 8 (roughly age 15) for work or attendance at special technical schools. About 9 percent attend the technical schools, while roughly 11 percent go to high schools (grades 9 and 10). The latter are often specialized schools that can lead to college degrees.

Institutions of Higher Education.   Nine institutions of higher education plus the University of Ashkabad stand at the top of the educational system. With total enrollment of about 50,000 (day students plus part-time and night students), these institutions provide specialized training for many of the top white-collar jobs. Other institutes cover fields such as medicine, languages, culture, music and the national economy. Early in 1992 these institutions were removed from the Ministry of Education. Higher education is headed by a Council of Rectors, created in September 1992, which substitutes for a Ministry. The chair of this council sits with the Cabinet of Ministers. Each institute is divided into several faculties. Faculty training was received mainly at the University of Ashkabad, but some proportion of faculty have degrees or have taken courses from universities in Moscow and St. Petersburg. There is no important representation of non-CIS training in these institutes. Faculty pay is modest; about R6,000 per month for full faculty and R5,000 for candidates in September 1992.

7.40   The basic structure of wages is heavily influenced by a cross-classification of worker occupations and physical exertion levels that specifies the minimum wage appropriate for each cell. The Ministry of Labor issues this "skill-exertion" matrix as a booklet that is distributed to each enterprise and to trade union representatives. The wage scales in the booklet change when the national minimum wage changes.

Collective Bargaining

7.41   The structure of collective bargaining is not yet well established. This is partly due to the absence of an independent trade union movement in Turkmenistan. At present, leaders of the trade unions are appointed by the President rather than elected by direct vote of by committee procedures. Thus the unions do not articulate policy options that are distinct from (and potentially in opposition to) positions taken by the Government. Collective bargaining between labor and management is not really feasible in Turkmenistan at present because enterprise managers and union leaders both are so closely tied to the existing institutions of Government.

Institutional Arrangements

7.42   At present the Ministry of Labor has responsibility for several areas of labor market regulation as well as for the provision of local employment office services such as job matching. It is anticipated that many of its functions will be transferred to the Ministry of Economics and Finance, in particular oversight of employment and unemployment, salary administration, definition of hazardous occupations, labor protection (including protection of three broad classes: women, youth and invalids), minimum wage determination and the setting of wage premiums for hazardous occupations. The main function to be reserved for the successor to the Ministry of Labor, the State Corporation on Training of Specialists, is the direction and coordination of job training and retraining. This state corporation will refer workers to one of 90 or so training institutions. The institutions have recently been removed from the Ministry of Education and are currently autonomous.

Recommendations

State Employment

7.43   State employment will have to decline significantly. However, until a private sector of some size has developed, a high proportion of state employees may face unemployment, although some may take early retirement.

Wage Policy

7.44   Wage policy is a complex issue. On one hand, real wages should rise because several benefits such as free housing will disappear. For now, however the exigencies of stabilization may have priority and justify continued wage controls. One option is a tax-based incomes policy, with guidelines for the maximum permissible rate of increase of the total wage bill at enterprises and taxation of enterprises for wage increases that exceed the guideline.

Layoffs

7.45   Special regulations need to be in place for mass redundancies. At the moment a firm contemplating a mass layoff or a complete shutdown must notify the Ministry of Labor and the Trade Union Federation. The Ministry of Labor can then delay the layoff for six months and for a second six months if the layoff would significantly harm the local labor market. Mass layoffs have not taken place yet, but these regulations should be in place before mass layoffs start. The key is the setting up of a standby program whereby the employment service could quickly move into mass redundancy situations to provide support and on-site services in counselling and job-matching.

Labor Mobility

7.46   One priority in the short run should be to encourage labor mobility. Furthermore, local labor offices should post job vacancies for all areas in Turkmenistan. Then workers would know where to migrate to find employment. To put this suggestion to operation, however, a computerized system is needed to make job availability known outside of local labor markets. Another important issue is training and retraining. The administrative constraints on labor mobility are high. The system of internal passports, which is in place due to internal security reasons, the lack of affordable housing and the overspecialization and rigid educational system, all contribute to these constraints and should be changed.

Unemployment Compensation

7.47   Unemployment insurance could be financed by either a payroll tax or general revenues. At present, the Government anticipates levying a new 2 percent payroll tax on enterprises to finance both unemployment insurance and the new training initiative. However, employees should pay part of this since they would be the beneficiaries of these new programs. Such a system should be evaluated promptly, since it will require years to accumulate sufficient funds to make it effective. Meanwhile, it would serve as a useful anti-inflationary device.

Training and Education

7.48   Education and training were monopolized by the state in the former Soviet Union, and the goal was to produce a "specialist" whose future was known and whose responsibilities were preordained by the state enterprises in the Ministry under whose auspices the trainee had been produced. The system of training and education was operating under an assumption of economic planning that will not exist in the future. With the restructuring of the economy will come a very large demand for training and retraining programs in conjunction with the climbing rate of unemployment. The content of training programs and courses will need to change to reflect the needs of a market-oriented economy. This is true both for pre employment training and for the retraining that will be needed as part of the transition. Training and retraining can provide crucial opportunities for workers to adapt to the new economic circumstances.

Elementary and Secondary Schools

7.49   The elementary and secondary school system is already undergoing a series of changes that will give it a more western structure, increased emphasis on vocational preparation and shorter curriculums. Economics and marketing are being introduced in secondary schools along with courses on ethics, family life and the relation between man and society. Curriculum changes are largely determined by two institutions located in Ashkabad: the Pedagogical Institute and the Central Institute for Retraining. Currently under consideration are the adoption of Western (Latin) script and ability tracking of students starting in grade 1.

7.50   Problems facing the elementary-secondary system include the following:

- High birth rate creates a continuing need for new classroom space. About 30 percent of the schools operate on double shifts.

- Many schools (230, or 13 percent) have such serious structural defects that they are dangerous for the conduct of classes.

- There is high turnover of teachers, which is associated with their chronically low pay. In 1990 their average monthly salary of R189 was 23 percent below the national average of R243.7.

7.51   Enterprises were building and running kindergartens and schools in the FSU. Structural change and the privatization process will require that enterprises disencumber themselves of these non-production related responsibilities. The public sector might have to take over some of these services. Provision will have to be made for the financing of these new public expenditures.

Technical Institutions

7.52   Students are recruited into the technical institutions through a special local commission. At the Polytechnical Institute, for example, the applicant to acceptance ratio had been about five in past years, but it dropped to two in 1992. This could be one indication of the general softening of the labor market in the past two years. Applications would tend to fall if placements are declining due to reduced numbers of new job openings.

7.53   Students receive stipends that depend on graded performance. In September 1992 the basic stipend of R800 per month increased to 940 for students rated as good and to R1,200 for those rated as excellent. The stipends change with the minimum wage. Additionally students receive subsidized food and rental subsidies (R200 per month) if they must secure apartments. Besides offering a full four- (formerly five-) year program for candidates, the institutes also provide for shorter (3-, 6- and 12-month) courses, supported by enterprises, for the retraining of experienced workers. Workers receive full salaries while enrolled. The importance of these teaching-training activities varies across institutions.

7.54   The primary problems facing these institutions have been:

- Lack of staff and high staff turnover.

- Low teacher qualifications.

- Lack of facilities, such as laboratories and computers.

7.55   Turkmenistan has about 90 technical colleges whose main function is to train blue-collar workers. Students usually enroll following completion of the eighth grade. The course of study is being shortened to two years from three years. Graduates who pass a qualification exam are guaranteed a job requiring their specialization in a state enterprise. These same institutions also offer shorter courses of instruction for experienced workers who are to learn new skills.

Training

7.56   Training programs for individual workers are to be selected in consultation with the local employment office and the prospective employers. Typically, training is expected to last three or six months. There are about 90 institutions of higher education that can provide training. The trainee is guaranteed a job if the training course is passed successfully.

7.57   The new training corporation is to be financed with part of the proceeds from a payroll tax on employers. The new payroll tax is also to finance an unemployment insurance program.

7.58   Under the new approach to training, participating institutions of higher education are to place greater emphasis on vocational preparation than in the past. Training for several specializations will be even shorter: 3, 6 or 12 months depending upon what is appropriate for the situation. Longer training will be offered for more difficult specializations.

7.59   Consideration should be given to establishing a training fund, financed jointly by employers and a direct budgetary contribution. Employer contribution would be reduced to the extent that companies provide their own training of workers. An area of concern is the training of the teachers. Ministry of Labor officials indicated that several foreign sources (EC, the German Employment Ministry) have been contacted for possible technical assistance. Their preference is for teacher training to be conducted in Turkmenistan in Turkmen or Russian. Teachers at all levels -- like civil servants in general -- appear to be underpaid at present. It is not clear that the changes contemplated by the Government include a substantial increase in teachers' salaries relative to other sectors. Apart from training for the potentially unemployed, there is a broader, though related, issue of skills training in the area of public administration, entrepreneurship and small business development, development of the infrastructure for professional services, and the financial sector. Training in areas of finance and management is very important, including such areas as modern methods of accounting (as an aid to managerial decisions rather than simple bookkeeping), banking and finance, investment choice, assessment of risks and marketing.

The Health Sector

7.60   There has been no basic change in the health system since the dissolution of the Soviet Union. Because of relative isolation from the outside world, health care practices are often somewhat outdated by Western standards. Shortage of medical equipment is a serious problem. Anaemia, diarrheal diseases, hepatitis and tuberculosis are not uncommon and remain the most important health problems.

7.61   Turkmenistan provides free health care and the sector is now in serious financial difficulty. The share of the Government budget devoted to health fell to 6.9 in 1992, down from 11.2 in 1989 and 9.6 in 1991. Issues of health care reform touch upon how to maintain acceptable standards and not to increase budgetary expenditures. This will involve substantial restructuring and reform in the financing arrangements of the sector.

7.62   Health care in Turkmenistan was previously directed by the Ministry of Health of the former USSR. Drugs, were provided by the Moscow Central Planning Pharmacy depot upon the request of the of pharmacy of the Turkmenistan Health Ministry. This practice has now been stopped, and the Ministry of Health needs to procure directly from producers. Many of the drugs used in Turkmenistan came from Poland, East Germany, Hungary and Czechoslovakia, and now require hard currency for their purchase. The Directorate of Pharmacy is investigating various procurement possibilities. In 1991 it purchased 700 types of pharmaceuticals from Japan on a trial basis. The Directorate should also work to negotiate individual contracts with pharmaceutical plants throughout the former Soviet Union.

7.63   The Directorate of Pharmacy sells drugs to hospitals, health centers and pharmacies. Collected funds constitute the revolving fund of the Directorate of the Pharmacy. The Directorate's Pharmacy is provided directly by the central Government and is not part of the Health Ministry's budget. Drugs are provided free of charge in hospitals. For outpatient services an individual buys the drug from an assigned pharmacy. However, drugs are provided free of charge to children up to three years old. In addition, children up to 12 months old get free infant formula and other baby food.

7.64   Another legacy of the former USSR is the system of Sanitation and Epidemiology Departments, which are distinct from hospitals. They are staffed by physician-hygienists who are responsible for epidemiology, nutrition and municipal or industrial hygiene. The main responsibilities of these departments include the control or observance of sanitary regulations, including food hygiene, control of infectious diseases, immunization and health education.

7.65   There is an abundant supply of medical personnel in Turkmenistan, but there is a lack of qualified personnel in the more remote or rural areas. There are 335 hospitals and 597 polyclinics and mobile hospitals in Turkmenistan. The number of available beds is 41,279, or 112.3 per 10,000 people. There are 13,701 physicians (36 per 10,000 population) and 37, 261 mid-level personnel (e.g., technicians, nurses, midwives: 10,6 per 10,000 population).

Health Indicators

7.66   Although mortality data reflect underreporting and methodological differences, it would seem that mortality rates and life expectancy in Turkmenistan are at best near the level of low-middle-income countries. Infant mortality has been rising. In 1970, the infant mortality rate was 46.1 per 1,000 live births, and in 1987 it was 56.4 deaths per 1,000 live births, the highest in the former USSR. The official infant mortality rate was about 45 per 1,000 live births in 1990, the highest in all the new independent states. There are major variations in the infant mortality rates from region to region with the mortality rate rising in rural areas and with distance from the capital city. Recalculation of 1986 data suggest that rates may have been as high as 103 per 1000, for rural Turkmenistan (see Table 7.2).

Table 7.2
Infant Mortality Rates, 1990

Turkmenistan	43.6
Ashkabad City	33.6
Balkanskya Oblast	34.8
Ashkabad Oblast	41.5
Mary Oblast	46.0
Tashauz Oblast	52.6

Source: Goskomstat.

7.67   The Government has historically endorsed a pronatalist position and still encourages large families. The average number of children per woman (total fertility rate) in 1969-70 was 5.9. The rate has fallen steadily: in 1979-80 it was 5.2; in 1984-85 it dropped to 4.7. Birth intervals are short, averaging less than 1.5 years. To account for underregistration of births, the Bureau of the Census adjusted the total fertility rates for 1990 to 4.2 children per woman.

7.68   The maternal mortality ratio for 1992 was 48 deaths per 100,000 live births. Women's health status is generally poor, with anaemia being found in 60 percent of urban pregnant woman, and in 75 to 80 percent of rural women.

7.69   The major cause of the high infant mortality rates and the associated morbidity is childhood diarrhea resulting from the poor quality of water. Limited availability of potable water and a lack of sewage treatment systems contribute to a high prevalence of diarrheal diseases. Gastro enteric disease is now a major health problem and frequent cause of death. Respiratory diseases cause 43 percent of infant deaths.

7.70   In the past five years infant deaths from respiratory disease declined 41 percent, but deaths from perinatal complications increased by 75 percent and from digestive system causes by 182 percent. The under-five mortality was 17.2 per 1,000 in 1989, a slight improvement over previous years. Children constitute 80 percent of patients with severe intestinal infections.

7.71   Dehydration is a major problem for children. Oral rehydration therapy (ORS) is widely known and used. However, the shortage of oral rehydration salts, previously imported from the USSR and Finland, is a real problem. The Government estimates that 2 million packets of ORS per year are needed. Regular supplies of ORS solution are very important. Turkmenderman in Ashkabad, the only pharmaceutical firm in the country, does not produce ORS.

7.72   In 1992, cardiovascular disease was the most common cause of death, followed by cancer, respiratory diseases, and accidents. 68 percent of homes in Turkmenistan have no indoor plumbing, running water or central heat.[3] The incidence of water borne diseases follows a seasonal cycle, with many children being stricken in the warm summer months. The incidence of tuberculosis is very high, particularly in children. Brucellosis is also widespread in rural areas. According to the health authorities, the two diseases are related mainly to animal diseases, and a specific program on animal immunization is needed. Acute respiratory infections and pneumonia increase rapidly during winter, and children are particularly affected.

Pharmaceutical and Equipment

7.73   The collapse of interrepublican trade ties is causing serious disruption in the health-delivery system. Disposable syringes and needles are virtually unavailable. In 1991, purchases of medicines amounting to only R32.2 million out of a required R58.1 million were received. The estimated amount for 1992 is R69.8 million.

7.74   Vaccination coverage for children has been high in the past, but it may become very difficult to maintain high levels of coverage without an assured supply of vaccine. Recently, measles vaccination coverage has dropped below 60 percent because of vaccine shortages and an improper cold

---

3.   Of all new housing built in 1985, only 28 percent was equipped with a sewage system, running water and central heating. Nineteen percent had only partial provision of these amenities, and 53 percent had no provision.

chain. Vaccines have to remain under refrigeration at all stages of their transport and storage. While a basic cold chain infrastructure exists, the lack of adequate hardware prevents the chain from functioning properly and vaccines are often received and shipped in an unrefrigerated state.

7.75   A shortage of medical equipment also seriously limits the ability to provide adequate care. Lists of requested equipment range from basic items such as gloves, sutures, transfusions and infusion sets, X ray, ultra sound and dental equipment and aspirators. At the same time existing materials need maintenance and repair, which is difficult to effect because of a lack of standardization. Health buildings also need repairs, and new buildings are not well constructed.

Health Care Reform

7.76   Turkmenistan plans to introduce a health care system that guarantees care for all. Canada was mentioned as a possible model. However, the issue is not being pushed as authorities feel that a health insurance system may be difficult to institute in a country with little industry and a widely dispersed rural population. In this context, possible negative health implications were feared for women, children and the elderly who might find it difficult to participate in such a system.

Recommendations

Shortages of Pharmaceuticals and Equipment

7.77   Shortages of drugs, particular those used to treat tuberculosis, pneumonia and other infectious diseases, and other medical supplies need to be addressed, to meet the demands created by the disruptions of traditional sources of supply.

- Vaccines for the immunization program must be supplied on a priority basis. Anti tuberculosis drugs are also required.

- Local production and distribution throughout the country should be urgently ensured, and the Government provided with technical advice.

Health Care Financing

7.78   There is an urgent need for a health care safety net. Currently, health services are financed mainly from local budgets. Responsibilities for important social services should not be given to local authorities without an assured means of funding the services. The central Government should have responsibility for maintaining the safety net during the transition period. With local governments depending on highly unstable income sources, the central Government needs to ensure the provision of social services.

Box 7.5
Technical Assistance Recommendations

Social Safety Net
- Develop a system to record the earnings histories of workers. With such a system in place, the determination of monthly benefit amounts for retirement and invalidity benefits would be accomplished more easily than by the non automated processes used at present. Having a record system of individual earnings histories would also allow the pension system to institute an effective benefit offset. This would reduce benefit payments to persons who continue to have substantial amounts of earnings after reaching retirement age.

- Develop an automated intake system for determinations of retirement and invalidity benefits. This system would complement the existing automated payment system for persons already receiving benefits. Officials at the local pension office in Ashkabad already seem to have thought through much of the computer programming needed for such a system.

Labor Market
- Develop an automated system for listing job vacancies, and network it to all local offices. Having such a system in place would increase the effectiveness of local employment offices in matching unemployed workers with available job vacancies. It would also increase the geographic scope of job matching.

- Provide assistance in developing administrative processes for unemployment insurance intake and payments. At present there is no design for a structure of unemployment insurance to process large numbers of applicants for cash benefits. At a minimum this involves the development of the intake form(s), operational definitions of suitable work and availability for work and a method for ascertaining previous earnings (the basis for the cash benefit payment).

Education/Training

- Review the elementary-secondary curricula. Since the authorities are already in the process of revising curricula, having access to information on non-FSU curriculums could prove helpful.

- Provide assistance on the organization of technical-vocational training. The Government is placing strong emphasis on vocational training to reduce unemployment and to facilitate improved worker performance in the labor market. Technical assistance could be provided in areas such as identifying the emerging occupations and skills for which training will be needed, developing performance standards for the content of training courses and ensuring the appropriate training of teachers in vocational training schools.

Part III

Sectoral Reforms

Part III focusses on the sectors which will be particularly important in helping to generate economic recovery. Furthermore, to ensure a supply response in the productive sectors, improvements in infrastructure are required to support the adjustments in the real economy, and more broadly, the emerging requirements of a market economy.

Agriculture (Chapter 8): The priority in agriculture is to change the structure and incentives governing production and processing. The adjustment of prices is crucial, state production orders should be phased out and input subsidies eliminated. The sectoral policy should include the withdrawal of the state from the direct distribution of agricultural inputs; privatization of small-scale agro-processing enterprises, input dealerships and retail food outlets; reform of agricultural credit; and, research and marketing services. Agricultural enterprise reform is important to create accountable and responsive agents. It should entail restructuring state and collective farms as well as other agricultural enterprises into either joint stock companies, private individual farms, or true cooperative farms with fully legal and tradable ownership rights.

Energy (Chapter 9): While increasing the value of gas exports to existing markets should be the main priority in the sector, in the longer term, investments in the diversification of transport options to enter new export markets is an appropriate objective. However, the economic viability of such investments needs to be carefully weighed by the Government before any commitments are made. Furthermore, the Government needs to attract foreign expertise and capital to regenerate the sector's production potential. It has to be ensured that energy prices fully reflect their cost of supply or, where the resource is traded in world or regional markets, their export value.

Telecommunication (Chapter 10): Turkmenistan's geographic remoteness from its potential hard currency markets and the need to integrate the economy more closely into the world economy make adequate international telecommunications particularly important. Before a long-term investment program can be developed, a sector restructuring program which includes sectoral policy, sector regulation, legislation, operations arrangements and private sector participation should be defined. It is necessary to develop a short-term investment program aimed at highest priority areas like the continued maintenance and operation of the existing network and the expansion of the higher revenue generating international services.

Environment (Chapter 11): A major reform of environmental policies and institutions is required concurrently with economic reforms. The appropriate pricing of resources, e.g. water and energy, will help induce efficiency in their use. The key reforms needed to promote greater economic efficiency and environmental protection are price reform, privatization and the establishment of a competitive industrial structure. It will be important to establish the mechanism needed for the development and implementation of environmental policy measures including an adequate monitoring system, effective standard setting and enforcement procedures. Pollution fees and fines will help finance administrative costs. User charges can help fund future environmental investments.

CHAPTER 8

AGRICULTURE

8.1   Half the population of Turkmenistan lives in rural areas with most of the activity concentrated in the irrigated oases along the Kara Kum Canal, the Amu Darya and other rivers. The remaining areas are non arable semi desert or desert that will only support extensive grazing, and then only if stock water exists. There were only about 36,000 hectares of non-state controlled arable land in 1991 when agriculture accounted for 24 percent of gross social product. High rural birthrates (37.6 per 1,000) put strong pressure on land resources.

8.2   Prior to independence, Turkmenistan and other Central Asian republics were required to supply as much cotton as possible to the former Soviet Union. Thus about half of the irrigated area was devoted to cotton. Cotton is still the major cash crop in Turkmenistan, and it is well suited to the climate. However, Turkmenistan's relatively mild climate would also allow a large variety of other crops to be grown. Turkmenistan now has the opportunity to take charge of its own destiny, but the country is left with a legacy of a heavily controlled command economy, a capital stock that is technologically inefficient and nearly depreciated, and a population largely dependent on cotton production for employment.

8.3   There has been little change in the command structure of state and collective farms inherited from the former Soviet Union. Collective and state farms still dominate the sector, controlling 37.7 million hectares of land, of which only 1.23 million hectares is arable (irrigated). Under the former Soviet Union, neither managers nor workers on state or collective farms had strong incentives to improve productivity, reduce costs or preserve capital and land. Inputs were provided according to the central plan and farm managers had little choice over quantities received or their quality. Furthermore, the high degree of agricultural specialization among the different countries of the former Soviet Union left the economy heavily dependent on food imports and security of food imports remains a principal concern. Under the former Soviet Union, approximately two thirds of cereals, 45 percent of dairy products, and one third of meat supplies were imported from other republics. Sugar and many processed food products were imported as well, while Turkmenistan produced fruits and vegetables for export to other republics.

8.4   Overall, while the Government has taken steps to reduce the country's dependence on food imports, little has been done to reform the agricultural sector. As a result, it is not likely that a successful agricultural adjustment towards a market economy will be made in the next few years. Production of cotton and other key crops is still controlled via state orders that set production quotas and prices. As an incentive, state and collective farms are only free to sell above-quota quantities as they wish. The principal change in priorities has been an increased emphasis on grain production to reduce dependence on outside sources. For non controlled crops, prices are negotiated on a cost-plus basis. Other than the provision of family plots of up to 0.5 hectare, the only move toward privatization has been to develop leasing schemes for land on some of the state and collective farms to individuals.

8.5   The sector's problems cannot be solved under the structure of a command economy. The solutions to the agricultural sector's problems lie not in tinkering with the existing system but in radical restructuring of the agricultural economy and of the economic incentives that govern it.

8.6   The overall strategy for a successful transition in agriculture might include the following elements:

- Macroeconomic stabilization and greater integration with world markets which should include price liberalization and the termination of state orders, demonopolization of trade and gradual removal of non tariff trade barriers to foreign trade in agricultural products. Without a suitable macroeconomic policy in place, investments in agriculture and agro-processing will have a high probability of being of the wrong kind, in the wrong place, and producing the wrong product after the economy has adjusted;

- A sectoral policy that provides the right signals by restructuring support services. This policy should include the withdrawal of the state from direct distribution of agricultural inputs; privatization of most processing, wholesale, retail trade and small-scale transport operations; and reform of agricultural credit, research, information and marketing services.

- Enterprise reform to create accountable and responsive economic agents by restructuring state and collective farms as well as other economic enterprises to establish either joint stock companies, private individual farms or true cooperative farms with full legal and tradeable rights of property ownership.

8.7   In implementing a structural reform program in agriculture along these lines, several major issues have to be addressed, such as whether to continue to administer some prices or fully liberalize prices all at once; whether to permit private land and property ownership or develop tradable land use-rights; and how to ameliorate adverse effects that major retail price reform may have on some segments of the population. There are few, if any, alternatives to making price adjustments, but the impact of higher prices on vulnerable groups can be cushioned by certain social safety net measures.

8.8   The most important steps needed to begin the transition are:

- Freeing input and output prices. The adjustment of prices is crucial, since prices influence all consumption and production decisions. The Government needs to phase out state production orders, eliminate input subsidies, adjust prices of food commodities to competitive levels and target available resources towards solving the most pressing problems.

- Liberalizing imports and exports. Price adjustments should be accompanied by the liberalization of imports and exports to provide alternative sources of commodities to state monopolies and to help develop the domestic private marketing system.

- Establishing hard budget constraints for all state and collective farms as well as other state enterprises. This action should be accompanied by lifting all restrictions on where state and collective farms and enterprises may purchase inputs and sell outputs.

8.9   While the above steps are being implemented, the institutional and legal framework required for a market economy to function need to be developed and put into place. If privatization of both land and state enterprises is to succeed, decision makers who control resources need to be assured that they will be able to retain the benefits of any investments made, while also knowing that they will not be directed to produce unprofitable commodities, and not be protected from failure. To foster competition, individuals and firms must have the means to enforce contracts fairly, be freely allowed to enter into any type of business and have free access to economic and market information services.

8.10   Once the legal framework is in place--which includes preparation of revised land legislation that would ensure full rights to buy, sell and mortgage land--other reforms can follow:

- Rapid privatization of small-scale agro-processing enterprises, input dealerships and retail food outlets; and adoption of a detailed strategy for privatizing larger enterprises.

- Introduction of measures to reduce remaining barriers to the efficient functioning of markets.

- Restructuring of State and Collective farms by separating out municipal and governmental functions from commercial operations. The commercial operations can then be converted to either joint stock companies, true cooperatives, individual private farms or some combination of the three.

The Current State of the Agricultural Sector

8.11   Agriculture is still the dominant economic sector, accounting for 38 percent of the net material product (NMP) in 1991. Agriculture and construction are the only two sectors that have been growing since 1985. The NMP for agriculture increased at approximately 3.2 percent a year from 1985 to 1991 compared with an overall increase in NMP of 3.0 percent for the same period. The crop sector accounts for approximately two-thirds of the gross value of output of the agricultural sector. Cotton contributes three-fourths of the gross value of crop production or about one half the gross value for all agricultural output (see Figure 8.1). For 1992, while there was a large increase in the gross value of agricultural output in nominal terms because of price increases; the value of agricultural output in real terms was limited because of large increases in input costs. The terms of trade are likely to continue to shift against agriculture since input costs will likely increase more than output prices. Current

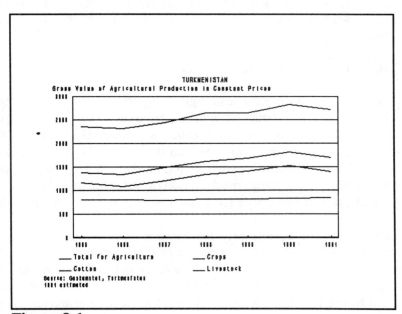

Figure 8.1

price levels are considerably below international prices, which means that substantial adjustment will be required before the economy will be integrated into the international marketplace.

Improving Efficiency and Increasing Output from Existing Resources

8.12   There is substantial room for increasing agricultural output from existing crops in the short run by using improved crop varieties, on-farm water management, integrated pest control and better production techniques. Current yields of most crops are below those attained by other countries with similar climatic and agronomic characteristics (See box 8.1). For example, the current level of cotton production could be attained with 20 percent less crop area if yields were increased to 900 kilograms per hectare of lint --slightly below the average yield now obtained in Turkey. Similar increases are possible for grains and fodder crops using existing varieties and genetic materials available from international agricultural research centers (IARC). The key is establishing linkages between Turkmenistan research and training institutions and those research centers.

8.13   There is also considerable room for improvement in livestock production. Output per unit of inventory is low, and much higher productivity could be obtained with better livestock manage-ment practices. Within the livestock sector, increasing the productivity of small ruminants appears to have the greatest potential. As for the beef and dairy sector, only milk production was profitable in 1991 on collective farms. Once prices adjust to market levels and subsidies are reduced, there will be considerable restructuring of cattle production, with only the more efficient units likely to survive. Since most cattle operations are dual meat and milk operations, specialization is also likely to occur. Poultry operations were the most inefficient and are not likely to survive as now organized. A thorough review of the livestock sector is needed to determine where the comparative advantage lies and how the state livestock sector should be privatized.

Irrigation and Water Management

8.14   As in most arid regions, agriculture is almost completely dependent on irrigation except for sheep and goat production in the desert areas. The current irrigated area of about 1.3 million hectares is dependent upon the Kara Kum canal, which stretches over 1,000 kilometers from the Amu Darya on the east to almost the Caspian Sea on the west. The Kara Kum canal project was part of the former Soviet Union's effort to increase cotton production regardless of cost. Although the Kara Kum canal is a remarkable undertaking, the diversion of water for irrigation in Uzbekistan and Turkmenistan from the Amu Darya and Syr Darya river had severe impacts on the Aral Sea (see Annex A).

8.15   Responsibility for irrigation development and water management is currently divided between the Ministry of Irrigation and the Irrigation Institute. The Ministry of Irrigation (MOI) is responsible for allocating water among users and for operating and maintaining the Kara Kum canal, other major canals and the major drainage canals. The Ministry also has the responsibility for interregional coordination with neighboring republics and riparian countries. The Irrigation Institute is responsible for designing, evaluating and building new projects. The Institute also maintains pumping stations for high-lift irrigation projects. These organizations are responsible for managing water delivery to the collective and state farms, other economic enterprises and municipalities. Once water is delivered to these entities, it becomes their responsibility. Thus the collective and state farms are responsible for the secondary canals and for establishing delivery schedules for individual fields. Collective and state farms may also own and operate groundwater pumps. The same is true for municipalities and other water-using economic enterprises.

8.16   At the system level, the Ministry's management of water allocation and irrigation-system operations is fairly efficient. Because of the interdependency of the water-delivery system, the MOI will continue to play a major role in development of the agricultural economy. At the collective and state farm level, even with privatization, a central organization will have to be maintained to order water from the main canal, schedule and control deliveries to farms and fields and maintain and operate the secondary canal system. The organization at this level could be a water users association with voting rights tied to the shares of water received. This organization will need to be able to assess fees to pay for water obtained from the main system, to maintain the secondary canals within its jurisdiction, and to pay operational personnel. Once privatization occurs, use of water received at the farm level becomes the individual's responsibility.

8.17   The total dependence of the agricultural sector on irrigation and the lack of additional water resources that can be developed means that irrigation losses need to be reduced from the current level of 45 percent. Technical assistance should be provided to the Ministry to improve its technical and management capabilities, particularly in the planning and environmental areas. Because water is a very scarce resource, improved drainage, water management and control, both on farm and at the system level, is of foremost importance. The introduction of water charges that reflect the scarcity of water in the Turkmen economy and increase the costs of water-intensive production would promote the most efficient use of water. The Government has indicated that water charges may be introduced for the next cropping season. If charges are established, this will be a very positive step for improving water efficiency. In addition to this step, a systemwide review should be undertaken by the Ministry of Irrigation to identify where efficiency improvements are possible and to develop a long-term water strategy for the next 25 to 30 years.

8.18   Investments in modern water savings techniques such as sprinkler and drip systems, are quite expensive ($2,000 to 3000 per hectare). Therefore, the most likely applications that will provide a positive return on investment will be in areas with high population densities and near cities to supply vegetables and for higher value crops, such as fruit and nut trees that can be grown for processing or export. Water saving under the existing system can be obtained through better controlled intakes, reducing losses through lining of canals and improving the drainage to reduce salinity levels. Improved efficiency of water use is also possible through better on-farm water management and changes in the cropping pattern.

8.19   Finally, there are several projects underway or under consideration to increase the area under irrigation, particularly the Kyzyl Etrek project in the southeast. It is doubtful whether these projects meet sound economic and environmental criteria. Because of the level of investment required, it is recommended that all currently approved and proposed projects be reviewed to see that they meet the economic and environmental criteria of a market economy and are consistent with long-term water needs.

Supply of Agricultural Inputs

8.20   The input distribution structure reflects the policy of the former Soviet Union for highly centralized, interdependent and specialized production. Thus, Turkmenistan is dependent on outside sources to supply almost all of its inputs except energy, urea and some agricultural chemicals. One company, Turkmen Selkosprom Service (TSS), which was the republican branch of the State Supply Agency (GOSNAB) of the former Soviet Union, has primary responsibility for the supply of all agricultural inputs to the state and collective farms and the rest of agricultural sector. TSS is not within the Ministry of Agriculture but supervised by the Cabinet of Ministers. TSS handles fertilizer and agricultural chemical sales and application. Most pesticides are imported, but some agricultural chemicals are exported. TSS is considering the feasibility of manufacturing more of its own pesticides and chemicals. Pesticide management seems reasonably well controlled because it is the responsibility of this single special service. For example, TSS has confiscated all banned pesticides. TSS decides on levels of imports, which fertilizer and pesticides should be used and, based on the availability of fertilizer, allocates supplies to state and collective farms and other enterprises.

Fertilizer

8.21   Compared with Western agricultural practices, average fertilizer rates were relatively high prior to the breakup of the former Soviet Union. In 1990, the average application of mineral fertilizers (nutrient basis) for all crops was 232 kg/ha, with the highest level of fertilization for cotton at 322 (192 N, 94 P_2O_5, 36 K) kg/ha and 314 kg/ha for rice. Comparing these application rates to the highest rates of use in California or Arizona, which produce irrigated cotton, Turkmenistan's rates were 37 percent higher for total fertilizer use in California, 26 percent higher than nitrogen use in Arizona and 21 percent higher than P_2O_5 use in California. Only 10 percent of the farmers in Arizona and 18 percent in California used Potassium (K).

8.22   Possible reasons for these high levels of fertilizer use are:

- More fertilizer may be required to maintain yields under the high cropping intensity for cotton in Turkmenistan.

- A relative "overdose" of nitrates may be applied to degraded saline soils in an effort to maintain productivity.

8.23   Without more information on actual field conditions and fertilizer response levels, it is not possible to determine whether these rates are economical[1]. State and collective farm managers and Ministry of Agriculture officials indicated that fertilizer was now being used more carefully and more organic fertilizers are being used because of the higher cost of chemical fertilizers.

Agricultural Chemicals (Pesticides, Herbicides, Defoliants, Growth Regulators)

8.24   Application rates of pesticides on cotton are high--5 to 10 kg/ha--comparable to those in Arizona--but have come down considerably as a result of increased cost and lack of foreign exchange. Because Turkmenistan has invested heavily in specialized cotton production, which requires the heavy use of agricultural chemicals, there will continue to be a high demand for these products. At this time, the MOA finds it difficult to visualize major changes in current agricultural practices, but efforts are being made to reduce the use of agro-chemicals, in particular hazardous defoliants, and apply stricter control on the use of pesticides. More use is also being made of biological pest control methods, although on small scale on a limited number of state cooperative farms.

---

1.   According to a group of USDA cotton experts who traveled extensively through Central Asia, including Turkmenistan, in September and October of 1992, the application rates for fertilizer and chemicals were not considered to be excessive.

8.25   Because of the limited information with which to evaluate economically and environmentally sound cropping intensity and input requirements for cotton and other crops, it is recommended that cooperative arrangements be established with Western research institutions with similar agronomic conditions.   The goal would be to review and compare existing research results, develop updated methodology that incorporates economic and environmental factors and then undertake new field trials using the updated methodology.   One practice that could be considered immediately is adopting the use of acid de-linted seeds, which would reduce seeding rates and allow the use of a systemic insecticide at the time of seeding.   This practice could reduce the need for the first two or three applications of pesticides and produce more-even plant populations.

Machinery and Equipment

8.26   TSS is also responsible for the distribution and repair of agricultural machinery. In 1991 there were 48,000 tractors and 13,000 cotton-picking machines, that is, one tractor for every 26 hectares and one cotton-picking machine for every 48 hectares.   Until 1989, Turkmenistan was receiving almost 7,500 new tractors of all types per year. This number declined to 6,600 in 1990.   Precise information is not available for 1991 and 1992, but the number of new tractors received has continued to decline. Based on the statistics on the number of machines delivered since 1985, more than half of the tractor fleet is less than 10 years old.

8.27   The situation is similar for cotton-picking machines.   However, there is considerable dissatisfaction with the cotton-picking machines because of the amount of trash in machine-picked cotton. It is not clear that the problem is due to the machine, since excess trash in machine-picked cotton may be the result of inadequate or improper defoliation. Regardless of the cause, these problems have resulted in large discounts for Central Asian machine-picked cotton in world markets.   As a result, the Government instituted a policy in 1992 to encourage hand picking of cotton.

8.28   Maintenance and repairs to equipment are performed either at the collective and state farm repair facilities or in centralized TSS stations.   TSS officials and collective and collective and state farm managers reported that machinery was out of service on the average of 20 to 25 percent of the time. These officials reported that repair and maintenance had become more difficult since the breakup of the former Soviet Union because it is difficult to obtain supplies of spare parts.

8.29   Since most machinery is from the former Soviet Union, it is energy inefficient and is larger than may be appropriate if farms are privatized. Over the longer term, this equipment will need to be replaced with modern, energy-efficient equipment suited to a restructured agriculture. TSS is considering a joint-venture plant with Kubota to manufacture tractors and spare parts for farm machinery. However, careful study should be given to this proposal since the Turkmenistan market is not large enough to support a tractor factory by itself, and machinery would need to be marketed to other countries of the former Soviet Union.

Box 8.1: Agriculture in Turkmenistan

In 1991, there were 365 collective farms (KolKhoz), 138 state farms (Sovkholz) and 23 interenterprise agricultural farms. Out of a total land area in Turkmenistan of 48.8 million hectares, these farms encompassed an area of 37.7 million hectares, of which only 1.23 million hectares is arable (see Box 1). The non arable area is semidesert or desert that will only support extensive grazing, and then only if stock water exists. There were only about 36,000 hectares of non state controlled arable land in 1991. Of the 1.23 million hectares of arable land, in 1991, cotton was the principal crop, followed by forage crops, grains, and fruits and vegetables (see Box 2).

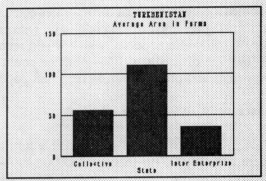

Box 1

Cotton. Cotton is still the major cash crop in Turkmenistan, and will likely remain so for some time. Turkmenistan ranks among the top 10 cotton producers and is climatically well suited for cotton production. The average yield of 650 to 700 kg/ha of lint cotton is higher than the world average for exporters of 600 kg/ha, but is less than most other major cotton producers. Worldwide, Israel and Australia obtained the highest yields-- 1,633 and 1,525 kg/ha of lint cotton, respectively in 1991/92 marketing year. Cotton production in both of these countries is primarily from irrigated areas. The 1991 crop of 1.43 million tons of raw cotton (428,000 tons lint) was very good, but by autumn of 1992 significant stocks remained to be sold--up to one quarter of production. The principal reason for the unsold stocks from 1991 was the unwillingness of the Russian Federation and other republics to purchase their usual share of cotton at world market prices. Thus, Turkmenistan has had to sell its cotton on the world market. While some use has been made of former Soviet Union agents and buyers, the international cotton sales board of the MOA has had to learn how to market Turkmenistan cotton to a sophisticated world market. In addition to finding buyers, Turkmenistan also has problems transporting its cotton to points that link up with international transportation nodes. Finally, between the extra supplies that both Turkmenistan and Uzbekistan have been offering on the world market and quality problems, prices of Turkmenistan cotton are near the bottom of the market[2]. As a result of lessons learned in marketing this year's

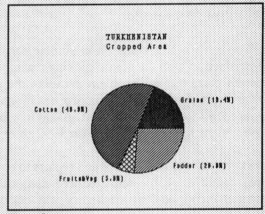

Box 2

cotton crop, the MOA has made significant changes in pricing policy from that of the former Soviet Union in order to emphasize quality. In 1992, the MOA is paying R37,000 per ton (equivalent to approximately $.28/lb. lint @ $1 = R200) for extra-long staple class I, grade I, hand-picked raw cotton versus R25,000 per ton for the same class of machine-picked cotton. In 1991, the price received by the state and collective farms for extra- long staple cotton was R3,885 per ton. For this class of cotton, the 1992 price is six to ten times the price in 1991, which is enough to cover increases in input costs. Price increases are less for lower grades of cotton. Major problems in the cotton sector are quality control, water control, insect control, development of better varieties and high use of chemicals and fertilizer. With better technology and production techniques, the same output could be obtained from less area. The emphasis is now on upstream investments, and several new cotton gins and textile mills are now under construction.

2.   The Liverpool price for Central Asian long staple cotton was $.59/lb or $1,300 per ton in September 1992. The cotton marketing board indicated the average Liverpool price was $1,235 per ton. The border price would be less because of transportation costs, which may be as much as one half the Liverpool price.

Box 8.1 (cont.)

Grains. Under the former Soviet Union, Turkmenistan only produced about half of the grain consumed. Production has been steadily increasing since 1987 when total grain production was only 324,000 tons. Planned production in 1992 was 1 million tons, and the MOA has set a target for self-sufficiency by 1995 at 1.5 million metric tons. Most of the additional hectarage is expected to come from increased areas brought under irrigation during the winter months. The main issue in the short term is whether increasing production by increasing irrigated area during the winter season is a cost-effective measure. Over the longer term, improved varieties and production technology are needed to increase productivity.

Fruits and Vegetables. Turkmenistan produces a variety of fruits and vegetables well in excess of domestic needs. Fresh vegetables and melons were exported to Siberia and other parts of the former Soviet Union, but have been curtailed because of increased transportation costs. Turkmenistan is also a major producer of grapes, which have been exported in the form of wine to the former Soviet Union. The current bottling capacity is insufficient to handle all of production because wine was exported in bulk. Handling and storage facilities are also inadequate, so losses of fresh fruits and vegetables are high---as much as 40 percent. The former Soviet Union made very few investments in cold storage and food processing in Turkmenistan. Thus, development of the processing industry is a high priority of the MOA, and some investments have been made. While Turkmenistan is climatically well suited for production of a wide variety of fruits and vegetables and has good potential, a careful evaluation of potential markets and potential competitors is needed before large investments in new crops and agro-processing are made.

Livestock. There are 5.6 million sheep and goats; 900,000 head of cattle, of which 360,000 are cows; 260,000 head of hogs, and 93,000 camels in Turkmenistan. A large proportion of the livestock are in the private sector, with three fourths of the cows, more than half the cattle and almost one third of the sheep and goats owned by individuals. However, production of meat and dairy products meets only about one half of consumption requirements at current subsidized prices. As elsewhere in former Soviet Union, much of livestock production is dependent on the production of fodder and is high cost. Calving and lambing rates are generally low -- 57 percent and 86 percent respectively in 1991. Poultry production is even more inefficient. The average production of eggs per hen per year is only 112 eggs compared to the average in the U.S. of over 200. Even these costs do not reflect the actual costs since feed and energy costs are still highly subsidized. Because prices for eggs and poultry meat are controlled at R3 and R60 respectively, most of the difference between production costs and the selling price was made up by state subsidies, with the remainder being borrowed.

Because domestic production in Turkmenistan was inadequate under the former Soviet Union to meet domestic consumption requirements there were large imports from other republics and outside sources that were sold at subsidized prices in state outlets. However, in Turkmenistan, a large percentage of meat and dairy products are produced by individuals and sold at higher open market prices. Thus, it is not clear how much of a production deficit would exist at non subsidized prices. Experience in other socialist countries suggests that when prices for livestock products in Turkmenistan are liberalized, a new equilibrium may be established with sharply lower demand and moderately reduced livestock numbers. As prices and demand adjust to new price levels, the livestock sector will need to adjust production and increase efficiency by updating management and technology. The MOA is now promoting development of extensive livestock production by providing stock watering stations in the desert and is considering privatizing the herds. In addition, there will also need to be better integration of extensive livestock production into the irrigated agricultural economy. Range conditions observed indicated that improved range management and control of overgrazing is needed. With careful management of small ruminant livestock, higher output probably can be obtained from the same animal population. In addition, there may be an imbalance in the N-P-K ratio in relation to phosphorus or deficiencies in other micro-nutrients which may limit increased yields. Finally, actual application rates may be less than reported because of diversion to other crops.

8.30   Key to improving efficiency in the farm machinery area is developing an independent dealer and service network that maintains adequate repair facilities and supplies of spare parts. Because of the emphasis on production under the former Soviet Union, the ratio of spare parts production and inventories to new equipment was much lower than in most market economies. Privatization of repair depots and promotion of independent repair services would be the most efficient way of providing farm machinery services. Even in most developing countries there are usually a large number of private repair facilities, many that can fabricate otherwise unavailable parts.

Agricultural Finance

8.31   Agroprombank, with 53 branches, provides the largest share of agricultural lending in Turkmenistan. Agroprom shareholders include the Ministry of Agriculture, state agricultural processing enterprises and state and collective farms. Agroprom's main liabilities include deposits of agricultural enterprises, Government deposits and lending from banks (predominantly from the Gosbank). The lending of this institution is directed to state and collective farms, to the agricultural processing industry and to support irrigation works.

8.32   Because of Turkmenistan's continuing policy of subsidizing agriculture, Agroprombank charges rates that, in many cases, are lower than those charged to other enterprises, particularly those of commercial banks. A special credit line has recently been introduced by presidential decree that supports lending to collective farms at a rate of 2.2 percent. Agricultural enterprises obtain only 1/2 percent for deposits placed with the bank even though they are required to deposit their funds in Agroprombank. In the first half of 1992, Agroprom's lending increased from R27.5 billion to R33.8 billion, while the capital base of the bank rose only marginally.

8.33   As privatization occurs, means will have to be developed to provide small producers with credit. Under the leasing system now being implemented, it appears that financing is being provided by the collective and state farms. In the future, as the number of private farmers increases, the rural banking system will have to change if it is to serve the needs of independent producers.

Research

8.34   Agricultural research is carried out under the Turkmenistan Academy of Science by the Desert Institute in Karakum and the Turkmenistan Academy of Agricultural Sciences. The Agricultural Academy has 1,500 research personnel, of which 15 percent are Ph.Ds and 500 are researchers. There are ten institutes, seven experimental stations, six experimental farms and eight orchards. In the past agricultural research was financed from budgetary allocations that came mostly from the former Soviet Union, with some contribution from republic levels, state and collective farms and sales of agricultural products. Replacement of funding from the Soviet Union level has been difficult. Most scientists had few linkages with other countries and only limited access to foreign scientific literature.

8.35   Most agricultural research has been directed toward the large state and collective farms and was geared toward obtaining maximum output, particularly of cotton. Little attention was paid to developing a more diversified crop production system, which could be economically and ecologically advantageous. Many of the researchers understand the problems, but funding is now limited. After funding, the main problems faced by the Agricultural Academy in transforming itself into a modern research institution are:

- Developing linkages with other scientific organizations in other countries in order to transfer experience.

- Retraining of existing research personnel.

- Training new specialists.

- Developing viable means of transferring new technology to a restructured agricultural sector. ·

Transport

8.36   Because of Turkmenistan's remoteness to major markets, the availability of transportation is critical for the competitiveness of its agriculture. Turkmenistan's only linkage to the ocean is via the Volga Don canal from the Caspian to the Black Sea. Shipping capacity is limited because the canal is frozen over during the winter months and can only handle vessels of no more than 5,000 tons. The other main means of transport of agricultural commodities is via rail through Kazakhstan, Uzbekistan and Russia to either the Black Sea ports or St. Petersburg. Road transport is possible, but is less developed, and it is used mainly for trade among the Central Asian countries. There are some road linkages now developing with Iran and Turkey. A rail link with Iran is also being constructed. Air transportation is also available, but would only be economical for high-value, perishable commodities.

8.37   Under the former Soviet Union, transportation costs were highly subsidized, and thus these costs were given little consideration in production decisions. As the actual economic costs of transportation are passed on to producers and consumers, these costs will become a major consideration in production decisions.

8.38   Logistics management and transportation of commodities under the former Soviet Union were handled by large enterprises at the All Union Level. The republic-level transportation branches have evolved into Turkmenistan air, rail and transport enterprises. Short-haul transport between collective and state farms and nearby cities are still handled by Agroprom, the collective and state farms themselves and some newly independent truckers. The transportation system inherited from the former Soviet Union is one of the major constraints to developing a more diversified agriculture, as demonstrated by the impact of increased transportation costs on the marketing of fruits and vegetables in the former Soviet Union. In Western economies, the most effective means of moving perishables over long distances from multiple suppliers to multiple markets, distributors and consumers is long-haul road transport. These low-cost road transportation services are provided by many independent trucking and service firms. Improvements in long-haul capability by rail and water are also important to reduce delivery costs and losses for cotton. There have been reports of substantial losses and water damage to cotton shipped via barge through the Volga Don canal, and rail transport is slow and expensive. Because of the distance of Turkmenistan from markets, the most efficient form of transportation is likely to be a combination of short-haul and long-haul road transport, rail and barge that uses efficient transfer terminals and containerized cargo.

8.39   Because the most efficient transportation system is a complete departure from that of the former Soviet Union, privatization is a key requirement. Thus, a program should be developed as rapidly as possible that legalizes and regulates individual ownership of transportation services, privatizes small and medium-sized trucking enterprises, auctions off excess inventories of trucks and spare parts (with preference given to currently employed drivers), and auctions off surplus military trucks. Encouragement should be given to the breakup of huge trucking enterprises and the spinning off of the transportation units of various Ministries, Agroprom, economic enterprises, municipalities and state and collective farms into independent companies. Even with these steps, large investments will be needed in road improvements, all sizes and types of trucks, service facilities, logistics management, long-haul tractor-trailers, refrigerated trucks and transfer nodes between different types of transportation facilities, (e.g. piggy-back rail cars and trailers, containers and terminals with modern loading and unloading systems).

Distribution

8.40   The marketing and distribution of agricultural commodities is still dominated by state enterprises (see Figure 8.2). In 1992, the state plans to purchase all of the cotton, 85 percent of the grapes and more than 75 percent of the melons and karakul pelts. Only for potatoes, fruit, milk, meat and grains are planned state purchases less than one half of production. The state purchases only limited quantities of grain because most production is used on the state and collective farms for feed or for individual consumption. There were only two main channels of distribution in the former Soviet Union: state managed chains of retail stores that served the urban areas and consumer cooperatives that served the non-urban areas. The amount of retail space per person in the former Soviet Union was one fifth that in Europe. In addition, particularly in Central Asia, there are a number of open markets run by the consumer cooperatives and municipalities. Consumers also receive commodities or food services through their work place as well as non market channels. There are now a number of roadside sellers who sell a variety of fresh fruits, vegetables and other goods, although prices are usually higher than in state shops. In Turkmenistan, marketing and distribution by the state sector is now handled by the Ministry of Trade in the urban areas and by the Cooperative Alliance in rural areas (see Box 8.2). A number of commodity exchanges have also come into being which are being used as a trading mechanism by the state enterprises and state and collective farms to sell above quota production and obtain needed materials.

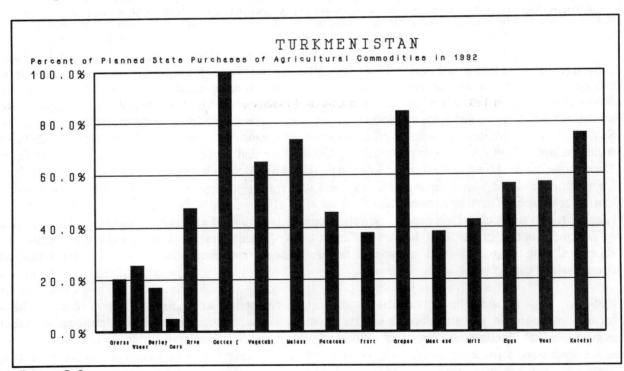

Figure 8.2

8.41   The development of a modern consumer-oriented marketing system will require service-oriented marketing, distribution firms linked by modern communications and information systems, and selling goods of consistent and known quality. Price liberalization by itself will not produce this result since marketing and distribution will remain under state control. Privatization of the retail sector is the easiest step that can be taken and should be pursued. However, of more importance is the development of wholesale and assembly markets that are not dominated by public sector enterprises already operating in this area. Actions needed to develop the distribution system are a privatization strategy that allows free entry of firms, a regulatory framework that provides for food safety, standardization and quality control, and support services such as market information, food inspection, financial services, training and technical assistance.

Box 8.2 : The Turkmen Cooperative Alliance

The Turkmenistan Cooperative Alliance (TCA) is a federation of rural cooperatives. In the pre-independence economic regime, the TCA was the only agent that could conduct foreign trade, which was done by barter. The Cooperative Alliance secured above-plan cotton from the collectives and traded the cotton for hard-currency imports that were sold to TCA members in a network of rural stores. The TCA was viewed as the business, or trading sector of the Turkmenistan economy. The Alliance was formed before 1917 and has been independent of the state.

TCA operations are small scale and dispersed in the rural areas. The Alliance has responsibility to supply consumer goods to the rural population. There are 700,000 members in a three-level organizational pyramid: the all-republic organization, the oblast and the town. The Law on Consumer Cooperatives specifies who can be a member of a cooperative. Membership fees are in effect shareholdings that determine the distribution of profits.

TCA has facilities for processing tomatoes, cucumbers, honey, olives, canned fruit and jams; a rest home on the Caspian Sea; a construction business; restaurants; and a wide chain of retail outlets. A cotton ginning mill is under construction as a joint-venture with a collective farm. TCA also has rural land for its cultivation. In 1991, these enterprises produced 140 tons of cotton on 40 hectares. In 1992, TCA has planted 500 hectares which are expected to produce 4,000 tons of cotton. TCA expect to barter 5,000 tons of cotton in 1992 for hard-currency imports that will be sold domestically via the Cooperative Alliance's retail outlets. Of TCA's total sales, 25 percent comes from its own production and 75 percent from distribution of goods provided by the state. TCA controls 45 percent of the total retail sales in Turkmenistan. The Turkmenistan Cooperative Alliance engages in barter trade in order to avoid the retention requirements for foreign exchange and has no difficulty obtaining export licenses.

8.42   Farmers markets are playing an increasing role in the marketing and distribution area, and support should be given to expanding their role. In this regard, consideration should be given to converting the National Market in Ashkhabad into a modern wholesale market. The National Market is centrally located near both the main highway and the rail line. There is also undeveloped space that can be used to expand the market area, improve access roads and build unloading docks, warehouses and cold storage facilities. The first step is to undertake a preliminary design and feasibility study of the area. If a wholesale market proves feasible, then financing from a variety of sources should be possible. Some improvement, such as better access and expansion of the market area, could be undertaken while plans are being developed.

Agro-Processing

8.43   There are only a limited number of agro-processing plants, and except for cotton ginning, the processing technology is relatively unsophisticated.   Only a limited number of processed food products of modest quality are produced, and losses of fresh fruits and vegetables are high because of poor handling and lack of cold-storage facilities. Quality is also a problem.

8.44   A substantial potential exists for developing the agro-processing industry in Turkmenistan because of the variety of agricultural crops that could be grown. However, because of the location of Turkmenistan and similar climatic conditions in other Central Asian Republics, potential areas for investment need to be carefully evaluated in terms of markets and alternative suppliers.   Since the states of the former Soviet Union are likely to be the major market for Turkmenistan products, predicting what the potential demand and prices will likely be after their structural adjustment has occurred will be a very difficult task.

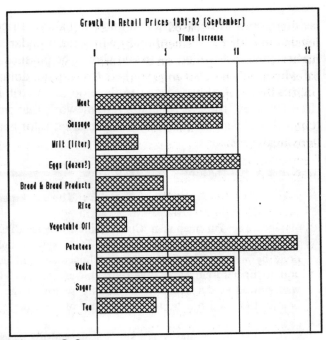

Figure 8.3

8.45   A number of investments are being considered by the Government in the processing area, for example, the proposed sugar beet and tanning factories. All proposed investments now being considered by the Government should be subjected to a full feasibility analysis based on market prices expected after adjustment. While the Government may provide assistance for carrying out the feasibility study, those investments that show potential should be left to the private sector and no additional investment undertaken by the existing state enterprises unless they are privatized. An efficient private agribusiness and processing sector in the long run will be in the best position to take advantage of Turkmenistan's comparative advantage producing subtropical agricultural products in competition with other Central Asian republics.

Incentive Framework

The Case for Price Liberalization

8.46   The pricing policy in the former Soviet Union has greatly reduced incentives to cut production costs besides misallocating resources. Although the retail price controls are the most damaging to the budget, the system of procurement prices and state orders are the most distorting for agricultural production.

8.47   One of the important issues during the transition process is the overall policy regarding relative food prices. Increased food prices are desirable for a number of reasons. Increased output prices would help to avert the substantial decline in agricultural production that could occur as budget constraints are hardened. Increased food prices would also help to move relative consumer prices toward world levels, an essential element of structural adjustment for the economy as a whole. The average impact of higher consumer prices on the average consumer may be less than feared, and devising an appropriate safety net will be vital to safeguard the welfare of these groups and make increases in food prices more politically acceptable.

8.48   Administered prices would mean that the command structure and control of farming and agro-industry would most likely continue. If the Government attempted to control only retail prices while freeing wholesale and producer prices, subsidies would expand. To control subsidies, the reinstatement of controls on wholesale and producer prices would then probably be unavoidable. With price controls in place, investment in the sector would be delayed. Without a clear signal on prices, farmers and processors cannot determine the potential value of privatized assets in agriculture. Agricultural and agro-industrial restructuring would be distorted under politically controlled prices. It would also mean forgoing the possibility of a rapid supply-side response in the agricultural and food economy in the early stage of transition. The only viable step is to free agricultural prices at all levels. The rationale for price liberalization lies in eliminating the increasing inefficiencies in production and processing caused by a highly distorted price structure, in redressing the regressive nature of the food subsidy and its continuing pressure on the Government's budget and in countering high costs with barter trade arising in part out of attempts to avoid price controls.

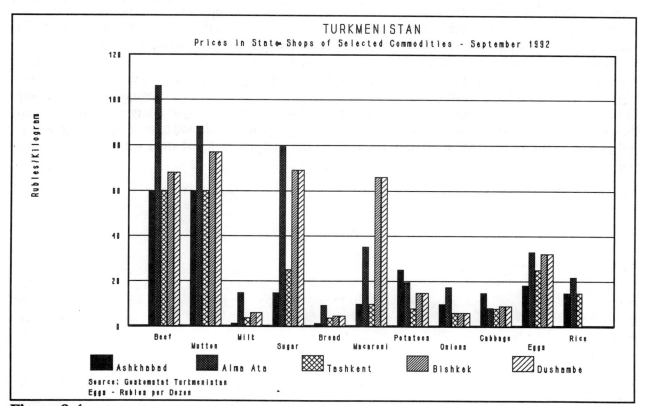

Figure 8.4

Food Availability, Prices and Wages

8.49   Except for fresh fruits and vegetables, most prices are still either established by the Government or negotiated between state enterprises. Several commodity exchanges exist that mainly serve state enterprises selling commodities that were produced above quota and buy needed supplies. Basically three sets of prices exist: state-controlled prices, free market prices and Cooperative Alliance prices, which are between the other two levels. In addition, many shops now have commercial market sections that sell goods, a number of which are imported, at uncontrolled prices. There is great concern in Turkmenistan that price liberalization will make food unaffordable for the more vulnerable parts of the population. Under the former Soviet Union, food supplies and per capita consumption levels for most commodities were adequate. While cereals provide the majority of calories in the Turkmen diet, consumption of meat, dairy products and vegetables are still well above minimum nutritional requirements and above other countries with comparable levels of economic development. In 1991, there were some shortages of cereals, sugar and livestock products, but supplies in 1992 were adequate and there were no reports of expected shortages.

Retail Price Increases for Food

8.50   Price data for the first six months of 1992 indicate that food prices were up overall in 1992 about eight to ten fold from those of a year earlier (see Figure 8.3). Uncontrolled prices for most items are two to four times higher than controlled prices. Prices of controlled food items are substantially below production costs. Principal among these are bread, meat and dairy products which are still highly subsidized (see Figure 8.3). Even though prices and wages are now adjusted quarterly based on the rate of inflation, Turkmenistan's controlled prices are still below those of other Central Asian countries and Russia (see Figure 8.4). Open market prices on the other hand are fairly uniform among the Central Asian countries, suggesting that private trade among the countries of the Former Soviet Union is occurring (see Figure 8.5). The growing gap between official prices and free market prices reflects the relative availability of food commodities in the state network. Because of better quality, variety and supplies, consumers have been turning to the open market or to barter for ordinary purchases of food except basic staples. As consumers become more dependent upon markets and have to pay higher prices, those segments of the population on fixed incomes become more at risk and steps will need to be taken to protect this group.

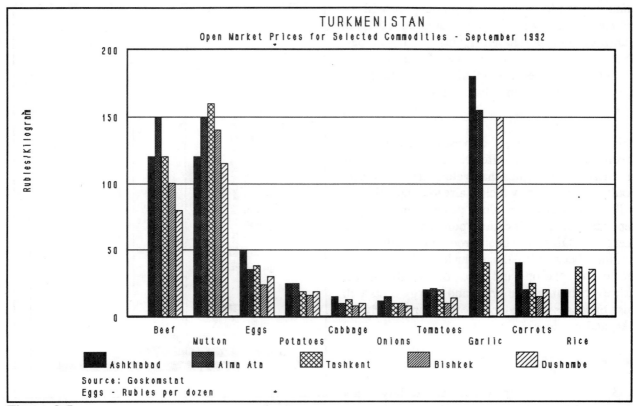

Figure 8.5

Decline in the Input Terms of Trade

8.51   Following the partial price liberalization early in 1992, food prices remained much more constrained than input prices due to Government control and limited increases in income (see Figure 8.6). Input prices are expected to continue to increase because of energy price increases in October, 1992. Prices for fertilizer and chemicals were on the order of 10 to 15 times higher than the same period in 1991. Machinery prices were 50 to 100 times higher, and spare parts were in short supply. The higher costs of inputs has already had some effect. Most farm managers indicated they were using fertilizer and chemicals more carefully and were not buying new machinery. Down time for tractors and other machinery under repair was reported to be 20 to 25 percent.

8.52   The deterioration in the input terms of trade has also put a severe squeeze on the profitability of some sectors of agriculture and will affect all sectors in the next few years. The increased costs of purchased inputs will have the greatest impact on those activities that account for a high proportion of costs and where profits are already low. Based on past profitability, the majority of collective farms, particularly those that are primarily crop based, will be able to absorb the increased costs. State farms and other agricultural enterprises will be affected more.

8.53   The impact on individual commodities will vary, depending on the same factors given above. While cotton has a high level of purchased inputs, it requires high levels of labor and is tied to the international market. Since cost increases are likely to be offset by increased prices, and cotton has been a profitable crop, the immediate impact of increased input costs will not be great. On the other hand vegetable and melon production will be affected quite severely by increased costs of transport and purchased inputs. For grapes, Turkmenistan should emerge as a low-cost producer. Grapes use relatively low levels of purchased inputs and have high productivity levels.

8.54   As for the livestock sector, sheep raising will be least affected since it uses few purchased inputs other than veterinary medicines. Poultry production, which is already unprofitable, will be most affected, since production is highly dependent on good location, purchased inputs and energy. Dairy and beef production will likely continue because of the inclusion of legumes in the crop rotation and use of family labor. However, higher feed grain and energy costs will raise expenses and reduce profits, particularly for marginal producers.

Trade

8.55   Turkmenistan is a large net exporter of agricultural commodities if exports are

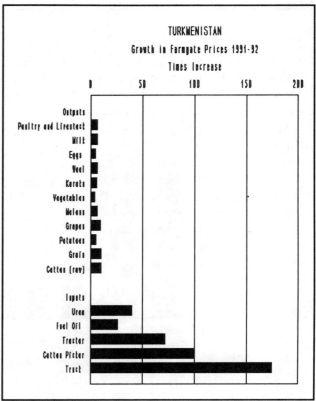

Figure 8.6

valued at world prices. In 1990, the net value of the 1.7 million bales of cotton sold to the former Soviet Union and internationally would have been between $600 and 700 million. If only one half of this had been sold on the international market, this would have netted Turkmenistan $300 million dollars. Turkmenistan provided 102,000 tons of vegetables, 139,000 tons of melons, and 32,000 tons of fresh grapes to the All Union Fund for trade purposes. For processed agricultural products, Turkmenistan exported most of the vegetable oil and wine produced to the former Soviet Union as well as some processed fruits and vegetables. Karakul pelts, hides and skins and wool were also exported to the former Soviet Union. The Government is pursuing a policy of import substitution to achieve self-sufficiency in cereal production by 1995, to become a net exporter of processed foods and become self-sufficient in cotton textile production.

8.56   Agricultural trade is constrained by barriers on both the import and export sides. One of the principal constraints is the lack of an international financing and banking system. For cotton, the main constraints are developing cotton grading standards that are acceptable on the international market, developing good transportation facilities and linkages through Russia, Ukraine, Kazakhstan, Uzbekistan or neighboring countries and developing international marketing experience. Regaining the market share for fresh fruits and vegetables will require developing new marketing channels to the other countries of the former Soviet Union, reducing shipping losses and improving marketing. Developing markets will require products that meet international standards, are low cost and are either easily transported or have high value. Imports are constrained by the lack of access to foreign exchange, import controls and price controls, lack of information on availability and cost of foreign goods and high transportation costs. Domestic prices are still much lower than international prices for both exported and imported commodities.

Land Reform and Privatization

8.57   The transition from a centralized command economy to a market-driven economy requires a continuous decentralization of decision making from the central planners to independent firms and individuals in all sectors of the economy. This requires that a set of legally defined property rights for land, water and intellectual services be developed and adopted by the Government. The first steps have been taken by allowing the leasing of and the allocation of private plots at the farm level in a pilot project. However, before economic actors will be willing to risk investing time and capital into an economic activity, there must be secure, tradable rights for that activity. If the ownership of property is not allowed, leases must have long-term, well-defined rights and be tradable. Second, privatizing only part of the economy will not have the desired results because decisions will still be subject to control of that part of the economy rather than the market. Thus, to obtain the benefits of a market economy, the Government would need to take the next step of freeing up wholesale-retail trade and allowing private firms to enter the processing, manufacturing and distribution sectors.

Agricultural Privatization

8.58   The Ministry of Agriculture is preparing two supplementary laws on agricultural privatization to complement the general privatization law passed in early 1992. The first concerns privatization of state farms and cooperatives and the second, the purchase of individual land plots by farmers.[3]

8.59   State farmland is currently owned and controlled by the oblasts. Collective farmland is leased by the oblast to the collective, who has no rights to sell it. Ownership of both will apparently shortly be transferred to the Ministry of Economics and Finance as described above. However, new legislation is expected to grant most of those living on the land a "private" allocation of 0.25 to 0.5 hectares, generally surrounding their houses, which will become their property (it also appears that urban dwellers will have the right to an allotment one half this size).

8.60   Options for dealing with the remaining land and equipment are set out below. Some state and cooperative farms have already introduced a degree of flexibility by permitting farmers to have one-to three-year leases. Farmers agree to sell a fixed share (for example, 30 percent) of their output to the state and collective farm and are free to sell the remainder on the free market, with no control from the state. This arrangement is most common for vegetables and grapes, though some state and collective farms are leasing cotton land.

8.61   The intention is that for a number (possibly 15 percent) of the 150 state farms Government will retain a controlling interest, to prevent shortages.[4] The remainder will have the option of privatizing fully, as described below. All forms of destatization will be voluntary. In the first stage, farm workers need to purchase the farm assets (buildings and machinery, but not land) from the state. Valuation will be conducted by taking the original value, minus depreciation, of the assets. Original value should not include reinvested profits (which are considered as already belonging to the workers).

---

3.   The first law is largely complete, and the second around 25% complete, with two Ministry officials working on them since April 1992, and apparently consulting widely with farmers themselves.

4.   Examples given were cotton seed production, which only two farms specialize in, and poultry.

A certain percentage (10 to 30 percent) of this residual value is given to the employees at no charge. The more profitable the farm, the less is distributed at no cost. Distribution is made, in the form of shares, according to employees' length of service, their job and various other factors. The remaining shares (70 to 90 percent of the residual value) must be paid for by the employees, unless the state wants to retain majority control, in which case only a minority share is offered for sale.

8.62   Cooperative farms will need to undergo the same process in order to value the shareholding and then distribute it all to cooperative members, according to length of service and other factors. It appears that one option open to cooperative members may be to withdraw entirely from the cooperative, following the valuation, taking their land immediately into private ownership and receiving cash from other members in return for their share of the equipment.

Box 8.3:
Privatization of Agricultural Assets
Draft Options for Farm Organization

Option I: Union of Leaseholders Paying a Fixed Share of Output

This option maintains the basic structure of the cooperative, run by an "association of leaseholders" elected by the farmers. Each farmer is given an individual lease on his or her land, for a minimum of 10 years, with an unspecified "right to buy" at some future point. Thirty percent of the farmer's produce is given to the state farm as a lease payment, which also covers the union's state land taxes. The remaining 70 percent of production can be sold privately or to the state farm. Payments for Value Added Taxes, services such as use of farm machinery and inputs such as fertilizer and irrigation are the responsibility of the tenant.

Option II: Union of Leaseholders Selling Produce Collectively

Under this arrangement, an agreed proportion of each farmer's output is sold to the management "company," which is estimated to be sufficient to cover the costs of all centrally provided services. The farmer is free to market any production in excess of the agreed-upon share however he wishes. The company then markets the products received, and at year end, the management presents all farmers with an account of the year and divides up any profits. Each farmer is responsible for paying a tax on the land he or she is using directly to the tax inspectorate.

Option III: Separate Leaseholders

This arrangement enables leaseholders to conduct their tax dealings with the state directly and to pay for or supply their own services (this will appeal particularly to machinery owners). This appears to be the most radical form of privatization, but may be subject to a number of practical problems (some central provision of "municipal" type infrastructure and social services, and some central purchasing of outputs, seem inevitable in the short and medium term).

Reorganization of Farm Services

8.63   After both state farms and cooperatives have transformed themselves into joint stock companies in this way, the next stage will be to create a separate farm-management services company, which sells inputs and markets output. Details of current thinking on the alternatives that may be open to both state and collective farms are given in Box 8.3. With each option, the use of long leases could achieve many of the benefits of selling land, assuming that leases are fully transferable and automatically extended at the end of their term. With such provisions, it is even possible that a very long lease could be used as collateral for borrowing.

Sale of Land

8.64   The final stage in this process would involve direct land sales to farmers. Although this appeared acceptable to officials in principle, the mechanisms for such sales, and other preparatory work (including a definitive survey of farm boundaries), have not been spelled out. In addition to irrigated land, the state and most cooperatives own very large areas of land suitable only for grazing. These public holdings are unlikely to be privatized. The main issue will be the sale or allocation of water and grazing rights. Some land may also be designated as natural parks for ecological or environmental reasons. Sale of urban land has not yet commenced, and plans for this are unclear.[5]

New Role of the Government

8.65   The transition from a centrally planned economy to a market economy will change the Government's role in agriculture substantially. The primary short-term need for developing the agricultural sector is a sound macroeconomic policy that will sustain the transition to a market economy. Without a suitable macroeconomic framework, investments in agriculture and agro-processing are likely to be the wrong kind, in the wrong place and to produce the wrong product after the economy has adjusted. The first step involves phasing out state production orders, eliminating input subsidies and adjusting the prices of wage goods to competitive levels, since these prices influence all consumption and production decisions. The next step is to establish a hard budget constraint for all state enterprises, that is, to limit or eliminate the subsidies granted through the state budget or through the banking system.

8.66   Liberalization of imports and exports will provide alternative sources of commodities to state monopolies and help develop the domestic private marketing system. As a starting point, all restrictions should be removed on state and collective farms and other economic enterprises for trading. This should be followed by allowing free entry of individuals into the import-export business. Consideration also should be given to setting up an international cotton exchange. Finally, consideration should be given to setting up an international commodity exchange covering a broad range of commodities in cooperation with other Central Asian countries.

8.67   The next priority is developing the institutions and legal framework needed for a market economy to function. If privatization of both land and state enterprises is to yield benefits, decision makers need to be assured that they will be able to retain the benefits of any investments made, not be

---

5.   Nonetheless some land has apparently been sold on a 99-year lease for industrial development, and some 50-year leases have been granted for house building.

directed to produce unprofitable commodities and not be protected from failure. Individuals and firms must have the means to enforce contracts fairly and be freely allowed to enter into any type of business in order to foster competition.

Management of the Transition

8.68   Turkmenistan, as other countries of the former Soviet Union faces a daunting task in restructuring its economy. While privatization and price liberalization are key requirements for the development of a market economy, equally important is a clear separation of Governmental functions from commercial functions. In the agriculture sector this is particularly true because the collective and state farms are both governmental and commercial units. Thus, at the same time that privatization programs are developed, equal attention needs to be paid to developing local Governments.. This will require laws establishing local governmental units, decisions on how governing bodies will be formed, identification of sources of revenue to support schools, roads, health and other services and determination of how pensioners of the state and collective farms will be compensated for goods and services now being provided by these farms.

Role of the Ministry of Agriculture

8.69   Another problem Turkmenistan faces is developing a functional Ministry of Agriculture from a number of disparate entities that were the republic-level branches of production and other Ministries and organizations of the former Soviet Union that operated under direction of Gosplan. There was often little coordination between these production agencies at the central level and almost no coordination at the republic level. While the republic-level branch of Gosplan would pass information to the central government, the central government did not feel obligated to follow these recommendations. The Turkmenistan Ministry of Agriculture was formed from three earlier ministries responsible for production agriculture, processing, and marketing and export sales (Agroprom). Some of these ministries in turn had been formed from other entities. Agricultural research is conducted by the Agricultural Academy of Sciences, and education and training is carried out by the Agricultural Institute.

8.70   A decentralized economy requires a new role for the Ministry of Agriculture as it moves from mandating production, distribution and pricing and into the role of regulating the market and promoting competition. In support of this role, the Ministry of Agriculture will need to develop a market information system that is freely available to individuals; establish and enforce grades and standards; establish a targeted safety net for those most affected by the reforms; orient research needs toward providing new technology that will increase the productivity of individual private producers and develop extension and other services to transmit the new technology to those producers.

Long-Run Policy Considerations

8.71   A successful transformation of the agriculture sector in Turkmenistan will result in large structural changes. Land-use patterns are likely to change and much more diversified patterns will result. Because of the scarcity of water and increasing demands for water for other uses, land-use patterns will evolve that most efficiently use water, and marginal areas will no longer be used for production. Cotton will likely continue as the major crop, but on fewer hectares than now. High-value speciality fruit, vegetable or tree crops that fill niche markets in Europe or the states of the former Soviet Union will be developed. The grape and wine industry will continue to expand. Winter grain and other crops will also expand.

8.72   The high proportion of people who now live in rural areas will decline as opportunities develop in the rest of the economy. This change will require production adjustments to less labor-intensive crops and livestock activities, unless migrant labor is used. The largest restructuring will likely occur in the livestock and poultry sectors. Livestock production will become more specialized, particularly the dairy industry. Sheep raising will require the fewest adjustments and, with improved management, will remain profitable. The poultry industry will require major restructuring and will not likely survive in its present form. The best long-term investments in the agricultural sector are likely to be in modern irrigation equipment and technology, modern fruit and vegetable processing, cold-storage and shipping facilities, wine and alcohol production facilities, modern tanning and wool processing facilities, cotton textiles, and modern dairy and milk-processing facilities.

Box 8.4
Technical Assistance Recommendations

The amount and type of technical assistance should be keyed to the transition to a market economy. In the short term, while the economy is in transition, technical assistance should be geared to those areas that can assist with the transition or areas where there is obvious need regardless of where the country is in the adjustment process. Once the transition is well under way, technical assistance can shift into those areas where the economic returns can be measured.

Short-Term Technical Assistance

- Because of the importance of using water more efficiently, technical assistance for conducting a systemwide review of water management and preparation of a national water strategy has high priority. The objective of this activity is to develop policies and procedures that will improve water use, control, operation, maintenance and environmental conditions. This activity should be coordinated with the development of an automated management system for the Amu Darya being undertaken by the Amu Darya River Basin Commission.

- Technical assistance for land and irrigation activities include assistance for improved drainage, both system wide and on farms; development of automated water-control and metering devices to improve water-delivery schedules; development and promotion of better irrigation and on-farm water-management practices; and cadastral and land-use surveys.

- The Ministry of Agriculture needs to improve its ability to evaluate proposed investments as to their feasibility, provide policy guidance on the Government's role in agriculture in a market economy, and develop new approaches to managing the transition to a market economy. Technical assistance could be provided for project evaluation, training of policymakers, development of proposals on the most efficient approach for divesture of its operational activities, legal assistance for developing commercial and privatization laws; and development of extension, market news, statistical and other services.

Box 8.4 (cont.)

- New approaches are required for the training and education of teachers, policy makers, and managers in marketing, business management, western accounting methods, agricultural economics, and related areas. Technical assistance would focus on training and exchanges of Ministry, Academy and Institute personnel in all areas; evaluation of the structure and content of ongoing training and research programs and development of a long-range plan; and development of recommendations for curricula changes appropriate to a market economy.

Medium-Term Technical Assistance

- Once sufficient structural adjustments have occurred so that projects can be evaluated as to their priority and economic feasibility, technical assistance can be provided for proposed investments in irrigation infrastructure, particularly for improving drainage and water efficiency.

- Technical assistance may be needed to identify specific investments in transportation and storage to support agricultural development. Potential areas for assistance are in building facilities needed to move commodities less expensively into international markets and obtain needed imports, on farm storage and farm-to-market roads.

- Once prices adjust and there is a more open economy, areas can be identified where crop and livestock diversification are possible. Technical assistance can then be made available for the development of a research, extension and training system to support a more diversified agricultural economy.

- In conjunction with the development of a more diversified agricultural economy, investments in agro-industry and food processing will be possible. Technical assistance could be provided to review all investments now being considered for their feasibility and to identify new areas for investment.

- Technical assistance may be needed to investigate the need for restructuring the current Agricultural Bank or establishing a different rural banking system or other rural financial institutions.

CHAPTER 9

ENERGY

9.1   Turkmenistan has a rich endowment of energy resources, primarily natural gas and oil, and ranks among the major energy producers of the former Soviet Union. Currently, Turkmenistan is the second largest natural gas producer among the new independent states of the former Soviet Union after the Russian Federation and the fourth largest producer in the world. It is also the fourth largest oil producer in the region.

9.2   With a small population and a relatively low level of industrialization, total domestic energy consumption is small. So Turkmenistan is a large net exporter of energy. In absolute terms it is the second largest net exporter of energy in the region, but per capita net energy exports are about five times as large as in the Russian Federation, the largest regional net exporter. Around 85 percent of the country's total external energy trade is with the other republics of the former Soviet Union. Exports of natural gas account for 95 percent of this trade and for about 95 percent of energy trade with countries outside the region, mostly in Central and Eastern Europe. Natural gas exports outside the former Soviet Union are the result of a swap by Gasprom of Russia of part of its exports for Turkmenistan supplies going to southern Russia.

9.3   Energy exports are estimated at R300 billion in 1992 against imports of about R5.0 billion.[1] Hard-currency revenues from exports of natural gas in 1992 are estimated at US$700 million and accounted for about 70 percent of the country's total hard-currency receipts during the year. If Turkmenistan's energy trade with the countries that used to make up the Soviet Union were valued at world market prices or prices that fully reflect the economic value of energy resources, the trade balance would have been about R540 billion (US$2 billion equivalent) higher.

9.4   The energy sector is the Government's most important source of ruble and hard- currency revenues. In 1992, the natural gas subsector is estimated to have contributed R22 billion to Government fiscal revenues through taxes and other levies on production and profits. In addition, about $0.5 billion of the subsector's hard-currency export revenues accrue directly to the Government. Other sources of fiscal revenues were comparatively small.

9.5   The prospects for the natural gas sector to become the motor of rapid economic growth and transformation are clouded by the relatively low remaining proven reserves in developed fields, the limited capacity of the domestic industry to identify and develop new reserves and the uncertainties surrounding export markets both in the former Soviet Union and elsewhere. Most of these challenges can, however, be met if the Government can create an environment that will attract both foreign expertise and capital to regenerate the gas sector's production potential and to help diversify the markets for the country's natural gas.

9.6   The potential for the country to expand its production of crude oil and petroleum products and reduce its narrow dependence on natural gas appears to be considerable. The Government recognizes that foreign investors will play a crucial role in developing this potential by providing capital for exploration and development and by introducing new technology. A satisfactory legal and fiscal

---

1.   Assuming an average exchange rate of US$1 = R267 for transactions through the year.

framework for external investment in the sector would be required to achieve this objective. The existing procedures for promoting the country's petroleum potential to foreign investors will also need to be changed to encourage wider investor interest. The domestic industry can also make an important contribution to expanding oil output, particularly in the medium term, through improvements in the efficiency of exploitation and timely investments in existing producing fields. However, this would require policy measures to improve the profitability of the industry and thereby its capacity to finance necessary investments and maintenance.

9.7   The sector has a large investment program under consideration at present. In most instances, the proof that these plans are economically and financially viable are not in place. Final decisions on these plans should be deferred until thorough assessments of their economic and commercial viability have been determined. It would seem wise for the Government as far as possible to seek to minimize the exposure of the public sector to the capital risk entailed in most of the proposals likely to be implemented, particularly where they are export oriented. One of the best tests of the likely viability of projects is whether investors are willing to risk their own capital in them.

9.8   Given the existing limited capacity in the country to assess the commercial aspects of export-oriented investments, the Government should seek to build up as rapidly as possible a central core of such expertise. In the interim, it would need to retain the services of independent expert advisors to assist it in screening, packaging and negotiating significant investment proposals in the sector.

9.9   The productivity of key sector assets, particularly in the oil and power subsectors, has been declining seriously in the recent past as a result of inadequate cash generation or retention for reinvestment by enterprises. The Government needs to take urgent measures to strengthen the profitability of sector enterprises to avoid the premature loss of sector capacity. In the interim, given the backlog of work that needs to be undertaken, these remedial investments should have priority over capacity expansions or new investments in the allocation of investment resources. The Government might well seek to attract foreign investment in the restoration of the condition of sector assets, particularly in the export-oriented sector. This would allow public sector resources to be freed for other, for example, the social-sectors.

Natural Gas Sector

Supply Issues

9.10   The recent history of natural gas production is illustrated in Figure 9.1. Production of natural gas increased consistently from 1966 to 1989, when it reached a peak of 89.9 billion cubic meters. Thereafter, production declined slowly to 84.3 billion cubic meters in 1991 and then fell sharply to 64 billion cubic meters in 1992. The decline in production reflects a shift in extraction policy from one based on exploiting the full production potential of the system to one driven by an aggressive objective to maximize unit prices and total revenues from gas exports. There was a serious dispute with the Ukraine when it refused to pay the higher price requested by Turkmenistan. Shipments to the Ukraine ceased from March to October 1992. Production is expected to increase only marginally to about 68 bcm in 1993, largely as a result of reduced export deliveries in the second half of the year. The reduction in exports reflects interruption to deliveries as a result of payments disputes and gas transport problems.

Natural Gas Reserves: Level and Composition

9.11   Turkmenistan ranks high in the world in the potential occurrence of natural gas. Total indicative resources of natural gas have been estimated at about 14 trillion cubic meters (tcm) based on the analysis of the country's geologic structures. As of January 1, 1993, a total of about 4.0 tcm of non-associated gas had been identified in the country through exploration activities. Currently, total remaining identified reserves of natural gas amount to 2.7 tcm following the cumulative production of 1.3 tcm since the beginning of large scale gas production in the country in the early 1960s. Of the remaining reserves of natural gas, an estimated 1.3 tcm or about 15 years of production at current production levels are assessed by Turkmengeologia (the Government's geological agency) as capable of being produced on an economic basis (i.e proven and probable).[2] The balance of remaining reserves are awaiting full appraisal through additional drilling and testing to determine whether they can be exploited commercially under current economic and technical conditions. About 75% of remaining reserves are in developed fields. However, at present, there are 25 producing fields, five of which account for 50% of total remaining reserves and over 50% of current gas production. The balance of the country's remaining identified reserves are distributed amongst 122 relatively small fields.

Constraints on Future Gas Production

9.12   There are two key potential constraints on future gas production capacity: (i) the technical capacity of the domestic gas producing industry to appraise and develop reserves on an efficient basis; (ii) the financial and technical capacity of the country to replenish and maintain an adequate level of reserves.

9.13   While the total remaining identified reserves (2.7 trillion cubic meters) can sustain production at recent levels until the mid-2010s, the capacity of the domestic industry to develop the remaining identified and undeveloped reserves appears limited. In

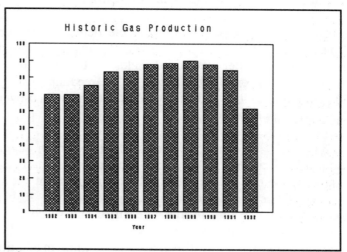

Figure 9.1

particular, at its current rate of productivity in drilling appraisal and development wells and with its complement of drilling rigs, the gas production enterprise can complete about 40 wells per annum. Compounding the problem of low productivity, the local industry does not have, at present, the requisite equipment or experience to drill in the high-pressure zones characteristic of most of the recent additions to identified reserves.

9.14   In addition to its limited capacity to develop identified reserves, the country has been experiencing a progressive liquidation of its base of identified reserves in the last decade. From 1986 to 1990, cumulative production exceeded additions to identified reserves by about 200 billion cubic meters. This deterioration in reserves replacement reflects an end to the period of easy gas discoveries

2.   In the system of reserves classification of Turkmenistan and the FSU, these reserves are termed Category A, B, and C1 reserves.

in Turkmenistan. The local exploration organizations have been encountering increasing difficulties in identifying and appraising geologically complex structures located in deeper horizons than encountered in the earlier period of petroleum exploration. The technology and know-how for effective exploration in such conditions is not generally available in the former Soviet Union. If this trend of poor reserves replacement continues, the industry will be effectively liquidated within the next 30 years.

The Prospects for Future Gas Production

9.15   Assuming that no significant policy or management actions are taken to improve the sector's operating performance, a likely future gas production profile is illustrated in Figure 9.2. The profile is based primarily on a field-by-field analysis of production from the producing gas fields in the Amu Darya basin, the base of the country's non-associated gas production.[3] This profile indicates that the country's main developed reserves will be depleted by around 2020. Total captured gas production will decline to 46 billion cubic meters by 2000, and slump to 23 billion cubic meters by 2005. Based on trends in domestic gas consumption, the exportable gas surplus will drop to 24 billion cubic meters by 2000 and there will be no exportable surplus by 2013. At that point, under this scenario, the country will need to import gas for domestic consumption.

9.16   Instead of allowing the depletion of existing producing fields and of its production capacity, Turkmenistan has the option of bringing into production currently proven and probable reserves in the other smaller developed fields. However, this will not make a material difference to the sustainability of exportable output in the medium term. Total gas production would decline to about 60 bcm by 2000 and 23 bcm by 2008 and the switch-over in domestic self-sufficiency in gas would be deferred by two years.

9.17   Production patterns could be further augmented by bringing identified possible reserves and newly discovered reserves into production. In particular, progressive development of about 1.0 bcm (equivalent to double the present discovered but not yet appraised reserves in non-producing fields) by the end of this decade could sustain production at 70 bcm per year until about the mid-2010s. This scenario would require further intensified and successful exploration efforts. Given domestic drilling productivity and capacity, field development on this scale would require external contracting to execute and would cost about an estimated US$3.0 billion in addition to substantial additional costs in finding new reserves. While this cost would represent only about 30% of the projected cumulative value-added of the natural gas sector over the next four years, much of this value-added is pre-empted by taxes for use in other sectors of the economy or appear to be earmarked for investments in more downstream activities in the gas subsector. It may be neither feasible nor economically prudent to re-invest such magnitude of resources in the gas sector. This scenario would thus require large scale foreign participation in exploration, development and financing in the gas sector.

---

3.   The balance of natural gas production emanates currently from associated gas fields in the western part of the country; production from this source is projected to amount to no more than 4 billion cubic meters a year. The production profile excludes the potential for greater production as a result of actual gas production that was significantly lower than the production potential in 1992.

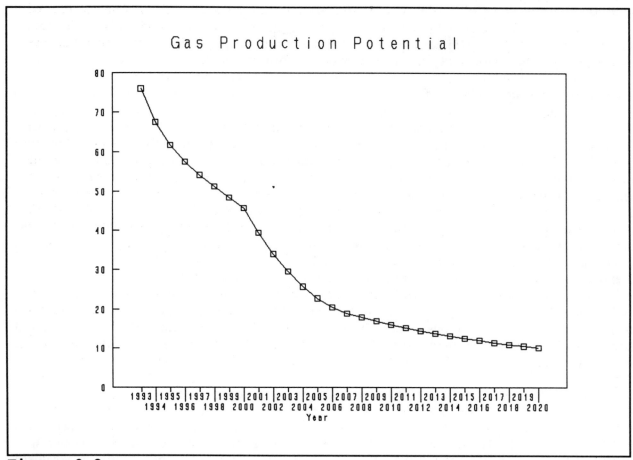

Figure 9.2

Government Gas Sector Development Strategy

9.18   The Government recognizes the impending crisis in the country's gas production potential and is engaged currently in formulating a revised long-term strategy for addressing the key underlying issues facing the domestic industry. Central to the evolving strategy is a large emphasis in attracting foreign technology and capital to relieve the key potential constraints on gas production capacity.   This strategy would need to address effectively four areas in order to set the basis for achieving its main objective: (i) the establishment of a clear and comprehensive legal, contractual and taxation framework to assure potential investors of a stable operating and commercial climate for their activities in the oil and gas sector; (ii) the required changes in the system of promotion of the country's petroleum resources from the one currently used to promote foreign participation in relatively small low-risk development and rehabilitation ventures in the oil sector to one more appropriate for high risk and large-scale exploration and development activities; (iii) the arrangements for pricing and marketing gas and the terms of access by third parties to the existing gas transmission network within the country; and, (iv) the Government's strategy for addressing the key export market risks in the short-term and for establishing alternative infrastructure access to export markets in the medium to long-term. The extensive experience of the World Bank in the development of natural gas resources suggests that, in the absence of a clear policy on the commercial aspects of gas production, promotional initiatives in gas-prone territories are unlikely to succeed.

9.19   Based on a revised strategy for development of the gas sector, the Government expects gas production to be progressively expanded to about 210 bcm per annum by 2006. This is a very high case scenario and would require all the key elements identified above to be in place in the very near term. In addition, it would require a highly successful outcome for investment promotion and exploration activities; a large growth in external gas markets; and solid improvement in Turkmenistan's competitive advantage in such markets. The implicit export market demand is very optimistic. Currently, the market for natural gas in Europe is estimated at about 350 bcm, of which Turkmenistan has a share of 3 percent. Projections of future growth in demand in the European market vary widely with the most optimistic indicating total demand for gas of 670 bcm by 2010. Turkmenistan's market share would need to increase to about 20% in order to absorb its exportable surplus over and above the demand from countries in the former Soviet Union. This would be extremely difficult to achieve given the level of competition from Russia and elsewhere. Finally, the gas investment program both to develop wells and create the infrastructure necessary for expanded exports is extremely large. Such a program of intensive development would cost at least US$20 billion spread over six to eight years. It may be too optimistic to expect the required magnitude of capital inflows over such a short period time or the ability of the economy to develop the large absorptive capacity to make such an inflow effective. Nonetheless, given the country's favorable geology, it is clear that with a well-articulated strategy for addressing the technical, market and financial constraints on gas production capacity, gas production could be maintained at recent levels in the medium term and significantly expanded in the longer term if prospective market conditions permit.

Gas Exports

9.20   No meaningful data on export patterns are available for the period prior to Turkmenistan's independence in 1991. The regional gas supply system was operated as an integrated organization with the primary emphasis on the optimization of gas flows over the system as a whole. Inter-republican gas trade reflected physical flows between contiguous republics. With gas priced on a uniform pan-territorial basis, there was little incentive in any event for the separation of physical gas flows and transport cost optimization from sales contracts. Under this system all Turkmenistan gas exports were assigned to Uzbekistan, which was self-sufficient in gas.

9.21   Turkmenistan started negotiating distinct gas sales, swapping and transport contracts in 1992 based on an allocation of the regional market by Gasprom in 1991. Under this allocation, gas exports from Turkmenistan accounted for about 27 percent of all gas exports by regional producers. More important, Turkmenistan gas exports accounted for about 65 percent of the apparent consumption of gas in the Central Asian and trans-Caucasus republics, excluding Uzbekistan. In addition, Turkmenistan supplied about 25 percent of the Ukraine's apparent gas Without these supplies, Gasprom would not have been able to expand gas exports outside the region to 104 billion cubic meters by 1991.

9.22   For exports outside of the region, Turkmenistan is allocated a quota based on its share of total production within the former Soviet Union. This quota amounted to 11.3 billion cubic meters in 1992 based on the country's relative share of 11 percent of regional natural gas production in 1991 and conforms to Gasprom's indicative allocation of intra-and extra-regional exports. The extra-regional export allocation is swapped with the Russian Federation for gas exports from Siberia.

9.23   The basis for allocating exports outside the region is essentially arbitrary in the sense that a number of other equally defensible ways of sharing an external market could be devised. One that is preferred by Turkmenistan is the allocation of exports to hard-currency markets based on relative shares of total gas exports by the producing republics. Using this basis would give Turkmenistan a hard-currency export allocation of 27 percent, or 27 billion cubic meters, based on exports for 1991. Gasprom of Russia has indicated, however, its strong opposition to increases in the absolute level of Turkmenistan's allocation. Thus, in the short to medium term, the prospects are limited for increasing exports (notional or actual) outside of the system. Turkmenistan not only depends on Gasprom of Russia for infrastructure access but is also totally reliant on Gasprom for sales and transport negotiations and contracting. One key risk factor for Turkmenistan regional gas exports is the possible impact of developments in the Russian domestic gas market on regional gas supplies. The domestic demand for natural gas in Russia is expected to decline significantly by 1996 as a result of economic pricing of gas supplies and industrial restructuring. The potential decline in demand has been projected as large as 200 billion cubic meters (bcm). If the anticipated restructuring in the Russian gas market actually occurs, a considerable volume of incremental gas supplies is expected to be released for export to the region. This eventually would probably reduce demand for Turkmenistan gas in the region as well as exports to outside the region. However, it should be noted that there is increasing, if implicit, cooperation in pricing between Turkmenistan and Gasprom, the effect of which may be to reduce competition on supply and raise prices to offset the impact on volumes.

9.24   Despite this outlook, Turkmenistan may well be able to improve the prospects for changing the allocation or limiting declines in its export market share by developing its own capacity to market its gas to Europe and to negotiate appropriate sales contracts that, for example, shift the responsibility for arranging transportation from itself to third parties that have greater negotiating leverage with the Gasprom of Russia system. The country would, however, require considerable external consultancy, advisory and training assistance to develop such a capacity.

9.25   With possible exports outside of the region constrained by competitive considerations by Gasprom, Turkmenistan exports have become increasingly defined by attainable prices, the payment capacity of potential importers and Turkmenistan expectations as to the direction of future prices. At the beginning of 1992, export prices to countries outside of the former Soviet Union were set at US$75 per 1 million cubic meters fob Uzghorod on the Ukrainian-Slovakia border. Reflecting the underlying allocation of ex-CMEA markets to Turkmenistan, 87 percent of deliveries were payable in convertible currency, with the balance to be settled by barter of goods. Gas transport tariffs were set on a one-year basis at R1,000 per million cubic meters plus a charge of 1.5 billion cubic meters of gas in kind (to be subtracted from the export allocation) for compressor fuel.

9.26   In contrast, prices for the former Soviet Union were established at the start of 1992 at R870 per million cubic meters at the Turkmenistan border for settlement in rubles except in the case of Armenia, which was to be supplied on the basis of barter. Similar to exports to the former Soviet Union, gas was provided in kind for transport fuel. The contract prices for former Soviet Union exports were changed in July 1992 to offset the severe erosion in the price of exports as a result of a substantial depreciation of the ruble and to differentiate between different markets, principally on their ability to pay for imports.

Box 9.1
The Utilization of Gas

The recent pattern of utilization of natural gas produced in Turkmenistan is shown in Figure 9.2 below. Large-scale production of natural gas in Turkmenistan was developed primarily to meet the industrial and power-generation needs of the more industrialized countries within the former Soviet Union. As a consequence, the industry has been highly export oriented with exports accounting for more than 90 percent of total production. Domestic natural gas utilization is dominated by the power sector, which accounts for around 57 percent of domestic consumption. The power sector is also the only significant gas-based exporting industry, with about 35 percent of its net output exported to neighboring countries. The balance of domestic gas consumption is more or less evenly distributed among residential use, district heating and industry and commerce.

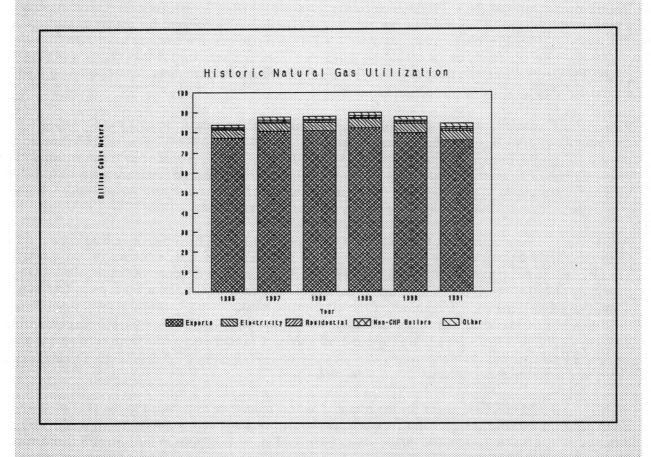

9.27   In January 1993, the export pricing basis was revised. Export prices to the former Soviet Union republics were again set on a uniform basis (at the Turkmenistan border) at 60 percent of the price of exports to areas outside of the former Soviet Union, based on an exchange rate for inter-republican trade of R400 to US$1. Prices are subject to change on a quarterly basis to reflect changes in the exchange rate and were changed in July 1993 to reflect an exchange rate of R800 to US$1. Exports to outside the former Soviet Union are priced at $80 per million cubic meter at Uzghorod. Transport charges for both categories of exports were set in January 1993 at R180 per thousand cubic meter per 100 kilometers with an underlying initial exchange rate of R400 to US$1 but have subsequently been revised to R980 per 1000 cubic meters per 100 kilometer subject. The revision reflects a change in the exchange rate and a decision to increase tariffs for transport services towards "world market" levels.

9.28   Turkmenistan's gas export pricing strategy has been dominated by one objective: to achieve progressive parity in pricing between exports to republics within the former Soviet Union and outside the former Soviet Union with settlement in convertible currency. The original goal of the Government was to achieve parity in prices by January 1993. Achievement of this objective proved elusive in 1992. However, toward the end of 1992, Gasprom of Russia adopted a much more aggressive pricing policy toward the former Soviet Union republics, in particular, Ukraine. Turkmenistan was able to speed up the rate of adjustment of its prices by linking its pricing strategy explicitly with that adopted by Gasprom of Russia.

9.29   While pricing gas uniformly across all export markets is simple and attractive, it is not necessarily an optimal policy. First, gas prices in the individual markets are shaped by different competitive factors. In particular, gas prices are determined by the price of close energy substitutes, mostly heavy fuel oil or various grades of gas oil. The prices of these substitutes are in turn determined by a combination of regulatory controls and market forces that varies dramatically from country to country. Pricing on a uniform basis runs the risk of undermining the competitiveness of Turkmenistan's gas exports in some export markets. The loss of export markets could constitute a serious loss of revenues to the Turkmenistan economy if there are no alternative export markets for such output and existing effective prices are greater than the economic value of gas. This is, to some extent, the case at the moment. Second while the competitiveness of Turkmenistan gas in export markets depends on its price relative to energy substitutes, Turkmenistan should be interested most in how much it gets for its exports at its border. The difference between these two prices is the cost of transport. This cost varies significantly from republic to republic. Reconciling the objective of maximizing revenues to the country and protecting the competitiveness of its gas implies accepting different prices at the Turkmenistan border for different republics depending on transport costs and domestic market conditions. This should apply as long as the revenue earned at the border is greater than the economic value of gas.

Gas Pricing Issues

9.30   Turkmenistan has already encountered significant problems in implementing its export pricing strategy. When the initial price increases were implemented, transmission and distribution entities in the importing republics proved unable to pay for delivered gas as domestic energy prices lagged significantly behind the border price of gas from Turkmenistan. As a result, the level of accounts receivable on export trade grew dramatically. At the same time, the importing countries found it increasingly difficult to finance the arrears of these enterprises as their external trade accounts and access to ruble balances deteriorated. But for political and economic reasons, Turkmenistan proved reluctant, aside from one or two dramatic cases, to interrupt supplies by substantial amounts.

9.31   As a result of this gas trade financing problem, the objective of conducting gas trade within the region in convertible currency has been practically abandoned, while trading has been switched largely from a ruble (monetary) basis to a clearing (essentially barter) basis. While all inter-former Soviet Union gas trade (except with Armenia) was to be settled in cash under the initial sales contracts for 1992, around 87 percent of contracted deliveries in 1993 are for settlement by clearing. Barter constitutes an inefficient basis for trading and a substantial deterrent to an effective national savings and investment strategy owing to a strong imperative to take goods irrespective of prevailing needs. While it is difficult to quantify, the effective price of gas under such a trading regime is probably substantially less than the notional price. Aside from the inherent problems of barter transactions, the country has been experiencing serious problems of non-performance of importers on barter transactions. As of November 30, 1993, the level of receivables for gas exports to the FSU was about US$0.9 billion equivalent, equal to about 40 percent of the value of gas exports (to the FSU). About 85 percent of this amount represented arrears in delivery of goods in exchange for gas.

Planned Diversification of Gas Use and Exports

9.32   In the medium term, the Government plans to overcome the constraints on the country's export of gas in two ways: (1) by developing alternative pipelines for access to existing and new hard-currency markets; and (2) diversifying into gas-based chemicals where transportation constraints are perceived as much less binding. The Government has already engaged consultants to review routing options, tentative costs and likely end market demand, competition and prices for a pipeline system to Europe through Turkey. However, while it addresses some commercial issues, the emphasis of this review is primarily technical. Until detailed market studies are undertaken, the conclusions of this study should be considered highly preliminary and cannot serve as a basis for investment or financing decisions. Other routes under consideration include a southern route to Pakistan through Afghanistan, and plans a pipeline to China and liquefaction facilities for onward export of liquefied natural gas (LNG) to Japan.

9.33   The initial indications are that an alternative transport system to European markets would cost within a range of US$4 billion to US$8 billion depending on routing, length and capacity. Given the likely investment size, the many combinations of possible markets and routes, and the economic and financial risks inherent in large fixed installations, the Government should conduct a detailed technical and commercial feasibility study of all promising choices before deciding on an option to be pursued. Also, it is unlikely that there will be any interest on the part either of potential external investors in a new pipeline system or of importers of gas unless the reserves position is assured. An appropriate gas exploration promotion strategy would need to be devised if export route diversification is to be a viable proposition. Finally, preliminary analysis suggests that, on the basis of the projected cost range for investments in alternative pipeline systems to European markets and existing prices, the effective netbacks are only marginally better than the notional amounts currently obtained in the former Soviet Union. Since these markets are likely to be substitutional given gas production constraints in the medium term, the Government should also carefully consider the options of improving price and settlement prospects in the former Soviet Union markets as opposed to assuming the additional risks of sizable infrastructure investment.

9.34   For diversification into petrochemicals, the Government's preferred option is the development of natural gas-based polyethylene production. A polyethylene project (200,000-ton capacity) is currently under detailed study. In addition to the production of granules for export, this project is envisaged as providing the basis for backward integration into domestic plastics manufacture. The preliminary results of the feasibility study indicate a likely cost of US$1.2 billion for the facility. Based on the assumptions of the study, the financial returns to this project are significantly less than should be expected from a capital-intensive investment in a highly cyclical industry. In particular, even if the natural gas input is free, the return to the processing activity will be marginal. The project under such conditions is a poor financial and economic option compared with keeping the proven gas fields designated to supply it dormant or exporting gas to the former Soviet Union.

9.35   The manufacture of polyethylene is an established process, and the viability of investments in it depend critically on commercial factors such as the attractiveness of the intended markets, the potential competitiveness of an entrant and the cost effectiveness of procurement arrangements for equipment, plant and process licenses. The Government should review these factors in detail before making an investment commitment. The Government should also consider alternatives to a direct and sizeable public investment in a project of this nature in order to reduce its capital exposure and risk while securing the benefit of providing an economic return to its gas reserves and the possibility of local access to inputs for downstream industrial processing. Finally, the choice of polyethylene as the project of choice appears to be largely historically determined. Other gas-processing options may prove to be equally or more attractive. The Government should consider undertaking a focused study of gas-utilization options to identify alternatives or future avenues for gas processing.

Domestic Gas Utilization

9.36   Domestic consumption of gas represents only about 10 percent of domestic production, with households accounting for about 12 percent of this consumption or about 1 percent of national gas production. Prior to independence, the expansion of the domestic distribution network was restricted by lack of funds and a policy emphasis on gas exports to the more industrialized republics in the Union. One of the Government's major policy objectives now is to expand the network to achieve universal coverage of households by 1996 from a current coverage of 52 percent of all households (an estimated 88 percent of urban and 22 percent of rural households). This is likely to cost about US$1 billion equivalent, about 30 percent of which will consist of the cost of imported inputs. The average incremental capital cost of gas supplies to household with this magnitude of investment will be about US$100 per 1,000 cubic meters and significantly higher for connections in the more remote and less densely populated settlements.

9.37   While it is implementing this expansion of the distribution system, the Government is also planning on a significant program of liquid petroleum gas (LPG) production to substitute for imports. Imported LPG is used predominantly by the household sector particularly in rural areas where it is a primary source of energy for around 77 percent of households. There is an established infrastructure for its distribution, and its production appears to be not only very import competitive but significantly less than the average unit incremental cost of supply of piped natural gas. However, while LPG may constitute an important investment option for the Government in reducing the cost of distribution expansion, any such investment would be a waste of resources if universal access to natural gas is going to be provided in any event (as appears to be the case). Important benefits will be gained by the economy if a clear policy is established on the role of LPG in the energy sector. The definition of such a policy would require detailed analysis of the potential energy requirements in rural settlements, the appropriate scale of investment in LPG recovery systems and the potential for savings in investments in distribution system expansion by the Government. This is the type of investigation that can be effectively undertaken within the framework of a comprehensive gas utilization study.

Investment Needs

9.38   Capital expenditures related to gas production and transmission activities are expected to amount to about US$100 million between 1993 and 1996. Most of this will be in conjunction with the limited ongoing drilling program. To maintain its medium-to long-term production capacity, the industry would need to invest around $3 billion in appraising and developing identified reserves in the next 5 to 10 years in addition to stepping up its exploration efforts. Given the uncertainties surrounding Government policy for attracting potential external operators into the sector and the existing export markets, it is unlikely that large-scale foreign investment would be forthcoming in the near future. It is also clear that given the uncertainties of the only available export markets (the former Soviet Union), it would be imprudent for the Government to devote large resources soon to gas field development.

9.39   The timing of significant investments in alternative pipeline systems or major petrochemical diversification is uncertain. However, while the incentives for such investments may be strong toward the end of the period covered by this medium-term scenario, particularly if the projected significant increases in exportable regional gas surpluses materialize, these investments will be beyond the capacity of the country to finance. In addition, there is little prospect of any investor being willing to finance such investments unless the outlook for gas production improves. In summary, the country may need to invest a total of at least US$8 billion in gas fields development and alternative export pipelines by the end of this decade to ensure the future of the gas industry. This can only be financed with significant external investor participation.

9.40   In the medium to long term, the realization of the potential for the sector to be the motor for the rapid transformation of the economy will depend on substantial investments to regenerate its production potential and, possibly, to gain access to new markets with few of the constraints on paying for imports facing the traditional markets. Given the claims of the Government on the sector's cash generation and the composition of such cash flow, the sector cannot finance such investments on its own. Again, the effective management of the surpluses that are generated by the sector in the next few years would be crucial to managing any future decline in gas export revenues and to establishing a degree of creditworthiness that would be crucial to mobilizing the magnitude of external financing that would be required to implement these investments.

The Oil Sector
Oil Reserves and Production Potential

9.41   Turkmenistan has substantial, if latent, oil production potential. Proven and probable oil reserves are estimated at 1.1 billion tons and ultimately recoverable oil from these reserves is estimated at between 315 million and 420 million tons (2.2 billion to 2.9 billion barrels).

9.42   Reflecting the general crisis in exploration activity, the pace of reserves replacement in the industry has declined sharply in the last five years, with net additions to reserves falling from 112 million tons in the period 1981--86 to 47 million tons in 1987--92. However, in contrast with the natural gas industry, the production potential from the existing oil reserves is substantial. The current proven reserves-to-production ratio is at least 60 based on recent production and a conservative assessment of commercially recoverable oil reserves.

9.43   Reserves-to-production (R-P) ratios of this magnitude are highly anomalous in countries with significant development financing needs. More typical ratios are in the range of 12 to 20. In the case of Turkmenistan, the high R-P ratio primarily reflects an unsatisfactory rate of exploitation and involuntary conservation of reserves. The involuntary conservation of oil reserves is counter to the country's best economic interest. Turkmenistan has substantial and economically worthwhile development needs. As long as the return to investments in satisfying these needs is greater than the expected increase in the future price of oil, deferral of development of economically viable oil reserves leads to a loss to the country's economy. Given the amount of potential incremental production involved from fuller exploitation of available reserves, the loss for Turkmenistan is substantial. For example, a reduction in the R-P ratio from 62 to 40 would generate additional gross export revenues of US$280 million per annum at present prices. Deferring production at the rate implied by this lower R-P ratio for five years will lead to a loss of at least US$400 million in foregone benefits from early use of these revenues. Such a loss can only be offset if oil prices grow at more than 10 percent per annum in real terms. Such growth is highly unlikely.

History and Performance

9.44   Recent crude oil production is illustrated in Figure 9.3.   Crude oil production in Turkmenistan has been in secular decline since the 1970s when output was as high as 15 million tons (300,000 barrels per day). Recent production (including gas condensate) has stagnated around 5.2 million tons (104,000 barrels per day).

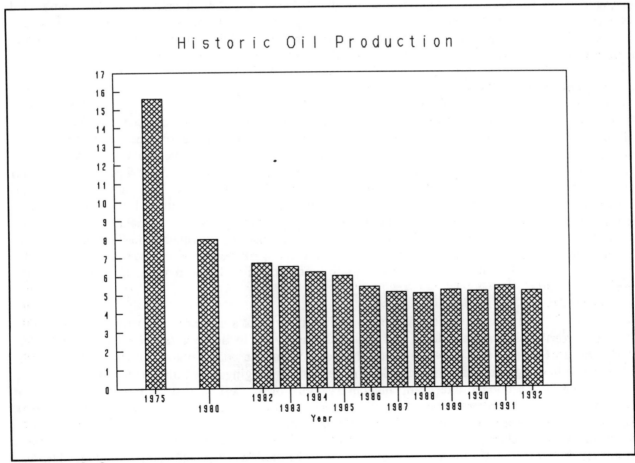

Figure 9.3

9.45   Present oil production is characterized by extremely low per-well productivity caused by a combination of poor well-completion practices, poor reservoir-management practices and sustained production from wells that are beyond their economic limits. At prevailing production rates and assuming international unit costs and output prices, more than 50 percent of active wells do not appear to justify expenditure on routine maintenance operations such as workovers. The underlying causes of widespread poor performance of producing wells, other than depletion of reservoirs beyond their economic limits, appear to need careful and urgent examination.

9.46   The financial performance of the oil industry has been highly unsatisfactory. While the costs of key operating inputs such as electricity are heavily subsidized, crude oil prices have been subject to stringent controls. Limited financial information made available to recent Bank missions indicates that for the first nine months of 1992, the onshore enterprise generated R1.4 billion in profits before drilling operations, or the equivalent of US$0.50 per barrel of oil produced. In contrast with the recent past, Turkmenistan now has to import practically all its maintenance and investment requirements for the industry at world market prices (explicitly or implicitly). Given this situation, the industry doesn't generate enough cash to adequately maintain wells and surface facilities and to expand field development programs that would sustain or expand production.

9.47   Reflecting a history of poor financial and operating performance, the attrition rate of producing wells has been high, with about 411 wells (16 percent of all wells in non depleted fields) idled for lack of maintenance as at November 1992. Compounding this problem, drilling productivity has been comparably low, leading to a substantial backlog in-fill development of existing fields and the development of new fields.

Strengthening Sector Performance

9.48   In the short run, the Government would need to address the industry's underlying lack of financial resources for essential maintenance activities in order stemming the declining trend in production. The Government increased the price of crude oil significantly in February 1993 from R2,000 per ton (US$5 equivalent per ton when set in August 1992 and equivalent to about 6 percent of the fob export price) to R15,000 per ton ($21, or 25 percent of the fob export price), but this price hike is not enough for producers to generate sufficient cash to finance imports of equipment and supplies. However, irrespective of the actions taken on pricing, the size of the backlog of work accumulated would require more resources than the capacity of the oil-producing enterprises could generate in the short term. In addition, to be done effectively, both remedial operations and workovers may require significant upgrades of technology and techniques. To reverse declining production will thus require considerable foreign capital and technology.

9.49   Notwithstanding the need for and the Government's interest in attracting foreign capital, the institutional structures and legal and financial framework to do so effectively are absent. The management of promotional activities needs changes to eliminate potential areas of conflicts of interest between the financial interest of the outside firm currently managing such activities for the Government and the long-term economic interest of the country. One of the best ways to eliminate this conflict of interest is for the management of all promotional work to revert to the Government. The Government would need external advisory assistance and training of its staff to manage such an activity effectively. A petroleum law to clarify the respective role and obligations of the Government, its operating agencies in the sector and potential external investors has yet to be drafted. A global natural resources law was recently enacted by the Government. This law is not appropriate, however, to the needs of the oil industry, and petroleum should ideally be removed from its ambit or, at the least, the areas of conflict between this law and provisions more appropriately tailored to the oil industry resolved explicitly. Also, the potential tax and financial arrangements governing the industry are unclear and would require some form of codification. Finally, large scale oil exploration and development would be contingent on the availability of adequate transport access to foreign markets. Work on defining possible export pipeline routes and financing strategies for such a project is only at a very early stage. Existing rail and sea (Caspian Sea) transport route options can·only handle very limited incremental production and at relatively high unit costs.

Foreign Investment in the Oil Sector

9.50   Foreign investment in the oil sector currently consists of three joint ventures with Turkmeneft, the onshore oil-producing enterprise. The contracts were awarded in January 1993 following a competitive tender based on signature bonuses paid beyond a minimum reservation amount. Signature bonuses paid (or payable) for the awarded contracts amounted to $65 million. The expected production performance of the three joint ventures based on analysis of limited but publicly available financial and geological information is summarized in Table 9.1.

9.51   O   i   l production from existing discovered fields is expected to be more than doubled by 1996. Total domestic crude production will then be equal to about 190,000 barrels per day assuming no precipitous decline in production from non joint venture fields compared with about 91,000 barrels per day currently. The   joint   ventures   are

Table 9.1
Incremental Production by Joint-Venture (JV) Projects

	1994	1996	1998	2000	2005
Production (mln tons)	1.3	5.2	8.1	6.3	4.4
Percentage of 1992 production	28.0	111.0	172.0	134.0	94.0

Source: World Bank Staff estimates.

expected to generate total discounted financial benefits (at 15 percent) over a 22-year period of about US$2 billion, or an average annual amount of US$320 million, assuming no upside to the reserves potential and the valuation of domestic sales of crude oil at the net export price of crude oil. About 76 percent of this sum (or US$240 million) will accrue to the country.

9.52   Given the above, the local joint-venture partner, Turkmeneft, should generate enough to finance most remaining oil fields remedial activities, given that most of its share of joint venture production will be exported, and if its share of production destined for the domestic market (and its production from non joint venture operations) are properly priced.

9.53   However, the benefits to the country identified above will only be fully realized if the joint venture contracts are effectively managed and facilitated. Delays in the startup of productive activities will reduce the returns to the joint venture foreign partners. Nonetheless, their returns may still be satisfactory, given their very high prospective returns (post-tax returns to their minimum required investments, including signature bonuses, are estimated at 40 percent and 60 percent, significantly greater than prospective returns for much higher risk petroleum operations). However, a decline in their total financial benefits from the projects will be mirrored by a corresponding decline in the value of the benefits accruing to the country. For example, a two-year delay in the startup of production activities will reduce the value of the benefits to the country by an average of US$64 million per annum. There is little experience in joint venture contract administration and facilitation in Turkmeneft or in the Government to ensure the minimal slippage in the agreed work program of the joint ventures. This is one area where the Government should seek to strengthen domestic capacity.

Refined Products

9.54   The country has two refineries with total effective capacity of about 8.2 million tons of crude oil. One refinery, dedicated to processing domestic crude, has matching capacity for the current level of crude production. The other refinery was recently commissioned and was sited to process crude oil from neighboring republics and Siberia. The processing efficiency of the domestic market-oriented refinery is low with high fuel input and high process losses. The refinery was starved of funds during most of the Soviet Union days, forcing it to defer or abandon the completion of major upgrading and rehabilitation work. Its current profitability, based on a fixed margin over crude oil and processing costs, is still very inadequate for it to start redressing the past neglect. The export-oriented refinery is currently facing severe problems in financing or obtaining crude oil inputs, which are imported at between 60 percent and 80 percent of world market prices. Its medium-term export prospects are clouded by the fact that its configuration leaves it with a basic facility with a high yield of low-value residual products. It will need major investments to upgrade its product slate to an attractive one. This should not be undertaken until its competitive prospects are carefully determined.

9.55   Domestic oil product demand is dominated by gasoline and diesel. While the domestic refinery produces enough diesel to meet domestic demand and to generate an exportable surplus, production of gasoline is now nearly outstripped by demand and has to be supplemented periodically by output from the export-oriented refinery. The current (August 1993) gasoline price at the refinery is set at about 46 percent of world market prices. Unless urgent action is taken to raise this price to encourage efficient consumption, the country could become a sizable gasoline importer in the medium term.

Power Sector

Structure and Operations

9.56   Turkmenistan has six generating stations operating within an integrated grid with total installed capacity of 2,548 megawatts. The system is interconnected with the power systems of Uzbekistan, southern Kazakhstan, the Kyrgyz Republic and Tajikistan within the Central Asia Integrated Power System (CAIPS). There is a small inter-tie with the power system of Afghanistan. The system developed rapidly over the last two decades based on the country's natural gas reserves. Household connection is near universal. Reserve capacity within the system is substantial with domestic peak load demand of about 1,500 megawatts. Total annual generation in 1992 was 13.1 billion kilowatt hours, about 4.0 billion kilowatt hours of which was exported to Kazakhstan under a bilateral agreement. The system operates with a reasonable degree of reliability, with transmission losses reported at less than 10 percent of net generation. However, average unit capacity factors in the system were only 54 percent in 1991, and the system is encountering significant problems with acquiring spare parts and supplies from the original equipment manufacturers in Russia and Ukraine.

Financial Viability

9.57   Prevailing tariffs for commercial and industrial customers, representing about 80 percent of demand, are low, at an average of about R8 per Kilowatt hour (56 percent of the estimated economic cost of electricity in Turkmenistan and 20 percent of international rates) but are a significant improvement on the position of late 1992, when they were less than 2 percent of comparable international rates. Tariffs for households, which were pegged at R0.08 per kilowatt hour throughout 1992, have been significantly eroded from 1 January 1993 under a Government program of free or heavily subsidized provision of basic utility services. The system's financial viability depends on two factors: 1) the supply of gas as a fuel input at a low effective rate of about R3 per kilowatt hour; and 2) the export of electricity at a rate of about US 3 cents per kilowatt hour.

9.58   Notwithstanding the favorable effect of these factors on its current profitability, the system is not viable in the long run under the present policy. Cash generation based on this cost structure and export revenues will not be sufficient to support extensive capital replacements. Without changes in the structure and level of prices, the system will be progressively decapitalized in the long run unless the Government subsidizes its investment requirements. The policy of virtual free of charge pricing for electricity would tend to accelerate the system's problems by (i) increasing load demand, limiting the scope for effective load management and thereby hastening the need for system expansion; whilst (ii) reducing reserves committed to earning higher export revenues.

Investment Plans

9.59   Despite the large reserve of capacity and the poor financial outlook, the system is planning for an expansion in capacity for the domestic market of 860 megawatts by 2000 at an estimated cost of about US$600 million. At present, this investment cannot be supported by anticipated growth in load in the domestic market where electricity demand fell substantially for the first time in 1992 and is not expected (based on the macroeconomic simulations in this report) to increase to 1991 levels before the end of the decade. Moreover, the regional export market is subject to considerable uncertainty with at least one major export-oriented power project in another power-surplus country planned and the system's major customer planning on rationalizing its power system to reduce and ultimately eliminate the need for imports. The Government should consider deferring the project until its viability as a least-cost source of needed power can be established.

9.60   Another investment proposal under consideration is a 900 megawatt system expansion and 200-kilometer transmission line (estimated total cost of $650 million) to supply electricity to Iran. Given the large reserves of the system, other options to meet this potential demand, including diversion of electricity from existing customers, should be considered. In addition, the alternative of supplying gas as well as other options for limiting the potential capital exposure of the country merit careful review before a final decision is made.

Energy Demand

9.61   Despite its relatively low level of industrialization and the lack of heavy industry, in particular, Turkmenistan's per capita energy consumption is very high. At about 3,800 kilograms of oil equivalent (kgOE) per capita, primary energy consumption is comparable to that of the United Kingdom and France, both of which have significantly higher GDPs. The energy intensity of the economy, at

3,000 kilogramsOE/US$000 GDP is significantly higher than in comparable middle-income countries and reflects the extensive availability and subsidized use of gas in the economy.

9.62   Unlike in almost all other republics of the former Soviet Union, overall energy demand in Turkmenistan continued to grow during 1990 and 1991. This growth reflects the relatively moderate reductions in national income, the progressive expansion of domestic supply and capacity and relatively low prices of energy supplies. With the prospect of large erosions in real energy prices over the next few years as a result of Government price control policies and possible expansion of supply, notably the addition of connections to the gas grid, energy demand is not expected to decline in the medium term unless dramatic policy measures are taken to curtail it. Growth in domestic energy demand will accelerate the need for capital investments in the sector. In particular, key sectors like power generation and oil refining are caught between the exigencies of supplying domestic demand and having to export to remain minimally viable. Unconstrained growth in demand can only be satisfied by these sectors through either significant Government subsidies to expand capacity or reductions in their exports and large operational subsidies to stay viable. ·

Energy Prices and Taxation

Pricing

9.63   Turkmenistan has maintained a system of highly centralized control of all domestic energy prices coupled with the administrative allocation of oil products. While prices are set to allow enterprises to cover their operating costs and be nominally profitable, the level of profitability on domestic operations is not large enough to allow for adequate maintenance expenditures and replacement investments. The operating performance of key sector entities with predominantly domestic sales and little or no access to foreign exchange has been deteriorating, and there is a substantial risk that energy supplies will be progressively restricted in the future. One feature of the present pricing framework is that it provides little incentive for the efficient management of enterprises and the efficient use of energy by consumers. Price controls, based on average enterprise operating costs, encourage the cross subsidization and continuation of non viable activities, particularly in the absence of competition or regulatory monitoring of efficiency. This is reinforced by Government policy that directs the cross subsidization of households by industrial customers, notably in the gas and electricity sectors.

9.64   In general, the Government's objective should be to ensure that energy prices fully reflect their cost of supply or, where the resource is easily traded in world or regional markets, their export or import-parity value. (The estimated economic value of key energy resources are provided in Table 9.2 below.) In applying this general principle, a distinction should be drawn between energy resources that can be supplied competitively either by domestic or foreign entities and those that can be supplied only with dedicated infrastructure that would be economically inefficient to duplicate. In the case of Turkmenistan, the latter situation would cover the network industries--electricity and natural gas supply-- which require extensive transmission and distribution systems and enjoy inherently large economies of scale. For these natural monopolies, regulation of prices and the efficiency of service provision would be required. However, the underlying pricing objective should be that prices for supplies to specific classes of consumers should cover the operating cost of such provision plus an appropriate allowance to finance the cost of investments to maintain an acceptable quality and level of service. Regulation would seek to balance the need for protection of consumers with the need to ensure that entities remain commercially viable and can take the actions necessary to promote this.

**Box 9.2
Technical Assistance**

- Development of a petroleum-exploration promotion strategy.

- Preparation of a petroleum law.

- Natural gas export marketing and export sales and transport contracting.

- Review of export pipeline options and advisory support in structuring implementation and financing arrangements for economically viable export pipeline options.

- Assistance in undertaking a detailed assessment of oil reserves production and undeveloped oil reserves, preparation of an oil sector development plan.

- Training in petroleum economics and forms of agreements; and assistance with administration of petroleum contracts.

- Assistance in developing a taxation framework and tax laws for petroleum operations.

9.65   The Government's recently implemented directive that the main natural monopolies in the sector--the power and gas distribution industries--supply electricity and gas on a more or less free-of-charge basis has important policy implications. The policy is based mainly on the position that, given the country's large natural gas potential, the value of the marginal quantities of gas involved is negligible. However, due to the relatively short horizon to the depletion of remaining proven and probable gas reserves, the economic value of gas at the wellhead in Turkmenistan is not trivial. The present value of the cost of offsetting the non availability of gas in the mid-2010s (when, on present consumption trends, production will start falling below domestic demand) through imports of gas or reduced exports of fuel oil is about $13 per 1,000 cubic meters. This cost can be avoided only by reducing gas exports now and forgoing export revenues to defer the depletion of reserves or developing new and large gas fields. The cost of either of these courses of action are also relatively large. Moreover, the costs of the power and gas distribution industries are dominated by capital inputs. These would need to be recovered from the consumers or more generally from public resources if they are to be able to sustain their level of service into the future. Currently, the estimated implicit subsidy for the supply of gas (excluding the economic value of gas) to residential and commercial consumers of gas is $40/per 1,000 cubic meters and $4/1000 cubic meters to industrial customers.[4] This amounts to a total subsidy of about US$100 million per annum. The level of the implicit subsidy will be doubled to an estimated $200 million with the full implementation of the distribution system expansion currently under way and assuming that the present policy of free gas to residential consumers is maintained.

9.66   Clearly, the Government may wish to have services to some classes of residential customers priced at below cost for a defined period of time. However, in order to avoid increasing the

---

4.   The implicit subsidy is defined as the difference between the current price and 1) the current operating costs of the system; plus 2) the annualized cost of the present value of future investments to maintain or expand the capacity of the system.

cost of service to other customers (and impairing their competitiveness) or reducing the efficiency and cost effectiveness with which such targeted services are provided and used, this subsidy should be provided directly by the Government to the consumer or the entity.   In the latter case, this should be accompanied by a detailed agreement on the cost of the service, the level of subsidy and payment procedures.   However, the present and prospective levels of implicit subsidies to domestic gas consumption are very high and, in the context of prospective Government revenues, probably unsustainable.

9.67   For crude oil and oil products, the primary objective should be the progressive adjustment of prices over a short, defined period to import price levels. Initial adjustments should be structured so as to ensure that the oil-producing and refining entities will be sufficiently profitable to cover their maintenance and rehabilitation expenses and capacity-replacement investments.   In the case of oil products, these adjustments should be accompanied by the removal of administrative allocation of products to ensure that products are put to their best use as demonstrated by users' relative willingness to pay. These actions should be complemented by measures to allow domestic distribution of oil products on a competitive basis; competition would ensure that efficiency and profit margins in domestic distribution activities are at reasonable rates. This goal can be achieved by restructuring petroleum product distribution into smaller competing wholesale and retail distribution units, the operation of which may be franchised or fully privatized.

Table 9.2:
Turkmenistan: Domestic Energy Prices

	1991	Nov 1992	August 93	Est. Economic Value[a]
Crude oil (R/ton)				
Producer	70	2,000	22,000	94,000
Refined oil Products (R/ton)[b]				
Gasoline: Domestic	109	5,017	75,300	164,000
Diesel	109	4,634	75,300	164,000
Heavy Fuel Oil	80	3,072	48,500	75,200
Natural gas (R/1000 cubic meters)				
Industry	34	235	770	16,000
Residential	50	150	free	--
Electricity (R/1000 Kwh)				
Industry (<750 Kva)	40	250	8,000	14,200
Residential	40	80	120	--

a/ Estimates as of August 1993.
b/ Ex-refinery; excluding any excise taxes.

Source: Data provided by Turkmengas, Goskomnefteproduct, Turkmenenergo, World Bank staff estimates.

9.68   As long as export prices for products are greater than domestic prices, there will be strong preferences to export compared with selling in the domestic market (see Table 9.2). As long as this exists, there will be a strong rationale for the administrative control of export trade. To avoid this, the Government should also consider creating a mechanism to equalize receipts from domestic and export sales. To ensure appropriate incentives for development of new fields (which would require, in general, prices close to current world market levels to be financially viable), such developments should be exempt from the application of such a claw-back mechanism. A considerable amount of work has been done by the Bank on feasible transitional pricing mechanisms for tradable products like oil, and the Government might benefit from a review of such work and its potential applicability to Turkmenistan.

Sector Taxation

9.69   The general enterprise taxation system produces no serious adverse effects on enterprise performance in the sector. A highly distortionary tax on Turkmengas, designed originally to capture the rent on gas exports, was repealed recently and replaced by a fixed royalty on regional exports. The level of the royalty is appropriate for Turkmengas's circumstances as an operator with more or less fully developed facilities that have been under production for a relatively long period. Indeed, the total tax liability of Turkmengas is relatively light. However, the level of the royalty (22 percent) could prove to be severely distortionary at certain output or price ranges and could be a deterrent to large-scale new investment in the sector.

9.70   While a high level of economic rents has not been a feature of the oil subsector due to the absence of crude oil exports and low domestic crude oil prices, this will change in the future with expanded output and price reform. There is no special tax regime in place for the subsector. The recent promotion of some of the country's producing and discovered acreage to the international oil industry provided for a flat corporate tax of 35 percent on the profits of the resulting ventures and sliding-scale royalties negotiated on a case-by-case basis.

9.71   A well-designed system for taxing rents from petroleum and ensuring reasonable after-tax profits for operators will be critical to protecting the operating viability of the gas company and to promoting domestic and foreign investment in the oil sector. Equally important, such a system should ensure that the Government shares appropriately in potential rents generated from its petroleum resources -- which may not be the case in the taxation arrangements provided for in the recent promotions of oil acreage. The design of a system that meets the requirements of both the Government and potential investors and the clarification of the rules for assessing taxable income are a high priority. In addition, there is a valid case for a regime of special taxes on the sector, which generates most of the country's foreign exchange but very little employment. But this special taxation would be related to preventing the country's equilibrium exchange rate settling at levels at which the employment-intensive sectors, such as agriculture and industry, become uncompetitive internationally. Such taxation should still follow the principle that the Government's share does not rise as profits fall.

9.72   In view of the limited sources of domestic tax revenues and the prevailing need to finance the domestic currency deficit in the budget, the Government might consider reinstating the excise tax on gasoline that was abolished in August 1992. The projected yield for a full year from this tax at the rates in force during its application, current (November 1992) prices and the current level of domestic consumption of gasoline is R3.2 billion. The yield could be expected to increase significantly as gasoline prices are decontrolled. In addition, the excise rate was significantly lower, at 62 percent, than typical rates in most countries. There is thus additional potential for further increases in future yield from such a tax.

CHAPTER 10

TELECOMMUNICATIONS

10.1   A well-functioning telecommunications system is crucial to Turkmenistan's economic development. The country's distance from its potential hard currency markets and the need to integrate the economy more closely into the world economy make adequate international telecommunications particularly important. Similarly, Turkmenistan's poorly developed transportation network increases the urgency of developing a network.

10.2   Telecommunications infrastructure in Turkmenistan is insufficient to support its needs. While local direct dialing is available to all 250,000 subscribers and interregional direct dialing facilities within the former Soviet Union are available to about 130,000 subscribers, international telecommunications facilities to other countries are extremely restricted, with almost all traffic routed through very limited routes via Moscow. One third of the exchanges and subscriber cables are 30 to 40 years' old and need to be replaced. Capacity utilization is high, and the quality of service is poor, especially to international destinations outside the former Soviet Union.

Current Status

Institutional Set up

10.3   The sector is now fully owned and operated by the state. The Ministry of Communications (MOC) is the monopoly provider of all telecommunication services. The MOC is responsible for strategic planning, policy, regulation and operational functions. It has accountability for local, long-distance and international telephone, telex, telegraph, mobile and data communication services. In addition, MOC has responsibility for postal services, special delivery service and delivery of press publications. The responsibility for radio and television broadcasting has recently been moved from the MOC to a state committee that reports directly to the President.

10.4   A range of enterprises under the MOC operate the telecommunications services on a local, long-distance or international basis. These include the Ashkabad city network, which provides local services in Ashkabad and five regional enterprises; Velajat, which replaced the previous oblast organization and which provides local services outside Ashkabad; the telegraph and telephone enterprise which oversees telex, telegraph, long-distance and international services; a construction enterprise and a few others. Planning and day-to-day operations are done at the enterprise level. Plans are submitted to MOC for comment and approval. The enterprises operate as separate profit centers. Results from all services (i.e., telecommunications and postal) are combined in the enterprise's accounts. The enterprise's accounts are then combined with the MOC Headquarters's accounts for the MOC's financial consolidated accounts. The enterprises have their own budgets, and they contribute to the MOC's budget.

10.5   The total number of telecommunications staff is about 5,000, of which some 700 have technical education: 30 percent higher (engineer) and 70 percent lower (technician) education. About 1,000 persons work for telex and telegraph. The staff ratio (number of telecommunications staff per 1,000 connected lines) is about 20. The figure is high compared with five to ten in industrialized countries but good compared with the thirty to eighty found in some developing countries.

Financial Issues

10.6   The financial and accounting systems are underdeveloped. The enterprises have no clear financial and accounting policy and they lack appropriate financial management systems and procedures as well as adequately trained financial staff at all levels. Those systems they do have are not organized or managed to be used as a regular management tool for planning and control. They provide very limited information on the overall performance of the different parts of MOC and its enterprises.

10.7   Tariffs in Turkmenistan, except tariffs for international calls, are low, although they were increased in 1992 and 1993. They are now 50 times for enterprises and 24 times for the population what they were in 1991. However, in light of the high inflation rates and the depreciation of the value of the ruble against the U.S. dollar and other foreign currencies, additional adjustments for tariffs are needed. A comprehensive tariff study should be carried out to develop a clear tariff policy, tariff level and structure and for reviewing and setting tariffs.

10.8   The Government's 1992 budget allocation to MOC is too low. It amounts to only 12 million rubles in local currency and no allocation in foreign currency. This means that MOC and its enterprises have to finance the investment in the telecommunications sector as well as its operations from internally generated resources. It will be difficult to achieve with the current tariffs, especially as MOC enterprises pay the Government a 35 percent tax on net income. The Government has spent R58.6 million in the first 9 months of 1993 to finance new investments in telecommunications.

Facilities

10.9   There are about 250,000 telephone lines for a population of 3.8 million that is 6.4 lines per 100 inhabitants. This figure is comparable to that in other Central Asian republics, but it is much lower than the average figure of 12 in the former Soviet Union. Ashkabad, with 66,000 connected lines, has a density of about 16 lines per 100 inhabitants. Urban areas have a higher density with 215,000 lines, while the rural areas, with 35,000 lines, have a density figure as low as 2.2 lines per 100 inhabitants. In rural areas, some 550 villages lack any telephone service. About 30 percent of the lines in the country are connected to business and Governmental subscribers, while 70 percent are connected to residential customers. About 28 percent of households have a phone. Party lines are being widely used because of the lack of cable capacity. However, in rural areas there are 550 villages without telephone service.

10.10   All telephone subscribers are connected to automatic exchanges, but more than one-third of the subscribers are in exchanges that are 30 to 40 year's old. Automatic long-distance dialing throughout the former Soviet Union is available to subscribers in Ashkabad and in velajat centers. The utilization of exchange capacity is about 86 percent and would be higher if there were enough cable capacity to connect new subscribers. International traffic to and from destinations outside the former Soviet Union is routed mainly through 11 outgoing and 6 incoming circuits via Moscow. There are two circuits from Ashkabad to Baku, Azerbaijan, for international traffic to and from Turkey and four manual circuits to and from Tehran, Meshad and Babul for traffic to and from Iran. Some relief in international and business communication will be provided in the near future when the new digital exchange in Ashkabad is put into commercial service along with its interconnection facilities via Intelsat IBS to Ankara, Turkey, with 15+15 circuits. The traffic to and from the former Soviet Union republics is routed through 245 circuits via Moscow, Tashkent, Dushanbe, Baku, Yerevan, Novosibirsk, Alma-Ata and St. Petersburg.

10.11   Other services include telex, telegraph, data communication and telefax services. Telex and telegraph services are provided by two telex networks. International services are provided to 20 subscribers through an ATK-20-U exchange, which is connected to an international AXB-20 exchange in Moscow. Services within the former Soviet Union are provided to 780 subscribers through an UKK exchange connected to Moscow, Tashkent and Baku. Data services are provided via the public switched telephone network and leased lines. Telefax services also are provided via the public switched network. Some dedicated networks are operated by other Government agencies. These include Aeroflot, the gas enterprise, railways, Ministry of Water Resources and the power enterprise (QUAT).

10.12   The network for TV and radio broadcasting has recently been moved from the MOC to the TV and Radio State Committee reporting to the President, except the wire radio outside Ashkabad. The TV and Radio State Committee is responsible also for the Orbita earth station providing transmission capacity between Ashkabad and Moscow for telephone services and for TV and radio program transfer. The wire radio service is provided to all offices and households throughout the country. Three radio programs are transferred via telephone network and distributed through two wires to residential, business and Governmental buildings. MOC is responsible for the distribution of the wire radio programs outside Ashkabad, and the customers pay a monthly fee to MOC.

10.13   MOC operates a mobile radio service based on the Soviet ALTAI system with one exchange and one base station in Ashkabad. The area covers Ashkabad with a diameter of 30 to 40 km the capacity is 300 channels in a 300 megahertz frequency band.

Performance

Technical

10.14   The local, long-distance and international networks are not operating satisfactorily. The local and long-distance (with the former Soviet Union) networks need constant maintenance. There are 90,000 lines connected to 30 to 40 year-old, unreliable exchanges. Frequent maintenance is also required to repair the damage (faults) caused by corrosion and water to the equally old cable network. The performance of the international network to and from outside the former Soviet Union is constrained by the limited circuit capacity in Moscow. No fault statistics are available. During recent years 12,000 to 17,000 new lines were connected yearly, an annual growth of 5 to 7 percent. The registered waiting list of applications is 100,000 lines. It is unclear to what extent this demand will remain if local tariffs are increased and the economy continues to deteriorate.

Financial

10.15   Financial performance indicators of MOC should be treated with caution, given the distortions in input and output price structures and differences in accounting practices compared with international systems. Nevertheless, the available data may give some broad indicators of the sector's past performance.

10.16   The profitability of the sector is quite low, mainly because of low tariffs. Net profit from all operations in the first half of 1993 was about R400 million. Postal services incurred a loss and were cross-subsidized by telecommunications services. The current annual fee for a telephone line, including unlimited number of local calls, is R1,440 (less than $2). The estimated revenue per telephone line in

1992 is about R1,200 per line compared with an estimated cost of $1,000 - to $1,500 to replace a line, most of which will need to be paid for in foreign currency.

10.17   Self-generated funds are not sufficient to finance the desired network rehabilitation and expansion. Funds are not available to purchase necessary spare parts and materials, contributing to the congestion of the network and decline in the quality of service. Funds needed for even a minimum capital investment program are not available. Billing and collection of subscriber accounts for local services are performed by the regions. Fixed monthly fees are expected to be paid by subscribers without billing. Bills for long-distance and international calls are produced monthly. A disconnection policy for non paying subscribers is in use.

Constraints to Sectoral Development

10.18   The development of telecommunications is constrained by the sector's inadequate structure, and finances and by a shortage of skilled staff.

Inadequate Structure

10.19   The structure of the telecommunications sector is an improved version of the structure inherited from the former Soviet Union. In the summer of 1992, several steps were taken to restructure the sector. Radio and TV broadcasting services were moved to a state committee. In 1993 telecommunications and postal services were separated. A new telecommunications law is currently under preparation.

10.20   These are steps in the right direction, but they should become part of a comprehensive and clearly defined sector-restructuring program that guides the sector's development in the medium and long term. The sector needs to be restructured so that the functions currently performed by the MOC (policy, regulation and operations) are reallocated and so that policy and regulation become separated from operations.

Inadequate Finance

10.21   The sector finances suffer from low profitability, low tariffs, lack of foreign exchange and an inadequate financing strategy that fails to identify potential sources of local and foreign funds and the steps necessary to mobilize these resources effectively.

10.22   The MOC (and future operators) needs to improve the sector's future financial position, taking into account the following issues:

- Resource mobilization policy.

- Tariff structure and levels charged for services.

- Revenue sharing (inter connect agreements with other operators and foreign telecommunications administrations.

- Cost of equipment and services procured.

- Contractual obligations with suppliers.

- Operational efficiency of the organization.

- Policy on private sector participation.

- Macroeconomic conditions.

Shortage of Skilled Staff

10.23   As is the case in many sectors of the Turkmenistan's economy, the telecommunications sector is short of staff with the skills needed in the new environment. This staff shortage includes accountants, financial analysts, commercial managers, most procurement and inventory managers, corporate planners and technical staff with knowledge and experience in new technology-related issues. The MOC needs to give top priority to developing its human resources.

Sector Development Strategy

10.24   The strategy for the development of the sector has two major elements: a sector-restructuring program and a physical investment program. Before a long-term investment program can be developed, the sector-restructuring program should be defined. It is necessary, however, to develop a short-term investment program that should aim only at highest priority areas. Some proposals for sector restructuring and a short-term investment strategy are presented below.

Sector Restructuring

10.25   The main elements of the sector-restructuring program are a sector policy, sector regulation, legislation, operations arrangements and private sector participation.

Sector Policy

10.26   The MOC should set the sector policy. It needs to formulate goals and create a conducive environment for achieving them, controlled by appropriate legislation and managed by appropriate entities, that should lead to Turkmenistan achieving those goals. This sector policy should cover the following areas:

- Clearly defined and quantified social objectives (including target groups and degrees of subsidization, if necessary).

- Competition and the role of the private sector.

- Consumer protection

- Technical standards

- Tariff principles

Regulatory Framework

10.27   In the absence of full competition in the sector, there is a need for regulation. The main objectives of the regulatory body are to implement the Government's sector policy, control tariffs, promote competition, avoid monopoly abuses, grant licenses, monitor quality of service, address customer concerns, approve equipment and allocate frequency spectrum.

10.28   The achievement of these objectives requires separating the regulatory function from operations. One fundamental issue, therefore, will be whether regulation is carried out by a separate and independent regulatory body. At this stage, and for practical considerations, the regulatory body may have to be retained within the MOC because people with the professional skills required to staff a regulatory body are in short supply; particularly accountants and lawyers. A regulatory body might now be set up as a unit within the MOC and headed by a director equivalent to deputy minister level. Under this arrangement, the MOC would retain responsibility for policy and regulation. The director of the regulatory unit would advise the minister of communications on regulatory issues.

10.29   **Legislation.** The Government recognizes that to achieve the sector policy objectives identified above, the telecommunications sector needs to be put on a sound and independent legal footing. The MOC is expected to present to the Government its proposals for new legislation shortly. Telecommunications should be treated in separate legislation, rather than in a general public utility law.

10.30   The telecommunications law should establish the responsibilities, duties and functions of MOC and the telecommunications operators. The law should also specify a comprehensive framework for licensing for the following reasons:

- To ensure technical standards and type approval for equipment and services provided meet international standards.

- To allow for the phased development of competition in line with the needs of the country.

- To secure a full financial contribution from licensees for the right to operate telecommunications services.

- To ensure effective regulation of the activities of telecommunications operations.

Operations

10.31   To promote efficiency, operational activities will need to be restructured to be autonomous and along more commercial lines. To achieve this objective, the following actions are required:

- Delegate autonomy and accountability to the operating entities including the ability to appoint top management; recruit, pay and motivate staff; conclude commercial contracts; determine investment decisions and enter into joint ventures.

- Assign the telecommunications corporation responsibility for all operational activities of local, long-distance and international services, including those currently performed by the Velajat. The Velajat and other enterprises may continue to operate as separate business units, but overall coordination and planning should be performed by the corporation's headquarters in consultation with the enterprises.

- Privatize ancillary, non core activities such as the press activities, construction and money transfers.

- Have an organizational structure and internal procedures (corporate planning, operational, commercial, financial, accounting, staffing) closely aligned with its objectives as an autonomous commercial company.

- Establish a board of directors with members chosen for their competence, and to reflect the interests of Government (and the shareholders, if any) and users. The distribution of responsibilities and the areas of jurisdiction between the board and the senior management would be clearly defined.

- Allow the corporation to have its own personnel regulations and wage and salary structure and to follow a personnel and human resource development policy consistent with its function and objectives.

- Produce annual financial statements, including an income statement, a funds statement and a balance sheet, and have its accounts audited by a firm of international standing.

- Establish capabilities and procedures for international traffic agreements and settlements.

- Have the corporation's contract awards and signatures, related to investments included in the annual budget, approved at different levels of authority, according to amounts involved.

- Introduce a comprehensive training program (including corporate planning, finance, management, operations and maintenance management, procurement and contract administration) to build the corporation's institutional capacity and ensure sustainability' of the commercialization effort.

Private Sector Participation

10.32   Allowing private investors to provide services and supply equipment in the sector is an important element in the restructuring program. The private sector can help in:

- Providing financial resources needed to meet investment and performance targets and thus ease the Government's financial burden.

- Managing operations more efficiently.

- Establishing effective separation between Government and operating management functions.

- Increasing prospects for introduction of competition.

10.33   Private sector involvement can begin in the supply of terminal equipment, mobile services, value-added services (such as packet switching, paging and electronic mail.) and non telecommunications services support operations. The MOC has taken steps in this direction. A joint venture, with a foreign private company, has already been signed for providing mobile cellular service.

Joint Ventures

10.34   Joint ventures can be useful for introducing new services with private participation. Joint ventures permit a pooling of knowledge and sharing of risks in an activity that is kept separate from the partners' mainstream businesses. In Turkmenistan, financial need is a strong motivation for forming joint ventures like the one for mobile cellular service.

10.35   Joint-venture agreements have implications for the future development of the sector in three main areas:

- Evolution of policy and regulation.

- Technical systems, standardization and interconnection.

- Financial performance.

It is therefore important that the joint-venture agreement, objectives, scope and license be consistent with telecommunications sector strategy, particularly with:

- The investment strategy in the sector;

- The sector regulation (including the regulation of tariffs, licensing, standards and performance evaluation).

- The sector policy on the private role and introduction of competition (when and in what parts of the network).

10.36   Agreements made before establishing new sector policy and regulatory framework (including a licensing regime) and before clearly identifying the desired role of the private sector would probably become obstacles to the consistent evolution of policy and the desirable reform of the sector. The MOC's short-term financial constraints should not therefore lead to long-term unbalanced commitments.

Short-Term Investment Strategy

10.37   Before completing its long-term plan -- which should await the restructuring of the sector -- the MOC should develop a long-term plan and a short-term investment plan (for the next 2 to 3 years). The MOC will require independent expert assistance to develop the long-term plan after the sector-restructuring program has been defined.

10.38   The short-term plan should aim at two main areas: (1) continued maintenance and operation of the existing network to avoid any major disruptions in services and to eliminate major bottlenecks, and (2) expansion of international services which generate higher revenue.

10.39   Based on the above criteria, Turkmenistan's short-term investment plan may emphasize the following key areas:

- International telephone service outside the former Soviet Union

- International telex service

- Packet-switched data service X.25

- Cable network in Ashkabad

10.40   International telephone traffic outside the former Soviet Union will be improved after completing the final testing of the DMS-100/200 exchange and Intelsat IBS earth station. In the beginning the system provides international circuit capacity to Ankara, Turkey, on 15 outgoing and 15 incoming circuits as well as 2,500 lines to Government and business customers. The MOC should discuss with Turkish PTT and other major correspondents how to route outgoing and incoming traffic via Ankara in addition to Moscow. Arrangements should be made to route international traffic from and to KVARTS exchange via the new satellite system by either establishing a direct C5 route from KVARTS to Ankara or routing via the DMS-100/200 exchange. Considering the potential international traffic, the MOC may consider acquiring DCME equipment to expand the circuit capacity to Ankara from 30 to 120 circuits. The MOC may wish to continue with its efforts to establish direct C5 circuits from the KVARTS exchange to Tehran, Iran. The MOC may also want to start negotiations with Turkey, Iran, Uzbekistan, Kazakhstan and Azerbaijan about the technical possibilities of routing traffic via their facilities to and from international destinations and about the relevant international accounting arrangements.

10.41   International telex service is at the moment limited to 20 customers, and the service is provided via Moscow. The MOC may want to study the feasibility of establishing a new international telex exchange with 100 to 200 terminals. Direct circuits can be established to Turkey via the above-mentioned satellite system and to Iran via the terrestrial network. To provide both national and international data services an X.25 packet-switched data node could be established. Connection to another international node is necessary (for example, via the above-mentioned satellite system to Turkey). Based on the information made available to the mission, it seems that there is a lack of cable capacity, especially in Ashkabad. The cable network may need to be rehabilitated before ordering significant new exchange capacity. A survey is required to evaluate the existing cable network and locate the areas where urgent replacement or additional capacity is required.

10.42   It is recommended that capacity in the new DMS-100/200 exchange be distributed to business and Government customers as soon as possible. Some major customers could be moved from the nearest old ATS-54 exchanges to the new digital one to provide better service and to relieve the old exchanges. The MOC may want to consider expanding the DMS-100/200 exchange instead of ordering a new System 12 exchange in the same building, subject to price, financing and technical considerations. Cellular mobile services could be provided by a joint venture interfacing with the MOC's fixed network for international traffic as well as traffic to and from the local fixed network.

Box 10.1
Technical Assistance

To facilitate institutional reform and development of new sector policy, regulation and operational arrangements, it is essential that a comprehensive technical assistance plan be implemented. The program should have two main components: manpower development and consultant services. Providing funding for such a program should be considered a priority.

Manpower development would concentrate on developing skills required to carry out the regulatory and policy functions as well as the internal restructuring of the Ministry and the operating entities. The elements of the manpower development program should include:

- Limited formal training abroad for some staff in key technical areas.

- On-the-job training through working with consultants.

- The offering of courses in Turkmenistan to be organized and conducted by foreign and local trainers.

- Establishment of an effective twinning arrangement for in-service training and exchange of professional knowledge and experience.

With reference to the twinning arrangement, a number of Turkmenistan's telecommunications staff would travel to and work within a "sister" telecommunications organization in another country. These staff members should be required to teach their colleagues on the subject of their assignment when they return to Turkmenistan. Staff from the "sister" organization will work with MOC's staff, teach them and provide the necessary support in carrying out the various functions. The organization selected should be operating more efficiently and effectively than MOC in an environment sharing at least some of the technical, economic and social characteristics of Turkmenistan.

Consulting assistance is required in preparing the new telecommunications law; preparing and implementing a regulatory framework; developing a tariff policy and determining sound tariff structure and level; developing adequate accounting and financial management systems and procedures; developing procedures for international traffic agreements and settlements and developing a management information system.

CHAPTER 11

ENVIRONMENT

11.1   Turkmenistan's environmental problems are largely the outcome of the command-and-control policies of the past, which placed heavy emphasis on intensive cotton production and industrial development without adequate consideration for their environmental implications. At the top of the priority list of environmental problems is the pollution of ground-water and surface water resources and the soil deterioration and salinization in the Tashauz area. The principal causes are poor irrigation/drainage methods and inappropriate application practices of agricultural chemicals. These causes are closely related to cotton production and encouraged by subsidized pricing of agricultural inputs and by lack of incentives for their prudent use in the absence of a market economy and a private sector. These two environmental problems are also reducing the volume of the Aral Sea and have destroyed its aquatic ecosystem, lowered soil quality in the surrounding areas and polluted surface and groundwater of the delta draining into the Aral Sea.

11.2   While the mitigation and prevention of industrial and urban pollution can be dealt with by specific technical and fiscal measures, addressing the quantity and quality problems of water resources will require important policy decisions about irrigation techniques and use of agricultural chemicals, the role of cotton in agricultural production, and the structural composition of the economy (agriculture and other sectors). Continuation of the current environmentally unsustainable agricultural practices is bound to increase the already heavy toll on human health and the degradation of natural resources. Furthermore, in the medium and long term, the high population growth will put additional pressure on the natural resource base and especially on the limited water resources. In Turkmenistan the birth rate in the rural areas is about 4 percent a year, and although the overall population density is low, the population basically concentrates in certain areas. Land use and occupation is intense in these areas. Increasing demands for water for drinking, economic activities and waste disposal are expected as a consequence of population growth and land-use patterns.

Current Status

Water Pollution

11.3   Water is very scarce in this arid country--Turkmenistan has very limited groundwater resources---and water pollution is severe. Currently, cotton irrigation requires 12 cubic meters of water per hectare. Using modern international irrigation practices, could reduce that to 7 cubic meters per hectare. The water, once diverted from the Amu Darya is sent through unlined canals, which allows seepage and mineral transfer. Forty percent of the diverted water is lost in arterial channels. Inadequate drainage has led to salination and mineralization of farm land and water tables, a decreased flow of the republic's principal water source, the Amu Darya River, and degradation of the Aral Sea. Turkmenistan's drinking water is highly contaminated with runoff from the cotton fields. Water tested in wells in the Tashauz Province showed sulfite levels 50 times higher than normal, chlorides 40 times higher, calcium 17 times higher and magnesium 10 times higher. Vegetables grown near the cotton fields have levitate nitrite levels, and pesticide residue is even showing up in breastmilk.

11.4   The Turkmen part of the Caspian Sea and the corresponding coastal zone are still relatively free of significant environmental problems except for pollution risks from offshore oil platforms. However, better coordination and active participation by all riparian states is required in the monitoring and control of the quality of the sea, which has until now been carried out largely by Azerbaijan.

Water Use

11.5   Water-use efficiency appears to be low. Household consumption is not metered, and there are no water charges for agriculture yet. The total water loss in conveyance from the place of diversion to the place of use was 6.8 cubic kilometers in 1989.

Aral Sea

11.6   The main environmental problems that affect the local population in the Aral Sea area are the salt-dust storms, contamination of drinking water by fertilizers and pesticides, the degradation of land in the deltas through salt deposition, and industrial pollution. In Tashauz oblast, in the lower Amu Darya, nine drainage water collectors discharge upstream the urban areas, and the polluted water is used for drinking. Turkmenistan's Government intends to allocate R1 billion for the pre-Aral area, to install pipelines for drinking water and provide social assistance for the people. The priorities defined are to provide clean drinking water and food products to the local population and to improve the sanitary and epidemiologic conditions (see Annex A on the problems of the Aral Sea).

Air Pollution

11.7   Although overall air pollution is not a major problem, there are localities with very high levels of atmospheric air pollution such as Chardzhou, where the pollution comes mainly from the mineral fertilizer industry, road transport and the power-generation industry. Industrial air pollution largely consists of three pollutants (in million tonnes in 1988): carbon monoxide (CO) 0.1; hydrocarbons (CxHx) 0.3; and suspended matter 0.1. Hydrocarbons are concentrated in the oil industry, the oil refining and petro-chemicals and the natural gas industry.

Protected Area/Wildlife

11.8   Flora and fauna are rather well protected by the joint efforts of Goskompriroda, the Academy of Sciences, and the Society for Nature Conservation. 1,108,000 have been designated as restricted nature reserves with strictly restricted human activity. The operating budget in 1990 was only R1,475,000.

Energy Efficiency

11.9   In 1991 Turkmenistan consumed 9.6 billion cubic meters of gas (equivalent to 9.6 million tons of oil). Oil consumption for the same year amounted to about 2 million tons. The total volume of primary energy consumption was equivalent to 11.6 MT oil. Net export of electricity was approximately 5 billion KWH (0.43 MT oil equivalent). The net local primary energy consumption (assuming it consists only of oil and gas) is about 11 MT oil equivalent. Per capita energy consumption in 1991 amounted to 2.9 tons of oil equivalent. Considering the low level of income of the population and relative weakness of the industrial sector, it seems that the amount of energy waste is quite substantial. Equivalent per capita energy consumption in 1985 (ton oil equivalent) for the following countries with much higher income and higher level of industrialization was: Turkey, 0.8; Portugal, 1.25; Greece, 1.85; and Spain, 1.93 (see Figure 11.1).

Agricultural Inputs

11.10   As noted, agricultural environmental issues focus primarily on use of agricultural chemicals and to a more limited extent on untreated or inadequately treated liquid wastes from livestock operations. Agrochemical soil inspection has indicated that about one third of the soil and two third of the plants contain pesticides. A number of pesticides are used, notably 7000 TPY magnesium chloride as a cotton defoliant (12 kg/ha), Targa-Super for fungus control, thiodan and chlorophos and parathion-methyl, a highly hazardous pesticide if applied by inexperienced applicators. Defoliant application rates have decreased by shifting from airborne application to ground-based tractor application, and further decreases are anticipated by developing shorter duration cotton varieties that defoliate themselves at an earlier stage. Application rates of pesticides have come down

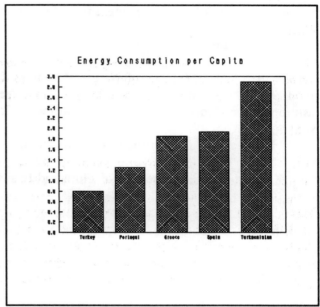

Figure 11.1

considerably (5-10 kg/ha) because of the lack of foreign exchange. Efforts are being made to reduce the use of agro chemicals, in particular of hazardous defoliants, and to apply stricter control on the use of pesticides. Attempts are also being made to use more organic manure and to adopt biological pest control methods, although on a relatively small scale on a number of state farms. However, laboratory results are not always reliable and seem to obscure the seriousness of the effect of high agro chemical application rates in the past (up to 30 kg/ha, excluding fertilizers).

11.11   There seems to be little capacity to monitor imported materials for composition and efficacy (amount of active ingredient) or to manage proper control of outdated or banned materials. Pesticide residues on food are monitored and analyzed to some extent with older, less accurate equipment. There is a list of banned pesticides that included DDT, butiphos and various organo-chlorines. Currently, those materials are buried in a concrete bunker near Tashauz (within the Aral Sea region). There is no routine monitoring program at the site, although it is claimed to be fenced and guarded. It is also claimed that the location is seismically stable. Pesticide management seems reasonably well controlled because it is the single responsibility of a special service. Previously all assay work was done in Russia; now it is done in laboratories in Turkmenistan. These laboratories are also responsible for residue work. Such arrangements are not considered trustworthy as residue work can easily be corrupted under these circumstances. Moreover, the regional laboratory facilities do not have sufficient capability to carry out greater number of analyses.

Health

11.12   The most important health problems are related to bacterial contamination of the ground water that is the source of drinking water for the population. The major cause of death in infants is diarrheal disease, that is closely correlated with the areas of the country with the water supplies most contaminated. The most pressing need from the health standpoint is clean drinking water. Longer range efforts to improve drinking-water quality should give priority to the design, construction and training in maintenance of small water-treatment units for use with piped water supplies.

Sector Organization

11.13   The Ministry of Nature Resources Use and Environmental Protection was created in July 1992. It integrated the former State Committees for Environmental Protection, for Forestry and Pasture and the Hydrometereological Department. It includes six departments:

- Environmental Protection.

- Protection of Flora and Fauna.

- Forestry.

- Hydrometeorology.

- Administrative Planning.

The Department for Environmental Protection has two divisions, one in charge of control and inspection and one for ecological expertise. The chief priority of the ministry is an adequate supply of potable water.

11.14   The Hydrometeorology Department is in charge of monitoring the air, the surface waters and radioactivity; underground waters are monitored by the Ministry of Geology. There are laboratories at all oblast offices, for climatic analysis and environmental pollution. The data produced are provided to interested ministries and research institutions to support their activities, as the Ministry of Environment has no specific units. Difficulties in coordination led to duplication of tasks, as the Ministry of Water Resources has set its own monitoring services.

11.15   Most of the institutions are operating inadequately, hampered by poor maintenance and shortage of equipment, instruments and supplies caused by serious budget constraints following the termination of funding from Moscow. Most technical staff are unfamiliar with the manner in which environmental problems are addressed in other countries. At present, there appears to be a focus on expensive, high technology solutions to problems that might be resolved as effectively with much less costly policy or simple technical interventions.

Environmental Fund

11.16   All the former republics recently created Environmental Funds to be replenished through fines and fees for the use of natural resources. Sources of income include fees for allowed discharges of wastes and fines for violations of the nature protection regulations. Funds were settled for five regions, in a total of about R1.2 million. There is a need to increase the fines and the control/monitoring system as a way to avoid violations of the established norms.

Environmental Policy

11.17   There is little innovation in the environmental policy. Standards and monitoring systems are similar for all the republics, which have adopted them largely unchanged from systems used in the Former Soviet Union. Many of these standards appear to be overly strict and are therefore extremely difficult to achieve and thus ignored.

11.18   Environmental expertise became mandatory in all the republics, for most types of projects, public and private. This includes both the construction of new urban, industrial and agricultural projects and their rehabilitation. Environmental permits are required to obtain funding for projects. About 60 percent of projects are refused at the first analysis. There are some difficulties in implementing this policy, given the lack of human resources. In Turkmenistan, the ecological expertise is centralized, as local specialists are not prepared to do this analysis.

11.19   Monitoring is considered a priority, specially of those aspects associated with water management and with the collection of fees and fines for the use of natural resources. The common problems include the following

- Obsolete laboratories and field equipment.

- Lack of chemical reagents.

- Inadequate standards and norms.

- Inadequate and uncoordinated methodologies.

11.20   The publicity given to the Aral Sea problem s prompted the acceptance of the new environmental laws, through the pressures of mass media and the demands of non-governmental organizations. At present, the Government is reviewing the standards and regulations for environmental protection adopted from the former Soviet Union. Some of these regulations, such as for air pollution, need to be brought closer to world standards. Others should be created, such as the laws on land use and the use of mineral resources. The main goals of the Government are to stop the increase of environmental pollution, to introduce waste-free, pollution-free technologies, to build treatment facilities and equipment and to introduce water-saving technologies. Higher fines are used to induce compliance with environmental law. There is an understanding that saving the Aral Sea itself is impossible, but saving water is possible.

Recommendations

11.21   It is vital not to see economic development and environmental protection as mutually exclusive policy objectives. The challenge is to find ways in which environmental considerations can be factored into a broader reform process, to find ways of promoting economic efficiency and environmental policy goals at the same time. A radical reform of the economy provides good opportunities for pursuing economic and environmental objectives at the same time. In many cases the mechanisms responsible for inefficiency and wastage are also responsible for pollution. These include central planning based on quantitative production targets, a pricing system that subsidizes the use of energy and raw materials and lack of any incentive to use clean technologies. From the policy perspective, market-based reforms of these policies and practices can help achieve environmental goals. Especially the appropriate (full cost) pricing of resources, such as water and energy, will promote economy and efficiency in their use.

11.22   The key reforms needed to promote greater economic efficiency and environmental protection are price reform, privatization and the establishment of a competitive industrial structure. Price reform and the reduction and abolition of subsidies would significantly reduce demand for energy, raw materials and other production inputs like pesticides and fertilizers. The establishment of enterprises operating within a competitive environment under market conditions would create a continuing pressure to reduce wastage and to make productive procedures more efficient.

11.23   At the same time it must be emphasized that market forces by themselves will not solve all environmental problems; indeed, left to themselves, market forces will generate their own kind of problems. A major reform of environmental policies and institutions is required concurrently with economic reforms. Economic reform is a necessary but not sufficient condition for environmental improvement. Steps to reform environmental institutions and to provide them with adequate powers must be made at the same time.

11.24   Most of the environmental standards are unrealistically high and incompatible with the enforcement capacity and the prevailing economic reality. This stems from the past practice of generalized environmental policies and uniform regulations across the former USSR without differentiation of physical, social or financial factors among the various republics. The result is the difficulty and inconsistence of compliance and the heavy burden on the relevant ministries' budgets of the high cost of adherence.

11.25   However, budgetary pressures will severely constrain resources,   and in the first stages of reform there might be a shortage of capital availability for major environmental investments. In these circumstances, environmental policy should focus on the following

- Establishing the mechanisms needed for the development and implementation of environmental policy measures including an adequate monitoring system and effective standard-setting and enforcement procedures. Pollution fees and fines will help finance administrative costs. User charges on environmental services like water and sewage treatment can help fund future environmental investments.

- Establishing priorities among the problems to be tackled in the major economic sectors and regions, focusing particularly on environmental health risks and degradation of critical natural resources.

- Steering industrial restructuring in an environmentally favorable direction, particularly through environmental audits of production facilities.

- Establishing environmental management schemes in priority areas.

- Promoting local initiatives.

- Elaborating and implementing a conservation strategy in conjunction with the privatization of land.

11.26   In the industrial sector emphasis should be placed on those processes that can be redesigned at little or no cost in order to achieve efficiency and waste and pollution reduction. Before specific recommendations for pollution control can be made, it must first be determined whether specific industrial operations are economically viable and will remain so, with proper pollution control measures, or whether national economies would be served by shutting certain facilities down. If it is the latter, pollution problems in large measure would be resolved as a part of economic restructuring when the industrial facility is closed.

11.27   Policies regarding chemicals must be developed and properly implemented. It is vastly cheaper to eliminate banned or hazardous pesticides before application than to remove them from the drinking water. Proper use of fertilizers and alternative strategies to pest management could likely lead to improved water quality at minimal cost.

ANNEX A

ARAL SEA ISSUES

.

Background:[1] The Aral Sea lies between Kazakhstan and Uzbekistan in a vast geological depression in the Kyzylkum and Karakum deserts. In 1960, the Aral Sea was the fourth largest inland lake in the world. Since then, however, it has shrunk significantly because of nearly total cutoff of river inflow from the Amu Darya (river) and Syr Darya as a result of heavy withdrawals for irrigation. By 1989 the sea level had fallen by 14.3 meters and the surface area had shrunk from 68,000 km^2 to 37,000 km^2. The salinity of the sea had increased to 2.8 times its 1960 level.

The Aral Sea basin extends over 690,000 km^2, including the republics of Kazakhstan, Kyrghyzstan, Tajikistan, Turkmenistan and Uzbekistan. A small portion of its headwaters is located in Afghanistan, Iran and China. The basin is formed by two of the largest rivers of Central Asia - Amu Darya and Syr Darya - both fed by the snow melts and glaciers from the mountains. The Amu Darya sources are mostly located in Tajikistan, with a few watercourses originating in northeastern Afghanistan. The Syr Darya originates mainly in Kyrghyzstan. It runs across small portions of Tajikistan and Uzbekistan and through the Kazakh provinces of Chimkent and Kzyl-Orda.

The total population of the Aral basin is estimated at 35 million based on the 1989 census. Uzbekistan, with 19.9 million, is the most populated among the countries in the region, Kazakhstan has a population of 16.5 million of which 2.48 million live in the Aral Basin. The rate of natural population increase in the region averaged 2.54% over the period 1979-89 compared to a national (FSU) rate of 0.87%. .

The Aral Basin has three distinctive ecological zones: the mountains, the deserts, and the Aral with its deltas. The Tian Shan and Pamir mountains in the south and southwest are characterized by high altitudes (with peaks over 7000 m) and by high moisture coefficients, with average annual precipitation ranging from 800 to 1600 mm. The mountains host large forest reserves and some national parks. In their foothills and valleys, soil and temperature conditions are favorable for agriculture. The lowland deserts of Karakum and Kyzylkum cover most of the basin area, and are characterized by low precipitation (under 100 mm/year) and high evaporation rates. Both the rivers' banks and deltas and the Aral Sea islands are characterized by a variety of vegetation and wildlife resources. For example, the Barsakelmes Island, in the main part of the Aral Sea, is a natural reserve for endangered species such as the Kulan (Asiatic wild burro) and Siagak, an ancient variety of antelope. The sea itself was the habitat for more than 24 species of fish, and a number of other aquatic organisms.

Issues

The main issues relating to the Aral Sea basin area are the following: the reduction of the sea, the destruction of its aquatic ecosystem, the lowering of soil quality in the Aral Sea Basin,

---

[1] For reference, the issues surrounding the Aral Sea Basin have been studied by a number of individuals and organization, in particular, UNEP has produced the Diagnostic Study for the Development of an Action Plan for the Aral Sea which was issued in July 1992. This report presents a comprehensive analysis of the causes of the Aral Sea crisis and provides a basis for elaboration and analysis of the strategies for future activities for mitigating the ecological disaster.

pollution of surface and groundwater of the delta draining into the Aral Sea, depressed economy and adverse health impact on the population due to lack of potable water and inadequate sanitation.

The causes as well as the regional effects of the Aral Sea shrinkage can be enumerated. Inefficient irrigation practices coupled with heavy chemical applications, cultivation of cotton and rice, and inappropriate development policies are among the important causes. For the last three decades, Soviet policy in the region focussed on massive irrigation projects along the Amu Darya and Syr Darya with the primary goal of creating a Central Asian cotton belt. Urban and industrial water use, though still a small fraction of total water use, has also risen. The irrigation techniques have lead to high rates of leakage and evaporation as well as waterlogging and salinity build-up. As a result, the two river flows that feed the Aral Sea are nearly completely expended before they ever reach the Sea.

Numerous reports and articles have been written by experts, both national and foreign, during the past decade on this crisis, attracting world-wide attention. Environmental experts, scientists, engineers and economists from all over the world have joined their counterparts from the FSU. Their findings have been presented in several publications during the past decade and discussed in many international seminars. Recently, in June 1992, the Stockholm Environment Institute, Boston Center, published the results of a microcomputer model for simulating current water balances and evaluating water management strategies in the Aral Sea region. The study presented a picture of an unfolding and deepening crisis situation and concluded that, in the absence of an action plan to save the Aral Sea, its surface areas would decrease from its 1987 level of 41 square kilometers to 9 square kilometers by the 2015 and that the sea would turn into several small residual brine lakes.

The United Nations Environment Program (UNEP) considers that, in terms of its ecological, economic, and social consequences, the Aral Sea is one of the most staggering ecological disasters of the twentieth century. Recognizing the crucial need to save the disappearing Aral Sea and the need to provide an overall perspective of the Aral Region, the UNEP issued a diagnostic study of the state of its environment, its population and its economics in July 1992. The report presents a comprehensive analysis of the causes of the Aral Sea crisis, but it does not recommend a specific action plan. It provides, however, a basis for elaboration and analysis of the strategies for future activities for mitigating the ecological disaster.

The Bank's Assessment of the Aral Sea Crisis[2]

Despite a decade of studies by national and international experts a viable plan for addressing the Aral Sea problems has not been formulated. Ideas and suggestions abound, but their technical, economic, financial and political feasibility has not been examined. The studies indicate that the solutions may be extremely costly, difficult to finance, and would take decades to implement. Thirty major action programs suggested in these reports broadly cover the following categories of action:

(a)   Actions proposed to increase the inflows to the Aral Sea (4 major projects and programs);

---

[2] This assessment is based on numerous reports written by experts and on the findings of the Aral Sea Reconnaissance Mission which visited the Aral Sea basin in September 1992.

(b)   Actions proposed to save a part of the water currently used for irrigation and other purposes and use the saved water to increase the inflows to the Aral Sea (14 major projects and programs);

(c)   Measures to improve the health and environment of the population in the Aral Sea Region (8 major projects and programs);

(d)   Rationalization of water rights in the Aral Sea Basin across off the Central Asia and Kazakhstan (4 major projects and programs);

The technical, economic, financial, and political feasibility of these programs have not been determined. They seem to constitute a master program costing, around 30 to 50 billion US dollars that would require a period of 40 to 50 years to implement. The authors of these programs have not considered how essential are these projects; who will finance them; and whether the Republics are willing to share such large costs.

The proposed projects and programs underline one overriding objective: to increase the inflows to the Aral Sea and restore it to its pre-disaster conditions, or to some level that would save the sea. The rational of this objective is not clear.

The feasibility of some grand schemes such as diverting the rivers flowing north to the Arctic Sea, or transferring water from the Caspian Sea, for increasing the inflows to the Aral Sea is questionable. Aside from their huge costs, these schemes could involve serious political and environmental issues.

The feasibility and sustainability of some proposals for increasing the inflows to the Aral Sea by reducing the existing uses is also questionable. They include, for example, limiting water deliveries from Amu and Syr rivers for irrigation and other purposes; and reducing the area of cotton and rice crops. It may be necessary to take these actions for other economic reasons, but it seems unrealistic to expect that the water saved from these actions would be available for increasing the inflows to the Aral Sea on a sustainable long term basis.

The Bank's assessment of the Aral Sea crisis is classified under three categories: (a) Aral Sea and Aral Sea related issues; (b) regional issues; and, (c) development issues that should receive high priority although not directly related to the Aral Sea problems.

A.   Aral Sea and Aral Sea Related Issues

(i)   There are differences in views and uncertainty on the extent of the existing and future adverse effects of the Aral Sea. The problems appear more manageable than what previous reports indicated.

(ii)   The proposals to divert water from outside the basin (from the Arctic rivers and Caspian Sea) to fill the Aral Sea do not appear viable.

(iii)   Conserving the water resources of the basin by reducing waste, improving water management, diversifying crops, and other measures are important and should receive priority. However, the political feasibility and economic justification of diverting the saved water to fill the Aral Sea is questionable.

(iv) The available information indicates that it is not possible to restore the Sea to its pre-disaster conditions. However, it may be necessary to stabilize the Sea at a sustainable level based on available flows.

(v) The living conditions of the people in the zone around the Aral Sea that has been seriously affected by the changes in the Aral Sea are deplorable. Lack of potable water, water borne diseases, inadequate health facilities, depressed economy, lack of employment opportunities, adverse effects of sand and salt storms and the deteriorating ecosystem are some of the major problems. This disaster zone covers parts of Kazakhstan, Uzbekistan and Turkmenistan. Improving the living conditions and environment of the people in this area should receive high priority. The suggestions made in some reports to shift the most severely affected population appear unrealistic. The people need development assistance, not migration assistance.

B.   Regional Issues

(i) The Agreement signed on February 15, 1992 between the Aral Sea Basin Republics, and the Protocol and Resolutions established during April-August, 1992 for cooperation on management, utilization and protection of water resources, and for joint measures for solution of the Aral Sea problems are commendable. Preliminary review, however, indicates that they are not adequate enough to constitute binding legal treaties. Some subdued complaints about the fairness of allocations are already simmering and other riparian (China, Afghanistan, and Iran) have not been consulted yet. It is advisable to improve these agreements to internationally accepted standards to avoid possible conflicts in the future.

(ii) The Republics have established an Inter-ministerial Committee and two River Basin Commissions* (BVOs) for allocating water, monitoring water use and quality and for data collection, analysis, management and forecasting. These arrangements are working satisfactorily and are commendable. However, the capacity and effectiveness of these institutions should be enhanced by increasing their decision making and regulatory powers and providing them with advanced equipment, facilities and technologies to play their role most effectively.

(iii) The need for comprehensive planning and management of water resources, both quantity and quality, and for short and long term, was stressed at some meetings. Given the scarcity of water resources, increasing demands, and the fact that the river flows have been almost fully diverted for irrigation and other purposes at present, the need and importance of developing strategies for comprehensive management of the water resources should be underscored.

(iv) The high caliber of researchers and scientists of research institutes and academies of sciences dealing with water resources, ecology and pollution control is impressive. However, there a continuing depletion of talent due to the lack of funds, advanced equipment and facilities, and career development opportunities. These problems require urgent attention.

(v)   The Central Asian Research Institute of the region has now become an institute of the Republic in which it was located. The need for a regional institution to address regional and Aral Sea research needs and to provide research support to the BVOs should be considered as a high priority.

C.   Development Issues

The Republics' concerns with their country-specific development issues and the high priority they attach to water supply and sanitation, health, ecology, population, salinity and waterlogging, drainage, pollution control and food self-sufficiency programs in their respective countries is overwhelming.   These programs should receive high priority for external assistance.

Statistical Annex Tables

Table of Contents

1/ Turkmenistan signed an agreement with Russia in July 1992 to transfer its share of FSU debt, and hence any servicing obligations, to Russia in exchange for relinquishing most claims on the financial and other assets of the FSU. Details of interrepublican financing arrangements are currently unknown.

TABLE 1-1: TURKMENISTAN - POPULATION AND EMPLOYMENT - SUMMARY TABLE

(in thousands)

	1980	1985	1986	1987	1988	1989	1990	1991	1992
Total Population	2,864	3,225	3,309	3,395	3,477	3,565	3,657	3,750	3,846
Males	1,407	1,585	1,627	1,671	1,757	1,803	1,805	1,850	1,897
Females	1,457	1,640	1,682	1,765	1,808	1,854	1,852	1,900	1,949
Urban	1,345	1,473	1,510	1,546	1,575	1,607	1,650	1,690	1,718
Rural	1,519	1,752	1,799	1,849	1,902	1,958	2,006	2,061	2,128
Total Labor Force	1,432	1,643	1,678	1,719	1,758	1,800	1,859	1,923	1,992
Below Working Ages	39	46	37	31	31	31	22	25	32
Working-Age Population a/	1,351	1,553	1,598	1,645	1,685	1,728	1,778	1,833	1,890
Above Working Ages	42	44	43	43	42	41	59	65	70
Total Employed Population	1,140	1,338	1,368	1,407	1,445	1,492	1,545	1,571	1,573
State Sector	750	857	879	898	914	918	926	920	886
Leased Enterprises	..	..	..	..	..	..	..	..	..
Joint-Stock Companies	..	..	..	..	..	..	..	..	..
Economic Associations	..	..	..	..	..	..	..	..	..
Social Organizations	..	..	..	..	..	..	..	..	..
Joint Ventures	..	..	..	..	..	..	..	..	..
Collective Farms	276	325	322	324	327	334	355	357	373
Cooperatives b/	..	..	..	1	2	16	33	49	59
Individual Labor Activities	1	1	1	1	2	2	2	2	2
Private Agriculture	113	155	166	183	197	221	229	243	252
Other	..	..	..	..	..	..	..	..	1

a/ Working age includes women aged 16-54 and men aged 16-59.
b/ Including consumer cooperatives.

Source: Goskomstat.

TABLE 1-2: TURKMENISTAN - EMPLOYMENT BY SECTOR, ANNUAL AVERAGE

(in thousands)

	1985	1986	1987	1988	1989	1990	1991	1992
Material Sphere	1,008	1,024	1,051	1,072	1,109	1,146	1,174	1,186
Agriculture including forestry	541	550	570	592	622	647	666	695
Agriculture excluding forestry	539	548	568	590	620	645	664	693
Forestry	2	2	2	2	2	2	2	2
Industry, total	280	286	293	289	309	321	327	318
Industry, other	150	153	157	158	160	166	159	154
Construction	130	133	136	131	149	154	168	164
Other, material sphere	187	188	188	191	178	178	181	173
Transportation of goods 1/	77	76	75	77	65	63	63	56
Maintenance of roads	..	..	..	..	..	..	..	..
Communication servicing material prod.	..	..	..	..	..	..	..	..
Wholesale trade	..	..	..	..	..	..	..	..
Retail Trade and catering	..	..	..	..	..	..	..	..
Material Supply	..	..	..	..	..	..	..	..
Procurement	..	..	..	..	..	..	..	..
Information and computing services	..	..	..	..	..	..	..	..
Other branches of material production	110	112	113	114	113	115	118	117
Nonmaterial Sphere	329	344	356	373	383	397	397	387
Transportation	..	..	..	..	..	..	..	..
Communication	..	..	..	..	..	..	..	..
Housing and municipal services	32	35	35	36	38	38	37	38
Health care, social security, physical culture and sports	64	67	71	77	81	86	87	82
Education, culture and art	135	141	149	159	168	176	182	172
Science and scientific services	27	26	27	27	28	28	23	21
Credit	..	..	..	..	..	..	..	..
Insurance	..	..	..	..	..	..	..	..
Private nonprofit institutions serving households	..	..	..	..	..	..	..	..
Other	72	75	74	74	68	69	68	74
Total Employment	1,338	1,368	1,407	1,445	1,492	1,542	1,571	1,573

1/ Includes Communication.

Source: Goskomstat.

TABLE 1-2A: TURKMENISTAN - PERCENTAGE DISTRIBUTION OF EMPLOYMENT BY SECTOR

(in percent)

	1985	1986	1987	1988	1989	1990	1991	1992
Material Sphere	75.3	74.9	74.7	74.2	74.3	74.3	74.8	75.4
Agriculture including forestry	40.4	40.2	40.5	41.0	41.7	41.9	42.4	44.2
Agriculture excluding forestry	40.3	40.1	40.4	40.8	41.6	41.8	42.3	44.1
Forestry	0.2	0.1	0.1	0.1	0.1	0.1	0.1	0.1
Industry, total	20.9	20.9	20.8	20.0	20.7	20.8	20.8	20.2
Industry, other	11.2	11.2	11.2	10.9	10.7	10.8	10.1	9.8
Construction	9.7	9.7	9.7	9.1	10.0	10.0	10.7	10.4
Other, material sphere	14.0	13.7	13.4	13.2	11.9	11.5	11.5	11.0
Transportation of goods 1/	5.8	5.6	5.3	5.3	4.3	4.1	4.0	3.6
Maintenance of roads	..	..	..	..	..	..	..	..
Communication servicing material prod	..	..	..	..	..	..	..	..
Wholesale trade	..	..	..	..	..	..	..	..
Retail Trade and catering	..	..	..	..	..	..	..	..
Material Supply	..	..	..	..	..	..	..	..
Procurement	..	..	..	..	..	..	..	..
Information and computing services	..	..	..	..	..	..	..	..
Other branches of material production	8.2	8.2	8.0	7.9	7.6	7.5	7.5	7.4
Nonmaterial Sphere	24.6	25.1	25.3	25.8	25.7	25.8	25.2	24.6
Transportation	..	..	..	..	..	..	..	..
Communication	..	..	..	..	..	..	..	..
Housing, public utilities & personal servic	2.4	2.6	2.5	2.5	2.5	2.5	2.4	2.4
Health care, social security, physical culture and sports	4.8	4.9	5.0	5.3	5.5	5.6	5.5	5.2
Education, culture and art	10.1	10.3	10.6	11.0	11.2	11.4	11.6	10.9
Science and scientific services	2.0	1.9	1.9	1.9	1.8	1.8	1.5	1.3
Credit	..	..	..	..	..	..	..	..
Insurance	..	..	..	..	..	..	..	..
Private nonprofit institutions serving households	..	..	..	..	..	..	..	..
Other	5.4	5.5	5.3	5.1	4.6	4.5	4.3	4.7
Total Employment	100.0	100.0	100.0	100.0	100.0	100.0	100.0	100.0

Source: Table 1-2

TABLE 1-3: TURKMENISTAN - WORKERS & EMPLOYEES IN STATE SECTOR, 1992

(in percent)

	Workers	Employees
Material Sphere	..	..
Agriculture including forestry	..	..
Agriculture excluding forestry	87.1	12.9
Forestry	80.2	19.8
Industry, total	..	..
Industry, other	82.5	17.5
Construction	82.4	17.6
Other, material sphere	..	..
Transportation of goods	82.1	17.9
Maintenance of roads	..	..
Communication servicing material production	75.0	25.0
Wholesale and Retail Trade	79.1	20.9
Material Supply	..	..
Procurement	..	..
Information and computing services	25.2	74.8
Other branches of material production	60.8	39.2
Nonmaterial Sphere	..	..
Transportation	..	..
Communication	..	..
Housing	80.3	19.7
Public utilities and personal services	..	..
Health care, social security,		
physical culture	33.5	66.5
Education	25.5	74.5
Culture and art	30.5	69.5
Science and scientific services	41.1	58.9
Credit and social insurance	14.7	85.3
General administration and defense	22.4	77.6
Private nonprofit institutions		
serving households	..	..
Other, material and nonmaterial spheres	..	..
Total	63.7	36.3

Source: Goskomstat.

TABLE 1-4: TURKMENISTAN - LABOR FORCE PARTICIPATION RATE

	Total	0-15	16-19	20-24	25-29	30-34	Age Groups 35-39	40-44	45-49	50-54	55-59	60-64	over 65
1989 Census													
Total Population (thous.)	3,523	1,505	290	326	322	253	185	106	109	114	97	84	132
Employed (thous.)	1,430	0	126	260	280	225	168	97	98	87	55	22	12
Labor Force Part. (%)	40.6%	0.0%	43.4%	79.8%	87.0%	88.9%	90.8%	91.5%	89.9%	76.3%	56.7%	26.2%	9.1%
Males:													
Population (thous.)	1,735	760	150	161	158	124	90	53	54	56	46	37	46
Employed (thous.)	788	0	66	137	153	122	89	52	53	53	41	15	7
Labor Force Part. (%)	45.4%	0.0%	44.0%	85.1%	96.8%	98.4%	98.9%	98.1%	98.1%	94.6%	89.1%	40.5%	15.2%
Females:													
Population (thous.)	1,788	745	140	165	164	129	95	53	55	58	51	47	86
Employed (thous.)	642	0	60	123	127	103	79	45	45	34	14	7	5
Labor Force Part. (%)	35.9%	0.0%	42.9%	74.5%*	77.4%	79.8%	83.2%	84.9%	81.8%	58.6%	27.5%	14.9%	5.8%
1979 Census													
Total Population (thous.)	2,765	1,219	261	262	200	120	120	130	111	102	65	52	123
Employed (thous.)	1,138	1	133	229	186	113	114	123	103	84	33	11	8
Labor Force Part. (%)	41.2%	0.1%	51.0%	87.4%	93.0%	94.2%	95.0%	94.6%	92.8%	82.4%	50.8%	21.2%	6.5%
Males:													
Population (thous.)	1,359	613	133	130	99	61	61	66	55	48	25	20	48
Employed (thous.)	599	1	68	117	97	60	60	65	54	44	21	7	5
Labor Force Part. (%)	44.1%	0.2%	51.1%	90.0%	98.0%	98.4%	98.4%	98.5%	98.2%	91.7%	84.0%	35.0%	10.4%
Females:													
Population (thous.)	1,406	606	128	132	101	59	59	64	56	54	40	32	75
Employed (thous.)	539	0	65	112	89	53	54	58	49	54	40	32	75
Labor Force Part. (%)	38.3%	0.0%	50.8%	84.8%	88.1%	89.8%	91.5%	90.6%	87.5%	74.1%	30.0%	12.5%	4.0%

Source: Goskomstat.

TABLE 2-1: TURKMENISTAN - GROSS SOCIAL PRODUCT, MATERIAL INPUT, AND NATIONAL INCOME, BY SECTORS

	1985	1986	1987	1988	1989	1990	1991	1992
				(current prices, millions of rubles)				
Total National Economy:								
Gross Social Product	8,891	9,305	9,819	10,307	10,534	11,381	29,739	461,714
Material Input 1/	4,896	5,107	5,349	5,590	5,706	6,059	17,440	180,183
National Income Produced	3,995	4,198	4,470	4,718	4,828	5,321	12,299	281,531
Industry:								
Gross Social Product	4,157	4,436	4,490	4,648	4,641	4,538	15,645	..
Material Input	3,029	3,181	3,216	3,414	3,543	3,705	13,130	..
National Income Produced	1,128	1,255	1,274	1,233	1,099	833	2,514	..
Construction:								
Gross Social Product	1,489	1,659	1,766	1,886	1,704	1,808	3,946	..
Material Input	816	828	920	919	829	858	1,722	..
National Income Produced	673	831	846	968	875	950	2,225	..
Agriculture:								
Gross Social Product	2,326	2,274	2,557	2,627	2,922	3,491	7,212	..
Material Input	685	709	771	786	828	943	1,532	..
National Income Produced	1,641	1,565	1,786	1,841	2,094	2,548	5,680	..
Transport and Communications:								
Gross Social Product	449	465	550	640	672	864	1,481	..
Material Input	260	272	315	345	363	413	666	..
National Income Produced	189	192	235	296	309	451	815	..
Other Sectors of Material Sphere:								
Gross Social Product	470	472	456	506	594	679	1,455	..
Material Input	106	117	127	126	143	140	390	..
National Income Produced	364	355	329	380	451	539	1,065	..
		(1983 prices, millions of rubles)			*(previous year's prices, millions of rubles*			
Total National Economy:								
Gross Social Product	9,013	9,412	9,796	10,492	9,989	10,869	11,992	..
Material Input	4,897	5,112	5,324	5,545	5,601	5,956	6,921	..
National Income Produced	4,116	4,300	4,472	4,947	4,389	4,913	5,071	..
Industry:								
Gross Social Product	4,264	4,499	4,610	4,829	4,503	4,530	5,076	..
Material Input	3,059	3,203	3,241	3,433	3,490	3,682	4,223	..
National Income Produced	1,205	1,296	1,368	1,396	1,013	848	853	..
Construction:								
Gross Social Product	1,492	1,671	1,726	1,831	1,647	1,733	1,783	..
Material Input	805	827	919	888	822	843	778	..
National Income Produced	687	844	807	943	824	890	1,005	..
Agriculture:								
Gross Social Product	2,357	2,315	2,429	2,638	2,635	3,123	3,334	..
Material Input	670	694	722	754	789	880	1,225	..
National Income Produced	1,687	1,620	1,707	1,885	1,846	2,244	2,109	..
Transport and Communications:								
Gross Social Product	449	465	550	640	662	854	1,091	..
Material Input	260	272	315	345	360	413	490	..
National Income Produced	189	192	236	296	302	441	601	..
Other Sectors of Material Sphere:								
Gross Social Product	451	463	481	553	544	629	708	..
Material Input	103	117	127	126	140	138	204	..
National Income Produced	348	346	354	428	403	490	504	..

1/ *Includes depreciation.*

Source: Goskomstat.

TABLE 2-2: TURKMENISTAN - NATIONAL INCOME ACCOUNTS, BY SECTORS

	1985	1986	1987	1988	1989	1990	1991	1992
				(current prices, millions of rubles)				
Gross Social Product	8,891	9,305	9,819	10,307	10,534	11,381	29,739	461,714
Material Inputs (incl. Depreciation)	4,896	5,107	5,349	5,590	5,706	6,059	17,440	180,183
National Income of Material Sphere	3,995	4,198	4,470	4,718	4,828	5,321	12,299	281,531
of which:								
Industry	1,128	1,255	1,274	1,233	1,099	833	2,514	..
Construction	673	831	846	968	875	950	2,225	..
Agriculture	1,641	1,565	1,786	1,841	2,094	2,548	5,680	..
Transport and Communications	189	192	235	296	309	451	815	..
Other Sectors of Material Sphere	364	355	329	380	451	539	1,065	..
National Income of Non-Material Sphere	..	..	1,363	1,456	1,722	1,915	3,145	23,932
Business Trips, Non-Mat. Services and Losses	..	..	585	553	594	672	2,212	23,818
Total National Income 1/	..	..	5,248	5,621	5,955	6,564	13,232	281,645
Depreciation 2/	..	..	1,163	1,190	1,226	1,173	1,434	2,568
Gross National Product	..	..	6,326	6,710	7,117	7,582	14,666	284,213
		(1983 prices, millions of rubles				*(previous year's prices, millions of rubl*		
Gross Social Product	9,013	9,412	9,796	10,492	9,989	10,869	11,992	..
Material Inputs	4,897	5,112	5,324	5,545	5,601	5,956	6,921	..
National Income of Material Sphere	4,116	4,300	4,472	4,947	4,389	4,913	5,071	..
of which:								
Industry	1,205	1,296	1,368	1,396	1,013	848	853	..
Construction	687	844	807	943	824	890	1,005	..
Agriculture	1,687	1,620	1,707	1,885	1,846	2,244	2,109	..
Transport and Communications	189	192	236	296	302	441	601	..
Other Sectors of Material Sphere	348	346	354	428	403	490	504	..
National Income of Non-Material Sphere	..	..	..	..	..	..	..	..
National Income of Mat.&Non-Mat.Sphere	..	..	..	..	..	..	..	..
Business Trips Non-Mat. Services and Losses	..	..	..	..	..	..	..	..
Total National Income 1/	..	..	..	..	..	..	..	..
Depreciation 2/	..	..	..	..	..	..	..	..
Gross National Product	..	..	..	..	..	..	..	..

1/ According to the UN System of National Accounts.
2/ Only Material Sphere; Non-Material already includes depreciation.

Source: Goskomstat.

TABLE 2-3: TURKMENISTAN - NATIONAL INCOME USED

	1985	1986	1987	1988	1989	1990	1991	1992
				(current prices, millions of rubles)				
National Income Produced	3,995	4,198	4,470	4,718	4,828	5,321	12,299	281,53
National Income Used	4,602	4,834	4,731	4,809	5,273	5,505	13,848	
Consumption	3,131	3,357	3,454	3,599	3,914	4,317	7,154	
of which								
Personal Consumption	2,740	2,947	3,015	3,149	3,426	3,764	6,370	
Savings	1,471	1,477	1,277	1,210	1,360	1,188	6,694	
Increase in Fixed Assets 1/	814	988	781	824	743	685	..	
Change in Inventories	657	489	496	386	617	503	..	
Difference (Produced-Consumed)	-607	-636	-261	-92	-446	-184	-1,549	
Losses 2/	127	145	199	158	198	788	..	
Trade Balance	-734	-781	-460	-250	-644	-972	..	
		(1983 prices, millions of rubles)				*(previous year's prices, millions of ruble*		
National Income Produced	4,116	4,300	4,472	4,947	4,389	4,913	5,071	
National Income Used	4,638	4,888	4,706	4,556	5,057	4,734	5,692	
Consumption	3,149	3,399	3,462	3,553	3,825	3,856	4,455	
of which								
Personal Consumption	2,758	2,988	3,022	3,102	3,345	3,328	3,712	
Savings	1,489	1,488	1,244	1,003	1,232	878	1,237	
Increase in Fixed Assets	841	959	741	760	698	518	550	
Change in Inventories	648	529	503	243	534	359	687	
Difference (Produced-Consumed)	(522)	(588)	(234)	391	(669)	179	(620)	
Losses	..	..	..	..	..	..	..	
Trade Balance	..	..	..	..	..	..	..	

1/ Including livestock.
2/ For 1990 includes balancing item.

Source: Goskomstat.

TABLE 2-4: TURKMENISTAN - NATIONAL INCOME USED

	1985	1986	1987	1988	1989	1990	1991	1992
	(in percent of National Income Produced, current prices)							
National Income Produced	100.0	100.0	100.0	100.0	100.0	100.0	100.0	..
National Income Used	115.2	115.1	105.8	101.9	109.2	103.4	112.6	..
Consumption	78.4	80.0	77.3	76.3	81.1	81.1	58.2	..
of which								
Personal Consumption	68.6	70.2	67.5	66.8	71.0	70.7	51.8	..
Savings	36.8	35.2	28.6	25.7	28.2	22.3	54.4	
Increase in Fixed Assets 1/	20.4	23.5	17.5	17.5	15.4	12.9	..	..
Change in Inventories	16.4	11.6	11.1	8.2	12.8	9.4	..	..
Difference (Produced-Consumed)	(15.2)	(15.1)	(5.8)	(1.9)	(9.2)	(3.4)	(12.6)	..
Losses	3.2	3.5	4.5	3.3	4.1	14.8	..	..
Trade Balance	(18.4)	(18.6)	(10.3)	(5.3)	(13.3)	(18.3)	..	..
	(percentage change at comparable prices) 2/							
National Income Produced	..	4.5	4.0	10.6	-7.0	1.8	-4.7	..
National Income Used	..	5.4	-3.7	-3.2	5.2	-10.2	3.4	..
Consumption	..	7.9	1.8	2.6	6.3	-1.5	3.2	..
of which								
Personal Consumption	..	8.3	1.1	2.6	6.2	-2.9	-1.4	..
Savings	..	0.0	-16.4	-19.4	1.8	-35.4	4.2	..
Increase in Fixed Assets	..	14.0	-22.7	2.6	-15.2	-30.2	-19.7	
Change in Inventories	..	-18.3	-4.9	-51.6	38.2	-41.7	36.7	
Difference (Produced-Consumed)	..	..	..	..	..	..	..	..
Losses	..	..	..	..	..	..	..	..
Trade Balance	..	..	..	..	..	..	..	..

1/ Including livestock.
7

Source: Goskomstat.

TABLE 2-5: TURKMENISTAN - NET MATERIAL PRODUCT AT CURRENT PRICES

(millions of rubles)

	1985	1986	1987	1988	1989	1990	1991	1992
By Industrial Origin:								
Agriculture including forestry	1,641	1,565	1,786	1,841	2,094	2,548	5,680	..
Agriculture excluding forestry	..	..	..	..	..	..	..	
Forestry	..	..	..	..	..	..	..	
Industry, total 1/	1,801	2,086	2,120	2,201	1,974	1,783	4,739	..
Industry, other	1,128	1,255	1,274	1,233	1,099	833	2,514	..
Construction	673	831	846	968	875	950	2,225	..
Other	553	547	564	676	760	991	1,881	..
Transportation of goods 2/	189	192	235	296	309	451	815	..
Maintenance of roads	..	..	..	..	..	..	..	..
Communication servicing material producti	..	..	..	..	..	..	..	..
Wholesale trade	..	..	..	..	..	..	..	..
Retail trade and catering	..	..	..	..	..	..	..	..
Material supply	..	..	..	..	..	..	..	..
Procurement	..	..	..	..	..	..	..	..
Information and computing services	..	..	..	..	..	..	..	..
Other branches of material production	364	355	329	380	451	539	1,065	..
Net Material Product	3,995	4,198	4,470	4,718	4,828	5,321	12,299	281,831
By Expenditure Category:								
Consumption	3,131	3,357	3,454	3,599	3,914	4,317	7,154	..
Consumption of population	2,740	2,947	3,015	3,149	3,426	3,764	6,370	..
Social consumption	391	411	439	450	488	554	784	..
Investment (accumulation)	1,471	1,477	1,277	1,210	1,360	1,188	6,694	..
Fixed capital	814	988	781	824	743	685	..	..
Changes in inventories and other	657	489	496	386	617	503	..	..
Losses 3/	127	145	199	158	198	788	..	..
Net exports	-734	-781	-460	-250	-644	-972	..	..

1/ Includes turnover taxes and understates value-added in natural gas sector
2/ Transportation and Communication.
3/ For 1990 includes balancing item.

Sources: Goskomstat.

ABLE 2-5A: TURKMENISTAN - DISTRIBUTION OF NET MATERIAL PRODUCT AT CURRENT PRICES

(percent)

	1985	1986	1987	1988	1989	1990	1991	1992
By Industrial Origin:								
Agriculture including forestry	41.1	37.3	39.9	39.0	43.4	47.9	46.2	..
Agriculture excluding forestry	..	..	..	..	..	..	..	..
Forestry	..	..	..	..	..	..	..	..
Industry, total 1/	45.1	49.7	47.4	46.7	40.9	33.5	38.5	..
Industry, other	28.2	29.9	28.5	26.1	22.8	15.7	20.4	..
Construction	16.8	19.8	18.9	20.5	18.1	17.9	18.1	..
	0.0	0.0	0.0	0.0	0.0	0.0	0.0	..
Other	13.8	13.0	12.6	14.3	15.7	18.6	15.3	..
Transportation of goods 2/	4.7	4.6	5.3	6.3	6.4	8.5	6.6	..
Maintenance of roads	..	..	..	..	..	..	..	..
Communication servicing material producti	..	..	..	..	..	..	..	..
Wholesale trade	..	..	..	..	..	..	..	..
Retail trade and catering	..	..	..	..	..	..	..	..
Material supply	..	..	..	..	..	..	..	..
Procurement	..	..	..	..	..	..	..	..
Information and computing services	..	..	..	..	..	..	..	..
Other branches of material production	9.1	8.5	7.4	8.1	9.4	10.1	8.7	..
Net Material Product	100.0	100.0	100.0	100.0	100.0	100.0	100.0	..
By Expenditure Category:								
Consumption	78.4	80.0	77.3	76.3	81.1	81.1	58.2	..
Consumption of population	..	..	..	..	..	..	..	..
Social consumption	..	..	..	..	..	..	..	..
Investment (accumulation)	36.8	35.2	28.6	25.7	28.2	22.3	54.4	..
Fixed capital	..	..	..	..	..	..	..	..
Changes in inventories and other	..	..	..	..	..	..	..	..
Losses	3.2	3.5	4.5	3.3	4.1	14.8	..	..
Net exports	-18.4	-18.6	-10.3	-5.3	-13.3	-18.3	..	..

Source: Table 2-5.

TABLE 2-6: TURKMENISTAN - NET MATERIAL PRODUCT AT CONSTANT PRICES 1/

(millions of rubles)

	1985	1986	1987	1988	1989	1990	1991	1992
	(1983 prices, millions of rubles)				(previous year's prices, millions of rubles)			
By Industrial Origin:								
Agriculture including forestry	1,687	1,620	1,707	1,885	1,846	2,244	2,109	..
Agriculture excluding forestry	..	..	..	..	..	..	..	..
Forestry	..	..	..	..	..	..	..	..
Industry, total 2/	1,891	2,141	2,175	2,339	1,837	1,738	1,858	..
Industry, other	1,205	1,296	1,368	1,396	1,013	848	853	..
Construction	687	844	807	943	824	890	1,005	..
								..
Other	537	539	590	723	705	932	1,104	..
Transportation of goods 3/	189	192	236	296	302	441	601	..
Maintenance of roads	..	..	..	..	..	..	..	..
Communication servicing material producti	..	..	..	..	..	..	..	..
Wholesale trade	..	..	..	..	..	..	..	..
Retail trade and catering	..	..	..	..	..	..	..	..
Material supply	..	..	..	..	..	..	..	..
Procurement	..	..	..	..	..	..	..	..
Information and computing services	..	..	..	..	..	..	..	..
Other branches of material production	348	346	354	428	403	490	504	..
Net Material Product	4,116	4,300	4,472	4,947	4,389	4,913	5,071	..
By Expenditure Category:								
Consumption	3,149	3,399	3,462	3,553	3,825	3,856	4,455	..
Consumption of population	2,758	2,988	3,022	3,102	3,345	3,328	3,712	..
Social consumption	391	411	440	451	480	528	743	..
								..
Investment (accumulation)	1,489	1,488	1,244	1,003	1,232	878	1,237	..
Fixed capital	841	959	741	760	698	518	550	..
Changes in inventories and other	648	529	503	243	534	359	687	..
								..
Losses and discrepancy 4/	-522	-588	-234	391	-669	179	-620	..
Net exports	..	..	..	..	..	..	..	..

1/ For 1985-88 in 1983 prices; for 1989-91 in previous year's prices.
2/ Including turnover taxes.
3/ Transportation and Communication.
4/ It is the difference between National Income Produced and National Income Used.

Sources: Goskomstat.

TABLE 2-6A: TURKMENISTAN - NET MATERIAL PRODUCT AT CONSTANT PRICES - GROWTH RATES

(in percent)

	1986	1987	1988	1989	1990	1991	1992
By Industrial Origin:							
Agriculture including forestry	-4.0%	5.4%	10.4%	0.3%	7.2%	-17.2%	..
Agriculture excluding forestry	..	..	..	..	..	..	..
Forestry	..	..	..	..	..	..	..
Industry, total	13.2%	1.6%	7.5%	-16.5%	-12.0%	4.2%	..
Industry, other	7.6%	5.6%	2.0%	-17.9%	-22.8%	2.4%	..
Construction	23.0%	-4.4%	16.9%	-14.8%	1.6%	5.8%	..
Other	0.3%	9.4%	22.7%	4.4%	22.5%	11.5%	..
Transportation of goods	1.9%	22.5%	25.4%	2.3%	42.9%	33.1%	..
Maintenance of roads	..	..	..	..	..	..	..
Communication servicing material production	..	..	..	..	..	..	..
Wholesale trade	..	..	..	..	..	..	..
Retail trade and catering	..	..	..	..	..	..	..
Material supply	..	..	..	..	..	..	..
Procurement	..	..	..	..	..	..	..
Information and computing services	..	..	..	..	..	..	..
Other branches of material production	-0.5%	2.2%	20.9%	6.0%	8.6%	-6.6%	..
Net Material Product	4.5%	4.0%	10.6%	-7.0%	1.8%	-4.7%	..
By Expenditure Category:							
Consumption	7.9%	1.8%	2.6%	6.3%	-1.5%	3.2%	..
Consumption of population	8.3%	1.1%	2.6%	6.2%	-2.9%	-1.4%	..
Social consumption	5.1%	7.0%	2.5%	6.8%	8.3%	34.2%	..
Investment (accumulation)	0.0%	-16.4%	-19.4%	1.8%	-35.4%	4.2%	..
Fixed capital	14.0%	-22.7%	2.6%	-15.2%	-30.2%	-19.7%	..

Source: Table 2-6.

TABLE 2-6B: TURKMENISTAN - NET MATERIAL PRODUCT - IMPLICIT PRICE DEFLATORS 1/

	1985	1986	1987	1988	1989	1990	1991	1992
By Industrial Origin:								
Agriculture including forestry	97.3	96.6	104.6	97.7	113.4	113.6	269.3	..
Agriculture excluding forestry	..	..	..	..	..	..	..	..
Forestry	..	..	..	..	..	..	..	..
Industry, total	95.2	97.4	97.5	94.1	107.4	102.6	255.1	..
Industry, other	93.6	96.8	93.1	88.3	108.5	98.2	294.9	..
Construction	98.0	98.4	104.8	102.6	106.2	106.8	221.3	..
Other	103.0	101.6	95.7	93.4	107.8	106.3	170.3	..
Transportation of goods	100.0	100.0	99.9	100.0	102.2	102.3	135.8	..
Maintenance of roads	..	..	..	..	..	..	..	..
Communication servicing material producti	..	..	..	..	..	..	..	..
Wholesale trade	..	..	..	..	..	..	..	..
Retail trade and catering	..	..	..	..	..	..	..	..
Material supply	..	..	..	..	..	..	..	..
Procurement	..	..	..	..	..	..	..	..
Information and computing services	..	..	..	..	..	..	..	..
Other branches of material production	104.6	102.5	92.9	88.9	112.0	110.0	211.4	..
Net Material Product	97.1	97.6	99.9	95.4	110.0	108.3	242.5	..
By Expenditure Category:								
Consumption	99.4	98.8	99.8	101.3	102.3	112.0	160.6	..
Consumption of population	99.3	98.6	99.8	101.5	102.4	113.1	171.6	..
Social consumption	100.0	99.9	99.7	99.7	101.5	104.8	105.5	..
								..
Investment (accumulation)	98.8	99.2	102.6	120.6	110.4	135.3	541.2	..
Fixed capital	96.8	103.0	105.4	108.4	106.4	132.2		..

1/ For 1985-88, 1983=100; for 1989-91, previous year = 100.

Sources: Tables 2-5 and 2-6.

TABLE 2-6C: TURKMENISTAN - NET MATERIAL PRODUCT - GROWTH RATES OF PRICE DEFLATORS

(in percent)

	1986	1987	1988	1989	1990	1991	1992
By Industrial Origin:							
Agriculture including forestry	-0.7	8.3	-6.6	16.1	0.1	137.1	..
Agriculture excluding forestry	..	..	..	..	..	..	..
Forestry	..	..	..	..	..	..	..
Industry, total	2.3	0.0	-3.5	14.2	-4.5	148.6	..
Industry, other	3.4	-3.8	-5.2	22.8	-9.5	200.3	..
Construction	0.5	6.5	-2.1	3.5	0.6	107.2	..
Other	-1.4	-5.8	-2.3	15.3	-1.3	60.1	..
Transportation of goods	0.0	-0.1	0.1	2.2	0.1	32.7	..
Maintenance of roads	..	..	..	..	..	..	..
Communication servicing material production	..	..	..	..	..	..	..
Wholesale trade	..	..	..	..	..	..	..
Retail trade and catering	..	..	..	..	..	..	..
Material supply	..	..	..	..	..	..	..
Procurement	..	..	..	..	..	..	..
Information and computing services	..	..	..	..	..	..	..
Other branches of material production	-2.0	-9.4	-4.3	25.9	-1.8	92.2	..
Net Material Product	0.6	2.4	-4.6	15.4	-1.5	123.9	..
By Expenditure Category:							
Consumption	-0.7	1.0	1.5	1.0	9.4	43.4	..
Consumption of population	-0.7	1.2	1.8	0.9	10.4	51.7	..
Social consumption	-0.1	-0.2	0.1	1.8	3.2	0.7	..
Investment (accumulation)	0.4	3.4	17.5	-8.5	22.6	300.0	..
Fixed capital	6.4	2.3	2.9	-1.9	24.2	..	..

Source: Tables 2-6B.

TABLE 2-7: TURKMENISTAN - GROSS NATIONAL PRODUCT

(in millions of current rubles)

	1987	1988	1989	1990	1991	1992
MATERIAL SPHERE:						
1.Gross Social Product	9,819	10,307	10,579	11,381	29,739	461,714
2.Intermediate Consumption	4,856	5,053	5,183	5,714	18,218	201,434
2.1. Material Inputs 1/	4,272	4,501	4,589	5,042	16,006	177,615
2.2. Business Trips	52	59	52	59	99	310
2.3. Household-Municipal Services	64	48	61	62	109	363
2.4. Socio-Cultural Services 2/	59	75	64	93	545	16,852
2.5. Deductions of Enterprises for Goelogical Research	201	201	201	201	205	1,226
2.6. Services of Science and Research	3	5	9	10	10	221
2.7. Interest paid Banks for Credit	1	1	1	1	1	346
2.8. Other Services	6	7	8	9	10	..
2.9. Losses	199	158	198	237	1,234	4,501
3.Value Added (1-2)	4,963	5,254	5,396	5,667	11,521	260,281
NON-MATERIAL SPHERE:						
1. Gross Output of Services	1,709	1,805	2,110	2,368	3,886	70,451
1.1. Wages	1,014	1,096	1,269	1,431	2,148	17,466
1.2. Deductions for Social Security	71	77	89	98	644	5,240
1.3. Profit	10	10	28	30	30	590
1.4. Payment for Non-material Services, including Business Trips	37	40	46	52	58	31,908
1.5. Material Inputs 1/	308	309	342	401	684	14,612
1.6. Depreciation	191	191	248	257	216	219
1.7. Depreciation of Individual Housing	29	34	41	49	57	67
1.8. Other Expenses	48	48	48	50	50	351
2. Intermediate Consumption	346	350	388	453	741	46,519
2.1. Payment for Non-Material Services and Business Trips	37	40	46	52	57	31,908
2.2. Material Inputs	308	309	342	401	684	14,612
3. Value Added (1-2)	1,363	1,456	1,722	1,915	3,145	23,932
Gross National Product	**6,326**	**6,710**	**7,117**	**7,582**	**14,666**	**284,213**
of which:						
Material Sphere	4,963	5,254	5,396	5,667	11,521	260,281
Non-Material Sphere	1,363	1,456	1,722	1,915	3,145	23,932

1/ Excluding depreciation but including non-depreciated value.
2/ Education, Public Health, Social Security

Source: Goskomstat.

TABLE 3-1: TURKMENISTAN - BALANCE OF PAYMENTS

(in millions of rubles)

| | Interrepublican transactions | | | | | Transactions with foreign countries | | | | |
	1987	1988	1989	1990	1991	1987	1988	1989	1990	1991
Trade balance	-269	-97	-328	-458	1,095	-208	-187	-348	-513	-197
Exports	2,327	2,389	2,418	2,469	6,731	120	245	241	172	1,105
Imports	2,596	2,486	2,746	2,927	5,636	328	432	589	685	1,302
Services, net	..	..	..	-172	-422	..	..	..	-77	-144
Transportation	..	..	..	-166	-415	..	..	..	-57	-97
Travel	..	..	..	-6	-8	..	..	..	-1	--
Interest	..	..	..	--	--	..	..	..	-19	-47
Other	..	..	..	--	--	..	..	..	--	--
Net public sector transfers	..	..	..	600	2,222	..	..	..	--	--
Current account balance:										
Including transfers	..	..	..	-30	2,894	..	..	..	-590	-341
Excluding transfers	..	..	..	-630	673	..	..	..	-590	-341
Capital account	..	..	..	-1,062	-447	..	..	..	18	60
Debt transactions (net) 1/	..	..	..	--	--	..	..	..	18	60
Disbursements	..	..	..	--	--	..	..	..	59	157
Amortization	..	..	..	--	--	..	..	..	44	100
Repayment from abroad	..	..	..	--	--	..	..	..	3	4
Interrepublican capital transactions	..	..	..	-1,062	-447	..	..	..	..	..
Inflows	..	..	..	--	--	..	..	..	..	..
Outflows 2/	..	..	..	-1,062	-447	..	..	..	..	..
Errors and omissions	..	..	..	542	113	..	..	..	86	22
Overall balance	..	..	..	-549	2,561	..	..	..	-487	-259
Financing	..	..	..	549	-2,561	..	..	..	487	259
Net foreign assets of the banking syste	..	..	..	549	-2,561	..	..	..	462	265
Arreas 1/	..	..	..	--	--	..	..	..	24	-10
Debt deferral 1/	..	..	..	--	--	..	..	..	--	4

1/ In the case of transactions with foreign countries, figures were imputed by applying Turkmenistan's share in external debt
   to flows for the USSR as a whole. This share was determined in the context of the interrepublican agreement on the external debt
   of the USSR in November 1991.
2/ Outflows reflect an increase in the State Bank of Turkmenistan claims on the USSR Gosbank.

Source: Goskomstat, Gosbank, Gosplan, Ministry of Finance, and IMF staff estimates.

TABLE 3-2: TURKMENISTAN - EXCHANGE RATES

(Rubles per U.S. Dollar)

	1987	*1988*	*1989*	*1990*	*1991*	*1992*
Official Exchange Rate	0.6328	0.6080	0.6274	0.5856	0.5819	..
Auction/MIFCE Rate 1/	n.a.	n.a.	8.9	19.4	54.6	268.7

	Russian Federation	
	1991	*1992*
	Nominal	
January	25.3	204.3
February	34.0	175.8
March	36.1	152.8
April	32.9	152.8
May	38.1	122.3
June	40.7	125.3
July	52.4	143.3
August	52.0	169.7
September	55.2	225.3
October	62.2	353.8
November	105.6	426.9
December	169.7	414.6
Annual Average	**58.7**	**222.2**

1/ *Weighted Average.*

Sources: World Bank staff estimates.

TABLE 3-3: TURKMENISTAN - TOTAL EXPORTS BY COMMODITY GROUPS AT DOMESTIC PRICES

(millions of current rubles)

	Interrepublic						Extrarepublic						Total Trade					
	1987	1988	1989	1990	1991	1992	1987	1988	1989	1990	1991	1992	1987	1988	1989	1990	1991	1992
INDUSTRY	2,188.3	2,245.9	2,197.4	2,271.7	6,334.5	96,290.0	118.2	213.0	228.5	163.7	1,078.7	115,836.0	2,306.5	2,458.9	2,425.9	2,435.4	7,413.2	212,126.0
POWER	64.7	58.9	69.6	67.0	151.5	6,780.0	0.0	0.0	0.0	0.0	0.0	:	64.7	58.9	69.6	67.0	151.5	6,780.0
OIL AND GAS	742.6	750.6	743.0	695.8	2,562.8	77,549.0	0.0	0.0	2.1	9.3	445.0	115,805.0	742.6	750.6	745.1	705.1	3,007.8	193,354.0
COAL	0.0	0.0	0.0	0.0	0.0	0.0	0.0	0.0	0.0	0.0	0.0	0.0	0.0	0.0	0.0	0.0	0.0	0.0
OTHER FUEL	0.0	0.0	0.0	0.0	0.0	0.0	0.0	0.0	0.0	0.0	0.0	0.0	0.0	0.0	0.0	0.0	0.0	0.0
FERROUS METALLURGY	3.3	3.3	3.4	3.4	7.3	78.0	0.0	0.0	0.0	0.0	0.0	0.0	3.3	3.3	3.4	3.4	7.3	78.0
NON-FERROUS METALLURGY	6.3	5.2	5.2	5.9	4.1	25.0	0.0	0.0	0.0	0.1	0.1	0.0	6.3	5.2	5.2	6.0	4.2	25.0
CHEMICAL & PETROLEUM	139.6	150.4	151.5	146.7	400.0	2,751.0	1.5	1.5	0.8	6.7	34.7	5.0	141.1	151.9	152.3	153.4	434.7	2,756.0
MACHINERY AND METAL WORKS	43.7	44.2	38.5	35.3	90.0	545.0	0.5	0.8	0.9	1.6	5.2	0.0	44.2	45.0	39.4	36.9	95.2	545.0
SAWMILL & LUMBER INDUSTRY	0.3	0.3	0.3	0.3	0.5	12.0	0.0	0.0	0.0	0.0	0.0	0.0	0.3	0.3	0.3	0.3	0.5	12.0
BUILDING MATERIALS	23.2	20.9	24.1	28.2	50.0	653.0	0.4	0.5	0.1	0.0	1.2	12.0	23.6	21.4	24.2	28.2	51.2	665.0
LIGHT INDUSTRY	1,074.1	1,116.1	1,076.0	1,082.5	2,767.3	1,685.2	112.7	206.6	223.1	138.9	576.0	14.0	1,186.8	1,322.7	1,299.1	1,221.4	3,343.3	1,699.2
FOOD PRODUCTION	89.8	95.3	85.1	205.9	300.0	6,211.3	3.1	3.6	1.5	7.1	16.5	39.1	92.9	98.9	86.6	213.0	316.5	6,250.4
OTHER INDUSTRIES	0.7	0.7	0.7	0.7	1.0	0.5	0.0	0.0	0.0	0.0	0.0	0.0	0.7	0.7	0.7	0.7	1.0	0.5
AGRICULTURE	133.2	137.2	127.6	123.6	370.0	:	2.0	22.0	4.9	3.5	42.0	:	135.2	159.2	132.5	127.1	412.0	0.0
OTHER MATERIAL PRODUCTION	5.8	6.1	93.2	73.7	80.0	24,354.0	0.0	10.0	7.8	4.7	0.0	20,418.0	5.8	16.1	101.0	78.4	80.0	44,772.0
TOTAL	2,327.3	2,389.2	2,418.2	2,469.0	6,784.5	120,644.0	120.2	245.0	241.2	171.9	1,120.6	136,347.0	2,447.5	2,634.2	2,659.4	2,640.9	7,905.1	256,991.0
Memo Items:																		
Share to Total Trade	95.1%	90.7%	90.9%	93.5%	85.8%	46.9%	4.9%	9.3%	9.1%	6.5%	14.2%	53.1%	100.0%	100.0%	100.0%	100.0%	100.0%	100.0%
Exchange Rate Used (Rubles per US$)	:	:	:	:	:	150	:	:	:	:	:	150	:	:	:	:	:	150

Sources: Goskomstat.

TABLE 3-4: TURKMENISTAN - TOTAL IMPORTS BY COMMODITY GROUPS AT DOMESTIC PRICES

(millions of current rubles)

	Interrepublic						Extrarepublic						Total Trade					
	1987	1988	1989	1990	1991	1992	1987	1988	1989	1990	1991	1992	1987	1988	1989	1990	1991	1992
INDUSTRY	2,529.4	2,457.0	2,611.5	2,693.1	4,246.3	65,454.8	324.6	389.8	538.8	625.2	810.2	7,207.1	2,854.0	2,846.8	3,150.3	3,318.3	5,056.5	72,661.9
POWER	8.6	8.9	9.6	10.0	15.7	139.6	0.0	0.0	0.0	0.0	0.0	..	8.6	8.9	9.6	10.0	15.7	139.6
OIL AND GAS	100.2	100.2	100.0	79.3	124.8	14,035.6	0.0	0.0	0.0	0.0	0.0	2.0	100.2	100.2	100.0	79.3	124.8	14,037.6
COAL	6.9	6.6	6.6	5.3	15.1	220.4	0.0	0.0	0.0	0.0	0.0	..	6.9	6.6	6.6	5.3	15.1	220.4
OTHER FUEL	0.0	0.0	0.0	0.0	0.0	0.0	0.0	0.0	0.0	0.0	0.0	..	0.0	0.0	0.0	0.0	0.0	0.0
FERROUS METALLURGY	105.9	107.0	83.9	105.8	166.6	2,869.0	9.8	8.3	18.5	7.3	8.9	23.0	115.7	115.3	102.4	113.1	175.5	2,892.0
NON-FERROUS METALLURGY	5.3	9.4	9.5	9.1	14.3	3,560.0	0.0	0.0	0.1	0.1	0.1	..	5.3	9.4	9.2	9.2	14.4	3,560.0
CHEMICAL & PETROLEUM	182.2	200.1	209.4	202.6	319.7	2,508.6	8.1	8.7	21.0	26.6	34.7	1,777.0	190.3	208.8	230.4	229.2	354.4	4,285.6
MACHINERY AND METAL WORKS	935.1	925.6	949.4	958.8	1,509.1	17,903.5	11.3	21.3	92.6	119.5	154.7	2,438.0	946.4	946.9	1,042.0	1,078.3	1,663.8	20,341.5
SAWMILL & LUMBER INDUSTRY	119.6	103.1	124.9	96.7	152.2	997.5	29.0	25.7	12.1	9.2	11.6	..	148.6	128.8	137.0	105.9	163.8	997.5
BUILDING MATERIALS	54.0	53.5	54.2	50.2	79.0	915.9	3.0	4.2	4.8	5.9	8.0	..	57.0	57.7	59.0	56.1	87.0	915.9
LIGHT INDUSTRY	466.8	395.1	453.3	550.7	866.8	6,412.7	136.4	195.6	243.3	254.5	330.0	840.4	603.2	590.7	696.6	805.2	1,196.8	7,253.1
FOOD PRODUCTION	436.9	433.9	477.9	444.7	699.9	15,892.0	123.7	122.8	143.9	185.1	240.0	2,126.7	560.6	556.7	621.8	629.8	939.9	18,018.7
OTHER INDUSTRIES	107.9	113.6	132.8	179.9	283.1	..	3.3	3.2	2.5	17.0	22.2	..	111.2	116.8	135.3	196.9	305.3	0.0
AGRICULTURE	66.7	28.2	33.6	132.1	207.7	14,038.0	3.7	42.4	50.7	60.1	78.3	2,660.1	70.4	70.6	84.3	192.2	286.0	16,698.1
OTHER MATERIAL PRODUCTION	0.8	0.8	98.8	97.9	154.1	915.7	0.0	0.0	0.0	0.0	0.0	..	0.8	0.8	98.8	97.9	154.1	915.7
TOTAL	2,596.9	2,486.0	2,743.9	2,923.1	4,608.1	80,408.5	328.3	432.2	589.5	685.3	888.5	10,914.5	2,925.2	2,918.2	3,333.4	3,608.4	5,496.6	91,323.0
Memo Items:																		
Share to Total Trade	88.8%	85.2%	82.3%	81.0%	83.8%	88.0%	11.2%	14.8%	17.7%	19.0%	16.2%	12.0%	100.0%	100.0%	100.0%	100.0%	100.0%	100.0%
Exchange Rate Used (Rubles per US$)	:	:	:	:	:	:	:	:	:	:	:	:	:	:	:	:	:	:

Sources: Goskomstat.

TABLE 3-4A: TURKMENISTAN - RESOURCE BALANCE BY COMMODITY GROUPS AT DOMESTIC PRICES

(millions of current rubles)

	Interrepublic						Extrarepublic						Total Trade					
	1987	1988	1989	1990	1991	1992	1987	1988	1989	1990	1991	1992	1987	1988	1989	1990	1991	1992
INDUSTRY	-341.1	-211.1	-414.1	-421.4	2,088.2	30,835.2	-206.4	-176.8	-310.3	-461.5	268.5	108,628.9	(548)	(388)	(724)	(883)	2,357	139,464
POWER	56.1	50.0	60.0	57.0	135.8	6,640.4	0.0	0.0	0.0	0.0	0.0	0.0	56	50	60	57	136	6,640
OIL AND GAS	642.4	650.4	643.0	616.5	2,438.0	63,513.4	0.0	0.0	2.1	9.3	445.0	115,803.0	642	650	645	626	2,883	179,316
COAL	-6.9	-6.6	-6.6	-5.3	-15.1	-220.4	0.0	0.0	0.0	0.0	0.0	0.0	(7)	(7)	(7)	(5)	(15)	(220)
OTHER FUEL	0.0	0.0	0.0	0.0	0.0	0.0	0.0	0.0	0.0	0.0	0.0	0.0	0	0	0	0	0	0
FERROUS METALLURGY	-102.6	-103.7	-80.5	-102.4	-159.3	-2,791.0	-9.8	-8.3	-18.5	-7.3	-8.9	-23.0	(112)	(112)	(99)	(110)	(168)	(2,814)
NON-FERROUS METALLURGY	1.0	-4.2	-4.3	-3.2	-10.2	-3,535.0	0.0	0.0	-0.1	0.0	0.0	0.0	1	(4)	(4)	(3)	(10)	(3,535)
CHEMICAL & PETROLEUM	-42.6	-49.7	-57.9	-55.9	80.3	242.4	-6.6	-7.2	-20.2	-19.9	0.0	-1,772.0	(49)	(57)	(78)	(76)	80	(1,530)
MACHINERY AND METAL WORKS	-891.4	-881.4	-910.9	-923.5	-1,419.1	-17,358.5	-10.8	-20.5	-91.7	-117.9	-149.5	-2,438.0	(902)	(902)	(1,003)	(1,041)	(1,569)	(19,797)
SAWMILL & LUMBER INDUSTRY	-119.3	-102.8	-124.6	-96.4	-151.7	-985.5	-29.0	-25.7	-12.1	-9.2	-11.6	0.0	(148)	(129)	(137)	(106)	(163)	(986)
BUILDING MATERIALS	-30.8	-32.6	-30.1	-22.0	-29.0	-262.9	-2.6	-3.7	-4.7	-5.9	-6.8	12.0	(33)	(36)	(35)	(28)	(36)	(251)
LIGHT INDUSTRY	607.3	721.0	622.7	531.8	1,900.5	-4,727.5	-23.7	11.0	-20.2	-115.6	246.0	-826.4	584	732	603	416	2,147	(5,554)
FOOD PRODUCTION	-347.1	-338.6	-392.8	-238.8	-399.9	-9,680.7	-120.6	-119.2	-142.4	-178.0	-223.5	-2,087.6	(468)	(458)	(535)	(417)	(623)	(11,768)
OTHER INDUSTRIES	-107.2	-112.9	-132.1	-179.2	-282.1	0.5	-3.3	-3.2	-2.5	-17.0	-22.2	0.0	(111)	(116)	(135)	(196)	(304)	1
AGRICULTURE	66.5	109.0	94.0	-8.5	162.3	-14,038.0	-1.7	-20.4	-45.8	-56.6	-36.3	-2,660.1	65	89	48	(65)	126	(16,698)
OTHER MATERIAL PRODUCTION	5.0	5.3	-5.6	-24.2	-74.1	23,438.3	0.0	10.0	7.8	4.7	0.0	20,418.0	5	15	2	(20)	(74)	43,856
TOTAL	-269.6	-96.8	-325.7	-454.1	2,176.4	40,235.5	-208.1	-187.2	-348.3	-513.4	232.1	125,432.5	(478)	(284)	(674)	(968)	2,409	165,668
Memo: Share to Total Trade	56.4%	34.1%	48.3%	46.9%	90.4%	24.3%	43.6%	65.9%	51.7%	53.1%	9.6%	75.7%	100.0%	100.0%	100.0%	100.0%	100.0%	100.0%

Sources: Tables 3-3 and 3-4.

TABLE 3-5: TURKMENISTAN - TOTAL EXPORTS BY COMMODITY GROUPS AT FOREIGN TRADE PRICES

(millions of current rubles)

	Interrepublic						Extrarepublic						Total Trade					
	1987	1988	1989	1990	1991	1992	1987	1988	1989	1990	1991	1992	1987	1988	1989	1990	1991	1992
INDUSTRY	:	:	2,330.4	2,645.9	:	:	:	:	113.2	108.9	:	:	:	:	2,443.6	2,754.8	:	:
POWER	:	:	105.1	100.5	:	:	:	:	0.0	0.0	:	:	:	:	105.1	100.5	:	:
OIL AND GAS	:	:	1,474.3	1,659.3	:	:	:	:	3.4	23.0	:	:	:	:	1,477.7	1,682.3	:	:
Oil Products	:	:	0.0	0.0	:	:	:	:	0.0	0.0	:	:	:	:	0.0	0.0	:	:
Refined Products	:	:	376.3	500.9	:	:	:	:	3.4	23.0	:	:	:	:	379.7	523.9	:	:
Gas Products	:	:	1,098.0	1,158.4	:	:	:	:	0.0	0.0	:	:	:	:	1,098.0	1,158.4	:	:
COAL	:	:	0.0	0.0	:	:	:	:	0.0	0.0	:	:	:	:	0.0	0.0	:	:
OTHER FUEL	:	:	0.0	0.0	:	:	:	:	0.0	0.0	:	:	:	:	0.0	0.0	:	:
FERROUS METALLURGY	:	:	3.4	3.6	:	:	:	:	0.0	0.0	:	:	:	:	3.4	3.6	:	:
NON-FERROUS METALLURGY	:	:	8.1	9.9	:	:	:	:	0.0	0.2	:	:	:	:	8.1	10.1	:	:
CHEMICAL & PETROLEUM	:	:	150.7	151.8	:	:	:	:	0.5	5.3	:	:	:	:	151.2	157.1	:	:
MACHINERY AND METAL WORKS	:	:	40.0	36.6	:	:	:	:	0.6	1.8	:	:	:	:	40.6	38.4	:	:
SAWMILL & LUMBER INDUSTRY	:	:	0.3	0.2	:	:	:	:	0.0	0.0	:	:	:	:	0.3	0.2	:	:
BUILDING MATERIALS	:	:	24.4	30.6	:	:	:	:	0.1	0.0	:	:	:	:	24.5	30.6	:	:
LIGHT INDUSTRY	:	:	492.5	541.2	:	:	:	:	108.1	75.0	:	:	:	:	600.6	616.2	:	:
FOOD PRODUCTION	:	:	30.9	111.7	:	:	:	:	0.5	3.6	:	:	:	:	31.4	115.3	:	:
OTHER INDUSTRIES	:	:	0.7	0.5	:	:	:	:	0.0	0.0	:	:	:	:	0.7	0.5	:	:
AGRICULTURE	:	:	41.5	44.4	:	:	:	:	0.8	0.7	:	:	:	:	42.3	45.1	:	:
OTHER MATERIAL PRODUCTION	:	:	94.8	83.1	:	:	:	:	9.8	4.6	:	:	:	:	104.6	87.7	:	:
TOTAL	:	:	2,466.7	2,773.4	:	:	:	:	123.8	114.2	:	:	:	:	2,590.5	2,887.6	:	:
Memo Items:																		
Share to Total Trade	:	:	95.2%	96.0%	:	:	100.0%	:	4.8%	4.0%	:	:	100.0%	:	100.0%	100.0%	100.0%	100.0%
Exchange Rate Used (Rubles per US$)	:	:	:	:	:	:	:	:	:	:	:	:	:	:	:	:	:	:

Sources: Goskomstat.

TABLE 3-6: TURKMENISTAN - TOTAL IMPORTS BY COMMODITY GROUPS AT FOREIGN TRADE PRICES

(millions of current rubles)

	Interrepublic						Extrarepublic						Total Trade					
	1987	1988	1989	1990	1991	1992	1987	1988	1989	1990	1991	1992	1987	1988	1989	1990	1991	1992
INDUSTRY	:	:	2,480.5	2,256.8	:	:	:	:	235.8	259.4	:	:	:	:	2,716.3	2,516.2	:	:
POWER	:	:	14.5	15.0	:	:	:	:	0.0	0.0	:	:	:	:	14.5	15.0	:	:
OIL AND GAS	:	:	162.0	176.6	:	:	:	:	0.0	0.0	:	:	:	:	162.0	176.6	:	:
Oil Products	:	:	0.0	0.0	:	:	:	:	0.0	0.0	:	:	:	:	0.0	0.0	:	:
Refined Products	:	:	162.0	176.6	:	:	:	:	0.0	0.0	:	:	:	:	162.0	176.6	:	:
Gas Products	:	:	0.0	0.0	:	:	:	:	0.0	0.0	:	:	:	:	0.0	0.0	:	:
COAL	:	:	6.0	5.0	:	:	:	:	0.0	0.0	:	:	:	:	6.0	5.0	:	:
OTHER FUEL	:	:	0.0	0.0	:	:	:	:	0.0	0.0	:	:	:	:	0.0	0.0	:	:
FERROUS METALLURGY	:	:	91.1	122.4	:	:	:	:	23.8	9.7	:	:	:	:	114.9	132.1	:	:
NON-FERROUS METALLURGY	:	:	14.7	15.2	:	:	:	:	0.1	0.1	:	:	:	:	14.8	15.3	:	:
CHEMICAL & PETROLEUM	:	:	160.2	168.8	:	:	:	:	14.2	19.0	:	:	:	:	174.4	187.8	:	:
MACHINERY AND METAL WORKS	:	:	1,427.4	1,191.7	:	:	:	:	73.4	85.0	:	:	:	:	1,500.8	1,276.7	:	:
SAWMILL & LUMBER INDUSTRY	:	:	71.2	63.8	:	:	:	:	6.6	5.2	:	:	:	:	77.8	69.0	:	:
BUILDING MATERIALS	:	:	52.4	43.2	:	:	:	:	1.8	2.2	:	:	:	:	54.2	45.4	:	:
LIGHT INDUSTRY	:	:	149.9	161.5	:	:	:	:	59.2	64.6	:	:	:	:	209.1	226.1	:	:
FOOD PRODUCTION	:	:	201.4	179.4	:	:	:	:	55.4	68.5	:	:	:	:	256.8	247.9	:	:
OTHER INDUSTRIES	:	:	129.7	114.2	:	:	:	:	1.3	5.1	:	:	:	:	131.0	119.3	:	:
AGRICULTURE	:	:	15.8	69.7	:	:	:	:	35.6	46.4	:	:	:	:	51.4	116.1	:	:
OTHER MATERIAL PRODUCTION	:	:	99.0	111.5	:	:	:	:	0.0	0.0	:	:	:	:	99.0	111.5	:	:
TOTAL	:	:	2,595.3	2,438.0	:	:	:	:	271.4	305.8	:	:	:	:	2,866.7	2,743.8	:	:
Memo Items:																		
Share to Total Trade	:	:	90.5%	88.9%	:	:	100.0%	:	9.5%	11.1%	:	:	100.0%	100.0%	100.0%	100.0%	100.0%	100.0%
Exchange Rate Used (Rubles per US$)	:	:	:	:	:	:	:	:	:	:	:	:	:	:	:	:	:	:

Sources: Goskomstat.

TABLE 3-6A: TURKMENISTAN - RESOURCE BALANCE BY COMMODITY GROUPS AT FOREIGN TRADE PRICES

(millions of current rubles)

	Interrepublic						Extrarepublic						Total Trade					
	1987	1988	1989	1990	1991	1992	1987	1988	1989	1990	1991	1992	1987	1988	1989	1990	1991	1992
INDUSTRY	::	::	-150.1	389.1	::	::	::	::	-122.6	-150.5	::	::	::	::	-272.7	238.6	::	::
POWER	::	::	90.6	85.5	::	::	::	::	0.0	0.0	::	::	::	::	90.6	85.5	::	::
OIL AND GAS	::	::	1,312.3	1,482.7	::	::	::	::	3.4	23.0	::	::	::	::	1,315.7	1,505.7	::	::
Oil Products	::	::	0.0	0.0	::	::	::	::	0.0	0.0	::	::	::	::	0.0	0.0	::	::
Refined Products	::	::	214.3	324.3	::	::	::	::	3.4	23.0	::	::	::	::	217.7	347.3	::	::
Gas Products	::	::	1,098.0	1,158.4	::	::	::	::	0.0	0.0	::	::	::	::	1,098.0	1,158.4	::	::
COAL	::	::	-6.0	-5.0	::	::	::	::	0.0	0.0	::	::	::	::	-6.0	-5.0	::	::
OTHER FUEL	::	::	0.0	0.0	::	::	::	::	0.0	0.0	::	::	::	::	0.0	0.0	::	::
FERROUS METALLURGY	::	::	-87.7	-118.8	::	::	::	::	-23.8	-9.7	::	::	::	::	-111.5	-128.5	::	::
NON-FERROUS METALLURGY	::	::	-6.6	-5.3	::	::	::	::	-0.1	0.1	::	::	::	::	-6.7	-5.2	::	::
CHEMICAL & PETROLEUM	::	::	-9.5	-17.0	::	::	::	::	-13.7	-13.7	::	::	::	::	-23.2	-30.7	::	::
MACHINERY AND METAL WORKS	::	::	-1,387.4	-1,155.1	::	::	::	::	-72.8	-83.2	::	::	::	::	-1,460.2	-1,238.3	::	::
SAWMILL & LUMBER INDUSTRY	::	::	-70.9	-63.6	::	::	::	::	-6.6	-5.2	::	::	::	::	-77.5	-68.8	::	::
BUILDING MATERIALS	::	::	-28.0	-12.6	::	::	::	::	-1.7	-2.2	::	::	::	::	-29.7	-14.8	::	::
LIGHT INDUSTRY	::	::	342.6	379.7	::	::	::	::	48.9	10.4	::	::	::	::	391.5	390.1	::	::
FOOD PRODUCTION	::	::	-170.5	-67.7	::	::	::	::	-54.9	-64.9	::	::	::	::	-225.4	-132.6	::	::
OTHER INDUSTRIES	::	::	-129.0	-113.7	::	::	::	::	-1.3	-5.1	::	::	::	::	-130.3	-118.8	::	::
AGRICULTURE	::	::	25.7	-25.3	::	::	::	::	-34.8	-45.7	::	::	::	::	-9.1	-71.0	::	::
OTHER MATERIAL PRODUCTION	::	::	-4.2	-28.4	::	::	::	::	9.8	4.6	::	::	::	::	5.6	-23.8	::	::
TOTAL	::	::	-128.6	335.4	::	::	::	::	-147.6	-191.6	::	::	::	::	-276.2	143.8	::	::
Memo: Share to Total Trade	::	::	46.6%	233.2%	::	::	::	::	53.4%	-133.2%	::	::	100.0%	100.0%	100.0%	100.0%	100.0%	100.0%

Sources: Tables 3-5 and 3-6.

TABLE 3-7: TURKMENISTAN - GEOGRAPHICAL DISTRIBUTION OF INTERREPUBLIC TRADE AT DOMESTIC PRICES

	EXPORTS						IMPORTS					
	1987	1988	1989	1990	1991	1992	1987	1988	1989	1990	1991	1992
	(millions of current rubles)											
T O T A L T R A D E	2,327.3	2,389.2	2,418.2	2,469.0	6,784.5	120,644.0	2,596.3	2,486.0	2,746.1	2,927.4	4,608.1	80,408.5
Armenia	..	..	..	..	..	2,791.4	..	..	..	..	..	341.2
Azerbaijan	..	..	..	..	..	4,676.0	..	..	..	..	..	6,812.2
Belarus	48.8	53.8	50.1	50.8	139.5	2,311.1	100.5	110.7	103.1	104.7	164.7	3,315.7
Estonia 1/	55.4	61.1	56.9	57.7	158.5	2,851.9	80.4	88.6	82.5	83.7	131.9	..
Georgia	..	..	..	..	..	8,123.4	..	..	..	..	..	..
Kazakhstan	61.3	67.5	62.9	63.8	175.2	9,829.5	112.7	123.5	115.1	116.8	184.1	9,519.2
Kyrgyzstan	..	..	..	..	..	3,689.5	..	..	..	..	..	1,126.6
Latvia 2/	..	..	..	..	..	..	..	..	..	..	..	..
Lithuania 2/	..	..	..	..	..	..	..	..	..	..	..	..
Moldova	..	..	..	..	..	6,969.1	..	..	..	..	..	37.6
Russia	1,179.4	1,300.0	1,211.6	1,229.7	3,377.9	24,189.9	1,172.6	1,291.5	1,203.7	1,221.7	1,925.4	28,201.6
Tajikistan	..	..	..	..	..	7,816.0	..	..	..	..	..	3,440.3
Ukraine	174.4	193.2	180.1	182.8	502.1	21,108.5	438.3	483.0	450.1	456.8	719.9	3,687.4
Uzbekistan	658.2	725.3	675.9	686.0	1,884.4	20,469.2	159.5	175.7	163.7	166.1	261.7	6,493.4
Statistical Discrepancy	..	..	..	..	..	..	..	..	..	..	..	..
	(Percentage Shares to Total Trade)											
T O T A L T R A D E	100.0	100.0	100.0	100.0	100.0	100.0	100.0	100.0	100.0	100.0	100.0	100.0
Armenia	..	..	..	..	..	2.3	..	..	..	..	..	0.4
Azerbaijan	..	..	..	..	..	3.9	..	..	..	..	..	8.5
Belarus	2.1	2.3	2.1	2.1	2.1	1.9	3.9	4.5	3.8	3.6	3.6	4.1
Estonia 1/	2.4	2.6	2.4	2.3	2.3	2.4	3.1	3.6	3.0	2.9	2.9	..
Georgia	..	..	..	..	..	6.7	..	..	..	..	..	..
Kazakhstan	2.6	2.8	2.6	2.6	2.6	8.1	4.3	5.0	4.2	4.0	4.0	11.8
Kyrgyzstan	..	..	..	..	..	3.1	..	..	..	..	..	1.4
Latvia 2/	..	..	..	..	..	..	..	..	..	..	..	..
Lithuania 2/	..	..	..	..	..	..	..	..	..	..	..	..
Moldova	..	..	..	..	..	5.8	..	..	..	..	..	0.0
Russia	50.7	54.4	50.1	49.8	49.8	20.1	45.2	52.0	43.8	41.7	41.8	35.1
Tajikistan	..	..	..	..	..	6.5	..	..	..	..	..	4.3
Ukraine	7.5	8.1	7.4	7.4	7.4	17.5	16.9	19.4	16.4	15.6	15.6	4.6
Uzbekistan	28.3	30.4	28.0	27.8	27.8	17.0	6.1	7.1	6.0	5.7	5.7	8.1
Statistical Discrepancy	..	..	..	..	..	..	..	..	..	..	..	..

1/ *Estonia, Latvia, and Lithuania.*
2/ *Included in Estonia.*

Sources: Goskomstat.

TABLE 5-1: TURKMENISTAN - CONSOLIDATED GOVERNMENT BUDGET 1/

(in millions of current rubles)

	1985	1986	1987	1988	1989	1990	1991	1992
Total Revenue	1,630	1,786	1,846	2,154	2,303	3,236	6,487	64,009
Tax Revenue	826	834	857	894	1,042	1,038	1,971	34,447
Turnover Tax 2/	583	576	593	619	711	780	669	..
Value-added Tax 3/	..	..	..	..	..	..	..	17,400
Company Profits Tax	..	..	..	..	..	..	518	12,568
Excise Tax 3/	..	..	..	..	..	..	..	1,187
Sales Tax 4/	..	..	..	..	..	..	314	..
Profit Tax from Cooperatives 5/	44	51	48	46	71	92	122	307
Personal Income Tax	199	207	215	230	260	166	349	2,985
Non-tax Revenue	607	712	744	896	802	1,471	3,106	29,562
Foreign Economic Activity 6/	..	..	..	..	..	..	11	56
State Duties	9	9	10	10	9	15	34	..
State Lottery	3	3	3	3	3	3	3	..
Funds from Social Security	104	116	126	140	172	187	..	..
Profit Transfers 7/	233	257	283	322	259	312	..	..
Fixed Payments 8/	..	..	..	..	..	..	1,551	18,253
Other Revenue	240	295	295	397	330	917	1,503	11,253
State Bonds 9/	17	32	28	24	28	36	6	..
Union Transfers	197	240	245	364	460	728	1,409	..
Total Expenditure	1,542	1,703	1,767	2,052	2,222	3,114	5,896	92,665
National Economy 10/	732	813	701	955	1,033	1,848	2,302	58,059
Social and Cultural	723	785	863	966	1,039	1,162	3,355	26,396
of which:								
Education and Science	431	467	518	573	602	655	1,159	13,423
Health, Physical Education	156	171	186	220	246	283	556	6,297
Social Security	119	131	141	155	173	207	1,572	5,256
Internal Security and Administration 11/	31	31	31	32	30	49	161	4,409
Other Expenditure	55	73	172	99	119	55	78	3,801
Surplus/Deficit	88	83	79	103	82	122	591	-28,656

1/ Includes all levels of government, but excludes the hard-currency fund.
2/ Abolished in 1992.
3/ Adopted in 1992.
4/ Introduced in 1991, abolished in 1992.
5/ Same as company income tax.
6/ Income arising from the sale of goods imported with hard currency.
7/ Transfers from state-owned enterprises (formerly of the Union).
8/ Transfers required from the state-owned gas and cotton corporations.
9/ Not a financing item: state bonds were issued by the former USSR government and sold in Turkmenistan.
   The receipts were divided evenly between the Union and Turkmenistan. However, these bonds were the liability
   of the Union government making Turkmenistan's share a transfer from the Union.
10/ Including development (capital) expenditure, and subsidies on account of price differentials.
11/ Includes police, administration, and defense since 1992.

Source: Ministry of Economics and Finance.

TABLE 5-2: TURKMENISTAN - CONSOLIDATED GOVERNMENT BUDGET 1/

(percentage shares)

	1985	1986	1987	1988	1989	1990	1991	1992
(percentage share of total revenue)								
Total Revenue	100.0	100.0	100.0	100.0	100.0	100.0	100.0	100.0
Tax Revenue	50.7	46.7	46.4	41.5	45.2	32.1	30.4	53.8
Turnover Tax 2/	35.8	32.3	32.1	28.7	30.9	24.1	10.3	..
Value-added Tax 3/	..	..	..	..	..	..	..	27.2
Company Profits Tax	..	..	..	..	..	..	8.0	19.6
Excise Tax 3/	..	..	..	..	..	..	..	1.9
Sales Tax 4/	..	..	..	..	..	..	4.8	..
Profit Tax from Cooperatives 5/	2.7	2.9	2.6	2.1	3.1	2.8	1.9	0.5
Personal Income Tax	12.2	11.6	11.7	10.7	11.3	5.1	5.4	4.7
Non-tax Revenue	37.2	39.9	40.3	41.6	34.8	45.4	47.9	46.2
Foreign Economic Activity 6/	..	..	..	..	..	..	0.2	0.1
State Duties	0.5	0.5	0.5	0.5	0.4	0.5	0.5	..
State Lottery	0.2	0.2	0.2	0.1	0.1	0.1	0.0	..
Funds from Social Security	6.4	6.5	6.8	6.5	7.5	5.8	..	..
Profit Transfers 7/	14.3	14.4	15.3	14.9	11.2	9.6	..	..
Fixed Payments 8/	..	..	..	..	..	..	23.9	28.5
Other Revenue	14.7	16.5	16.0	18.4	14.3	28.3	23.2	17.6
State Bonds 9/	1.0	1.8	1.5	1.1	1.2	1.1	0.1	..
Union Transfers	12.1	13.4	13.3	16.9	20.0	22.5	21.7	..
(percentage share of total expenditure)								
Total Expenditure	100.0	100.0	100.0	100.0	100.0	100.0	100.0	100.0
National Economy 10/	47.5	47.7	39.7	46.5	46.5	59.4	39.1	62.7
Social and Cultural of which:	46.9	46.1	48.9	47.1	46.8	37.3	56.9	28.5
Education and Science	28.0	27.4	29.3	27.9	27.1	21.0	19.7	14.5
Health, Physical Education	10.1	10.0	10.5	10.7	11.1	9.1	9.4	6.8
Social Security	7.7	7.7	8.0	7.6	7.8	6.6	26.7	5.7
Internal Security and Administration 11	2.0	1.8	1.7	1.5	1.4	1.6	2.7	4.8
Other Expenditure	3.6	4.3	9.7	4.8	5.4	1.8	1.3	4.1

Source: Table 5-1.

TABLE 5-3: TURKMENISTAN - CONSOLIDATED GOVERNMENT BUDGET 1/

(in percent of GDP)

	1985	1986	1987	1988	1989	1990	1991	1992
Total Revenue	..	..	29.6	32.1	32.4	42.7	44.2	22.5
Tax Revenue	..	..	13.7	13.3	14.6	13.7	13.4	12.1
Turnover Tax 2/	..	..	9.5	9.2	10.0	10.3	4.6	..
Value-added Tax 3/	..	..	..	..	..	..	..	6.1
Company Profits Tax	..	..	..	..	..	..	3.5	4.4
Excise Tax 3/	..	..	..	..	..	..	..	0.4
Sales Tax 4/	..	..	..	..	..	..	2.1	..
Profit Tax from Cooperatives 5/	..	..	0.8	0.7	1.0	1.2	0.8	0.1
Personal Income Tax	..	..	3.5	3.4	3.7	2.2	2.4	1.1
Non-tax Revenue	..	..	11.9	13.3	11.3	19.4	21.2	10.4
Foreign Economic Activity 6/	..	..	..	..	..	..	0.1	0.0
State Duties	..	..	0.2	0.1	0.1	0.2	0.2	..
State Lottery	..	..	0.0	0.0	0.0	0.0	0.0	..
Funds from Social Security	..	..	2.0	2.1	2.4	2.5	..	..
Profit Transfers 7/	..	..	4.5	4.8	3.6	4.1	..	..
Fixed Payments 8/	..	..	..	..	..	..	10.6	6.4
Other Revenue	..	..	4.7	5.9	4.6	12.1	10.2	4.0
State Bonds 9/	..	..	0.4	0.4	0.4	0.5	0.0	..
	..	..						
Union Transfers	..	..	3.9	5.4	6.5	9.6	9.6	..
Total Expenditure	..	..	28.3	30.6	31.2	41.1	40.2	32.6
National Economy 10/	..	..	11.2	14.2	14.5	24.4	15.7	20.4
Social and Cultural of which:	..	..	13.8	14.4	14.6	15.3	22.9	9.3
Education and Science	..	..	8.3	8.5	8.5	8.6	7.9	4.7
Health, Physical Education	..	..	3.0	3.3	3.5	3.7	3.8	2.2
Social Security	..	..	2.3	2.3	2.4	2.7	10.7	1.8
Internal Security and Administration 11	..	..	0.5	0.5	0.4	0.6	1.1	1.6
Other Expenditure	..	..	2.8	1.5	1.7	0.7	0.5	1.3
Surplus/Deficit	..	..	1.3	1.5	1.1	1.6	4.0	-10.1
Memorandum items:								
GNP (current prices) 1/	..	..	6,236	6,710	7,117	7,582	14,666	284,213

1/ GNP for 1992 was estimated.

Source: Table 5-1.

TABLE 6-1: TURKMENISTAN - MONETARY SURVEY, 1989-91 1/

	Absolute Changes			Changes			
	1989	1990	1991	1989-90	1990-91	1989-90	1990-91
	(in millions of rubles)			*(in millions of rubles)*		*(in percent)*	
Net external claims 2/	3,780	2,768	5,064	(1,012)	2,295	-26.8	82.9
Net domestic assets	1,706	4,044	13,261	2,285	9,271	133.9	232.3
Net credit to government (net)	..	360	21	..	(285)	..	-33.1
Credit to the economy	2,950	3,240	9,548	290	6,308	9.8	195.3
Other items (net)	..	444	3,692	..	3,248	..	731.5
Broad money (M2)	5,486	6,759	18,325	1,273	11,566	23.2	171.1
Currency in circulation	1,604	1,823	4,471	219	2,648	13.6	145.3
Deposits	3,881	4,936	13,854	1,055	8,918	27.2	180.2
Memorandum items:							
Narrow money (M1)	4,011	4,883	13,060	872	8,178	21.8	167.5
Broad money in 1990 prices	5,957	6,759	7,037	801	279	13.5	
Currency deposits ratio	0.41	0.37	0.32				
Velocity of broad money	1.6	1.5	1.5				

1/ Data refer to January 1 of the following year.

2/ Includes foreign exchange held by the Government. This item also includes certain ruble claims
   and liabilities in Turkmenistan viv-a-vis other republics of the former USSR.

Source: IMF, 1992; State Bank of Turkmenistan.

TABLE 7-1: TURKMENISTAN - AGRICULTURAL PRODUCTION

(in millions of rubles, current prices)

	1985	1986	1987	1988	1989	1990	1991	1992
Total Gross Agricultural Production	2,314.8	2,302.3	2,556.9	2,616.7	2,921.5	3,491.1	7,163.2	57,795.0
Crop Production	1,773.3	1,763.6	1,958.6	2,004.4	2,237.9	2,624.8	5,573.2	43,732.0
Grains	56.7	56.4	62.7	64.1	71.6	90.5	211.8	7,528.0
Potatoes	4.7	5.6	7.9	7.9	8.6	9.5	31.3	165.0
Vegetables	86.8	86.4	96.0	98.2	109.7	139.1	297.8	1,011.0
Fruits (without grapes)	24.2	31.7	33.5	36.1	29.8	52.2	87.7	352.0
Grapes	60.3	83.3	85.9	84.9	70.8	112.2	254.2	1,164.0
Tobacco	0.0	0.0	0.0	0.0	0.0	0.0	0.0	0.0
Cotton	1,388.5	1,380.9	1,533.6	1,569.4	1,752.3	2,222.8	4,758.4	31,910.0
Sugarbeets	0.0	0.0	0.0	0.0	0.0	0.0	0.0	0.0
Oilseeds	0.0	0.0	0.0	0.0	0.0	0.0	0.0	0.0
Livestock Production	541.5	538.7	598.3	612.3	683.6	866.3	1,590.0	14,063.0
Livestock	279.0	277.4	308.1	315.3	352.0	446.1	738.7	6,791.0
Cattle	125.6	124.8	138.6	141.8	158.4	200.7	383.3	3,362.0
Pigs	19.6	19.0	24.0	23.9	28.8	33.9	45.6	510.0
Sheep and goats	101.8	101.3	112.4	115.0	128.5	162.8	234.5	2,385.0
Poultry	19.8	19.7	21.9	22.4	25.0	31.7	43.7	201.0
Milk	102.4	101.8	113.0	115.7	129.2	163.4	269.4	2,694.0
Eggs	21.7	21.5	24.0	24.5	27.3	34.3	71.1	359.0
Wool	87.1	91.9	100.7	100.7	109.5	141.5	382.2	1,465.0
Agriculture Services	..	..	..	..	..	..	..	..
Material Inputs of which:	684.5	709.3	771.4	786.2	827.8	943.1	1,514.8	12,545.0
Crop Production	407.7	423.0	413.8	475.5	488.0	744.3	1,009.2	8,651.0
Animal Production	283.4	294.2	357.6	330.4	339.8	517.2	505.6	3,894.0
Net Material Product of which:	1,641.1	1,564.9	1,785.5	1,841.0	2,093.7	2,548.0	5,648.4	45,250.0
Crop Production	1,365.6	1,340.6	1,544.8	1,528.9	1,749.9	2,091.5	4,564.0	35,081.0
Animal Production	258.3	244.5	240.7	281.9	343.8	477.5	1,084.4	10,169.0

Source: Goskomstat.

TABLE 7-2: TURKMENISTAN - AGRICULTURAL PRODUCTION

(in millions of 1983 rubles)

	1985	1986	1987	1988	1989	1990	1991	1992
Total Gross Agricultural Production	2,357.0	2,314.5	2,429.2	2,638.1	2,647.8	2,832.6	2,713.7	2,482.0
Crop Production	1,547.7	1,503.4	1,634.8	1,819.7	1,826.5	2,000.1	1,865.1	1,612.0
Grains	45.4	45.8	49.2	58.9	53.3	60.5	67.9	98.0
Potatoes	4.1	4.8	6.6	7.2	7.0	6.7	5.8	7.5
Vegetables	92.0	99.0	114.6	112.2	125.0	122.4	115.8	94.0
Fruits (without grapes)	21.1	27.0	28.0	30.2	24.3	28.1	32.1	27.0
Grapes	52.6	71.0	71.7	71.1	57.8	79.1	78.1	59.0
Tobacco	0.0	0.0	0.0	0.0	0.0	0.0	0.0	..
Cotton	1,161.8	1,086.6	1,210.2	1,337.4	1,408.9	1,519.3	1,392.3	1,126.0
Sugarbeets	0.0	0.0	0.0	0.0	0.0	0.0	0.0	..
Oilseeds	0.0	0.0	0.0	0.0	0.0	0.0	0.0	..
Livestock Production	809.3	811.1	794.4	818.4	821.3	832.5	848.6	870.0
Livestock:								
Cattle	200.4	191.2	177.9	178.8	175.6	181.1	182.6	187.0
Pigs		28.6	32.0	32.0	34.6	32.6	26.2	25.6
Sheep and goats	144.3	152.0	133.5	147.1	149.3	147.5	154.2	171.0
Poultry	21.7	28.8	24.4	27.0	29.2	29.0	25.1	21.0
Milk	138.0	147.9	159.4	163.1	167.8	172.3	181.5	187.0
Eggs	26.3	28.8	30.5	31.4	31.4	31.4	28.7	28.0
Wool	..	138.3	136.4	134.6	131.6	136.0	138.7	141.1
Agriculture Services	..	..	..	..	..	..	..	..
Material Inputs	669.7	694.3	721.9	753.6	788.6	879.6	1,073.2	958.0
of which:								
Crop Production	424.0	417.0	446.0	465.0	468.0	483.0	589.0	590.0
Animal Production	262.7	257.4	275.9	287.0	289.1	298.3	335.6	368.0
Net Material Product	1,687.4	1,620.2	1,707.3	1,884.6	1,846.2	2,243.8	1,978.2	1,524.0
of which:								
Crop Production	1,123.7	1,086.4	1,188.8	1,354.6	1,358.4	1,517.1	1,337.2	1,022.0
Animal Production	546.7	453.7	518.5	531.5	532.4	534.2	570.0	502.0

Source: Goskomstat.

TABLE 7-3: TURKMENISTAN - AGRICULTURAL PRODUCTION, BY TYPE OF FARM

(in millions of 1983 rubles)

	1985	1986	1987	1988	1989	1990	1991	1992
Total Agriculture	**2,357.0**	**2,314.5**	**2,429.2**	**2,638.1**	**2,647.8**	**2,832.6**	**2,713.7**	**2,582.2**
Crop Production	1,547.7	1,503.4	1,634.8	1,819.7	1,826.5	2,000.1	1,865.1	1,723.8
Livestock Production	809.3	811.1	794.4	818.4	821.3	832.5	848.6	858.4
Total Public Sector	**1,901.2**	**1,850.7**	**1,979.1**	**2,188.3**	**2,204.8**	**2,375.3**	**2,240.1**	**1,947.3**
Collective Farms	1,501.7	1,441.8	1,546.7	1,700.7	1,759.9	1,906.4	1,790.9	1,528.3
Crop Production	1,231.5	1,167.2	1,270.2	1,410.7	1,461.9	1,603.7	1,486.4	1,251.4
Livestock Production	272.2	274.6	276.5	289.9	298.0	302.7	304.5	276.9
State Farms	353.6	337.5	385.0	436.0	397.5	433.4	415.2	389.0
Crop Production	229.2	218.2	264.0	298.7	259.6	304.8	292.0	263.5
Livestock Production	124.4	119.3	121.0	138.3	137.9	128.6	123.2	125.5
Other State Enterprises	45.9	71.4	47.4	51.6	47.4	35.5	34.0	30.0
Crop Production	29.4	53.2	33.2	40.7	34.0	20.6	20.0	7.4
Livestock Production	16.5	18.2	14.2	10.9	13.4	14.9	14.0	22.6
Individual Farms	**455.8**	**463.8**	**450.1**	**448.9**	**443.0**	**457.3**	**473.6**	**525.7**
Crop Production	59.6	64.8	67.4	69.6	71.0	71.0	66.7	102.3
Livestock Production	396.2	399.0	382.7	379.3	372.0	386.3	406.9	423.4

Source: Goskomstat.

TABLE 7-4: TURKMENISTAN - MAIN INDICATORS OF AGRICULTURAL FARMS

1990	Total	Collective farms (kolhozes)	State Farms (sovhozes)	Other (state farms)	Private Plots	Private Farms
Number of farms	..	361	136	..	..	..
Gross Output (million 1983 rubles)	2,833	1,906	433	36	457	..
Fixed Capital (million rubles)	..	..	..	..	..	..
Profits (million rubles)	..	635	115	..	..	..
Number of loss-making farms	..	3	7	..	..	..
Production (thousand tons)						
Grain	449.1	321.4	101.6	21.5	4.6	..
Sugar beets	..	..	..	..	..	..
Sunflowers	..	..	..	..	..	..
Cotton(raw)	1,457.2	1,294.9	162.2	0.1		
Flax	..	..	..	..		..
Potatoes	35.1	8.2	2.0	..	24.9	..
Vegetables	407.1	272.3	56.0	4.8	74.0	..
Watermelon	314.7	21`4.7	63.3	18.0	18.7	
Meat	104.3	29.2	18.0	14.1	43.0	..
Milk	435.5	154.9	36.7	6.8	237.1	..
Eggs (millions)	327.6	128.2	85.1	7.6	106.7	..
Cattle (thousand heads)	829.3	255.1	57.9	63.1	453.2	..
Cows	331.1	72.6	15.4	5.1	238.0	..
Pigs	266.8	* 152.4	62.6	47.6	4.2	..
Sheep, goats	5,481.1	2,166.7	1,391.1	272.9	1,650.4	..
Poultry	7,390.3	2,792.9	1,863.4	234.8	2,499.2	..

1991	Total	Collective farms (kolhozes)	State Farms (sovhozes)	Other (state farms)	Private Plots	Private Farms
Number of farms	..	369	137	..	..	..
Gross Output (million 1983 rubles)	2,714	1,791	415	34	473.5	..
Fixed Capital (million rubles)	..	..	..	..	..	..
Profits (million rubles)	..	1,260	248	..	..	..
Number of loss-making farms	19	4	10	4	..	..
Production (thousand tons)						
Grain	516.6	374.1	..	..	4.5	..
Sugar beets	..	..	..	..	..	..
Sunflowers	..	..	..	..	..	..
Cotton(raw)	1,432.8	1,267.9	164.8	0.1		
Flax	..	..	..	..	..	..
Potatoes	30.3	6.2	..	..	23.4	..
Vegetables	388.4	263.4	..	..	79.2	..
Watermelon	..	..	..	..	..	..
Meat	99.5	27.9	15.3	11.8	44.5	..
Milk	458.2	157.2	44.3	6.4	250.3	..
Eggs (millions)	300.0	115.5	72.5	5.0	107	..
Cattle (thousand heads)	898.6	260.4	54.9	62.5	520.5	0.3
Cows	360.2	72.8	14.7	5.2	267.4	0.1
Pigs	259.6	152.4	60.0	41.2	6.0	..
Sheep, goats	5,599.3	2,176.0	1,378.9	267.7	1776.6	..
Poultry	7,790.9	2,851.6	1,948.3	229.5	2761.5	..

(continued)

TABLE 7-4: TURKMENISTAN - MAIN INDICATORS OF AGRICULTURAL FARMS, continued

1992	Total	Collective farms (kolhozes)	State Farms (sovhozes)	Other (state farms)	Private Plots	Private Farms
Number of farms	..	372	147	..	..	..
Gross Output (million 1983 rubles)	2,482	1,528	389	30	534.3 1/	..
Fixed Capital (million rubles)	..	..	..	..	..	..
Profits (million rubles)	..	6,227	2,229	..	..	..
Number of loss-making farms	..	25	16	..	..	..
Production (thousand tons)						
Grain	636.9	550.5	152.6	14.3	19.5 1/	..
Sugar beets	..	..	..	..	..	..
Sunflowers	..	..	..	..	..	0.1
Cotton (raw)	1,300.0	1,149.6	149.2	1.1	..	..
Flax	..	..	..	..	..	..
Potatoes	39.5	7.8	0.7	0.1	30.9 1/	..
Vegetables	319.7	204.8	30.9	2.2	801.8 1/	..
Watermelon	213.1	130.9	42.7	6.4	33.1 1/	..
Meat	97.9	24.6	14.7	7.2	51.3	0.1
Milk	471.1	150.6	32.5	5.6	282.3	0.1
Eggs (millions)	292.0	104.0	60.8	4.5	122.7	..
Cattle (thousand heads)	1,004.1	268.6	61.3	56.3	615.8	1.1
Cows	416.0	73.0	14.7	4.9	322.9	0.5
Pigs	212.0	119.8	52.6	32.9	6.6	0.1
Sheep, goats	6,265.0	2,363.3	1,511.2	1,214.7	2,175.4	0.4
Poultry	6,964.5	2,113.9	1,696.0	194.3	2,960.3	..

1 9 9 3	Total	Collective farms (kolhozes)	State Farms (sovhozes)	Other (state farms)	Private Plots	Private Farms
Number of farms	..	..	..	..	..	..
Gross Output (million 1983 rubles)	..	..	..	..	..	..
Fixed Capital (million rubles)	..	..	..	..	..	..
Profits (million rubles)	..	..	..	..	..	..
Number of loss-making farms	..	..	..	..	..	..
Production (thousand tons)						
Grain	..	..	..	..	..	..
Sugar beets	..	..	..	..	..	..
Sunflowers	..	..	..	..	..	..
Flax	..	..	..	..	..	..
Potatoes	..	..	..	..	..	..
Vegetables	..	..	..	..	..	..
Watermelon	..	..	..	..		
Meat	..	..	..	..	..	..
Milk	..	..	..	..	..	..
Eggs (millions)	..	..	..	..	..	..
Cattle (thousand heads)	..	..	..	..	..	..
Cows	..	..	..	..	..	..
Pigs	..	..	..	..	..	..
Sheep, goats	..	..	..	..	..	..
Poultry	..	..	..	..	..	..

1/ *Includes private farms.*

Sources: Goskomstat.

TABLE 7-5: TURKMENISTAN - PRODUCTION AND AVERAGE YIELD OF MAJOR AGRICULTURAL CROPS

	1980	1985	1986	1987	1988	1989	1990	1991	1992
Production (thousands of tons)									
Grain - Cleanweight	..	..	293	324	408	379	449	517	737
Winter wheat	..	..	89	93	92	86	130	195	370
Spring wheat	..	..	..	..	..	..	..	11	7
Coarse grain									
Rye	..	..	..	..	..	..	..	..	5
Corn	..	..	98	95	159	140	135	126	159
Winter barley	..	..	66	88	105	105	139	127	126
Spring barley	..	..	..	..	..	..	..	1	1
Oats	..	..	..	..	..	..	..	..	..
Millet	..	..	..	..	..	..	..	..	..
Rice			38	45	50	45	42	54	64
Flax	..	..	..	..	..	..	..	..	..
Oilseeds	..	..	..	..	..	..	..	..	..
Sunflowerseed	..	..	..	..	..	..	..	..	..
Soybeans	..	..	..	..	..	..	..	..	..
Other	..	..	..	..	..	..	..	..	..
Cotton (raw)	..	..	1,138	1,272	1,341	1,382	1,457	1,433	1300
Cotton fiber	..	..	354	380	410	397	437	430	404
Sugarbeets	..	..	..	..	..	..	..	..	..
Potatoes	..	..	25	34	38	37	35	30	39
Pulses	..	..	..	..	..	..	..	..	..
Vegetables	..	..	334	354	372	414	411	388	320
Fruit	..	..	197	201	215	166	216	223	174
Grapes	..	..	152	154	165	124	169	167	125
Other	..	..	45	47	50	42	47	56	49
Corn (silage and greenchop)	..	..	..	..	..	..	..	..	..
Hay	..	..	..	..	..	..	..	..	..
Average yield (centners per hectare)									
Grain									
Winter wheat	..	..	17.8	17.1	20.6	21.2	23.6	19.0	19.4
Spring wheat	..	..	15.0	14.7	15.3	15.4	21.6	8.5	7.3
Coarse grain									
Rye	..	..	..	..	..	..	..	..	19.8
Corn	..	..	25.3	21.0	32.8	32.3	31.0	33.3	36.4
Winter barley	..	..	13.7	14.9	15.4	17.4	21.0	19.9	20.5
Spring barley	..	..	..	..	..	..	..	16.2	13.7
Oats	..	..	..	..	..	..	..	..	..
Millet	..	..	..	..	..	..	..	..	..
Rice			24.9	25.3	26.	22.5	26.0	28.3	23.0
Flax	..	..	..	..	..	..	..	..	..
Oilseeds	..	..	..	..	..	..	..	..	..
Sunflowerseed	..	..	..	..	..	..	..	..	..
Soybeans	..	..	..	..	..	..	..	..	..
Other	..	..	..	..	..	..	..	..	..
Cotton (raw)	..	..	17.5	20.1	21.1	21.8	23.4	28.3	23.0
Cotton fiber	..	..	5.4	6.0	6.4	6.3	7.0	..	..
Sugarbeets	..	..	..	..	..	..	..	..	..
Potatoes	..	..	69.0	81.0	100.0	91.0	78.0	98.0	93.8
Pulses	..	..	..	..	..	..	..	..	..
Vegetables	..	..	140.0	122.0	124.0	136.0	111.0	141.0	114.7
Fruit	..	..							
Grapes	..	..	89.5	78.2	80.8	72.5	81.8	83.1	59.7
Other	..	..	30.8	30.4	34.2	28.4	32.8	38.9	31.1
Corn (silage and greenchop)	..	..	..	..	..	..	..	..	..
Hay	..	..	..	..	..	..	..	..	..

Source: Goskomstat.

TABLE 8-1: TURKMENISTAN - GROSS INDUSTRIAL PRODUCTION BY SECTOR 1/

(in millions of current rubles)

	1980	1985	1986	1987	1988	1989	1990	1991	1992
All Industry	3,033	3,983	4,205	4,326	4,525	4,645	4,799	14,703	186,798
Heavy Industry	1,263	1,880	1,973	2,059	2,047	2,060	2,081	6,544	126,599
Fuel- Energy Industry	740	1,138	1,190	1,207	1,196	1,243	1,239	4,931	107,932
Electricity	103	170	211	218	212	242	250	565	8,736
Fuel Industry	638	969	978	990	984	1,001	989	4,366	99,196
Metallurgy	5	6	6	6	7	8	9	16	184
Machinery	37	47	51	52	53	58	58	115	1,365
Chemical and Petrochemical	113	154	175	202	207	201	204	404	5,720
Forestry/Wood Products	33	56	64	68	65	67	64	95	531
Construction Materials	177	259	269	286	293	272	285	583	7,130
Other Production	158	219	218	238	227	211	223	400	3,737
Light Industry	1,353	1,560	1,695	1,674	1,845	1,906	2,028	6,072	36,519
Textiles	1,168	1,323	1,454	1,433	1,587	1,638	1,745	5,488	33,623
Clothing	126	171	185	188	212	222	235	462	2,221
Leather and Shoe	60	66	56	54	46	47	48	122	675
Food Industry	417	543	538	592	632	679	690	2,087	23,680
Food processing	172	225	213	249	272	292	303	690	8,612
Meat and dairy products	120	159	165	174	185	192	196	876	7,397
Fish	27	36	31	38	32	39	34	57	397
Flour, groats and fodder	98	123	129	131	144	157	157	464	7,274

1/ *Data includes intermediate inputs.*

Source: Goskomstat.

TABLE 8-2: TURKMENISTAN - GROSS INDUSTRIAL PRODUCTION BY SECTOR 1/

(in millions of 1982 rubles)

	1980	1985	1986	1987	1988	1989	1990	1991	1992
All Industry	3,650	4,149	4,347	4,484	4,674	4,796	4,963	5,201	4,426
Heavy Industry	1,699	2,013	2,084	2,198	2,192	2,202	2,216	2,350	1,884
Fuel- Energy Industry	1,145	1,268	1,300	1,334	1,325	1,373	1,362	1,454	1,122
Electricity	121	192	215	229	224	253	258	269	265
Fuel Industry	1,024	1,076	1,085	1,105	1,101	1,121	1,104	1,186	899
Metallurgy	5	6	6	6	8	8	8	9	7
Machinery	40	48	51	52	53	58	58	65	59
Chemical and Petrochemica	130	154	175	203	207	201	204	194	126
Forestry/Wood Products	40	57	65	69	67	67	63	65	62
Construction Materials	191	260	271	292	300	278	288	305	325
Other Production	148	221	217	242	233	217	233	257	143
Light Industry	1,512	1,565	1,702	1,684	1,838	1,908	2,033	2,096	2,181
Textiles	1,317	1,328	1,460	1,439	1,575	1,637	1,748	1,787	1,858
Clothing	121	171	186	192	217	225	237	258	270
Leather and Shoe	74	66	56	54	46	47	48	53	57
Food Industry	439	570	560	603	643	686	714	756	765
Food processing	187	255	234	261	281	300	329	359	348
Meat and dairy products	120	157	164	173	183	191	194	194	205
Fish	33	35	34	39	37	39	34	32	39
Flour, groats and fodder	99	123	128	131	142	157	157	175	178

1/ *Data includes intermediate inputs.*

Source: Goskomstat.

TABLE 8-3:   TURKMENISTAN - ELECTRICITY PRODUCTION AND CONSUMPTION

(in millions of kwh)

	1980	1985	1986	1987	1988	1989	1990	1991
Production	6,712	10,987	12,396	13,267	12,891	14,508	14,611	14,954
of which:								
Thermal	6,707	10,986	12,395	13,264	12,888	14,503	14,606	14,950
Hydro	5	1	1	3	3	5	5	4
Nuclear	..	..	..	..	..	..	..	..
Imports	563	807	888	944	979	1,058	1,113	1,132
of which: Interrepublic								
Total Supply	7,275	11,794	13,284	14,211	13,870	15,566	15,724	16,086
Domestic Consumption	5,707	7,375	8,076	8,331	8,535	9,264	9,653	9,587
of which:								
Industry	1,903	2,464	2,703	2,896	3,402	3,865	3,733	3,657
Construction	205	211	222	188	201	218	247	233
Agriculture	855	1,297	1,405	1,467	1,610	1,643	1,817	1,853
Transport	877	1,090	1,337	1,236	797	809	1,044	945
Other Sectors	1,083	1,356	1,404	1,459	1,453	1,520	1,575	1,577
Municipal	677	879	897	951	947	987	1,020	1,036
Other	407	477	507	508	506	533	555	541
Losses	783	957	1,005	1,085	1,072	1,209	1,238	1,322
Exports	1,568	4,419	5,208	5,880	5,335	6,302	6,071	6,499
of which: Interrepublic	..	..	..	..	..	..	..	..
Total Uses	7,275	11,794	13,284	14,211	13,870	15,566	15,724	16,086

Source: Energy Balance of National Economy.

TABLE 9-1A: TURMNENISTAN - DEVELOPMENTS IN WHOLESALE AND RETAIL PRICES

ANNUAL	1980	1985	1986	1987	1988	1989	1990	1991	1992
				(previous year = 100)					
Wholesale prices - Total	..	..	..	..	..	..	100.0	310.9	1094.3
Electro-energy	..	..	..	..	..	..	100.0	210.9	580.5
Fuel	..	..	..	..	..	..	100.0	447.8	1651.1
Ferrous Metallurgy	..	..	..	..	..	..	100.0	..	..
Non-ferrous Metallurgy	..	..	..	..	..	..	100.0	..	..
Chemical	..	..	..	..	..	..	100.0	252.5	2690.7
Petro-chemical	..	..	..	..	..	..	100.0	210.0	1239.9
Machine Building	..	..	..	..	..	..	100.0	194.6	3983.2
Forestry, Wood & Paper	..	..	..	..	..	..	100.0	194.7	1042.0
Construction Materials	..	..	..	..	..	..	100.0	217.3	944.9
Glass Industry	..	..	..	..	..	..	100.0	195.3	1731.8
Light Industry	..	..	..	..	..	..	100.0	293.8	598.0
Food Industry	..	..	..	..	..	..	100.0	225.6	1131.8
Meat Industry	..	..	..	..	..	..	100.0	423.1	1664.3
Dairy Industry	..	..	..	..	..	..	100.0	316.6	959.2
Grain Processing	..	..	..	..	..	..	100.0	214.5	1432.5
Consumer prices - Total	..	..	..	..	..	..	..	100.0	931.3
Aggregated goods	..	..	..	..	..	..	..	100.0	979.4
Food products	..	..	..	..	..	..	..	100.0	906.6
Non-food products	..	..	..	..	..	..	..	100.0	1064.9
Paid Services	..	..	..	..	..	..	..	100.0	609.6

MONTHLY	1991 Jan.	1991 Feb.	1991 Mar.	1991 Apr.	1991 May	1991 June	1991 July	1991 Aug.	1991 Sept.	1991 Oct.	1991 Nov.	1991 Dec.
					(same month of the preceding year = 100)							
Wholesale prices - Total	253.2	250.3	227.6	259.9	289.1	292.7	295.6	300.2	343.0	363.8	443.1	412.6
Electro-energy	190.8	190.6	202.8	237.5	244.9	244.9	230.9	208.0	199.0	200.0	193.9	187.3
Fuel	406.6	406.6	411.4	411.4	411.4	412.0	412.9	413.1	410.5	411.5	632.9	632.9
Ferrous Metallurgy	..	..	..	..	..	..	..	..	..	..	..	..
Non-ferrous Metallurgy	..	..	..	..	..	..	..	..	..	..	..	..
Chemical	171.0	170.6	181.2	168.9	169.3	173.0	176.7	176.7	171.0	175.0	882.3	414.8
Petro-chemical	210.0	210.0	210.0	210.0	210.0	210.0	210.0	210.0	210.0	210.0	210.0	210.0
Machine Building	161.7	162.1	162.6	186.4	192.6	211.5	207.4	215.2	188.9	183.4	193.5	270.0
Forestry, Wood & Paper	161.2	175.8	179.9	203.4	194.1	185.8	190.3	180.1	175.0	214.3	204.8	272.1
Construction Materials	211.5	196.5	207.5	209.2	209.4	216.5	237.4	221.7	221.1	220.4	220.5	235.8
Glass Industry	194.7	192.3	194.3	200.6	192.1	193.5	193.7	192.0	192.0	198.9	199.6	199.4
Light Industry	226.3	223.4	166.1	194.0	261.1	265.5	263.7	276.3	376.3	434.1	435.6	402.9
Food Industry	187.0	187.7	172.2	223.5	224.3	233.8	235.1	246.1	268.5	248.4	237.5	238.2
Meat Industry	100.4	103.1	100.1	444.5	439.0	444.3	552.8	567.8	582.5	578.1	575.0	589.6
Dairy Industry	98.8	98.6	98.4	427.5	434.3	432.4	390.6	378.3	361.1	358.0	357.8	369.3
Grain Processing	264.3	223.0	229.5	240.3	238.0	238.4	237.2	240.8	236.2	143.4	143.9	139.1
Consumer prices 1/	..	..	..	..	..	..	..	..	..	..	200.5	..
Aggregated Goods	..	..	..	..	..	..	..	..	..	..	226.0	201.6
Food products											232.6	185.3
Non-food products											222.9	210.5
Paid Services	..	..	..	..	..	..	..	..	..	..	177.0	..

No calculations to the same month of the preceding year were made until November 1991.

(cont.)

TABLE 9-1A: TURKMENISTAN - DEVELOPMENTS IN WHOLESALE AND RETAIL PRICES, continued

MONTHLY	1992 Jan.	1992 Feb.	1992 Mar.	1992 Apr.	1992 May	1992 June	1992 July	1992 Aug.	1992 Sept.	1992 Oct.	1992 Nov.	1992 Dec.
(same month of the preceding year = 100)												
1. Wholesale prices - Total	740.8	769.7	847.5	775.7	807.9	764.0	820.5	1119.1	1601.3	1666.6	1610.1	1615.0
Electro-energy	900.9	348.3	440.8	376.2	365.0	344.9	454.6	454.8	788.0	701.6	893.0	898.1
Fuel	829.7	883.3	997.8	1053.9	899.4	883.9	1002.6	1861.1	3437.2	3118.2	2352.9	2487.6
Ferrous Metallurgy	..	..	..	..	..	..	..	..	..	..	..	..
Non-ferrous Metallurgy	..	..	..	..	..	..	..	..	..	..	..	..
Chemical	1367.7	2111.1	2155.4	3015.0	3120.2	2932.2	2941.8	3321.0	3972.2	3657.2	1543.1	2151.0
Petro-chemical	738.1	738.1	1195.3	1265.2	1235.9	1282.6	1249.6	1176.3	1171.4	1410.9	1665.6	1749.2
Machine Building	320.6	845.6	3048.8	2265.0	3893.8	3424.8	4001.6	4497.5	4945.4	11306.7	7491.5	1757.6
Forestry, Wood & Paper	550.7	555.7	725.4	719.6	932.3	1074.0	1016.0	997.6	1204.2	1067.7	1727.6	1932.8
Construction Materials	318.6	565.8	596.9	629.2	671.5	669.0	885.0	1065.5	1325.0	1338.3	1646.3	1628.2
Glass Industry	681.2	1136.8	1367.5	1538.9	1562.6	1766.9	1830.8	1999.0	2007.0	2045.3	2420.9	2424.9
Light Industry	581.8	587.1	611.3	502.9	533.5	509.4	528.7	516.8	452.7	607.4	847.9	896.1
Food Industry	747.4	680.6	653.5	568.3	654.0	403.9	793.5	1488.2	1641.2	1656.0	2151.1	2144.2
Meat Industry	2295.4	2254.2	2224.2	1016.3	1045.1	1093.1	491.7	473.5	2245.6	·2185.7	2443.7	2203.6
Dairy Industry	1459.5	1152.5	1107.8	280.1	266.7	267.1	298.5	322.7	1514.8	1476.0	1571.7	1793.5
Grain Processing	509.2	576.1	558.8	557.1	563.3	543.6	546.1	1522.3	2022.0	2158.0	3708.4	3925.2
2. Consumer prices - Total	..		..		..		..		..		..	..
Aggregated Goods	663.2	675.5	731.0	478.1	515.1	545.0	656.9	781.8	846.7	894.5	927.7	964.1
Food products	632.5	671.2	692.6	431.8	475.4	483.9	557.1	699.9	837.6	901.7	880.4	926.5
Non-food products	682.9	678.0	756.0	534.7	560.6	624.2	800.1	885.8	856.0	887.4	981.1	1006.0
Paid Services	..	291.1	392.2	378.4	386.4	412.4	376.5	567.2	550.6	790.7	779.6	813.1

MONTHLY	1993 Jan.	1993 Feb.	1993 Mar.	1993 Apr.	1993 May	1993 June	1993 July	1993 Aug.	1993 Sept.	1993 Oct.	1993 Nov.	1993 Dec.
(same month of the preceding year = 100)												
1. Wholesale prices - Total	1672.3	1411.0	1324.5	1300.5	1430.3	2178.2	2391.1	1680.1	1251.8	1915.2	1811.0	..
Electro-energy	5958.7	1175.8	1537.5	1353.8	1824.7	1891.1	3328.9	3329.4	2174.7	1404.0	1338.3	..
Fuel	1918.5	2053.0	1717.8	1499.6	1917.4	3212.0	2833.6	1693.8	1499.0	1512.3	1763.7	..
Ferrous Metallurgy	..	..	..	..	..	..	..	..	..	..	..	..
Non-ferrous Metallurgy	..	..	..	..	..	..	..	..	..	..	..	..
Chemical	1129.3	566.7	541.7	805.3	616.6	719.4	728.8	879.6	677.7	642.1	1533.1	..
Petro-chemical	224.0	185.4	173.8	359.7	447.2	530.4	805.1	850.1	852.8	1528.0	1428.4	..
Machine Building	8743.9	10453.3	4351.2	9417.7	853.2	1166.5	1204.0	1834.2	7517.9	764.1	1410.2	..
Forestry, Wood & Paper	1639.5	1597.8	3094.8	2334.7	1525.8	1825.8	1468.3	1827.2	1389.2	2378.7	3381.9	..
Construction Materials	1578.6	711.3	1147.6	1112.9	1179.5	1738.8	1721.5	1485.6	1400.2	1440.0	4241.5	..
Glass Industry	397.0	351.0	451.4	406.1	405.3	417.0	426.1	728.4	728.4	705.2	1114.4	..
Light Industry	492.2	428.0	597.7	645.7	655.3	631.3	643.9	694.9	708.0	3518.6	1450.8	..
Food Industry	737.9	1267.3	1105.3	1142.5	1168.8	837.6	2018.7	1160.0	760.0	773.3	4354.5	..
Meat Industry	988.9	593.1	1514.1	1668.7	1704.6	1739.9	4964.7	5241.3	996.5	967.0	1426.1	..
Dairy Industry	623.2	574.1	615.6	1816.0	1891.9	1682.2	6634.5	8178.0	2216.2	1650.8	1320.7	..
Grain Processing	1547.2	1643.1	1640.4	1617.6	1620.6	4810.0	5726.1	1754.2	1516.8	1493.5	1099.8	..
2. Consumer prices	..	..	..	..	..		..	..	..	..	..	..
Aggregated Goods	..	..	..	..	..							
Food products												
Non-food products												
Paid Services	..	..	..	..	..		..	..	..	..	..	..

Sources: Goskomstat.

ABLE 9-1B: TURKMENISTAN - DEVELOPMENTS IN WHOLESALE AND RETAIL PRICES

ANNUAL	1980	1985	1986	1987	1988	1989	1990	1991	1992
				(1990 = 100)					
Wholesale prices - Total	..	..	..	..	..	..	100.0	310.9	1094.3
Electro-energy	..	..	..	..	..	..	100.0	210.9	580.5
Fuel	..	..	..	..	..	..	100.0	447.8	1651.1
Ferrous Metallurgy	..	..	..	..	..	..	100.0	..	..
Non-ferrous Metallurgy	..	..	..	..	..	..	100.0	..	..
Chemical	..	..	..	..	..	..	100.0	252.5	2690.7
Petro-chemical	..	..	..	..	..	..	100.0	210.0	1239.9
Machine Building	..	..	..	..	..	..	100.0	194.6	3983.2
Forestry, Wood & Paper	..	..	..	..	..	..	100.0	194.7	1042.0
Construction Materials	..	..	..	..	..	..	100.0	217.3	944.9
Glass Industry	..	..	..	..	..	..	100.0	195.3	1731.8
Light Industry	..	..	..	..	..	..	100.0	293.8	598.0
Food Industry	..	..	..	..	..	..	100.0	225.6	1131.8
Meat Industry	..	..	..	..	..	..	100.0	423.1	1664.3
Dairy Industry	..	..	..	..	..	..	100.0	316.6	959.2
Grain Processing	..	..	..	..	..	..	100.0	214.5	1432.5
Consumer prices - Total	..	..	..	..	..	..	..	100.0	931.3
Aggregated goods	..	..	..	..	..	..	..	100.0	979.4
Food products	..	..	..	..	..	..	..	100.0	906.6
Non-food products	..	..	..	..	..	..	..	100.0	1064.9
Paid services	..	..	..	..	..	..	..	100.0	609.6

MONTHLY	1991 Jan.	1991 Feb.	1991 Mar.	1991 Apr.	1991 May	1991 June	1991 July	1991 Aug.	1991 Sept.	1991 Oct.	1991 Nov.	1991 Dec.
					(previous month = 100)							
Wholesale prices - Total	172.2	101.0	101.6	127.4	99.6	101.2	104.1	102.1	115.6	102.0	137.7	101.1
Electro-energy	192.6	100.0	103.8	118.2	103.1	103.1	100.0	102.2	100.0	102.4	96.9	96.6
Fuel	406.6	100.0	100.0	100.0	100.0	100.2	100.0	101.7	100.4	100.0	196.4	100.0
Ferrous Metallurgy	..	..	..	..	..	..	..	..	..	..	..	..
Non-ferrous Metallurgy	..	..	..	..	..	..	..	..	..	..	..	..
Chemical	171.0	99.6	106.0	99.0	99.8	102.2	101.6	100.0	99.6	100.1	471.6	114.4
Petro-chemical	210.0	100.0	100.0	100.0	100.0	100.0	100.0	100.0	100.0	100.0	100.0	100.0
Machine Building	133.4	99.3	99.8	100.3	102.0	109.3	98.7	112.0	86.4	98.7	102.4	130.1
Forestry, Wood & Paper	153.3	163.9	97.4	111.8	96.7	98.6	107.4	101.4	82.4	114.3	108.6	113.8
Construction Materials	197.4	98.9	101.0	99.9	100.5	105.8	102.7	102.1	99.5	102.8	101.3	109.6
Glass Industry	149.5	100.6	99.7	103.2	99.4	100.9	100.6	101.3	100.0	104.5	99.5	101.3
Light Industry	228.2	100.9	102.5	123.4	98.6	100.8	99.7	102.5	137.2	104.1	100.9	98.6
Food Industry	183.5	100.5	98.7	122.8	101.3	101.4	100.3	103.0	100.4	99.8	98.7	100.4
Meat Industry	99.5	101.2	99.1	441.4	101.1	99.6	222.0	100.5	100.8	100.5	99.1	102.9
Dairy Industry	98.7	99.4	99.5	424.8	101.1	100.3	91.6	97.6	100.9	101.5	99.8	99.3
Grain Processing	130.1	97.8	103.2	102.2	98.3	97.2	99.5	101.1	99.5	98.5	101.0	98.4
Consumer prices	103.1	106.9	106.1	165.4	110.8	110.2	99.2	100.0	101.1	103.4	102.5	101.6
Aggregated Goods	105.6	108.7	109.1	173.1	111.1	99.9	100.0	99.5	103.8	102.0	102.7	104.9
Food products	101.3	106.2	104.3	152.7	101.2	99.3	93.8	96.8	100.9	102.4	103.1	105.9
Non-food products	108.3	110.3	112.3	188.4	118.3	100.3	101.0	101.2	105.7	101.9	102.5	104.3
Paid Services	102.9	104.9	109.1	125.5	101.1	101.6	100.9	100.8	100.9	100.8	102.1	101.9

(cont.)

TABLE 9-1B: TURKMENISTAN - DEVELOPMENTS IN WHOLESALE AND RETAIL PRICES, continued

MONTHLY	1992 Jan.	1992 Feb.	1992 Mar.	1992 Apr.	1992 May	1992 June	1992 July	1992 Aug.	1992 Sept.	1992 Oct.	1992 Nov.	1992 Dec.
					(previous month = 100)							
1. Wholesale prices - Total	375.9	167.2	129.3	101.2	136.8	102.8	121.9	151.5	168.7	130.8	177.3	106.6
Electro-energy	478.7	100.0	131.4	100.9	100.1	97.4	100.6	100.1	173.3	91.2	100.0	101.4
Fuel	612.4	107.2	117.2	100.8	90.6	99.9	107.4	247.7	269.4	92.8	100.1	101.9
Ferrous Metallurgy	..	..	..	..	..	..	..	..	..	..	..	..
Non-ferrous Metallurgy	..	..	..	..	..	..	..	..	..	..	..	..
Chemical	592.4	178.5	109.7	145.3	99.8	96.5	107.6	119.1	116.3	111.9	97.6	110.5
Petro-chemical	738.1	100.0	100.0	100.0	100.0	100.8	100.0	102.7	99.7	120.6	106.9	105.0
Machine Building	243.3	149.3	1556.0	98.2	2625.6	100.0	103.6	151.9	90.8	287.1	85.9	117.0
Forestry, Wood & Paper	240.2	110.8	148.1	128.4	99.6	104.1	100.0	100.0	126.4	102.0	198.0	137.4
Construction Materials	190.9	286.2	114.8	107.2	109.4	111.5	126.5	130.0	136.0	102.2	122.2	109.1
Glass Industry	519.6	167.5	120.0	113.3	100.7	109.4	105.7	106.9	100.6	104.3	122.9	101.5
Light Industry	255.8	208.5	105.7	95.5	104.2	105.1	108.6	100.2	105.2	165.8	258.7	108.0
Food Industry	432.2	105.6	113.8	100.8	160.0	100.0	128.4	222.3	167.3	102.7	123.3	108.6
Meat Industry	395.3	99.6	97.5	101.7	103.9	101.2	100.0	116.9	463.0	109.8	106.8	99.0
Dairy Industry	393.7	82.8	97.3	106.5	100.9	100.0	101.6	100.0	478.2	99.0	106.0	103.8
Grain Processing	352.5	114.4	100.3	102.9	100.0	99.6	100.2	289.9	170.2	102.5	171.4	106.9
2. Consumer prices	280.7	117.9	106.3	107.3	107.1	101.6	101.8	124.6	108.9	104.9	109.0	114.7
Aggregated Goods	280.1	117.3	106.7	107.5	105.8	103.7	102.0	120.6	109.0	104.6	109.0	114.8
Food products	281.0	102.4	105.4	101.5	102.8	96.0	100.4	145.5	111.4	105.8	104.5	111.8
Non-food products	277.4	137.3	110.5	118.6	110.0	110.3	105.0	105.1	106.8	103.5	113.9	118.0
Paid Services	278.5	125.8	101.9	105.0	122.9	107.2	99.2	145.8	104.9	119.7	111.5	108.1

MONTHLY	1993 Jan.	1993 Feb.	1993 Mar.	1993 Apr.	1993 May	1993 June	1993 July	1993 Aug.	1993 Sept.	1993 Oct.	1993 Nov.	1993 Dec.
					(previous month = 100)							
1. Wholesale prices - Total	299.1	182.9	165.0	134.7	119.0	141.3	130.7	108.9	102.8	164.9	203.3	..
Electro-energy	154.8	100.1	802.1	128.4	92.6	102.0	175.9	100.0	108.9	106.4	101.7	..
Fuel	516.1	238.6	97.4	146.8	135.3	159.5	117.1	108.9	101.4	94.9	163.5	..
Ferrous Metallurgy	..	..	..	..	..	..	..	..	..	..	..	..
Non-ferrous Metallurgy	..	..	..	..	..	..	..	..	..	..	..	..
Chemical	152.6	118.3	104.9	142.0	111.6	124.0	103.2	116.3	102.8	105.7	402.5	..
Petro-chemical	123.7	109.3	100.0	213.4	156.4	115.8	151.8	108.5	100.0	214.3	100.0	..
Machine Building	160.2	106.8	109.5	166.7	109.0	150.3	106.6	185.0	90.1	176.1	154.3	..
Forestry, Wood & Paper	108.6	114.5	369.2	103.1	194.3	127.4	86.0	129.3	100.0	208.4	166.0	..
Construction Materials	139.3	123.0	208.5	111.4	118.8	163.8	165.8	122.2	107.8	105.3	402.2	..
Glass Industry	101.2	151.5	157.8	101.0	100.3	114.1	106.4	171.7	100.0	100.0	175.7	..
Light Industry	106.5	130.6	137.4	127.4	104.4	101.3	100.9	108.9	104.4	354.9	163.6	..
Food Industry	148.9	239.7	154.0	111.2	119.3	120.8	169.7	102.4	106.6	103.0	746.4	..
Meat Industry	101.4	100.9	263.9	100.4	104.5	102.4	287.3	101.2	96.1	103.6	151.9	..
Dairy Industry	92.1	103.9	104.9	315.7	103.6	93.0	409.4	100.1	101.0	106.0	84.0	..
Grain Processing	112.3	195.9	100.9	101.3	100.0	288.3	122.3	99.4	100.6	100.3	113.2	..
2. Consumer prices	114.6	241.3	115.1	128.0	114.0	155.8	115.4	116.0	121.7	127.7	..	..
Aggregated Goods	114.5	227.4	113.0	115.7	115.4	149.0	116.3	115.1	124.3	127.9	..	..
Food products	108.2	233.3	112.1	115.9	115.2	150.8	109.5	113.6	111.6	121.8	..	..
Non-food products	123.2	219.4	113.9	115.6	115.6	147.3	122.3	116.4	135.8	132.4	..	..
Paid Services	117.0	343.8	128.8	238.7	101.6	240.0	109.3	121.7	105.1	125.7	..	..

Sources: Goskomstat.

TABLE 9-2A: TURKMENISTAN - INDICES OF RETAIL PRICES BY GROUPS OF GOODS , continued

	ANNUAL 1)			MONTHLY 1993 2)											
	1990	1991	1992	Jan.	Feb.	Mar.	Apr.	May	June	July	Aug.	Sept.	Oct.	Nov.	Dec.
All Goods	104.2	200.5	1402.3	113.8	230.6	112.1	115.7	115.4	148.5	116.7	114.6	123.4	125.9	..	..
Food															
Meat and Fowl	102.8	185.7	1034.9	106.6	236.5	111.7	116.0	114.8	153.4	109.7	113.2	107.2	113.7	..	..
Fish	109.7	261.3	1054.8	104.4	180.8	108.5	105.3	120.1	221.5	109.5	113.4	111.1	108.8	..	..
Butter	100.3	243.4	1188.0	158.4	172.6	423.9	118.0	138.9	124.4	113.2	168.2	120.3	135.5	..	..
Vegetable Oil	100.0	233.5	706.2	100.0	250.0	100.0	100.0	100.0	200.0	100.0	100.0	104.2	100.0	..	..
Margarine and Margarine Go	100.6	163.3	271.2	100.0	333.3	100.0	100.0	100.0	350.0	100.0	100.0	100.0	100.0	..	..
Milk and Milk Goods	100.4	172.7	1314.1	113.0	100.0	100.0	119.2	100.0	109.7	100.0	120.8	100.0	100.0	..	..
Eggs	100.1	167.1	521.6	100.0	351.0	108.7	100.0	102.4	118.6	102.2	141.0	197.1	121.2	..	..
Sugar	100.1	232.2	781.0	128.6	114.4	100.0	103.6	103.4	108.3	107.7	100.0	100.0	133.3	..	..
Confectionery	100.0	223.4	665.1	100.0	266.7	106.7	100.0	100.0	116.8	103.4	106.8	113.9	123.3	..	..
Flour	101.2	213.8	1916.3	125.2	158.4	100.0	150.7	136.9	100.0	100.0	100.0	100.0	100.0	..	..
Natural Tea	102.0	188.7	404.1	100.0	443.3	102.5	100.4	102.6	158.2	102.0	100.9	107.6	109.9	..	..
Bread and Bread Products	100.1	183.0	491.4	105.4	134.0	100.0	103.0	102.6	102.7	157.3	163.9	138.0	157.4	..	..
Potato	131.3	317.5	1061.3	109.2	235.8	146.3	241.7	151.6	110.4	101.6	140.0	135.0	119.7	..	..
Vegetables	129.7	241.8	995.3	100.3	118.0	123.4	177.2	152.8	98.6	98.6	115.9	103.7	131.7	..	..
Non-Food Goods	105.5	213.7	1687.9	123.6	116.7	112.5	115.4	116.0	144.1	122.9	118.4	111.8	124.5	..	..
Cotton Fabric	109.9	281.1	1124.1	112.3	222.5	109.9	107.2	120.9	133.0	116.6	105.1	121.6	119.6	..	..
Woolen Fabric	105.0	252.8	906.6	141.9	158.2	101.8	109.6	103.9	133.4	102.6	113.7	139.2	118.3	..	..
Silk	110.3	213.9	969.1	116.8	122.6	107.7	109.7	110.8	132.7	102.7	120.7	100.0	133.4	..	..
Clothes and Underwear	103.9	259.2	1141.5	119.1	120.4	116.5	129.9	113.3	136.7	117.4	100.0	105.9	120.7	..	..
Furs and Fur Goods	101.3	268.3	961.1	104.1	125.0	114.3	106.8	208.2	100.0	431.3	127.1	142.4	100.3	..	..
Head-Dresses	100.8	181.0	959.3	103.4	128.9	109.1	140.2	112.7	137.4	110.9	113.1	151.5	152.1	..	..
Knit Wear	103.5	248.1	936.5	112.1	139.3	120.3	112.3	121.8	141.2	156.4	107.2	136.5	174.6	..	..
Stockings, Socks	103.4	228.5	1088.2	118.0	177.4	112.7	126.0	106.0	112.1	112.7	144.4	110.7	132.7	..	..
Leather Footwear	106.7	238.1	652.3	114.0	128.7	125.2	126.6	125.2	144.1	112.1	105.7	110.5	130.8	..	..
Rubber Footwear	104.8	227.5	946.9	198.0	148.5	107.3	104.6	100.2	110.0	128.5	126.3	130.8	236.0	..	..
Synthetic Detergents	101.9	192.5	1739.9	106.2	122.5	100.7	100.0	100.4	295.6	126.5	127.2	126.5	115.8	..	..
Perfume and Cosmetics	107.4	214.3	845.0	137.2	146.6	109.2	112.4	109.3	112.1	124.9	140.8	127.1	115.8	..	..
Haberdashery	102.1	194.5	834.4	106.0	128.8	115.1	116.9	115.6	215.2	117.1	140.8	182.7	143.4	..	..
Thread	113.9	176.1	1227.8	..	..	..	..	..	..	..	..	..	..	..	..
Tobacco and Cigarettes	100.3	186.6	8098.6	103.2	182.7	102.5	106.7	104.4	118.5	107.3	104.7	162.0	138.8	..	..
Exercise - Books	99.8	324.2	8098.6	100.0	100.0	124.7	100.0	100.0	100.0	100.0	178.3	246.3	166.4	..	..
Printed Matter	107.7	196.0	794.1	110.2	177.2	142.1	108.1	106.7	162.7	107.9	119.2	119.2	115.0	..	..
Sports Goods	100.3	190.6	1038.6	150.4	107.8	105.3	113.0	101.2	121.6	102.4	100.1	102.5	100.3	..	..
Radio Goods	101.5	174.7	1034.1	101.7	168.8	112.7	105.5	112.5	106.9	118.9	104.5	166.4	111.1	..	..
Music Instruments	102.2	185.9	1170.4	119.9	116.7	108.6	105.3	102.6	104.5	118.8	151.4	104.2	100.3	..	..
Furniture	105.0	286.4	1359.8	119.3	217.4	107.3	133.9	211.0	131.3	131.6	135.0	168.4	104.2	..	..
China Ware and Faience	110.9	276.4	2143.7	137.2	128.6	113.2	100.2	102.2	109.3	145.3	110.2	162.8	111.9	..	..
Bicycles and Motorcycles	107.7	197.7	1558.8	120.0	299.3	110.2	133.8	101.4	109.5	103.8	159.0	172.9	107.8	..	..

1) ANNUAL: Preceding year = 100.
2) MONTHLY: Preceding month = 100. January 1993 is linked to December 1992.

Source: State Statistical Committee.

TABLE 9-2B: TURKMENISTAN - INDICES OF RETAIL PRICES BY GROUPS OF GOODS, continued

	ANNUAL 1)	MONTHLY 1993 2)												QUARTERLY 1993 3)			
	1992	Jan.	Feb.	Mar.	Apr.	May	June	July	Aug.	Sept.	Oct.	Nov.	Dec.	I	II	III	IV
All Goods	1402.3	550.9	1038.2	883.6	1169.9	998.2	1402.1	1345.6	1330.4	1465.4	1820.2	..	..	769.8	1035.2	1312.1	..
Food																	
Meat and Fowl	1034.9	469.0	630.2	741.8	1006.8	921.3	1369.8	1414.3	1249.4	1225.8	1571.0	..	..	625.6	1050.4	1260.2	..
Fish	1049.6	1153.7	525.1	583.2	583.1	607.7	1291.5	1234.6	1220.7	1291.8	1168.6	..	..	471.8	937.2	1181.4	..
Butter	1188.0	788.1	758.6	2453.4	2162.6	2312.7	2971.6	3680.0	3576.4	4740.0	6348.5	..	..	1187.6	3572.8	4422.6	..
Vegetable Oil	702.6	133.3	333.3	320.0	315.8	315.8	631.6	631.6	500.0	520.8	495.0	..	..	263.0	421.1	540.7	..
Margarine and Margarine Go	271.2	107.1	357.1	346.0	346.0	142.2	149.1	149.0	1138.2	1166.7	1166.7	..	..	270.8	507.9	1180.4	..
Milk and Milk Goods	1314.1	260.0	562.4	549.1	539.9	533.4	707.5	733.7	477.0	424.2	644.3	..	..	114.5	596.1	487.2	..
Eggs	522.4	182.8	872.9	881.6	877.7	951.2	1030.4	1118.3	1441.8	2238.5	2559.5	..	..	375.6	944.3	1618.3	..
Sugar	774.1	803.6	459.8	391.8	450.5	475.6	951.1	920.5	520.6	533.3	533.3	..	..	871.6	684.7	604.0	..
Confectionery	665.1	168.9	1217.1	1255.2	1532.8	2042.3	2578.8	2634.0	2364.1	2519.7	3184.6	..	..	267.6	2239.9	2517.2	..
Natural Tea	1916.3	813.2	483.8	1474.0	1190.6	512.7	791.8	691.9	668.8	691.6	701.3	..	..	1037.0	865.7	684.4	..
Bread and Bread Products	404.1	245.3	491.4	516.7	618.2	831.9	1116.7	2695.7	3053.8	2346.7	2148.6	..	..	1419.2	1086.6	2391.6	..
Potato	491.4	321.0	586.0	888.6	1611.1	1716.2	2390.8	3403.4	3140.2	2070.8	2430.6	..	..	497.5	2109.4	2920.8	..
Vegetables	1027.5	479.9	838.8	1085.1	1568.4	1407.7	3109.9	1033.1	3073.6	3564.8	4449.7	..	..	805.7	1519.6	2715.1	..
Non-Food Goods	874.8	662.9	1595.8	1040.9	1319.6	1068.9	1431.8	1285.5	1401.2	1643.3	1997.1	..	..	913.8	1021.2	1357.5	..
Cotton Fabric	1687.9	693.2	322.9	328.3	283.2	324.5	346.8	483.4	586.6	684.1	662.0	..	..	929.3	667.8	637.0	..
Woolen Fabric	1124.1	1022.8	532.0	411.8	526.6	456.4	598.8	878.7	965.0	809.6	879.3	..	..	720.3	707.6	906.7	..
Silk	906.6	409.2	480.7	749.9	540.4	449.5	688.4	668.4	601.9	682.6	807.6	..	..	569.4	559.8	650.0	..
Clothes and Underwear	969.1	469.6	640.9	744.3	766.1	658.4	987.0	938.7	1001.4	1139.4	1313.0	..	..	710.8	793.5	1032.4	..
Furs and Fur Goods	1141.5	565.8	1250.0	1359.6	983.7	2429.4	1106.8	4170.2	9761.5	9761.5	8929.5	..	..	650.4	2426.7	10740.5	..
Head-Dresses	961.1	430.4	292.9	260.6	444.4	451.8	637.7	597.9	823.2	795.3	452.4	..	..	499.4	512.8	810.8	..
Knit Wear	959.3	383.1	435.1	1002.8	735.9	693.6	967.5	958.1	934.7	1001.6	1442.2	..	..	856.5	827.1	946.2	..
Stockings, Socks	936.5	996.5	1372.0	427.4	567.3	546.1	656.7	961.9	607.3	806.0	1621.2	..	..	888.8	551.9	598.0	..
Leather Footwear	1088.2	360.4	454.7	1016.2	1089.3	1203.8	1667.8	1543.3	2081.2	2183.3	2487.4	..	..	931.9	1328.1	1810.2	..
Rubber Footwear	652.3	887.5	837.4	487.8	926.1	992.2	1947.0	792.5	901.8	932.2	1403.8	..	..	611.9	1062.7	882.3	..
Synthetic Detergents	946.9	503.2	556.4	519.6	272.9	322.5	689.5	659.4	794.3	789.9	1999.8	..	..	559.6	453.4	775.7	..
Perfume and Cosmetics	1739.9	1289.5	764.1	936.0	851.8	890.7	1023.4	834.8	934.3	1598.2	1881.4	..	..	941.7	1201.1	1240.5	..
Haberdashery	845.0	541.3	793.8	863.3	993.1	910.4	1537.2	989.2	1320.6	1656.2	1864.1	..	..	640.4	1274.6	1413.2	..
Thread	834.4	516.3	1082.1	1231.3	3464.6	1132.1	3464.6	658.7	658.7	310.2	956.7	..	..	817.9	713.4	982.5	..
Tobacco and Cigarettes	8098.6	598.8	564.0	867.9	811.1	829.9	878.3	976.2	960.2	1362.3	2106.0	..	..	695.3	883.2	1114.6	..
Exercise - Books	1634.1	1034.5	1111.1	925.0	421.7	204.7	136.0	173.7	196.6	303.3	747.0	..	..	1056.7	287.3	221.6	..
Printed Matter	794.1	336.1	561.6	556.8	509.8	511.3	701.7	587.6	665.2	766.8	839.5	..	..	539.7	575.8	684.7	..
Sports Goods	1038.6	284.7	330.7	419.6	1317.8	1017.9	2000.0	2804.0	3306.6	3022.2	4526.9	..	..	375.8	2692.0	2981.9	..
Radio Goods	1043.1	1418.0	645.4	891.2	1451.7	1475.9	1640.1	1693.6	2042.3	2020.7	1799.0	..	..	941.1	1213.6	1859.0	..
Music Instruments	1170.4	865.3	1944.4	952.3	1002.2	791.3	605.6	762.1	1045.1	1421.3	1420.3	..	..	862.0	951.6	1414.3	..
Furniture	1359.8	490.9	1207.0	1141.8	1348.2	2687.0	2482.1	2487.8	3275.5	3962.6	4793.8	..	..	856.1	1703.4	3257.2	..
China Ware and Faience	2143.7	1489.0	1725.3	1432.7	1029.2	1015.9	1505.6	1452.8	1614.1	3145.2	3772.9	..	..	1416.3	1059.2	2623.8	..
Bicycles and Motorcycles	1558.8	626.5	1902.4	1179.0	2155.9	886.7	1024.0	699.8	1099.3	1740.5	1529.9	..	..	919.4	988.4	1145.1	..

1) ANNUAL: 1991 = 100.
2) MONTHLY: Same month of the preceding year = 100.
3) QUARTERLY: Same quarter of the preceding year = 100.

Source: State Statistical Committee.

TABLE 9-3: TURKMENISTAN - AVERAGE MONTHLY WAGES, BY SECTORS

(in current rubles)

	1987	1988	1989	1990	1991	1992
Total	198.4	208.4	221.3	243.7	414.8	3,982.8
Material Sector	210.0	223.0	240.0	266.0	532.5	4,492.2
of which:						
Industry	212.6	228.0	241.5	264.9	488.4	5,405.8
Electric Energy	237.9	273.1	296.9	367.1	711.0	8,238.9
Fuel Industry	291.6	336.0	355.0	387.0	787.0	8,600.0
Chemical and Petrochemical	255.6	283.0	300.0	305.0	559.0	5,670.8
Machine-Building	214.0	230.0	242.0	263.0	412.0	4,264.2
Wood Processing and Paper	216.0	216.8	231.9	252.5	406.0	4,323.0
Construction Materials	241.0	250.0	268.0	291.9	479.0	5,502.7
Light	179.0	189.0	201.0	220.3	364.0	4,402.4
Textiles	194.2	207.1	225.1	253.4	437.2	4,817.8
Clothing	149.0	160.0	168.0	178.0	262.0	..
Leather, Fur and Shoe	201.0	199.0	200.0	207.0	373.0	..
Food Industry	199.0	209.0	219.0	234.0	372.0	4,628.6
Food Processing	191.0	199.0	203.4	218.0	333.0	..
Meat and Dairy	176.7	191.0	216.0	221.0	394.0	..
Fish	262.0	267.0	299.0	330.0	472.0	..
Flour, Groats and Fodder	233.0	237.0	233.0	265.0	471.0	5,914.8
Construction	264.4	287.7	291.9	314.9	534.5	4,671.6
Agriculture	192.3	208.8	242.4	274.6	418.9	4,002.0
Transport	224.2	236.9	249.9	282.4	494.1	4,590.6
Communications	178.8	205.7	223.0	243.1	466.8	4,342.8
Trade, Material-Technical Supply	152.7	153.6	174.4	205.7	348.4	3,487.1
Information-Computer Services	153.2	160.9	192.6	209.8	369.0	3,697.4
Other	126.5	124.6	128.4	150.3	309.1	3,335.2
Non-Material Sector	180.0	185.0	192.0	205.0	238.6	3,230.2
of which:						
Housing-Communal	159.5	170.4	182.4	196.4	326.9	3,081.1
Health Care, Physical Culture and Social Security	141.7	143.3	148.8	164.5	324.3	2,647.4
Education	185.9	185.6	185.5	188.8	293.1	2,924.1
Culture 1/	130.4	119.2	129.2	153.2	278.0	2,730.0
Art 1/	150.3	154.5	155.1	182.6	303.5	..
Science and Science Services	235.2	265.6	297.6	319.5	374.4	4,469.4
Banking and Social Insurance	171.2	174.1	195.7	321.0	845.5	6,348.2
Administration	176.1	184.6	213.7	305.8	460.4	4,422.7

1/ *For 1992 Culture and Art.*

Source: Goskomstat.

TABLE 10-1: TURKMENISTAN - MONETARY INCOMES AND EXPENDITURES OF THE POPULATION

(in millions of current rubles)

	1985	1986	1987	1988	1989	1990	1991	1992
INCOMES								
State wages and salaries	2,019.7	2,104.4	2,211.6	2,376.9	2,544.6	2,779.5	4,803.3	39,953.3
Payments to cooperative members	..	..	..	16.5	78.1	174.4	148.4	2,454.5
Income over wages and salaries	62.8	65.9	72.0	77.4	100.7	124.7	271.3	2,321.0
Money wage payment by collectives	661.9	646.9	591.1	675.0	740.3	928.8	1,678.6	22,670.9
Income from sale of farm products	194.7	189.1	208.3	219.3	295.3·	341.9	977.7	5,855.6
Pension and allowances 1/	382.7	406.7	430.1	459.5	484.2	562.4	2,772.6	11,966.8
Stipends	23.5	24.0	22.5	25.0	24.6	28.4	90.3	646.4
Income from finance system	78.3	82.8	89.7	130.6	103.5	203.6	249.2	1,678.9
Other income	90.6	91.1	78.3	130.5	246.7	157.2	758.0	385.2
Money by mail	..	..	..	..	..	..	..	..
Compensation	..	..	..	..	..	..	..	..
Total Income	3,514.2	3,610.9	3,703.6	4,110.7	4,618.0	5,300.9	11,749.4	87,932.6
OUTLAYS								
Purchases of goods and services	2,689.9	2,887.9	2,945.0	3,241.9	3,565.7	3,976.7	6,821.8	36,799.3
Retail sales of goods for consumption	2,423.2	2,600.8	2,620.2	2,879.8	3,160.6	3,540.3	6,129.6	31,170.0
Purchases from collective farms	11.5	15.0	28.5	30.5	39.0	54.8	126.2	867.1
Consumer services	255.2	272.1	296.3	331.6	366.1	381.6	566.0	4,762.2
Obligotary and voluntary payments	292.4	304.8	319.0	349.0	393.5	456.2	609.8	4,227.2
Savings and loans	101.0	160.3	144.5	218.5	305.5	413.3	1,911.9	7,843.2
Postal money order	45.4	29.0	14.2	11.0	12.5	13.8	-46.1	109.3
Total Outlays	3,128.7	3,382.0	3,422.7	3,820.4	4,277.2	4,860.0	9,297.4	48,979.0
Income less expenditures	385.5	228.9	280.9	290.3	340.8	440.9	2,452.0	38,953.6

Source: Goskomstat.

TABLE 11-1: TURKMENISTAN - CAPITAL INVESTMENTS BY STATE ENTERPRISES AND ORGANIZATIONS

(in millions of rubles)

	1987	1988	1989	1990	1991	1992
		(1984 prices)		*(1991 prices)*	*(current prices)*	
Total of which:	1,694	1,675	1,678	2,450	3,491	41,120
Industry	757	818	731	999	1,263	11,872
Agriculture	366	301	297	514	897	12,477
Construction	21	41	53	22	13	440
Transport and Communications of which	152	139	134	170	152	2,335
Communications	22	25	18	32	30	190
Trade and Catering	17	16	20	27	32	401
Housing	173	177	189	299	442	4,783
Municipal Services	63	69	95	182	267	4,644
Health Protection and Social Maintenance	33	29	32	51	104	1,003
Public Education	100	68	80	137	250	2,596
Culture and Art	11	8	10	20	36	252

Source: Goskomstat.

TABLE 11-2: TURKMENISTAN - CHANGE IN STOCKS BY TYPE AND ECONOMIC SECTOR

(in millions of current rubles)

	1990	1991
Total Change	**502.5**	**6,366.9**
of which:		
By Type:		
Raw Materials	112.8	2,351.8
Unfinished Production and Semiproducts	34.3	1,353.7
Finished Production, Goods	355.4	2,661.4
By Sector:		
Agriculture	124.8	261.1
Industry	205.8	2,949.9
Construction	92.2	1,376.4
Transport and Communication	4.2	45.6
Trade and Catering	-158.2	415.9
Other	233.7	1,318.0

Source: Goskomstat.

TABLE 11-3: TURKMENISTAN - CAPITAL INVESTMENT FOR UNFINISHED CONSTRUCTION

(in millions of rubles)

	1987	1988	1989	1990	1991	1992
	(1984 prices)				(current prices)	
Total	1,558.7	1,683.3	1,927.4	1,969.6	2,892.3	20,777.0
Capital Investment for Unfinished Construction in percent of Total Capital Investment (%)	103.0	108.0	125.0	116.0	83.0	50.5
of which:						
Industry	101.0	114.0	139.0	134.0	100.3	60.9
Agriculture	134.0	153.0	183.0	143.0	85.5	52.9
Forestry	..	..	..	..	..	..
Construction	191.0	109.0	82.0	28.0	60.7	64.8
Transport and Communications	80.0	71.0	92.0	85.0	77.3	45.3
of which						
Communications	82.0	..	..	66.0	101.2	62.1

TABLE 11-3A: TURKMENISTAN - CAPITAL INVESTMENT FOR UNFINISHED CONSTRUCTION

(in millions of current rubles)

	1991	1992
Material Sphere	2,212.1	15,449.1
Industry	1,266.5	7,235.0
Construction	7.9	285.2
Agriculture	767.3	6,600.6
Forestry	..	..
Transport	86.9	939.8
Communications	30.7	118.2
Other	52.8	283.0
Non-Material Sphere	680.2	5,327.9
Housing and Municipal Services	438.8	3,630.0
Public Health, Social Security	87.9	708.1
Physical Culture and Turism	..	..
Education	84.3	567.6
Culture and Art	34.9	239.7
Other	34.3	182.5

Source: Goskomstat.

TABLE 11-4: TURKMENISTAN - CONSTRUCTION INVESTMENT

(in millions of rubles)

	1980	1985	1986	1987	1988	1989	1990	1991	1992
	(prices as of January 1, 1991)							*(current prices)*	
Construction Investment	1,915	2,517	2,579	2,681	2,847	2,882	3,150	4,318	51,067
of which:									
State Construction	1,536	2,037	2,132	2,237	2,283	2,254	2,464	3,491	41,120
Cooperatives, Collective Farms, Consumer Unions	248	306	288	263	312	366	406	444	3,661
Social Organizations	1	5	2	2	4	8	6	1	..
Private Construction	130	169	157	179	248	254	274	382	6,286
Maintenance and Service	..	..	..	..	..	..	..	..	..
Other	..	..	..	..	..	..	..	..	..
	(current prices)								
Gross Product of Construction	964	1,489	1,659	1,766	1,886	1,704	1,808	3,946	48,101
Material Production	411	677	686	762	760	677	726	1,593	..
Depreciation	101	139	142	158	159	152	132	129	..
Net Material Production	452	673	831	846	968	875	950	2,225	..
Gross Product of Construction	964	1,489	1,659	1,766	1,886	1,704	1,808	3,946	48,101
of which:									
State Construction	832	1,254	1,381	1,483	1,544	1,324	1,387	2,966	35,248
Cooperatives and Collective Farms	106	155	171	163	178	197	228	579	5,989
Private Construction	26	80	108	119	164	183	193	401	6,864

Source: Goskomstat.

Distributors of World Bank Publications

ARGENTINA
Carlos Hirsch, SRL
Galeria Guemes
Florida 165, 4th Floor-Ofc. 453/465
1333 Buenos Aires

**AUSTRALIA, PAPUA NEW GUINEA,
FIJI, SOLOMON ISLANDS,
VANUATU, AND WESTERN SAMOA**
D.A. Information Services
648 Whitehorse Road
Mitcham 3132
Victoria

AUSTRIA
Gerold and Co.
Graben 31
A-1011 Wien

BANGLADESH
Micro Industries Development
   Assistance Society (MIDAS)
House 5, Road 16
Dhanmondi R/Area
Dhaka 1209

   Branch offices:
   Pine View, 1st Floor
   100 Agrabad Commercial Area
   Chittagong 4100

BELGIUM
Jean De Lannoy
Av. du Roi 202
1060 Brussels

CANADA
Le Diffuseur
151A Boul. de Mortagne
Boucherville, Québec
J4B 5E6

Renouf Publishing Co.
1294 Algoma Road
Ottawa, Ontario
K1B 3W8

CHILE
Invertec IGT S.A.
Av. Santa Maria 6400
Edificio INTEC, Of. 201
Santiago

CHINA
China Financial & Economic
   Publishing House
8, Da Fo Si Dong Jie
Beijing

COLOMBIA
Infoenlace Ltda.
Apartado Aereo 34270
Bogota D.E.

COTE D'IVOIRE
Centre d'Edition et de Diffusion
   Africaines (CEDA)
04 B.P. 541
Abidjan 04 Plateau

CYPRUS
Center of Applied Research
Cyprus College
6, Diogenes Street, Engomi
P.O. Box 2006
Nicosia

DENMARK
SamfundsLitteratur
Rosenoerns Allé 11
DK-1970 Frederiksberg C

DOMINICAN REPUBLIC
Editora Taller, C. por A.
Restauración e Isabel la Católica 309
Apartado de Correos 2190 Z-1
Santo Domingo

EGYPT, ARAB REPUBLIC OF
Al Ahram
Al Galaa Street
Cairo

The Middle East Observer
41, Sherif Street
Cairo

FINLAND
Akateeminen Kirjakauppa
P.O. Box 128
SF-00101 Helsinki 10

FRANCE
World Bank Publications
66, avenue d'Iéna
75116 Paris

GERMANY
UNO-Verlag
Poppelsdorfer Allee 55
D-5300 Bonn 1

HONG KONG, MACAO
Asia 2000 Ltd.
46-48 Wyndham Street
Winning Centre
2nd Floor
Central Hong Kong

HUNGARY
Foundation for Market Economy
Dombovari Ut 17-19
H-1117 Budapest

INDIA
Allied Publishers Private Ltd.
751 Mount Road
Madras - 600 002

   Branch offices:
   15 J.N. Heredia Marg
   Ballard Estate
   Bombay - 400 038

   13/14 Asaf Ali Road
   New Delhi - 110 002

   17 Chittaranjan Avenue
   Calcutta - 700 072

   Jayadeva Hostel Building
   5th Main Road, Gandhinagar
   Bangalore - 560 009

   3-5-1129 Kachiguda
      Cross Road
   Hyderabad - 500 027

   Prarthana Flats, 2nd Floor
   Near Thakore Baug, Navrangpura
   Ahmedabad - 380 009

   Patiala House
   16-A Ashok Marg
   Lucknow - 226 001

   Central Bazaar Road
   60 Bajaj Nagar
   Nagpur 440 010

INDONESIA
Pt. Indira Limited
Jalan Borobudur 20
P.O. Box 181
Jakarta 10320

IRAN
Kowkab Publishers
P.O. Box 19575-511
Tehran

IRELAND
Government Supplies Agency
4-5 Harcourt Road
Dublin 2

ISRAEL
Yozmot Literature Ltd.
P.O. Box 56055
Tel Aviv 61560

ITALY
Licosa Commissionaria Sansoni SPA
Via Duca Di Calabria, 1/1
Casella Postale 552
50125 Firenze

JAPAN
Eastern Book Service
Hongo 3-Chome, Bunkyo-ku 113
Tokyo

KENYA
Africa Book Service (E.A.) Ltd.
Quaran House, Mfangano Street
P.O. Box 45245
Nairobi

KOREA, REPUBLIC OF
Pan Korea Book Corporation
P.O. Box 101, Kwangwhamun
Seoul

Korean Stock Book Centre
P.O. Box 34
Yeoeido
Seoul

MALAYSIA
University of Malaya Cooperative
   Bookshop, Limited
P.O. Box 1127, Jalan Pantai Baru
59700 Kuala Lumpur

MEXICO
INFOTEC
Apartado Postal 22-860
14060 Tlalpan, Mexico D.F.

NETHERLANDS
De Lindeboom/InOr-Publikaties
P.O. Box 202
7480 AE Haaksbergen

NEW ZEALAND
EBSCO NZ Ltd.
Private Mail Bag 99914
New Market
Auckland

NIGERIA
University Press Limited
Three Crowns Building Jericho
Private Mail Bag 5095
Ibadan

NORWAY
Narvesen Information Center
Book Department
P.O. Box 6125 Etterstad
N-0602 Oslo 6

PAKISTAN
Mirza Book Agency
65, Shahrah-e-Quaid-e-Azam
P.O. Box No. 729
Lahore 54000

PERU
Editorial Desarrollo SA
Apartado 3824
Lima 1

PHILIPPINES
International Book Center
Suite 1703, Cityland 10
Condominium Tower 1
Ayala Avenue, H.V. dela
   Costa Extension
Makati, Metro Manila

POLAND
International Publishing Service
Ul. Piekna 31/37
00-677 Warzawa

For subscription orders:
IPS Journals
Ul. Okrezna 3
02-916 Warszawa

PORTUGAL
Livraria Portugal
Rua Do Carmo 70-74
1200 Lisbon

SAUDI ARABIA, QATAR
Jarir Book Store
P.O. Box 3196
Riyadh 11471

**SINGAPORE, TAIWAN,
MYANMAR,BRUNEI**
Gower Asia Pacific Pte Ltd.
Golden Wheel Building
41, Kallang Pudding, #04-03
Singapore 1334

SOUTH AFRICA, BOTSWANA
For single titles:
Oxford University Press
   Southern Africa
P.O. Box 1141
Cape Town 8000

For subscription orders:
International Subscription Service
P.O. Box 41095
Craighall
Johannesburg 2024

SPAIN
Mundi-Prensa Libros, S.A.
Castello 37
28001 Madrid

Librería Internacional AEDOS
Consell de Cent, 391
08009 Barcelona

SRI LANKA AND THE MALDIVES
Lake House Bookshop
P.O. Box 244
100, Sir Chittampalam A.
   Gardiner Mawatha
Colombo 2

SWEDEN
For single titles:
Fritzes Fackboksforetaget
Regeringsgatan 12, Box 16356
S-103 27 Stockholm

For subscription orders:
Wennergren-Williams AB
P. O. Box 1305
S-171 25 Solna

SWITZERLAND
For single titles:
Librairie Payot
Case postale 3212
CH 1002 Lausanne

For subscription orders:
Librairie Payot
Service des Abonnements
Case postale 3312
CH 1002 Lausanne

THAILAND
Central Department Store
306 Silom Road
Bangkok

**TRINIDAD & TOBAGO, ANTIGUA
BARBUDA, BARBADOS,
DOMINICA, GRENADA, GUYANA,
JAMAICA, MONTSERRAT, ST.
KITTS & NEVIS, ST. LUCIA,
ST. VINCENT & GRENADINES**
Systematics Studies Unit
#9 Watts Street
Curepe
Trinidad, West Indies

UNITED KINGDOM
Microinfo Ltd.
P.O. Box 3
Alton, Hampshire GU34 2PG
England